Health Insurance Answer Book

Third Edition

John D. Reynolds, CLU
Robin N. Bischoff, CLU

The Panel Answer Book Series
Panel Publishers, Inc.

Library of Congress Cataloging-in-Publication Data

Reynolds, John D.
    Health insurance answer book -- 3rd ed. / John D. Reynolds, Robin N. Bischoff.
      p.   cm. -- (Panel answer book series)
    Rev. ed. of: The health insurance answer book / Charles E. Vadakin II, Zelda Lipton. c1986.
    ISBN 1-878375-18-0
    1. Insurance, Health--United States--Handbooks, manuals, etc.
I. Bischoff, Robin N. II. Vadakin, Charles E. Health insurance answer book. III. Title. IV. Series.
    [DNLM: 1. Insurance, Health--United States--Handbooks.
W 39   R463h]
HG9396.V33   1989
368.3′82′00973--dc20
DNLM/DLC
for Library of Congress   89-26472
                                                                       CIP

This publication is designed to provide accurate and authoritative information in regard to the subject matter covered. It is sold with the understanding that the publisher is not engaged in rendering legal, accounting or other professional services. If legal advice or other professional assistance is required, the services of a competent professional person should be sought.

> — *From a Declaration of Principles jointly adopted by a Committee of the American Bar Association and a Committee of Publishers and Associations.*

Copyright © 1986, 1990, 1991

by
PANEL PUBLISHERS, INC.
A *Wolters Kluwer* Company

All rights reserved. No part of this book may be reproduced in any form or by any means without permission in writing from the publisher.

Printed in the United States of America

For more information on other titles in the
Panel Answer Book Series

Contact: Panel Publishers, Inc.
Customer Service
36 West 44th Street
New York, NY 10036
(212) 790-2090

About the Authors

JOHN D. REYNOLDS, CLU, is an employee benefits consultant and a writer on pension and health care topics. He has worked in the employee benefits field since 1973, and was associated with The Prudential Insurance Company and Noble Lowndes prior to becoming an independent consultant in 1988. He received a BS/MA in economics from West Virginia University and a JD from Rutgers School of Law.

ROBIN N. BISCHOFF, CLU, is an employee benefits consultant specializing in health and welfare issues. She writes and speaks on flexible benefits and other health care topics and has been employed in the field since 1975 by The Prudential Insurance Company and Noble Lowndes. She attended Georgetown University School of Foreign Service, received her BA from Upsala College and is currently pursuing her Ph.D. at Drew University.

Table of Contents

About the Authors iii

How to Use the Health Insurance Answer Book ix

Health Care Reform: 1990 and Beyond xi

Listing of Questions xix

Introduction lvii

Chapter 1: An Overview of Group Health Insurance 1

Chapter 2: The Health Insurance Marketplace 9
Types of Insurance Professionals 9
Choosing and Compensating Intermediaries 14
HMOs, PPOs, and Health Care Coalitions 18

Chapter 3: Factors Influencing Insurance Plan Design 21
Legal Factors Affecting Design 21
State Laws 24
Workers' Compensation 27
Federal Law 30

Health Insurance Answer Book

Pregnancy Discrimination Act 34
Occupational Health and Safety Act 41
Americans with Disabilities Act 42
    Taxation of Group Health Plans 44
Nonlegal Factors Affecting Design 45
    Restrictions on Coverage 47
    Paying for Insurance 51

Chapter 4: Types of Health Insurance Plans and Related Benefits 55
Medical Benefits 55
    Blue Cross/Blue Shield Plans 58
    Coverage 61
    Outpatient Care, Extended Care, and HMOs/PPOs 65
    Deductibles, Copayments, and Reimbursements 67
Dental Benefits 71
Vision and Hearing Benefits 76
Prescription Drug Plans 76
Mental Health Benefits 81
    Mental Health Management 84
Life Insurance Benefits 86
Disability Benefits 88
    Disability Management 92

Chapter 5: Plan Rating and Funding 97
Fully Insured Plans 97
Alternatives to Fully Insured Plans 113
    Stop-Loss Insurance 115
    Deferred Premium Arrangements 117
    Shared Funding Arrangements 118
    Retrospective Premium Arrangements 120
    Reserve Reduction Agreements 123
    Minimum Premium Plans 125
Voluntary Employee Benefit Associations (VEBAs) 129

Chapter 6: Plan Implementation and Administration 137
Setting Up the Plan 137
Reporting and Disclosure 141
Enrollment 144

Table of Contents

Billing 147
Claims 150
Renewals, Changes, and Termination of Coverage 154
Terminated Employees 157
COBRA 159
Computerized Administration 177

Chapter 7: Managing Health Insurance Costs **181**
Health Care Data 187
Cost-Sharing Strategies 190
Coordination of Benefits 194
Outpatient Surgery/Preadmission Testing 197
Second Surgical Opinions 198
Utilization Review and Case Management 202
Additional Cost-Management Strategies 207
Billing Codes 210

Chapter 8: Alternative Health Care Systems: HMOs and PPOs **213**
Health Maintenance Organizations 214
  Adverse Selection 224
  Legal Standards 225
  Evaluating HMOs 231
Preferred Provider Organizations 235
HMOs vs. PPOs 247

Chapter 9: Flexible Benefits **251**

Chapter 10: Medicare **279**
Medicare Order of Benefit Determination 282
OBRA '89 283
Medicare Cost Containment 289

Chapter 11: Nondiscrimination Rules **297**
Accident and Health Plans 297
Group Term Life Plans 301
Cafeteria Plans 304
Dependent Care Assistance Plans 307

Health Insurance Answer Book

    Educational Assistance Plans 309
    Group Legal Services Plans 310
    VEBAs 311
    Nondiscriminatory Classification 312

Chapter 12: Other Benefits Issues 317
    Substance Abuse Treatment 317
    Employee Assistance Programs 322
    Health Promotion and Wellness 324
    Retiree Health Benefits 331
    Long-Term Care 338
    Impact of AIDS on Insurance 343

Appendix: Health Information Resources 349

Glossary 359

Index 381

How to Use the *Health Insurance Answer Book*

In the following pages, the Health Insurance Answer Book will provide you with the answers to the many questions raised by even a short trip through the health care maze. This third edition has revised and expanded all the material in the second edition and has added new material as well.

The book concentrates primarily on issues facing the health insurance plan sponsor—generally a nongovernment employer or a union. Although the book does not ignore individual insurance programs, the emphasis is on group programs. And although the word "insurance" in the title suggests a program purchased through a commercial insurer, it also means those plans that the sponsor self-insures without commercial insurer involvement.

The types of issues the plan sponsor faces in implementing and maintaining a health care plan include:

- Whom to work with in designing and purchasing a plan;
- What benefits to provide;
- How much to spend;
- How to fund the plan costs;
- What cost-control mechanisms to implement; and
- How to deal with ongoing administration, including government compliance.

Health Insurance Answer Book

This book is designed to answer the questions surrounding these basic decisions.

Organization of the Book: The book is divided into 12 chapters, that are intended to take the reader from the fundamental concepts of group insurance through the selection and buying process, financing, and administration. These basics are followed by discussions of how to manage costs, alternative approaches to providing health care benefits, Medicare, and finally some thoughts on current issues of special interest.

Numbering System: The questions are numbered in a consecutive sequence within each chapter. Subheadings before groups of related questions are provided to help in locating specific material. In addition, the question numbers beginning each left page and ending each right page appear in the upper left and right corner of each page, respectively, for easy reference.

Detailed Listing of Questions: The list of questions that follows the Table of Contents in the front of the book helps the reader locate areas of immediate interest. Each question is identified by a question number and the corresponding page number on which it appears. Thus, the reader can easily locate an area of interest and the specific questions relating to it.

Appendix: An appendix provides a listing of health insurance resources.

Glossary: An alphabetical glossary of terms is included to help explain the terms, abbreviations, and acronyms that are frequently used in the health care industry.

Index: At the back of the book, a traditional topical index is provided as a further aid to locating specific information. All references in the index are to question numbers rather than page numbers.

This question-and-answer format offers a clear and useful guide to understanding the complex, but extremely important, area of health insurance.

Health Care Reform: 1990 and Beyond

In addition to the legislation that has already been enacted, there are some proposed statutes that could become law within the next year or so that may be even more interesting. The drive to reform the way health care benefits are provided to Americans, both employees and non-employees, is picking up momentum. Driven by the growing demands on the health care delivery system, the burgeoning costs of meeting those demands, and the increasing number of Americans who enjoy no health care coverage at all, there has been a rush by government agencies, professional associations and industry groups to propose new ways of offering health insurance.

According to the U.S. Department of Commerce, national health care outlays were around $600 billion in 1989, or roughly $2,400 for every American. That was 11.5% of the U.S. gross national product, up from 10.1% in 1988. Thus, the rate of growth for health care costs was almost twice that of the GNP.

The employer share of health care plan costs rose 20.4% in 1989 according to a survey by A. Foster Higgins & Co., Inc. The survey of 1,943 employers with plans covering 12.5 million employees showed that the average cost of medical indemnity plans rose from $2,160 per employee in 1988 to $2,600 in 1989. With dental plans and HMOs included, the averages were $2,748 and $2,354 respectively.

Meanwhile, despite the huge expenditure, there are over 30 million Americans who have no coverage at all. Recognizing that buying more health care for these people is simply beyond our resources without some rearrangement of and economizing in the current system, a number of organizations have issued reform proposals, with more due out later this year. (Some reforms have already been introduced at the state level.) The following is a summary of some of these reform initiatives.

1. The *Pepper Commission* (U.S. Bipartisan Commission on Comprehensive Health Care) reported to Congress on its plan for expanding the availability of health care and providing coverage for the estimated 30 million people who are now uninsured. The panel proposed:

- three months of free nursing home care for those with severe disabilities;
- free nursing home care for the elderly with low or moderate incomes (less than $30,000 for single persons; $60,000 for couples);
- businesses with over 100 employees would be required to provide minimum levels of physician and hospital coverage, as well as primary and preventive care;
- there would be a public plan to provide coverage for those who are not now covered;
- there would be temporary tax credits and subsidies to offset the costs of providing benefits for small employers,
- self-employed health insurance premiums would be 100% deductible, and
- health insurance reform would prohibit medical underwriting, deny exclusions for pre-existing conditions, and preempt state insurance laws.

Some of these provisions would be phased in over a period of time (the tax credits and subsidies would begin immediately and then be phased out).

The nursing home coverage was projected to cost $42.8 billion over a 4-year period. The public health care coverage would cost $43 billion over 7 years, of which the government would pay $23 billion, with the rest coming through private employers, with employees paying 20%.

Health Care Reform: the 1990s and Beyond

While there has been some support for the proposal, businesses have criticized it as being too expensive, and members of Congress have complained that it offered no suggestions as to where the government's $66 billion share would come from.

2. Medical associations have offered their own versions of health care reform. The *American Medical Association* reform proposal would:

- reform Medicaid to provide uniform, adequate benefits to all persons whose incomes fall below the poverty level;
- require employers to provide health care coverage for full-time employees and their families;
- create tax incentives and state risk pools to enable new and small businesses to afford coverage; and
- create risk pools for those who are uninsurable, or insurable only at prohibitive cost.

A recent position paper from the *American College of Physicians* went further and called for a national program similar to the Canadian model.

3. The *Health Insurance Association of America* (HIAA) has offered a proposal for the reform of the small business (employers with under 25 employees) health insurance market. The plan calls for federal and state legislation that would:

"1. guarantee that employers with fewer than 25 employees who seek to purchase health insurance for their employees will not be denied such health insurance coverage even if one or more employees might otherwise be either uninsurable or a high risk in today's world;

2. provide that once insured, neither the group nor an individual in the group may be denied continued coverage because the group's or the individual's health deteriorates;

3. limit the rate of year-to-year premium increases relative to other groups insured by the same carrier;

4. permit medical underwriting only for the purpose of determining the level of risk, and thus anticipated health claims;

5. not deny coverage or apply new preexisting condition re-

strictions to an insured individual in a group changing either employers or insurance carriers;

6. establish a privately funded and administered reinsurance mechanism through which insurers could reinsure high risk persons;

7. ensure that any group would pay no more than 150% of the average cost of similar groups for basic coverage."

The HIAA proposal would assure that a company's premiums would not exceed by more than 50% those of other employers with similar age and occupational groupings. Workers with a serious illness who wished to change jobs would not have to worry about losing coverage because of a new employer's pre-existing condition clause. The entire system would be backed by a new reinsurance scheme to protect the insurers themselves.

This proposal, intended to make affordable insurance available to as many as 10 million employees of small firms, may have the best chance in the near term. Already the National Association of Insurance Commissioners (NAIC) is considering model legislation along these lines.

More reports and proposals are expected. Reports from the Social Security Advisory Council and a task force from the Department of Health and Human Services are scheduled to be presented to Congress and the Administration shortly after this book goes to press. These will be placed alongside mandatory coverage proposals which have been around for quite a while. Senator Edward Kennedy (D-MA) introduced a bill which would require employers to provide minimum levels of hospitalization, physician and mental health coverage to employees who work 17-1/2 hours a week or more.

The sticking point to date has been concern over cost. Government has shown itself unable to fund the commitments it has already made, and has engaged in an almost annual ritual of shifting obligations from Medicare to private employers. Those employers are still reeling from double-digit growth in health care costs and are not willing to take on any more expense.

A Buck Consultants, Inc. survey of Fortune 1000 employers found that 59.8% of the respondents were opposed to a national health insurance program, while only 29.5% favored it. 82.6% (including

Health Care Reform: the 1990s and Beyond

64.6% of those who were in favor of national health care) said they did not believe that the federal government could manage health care costs any more effectively than could the private sector, and 58.3% felt that the quality of health care under a national health care program would not be as good as what we have now.

State Initiatives

While the debate on health care reform has recently heated up at the national level, states have been busy with initiatives of their own. 1988 alone saw 34 states pass 320 bills governing mandatory coverages. These laws generally apply to insured plans rather than self-funded arrangements. Most states have mandates covering treatment for alcoholism and drug abuse, mental health, and coverage of newborn and adopted children. Many others also require coverage for chiropractic services, treatment for mental and physical handicaps, optometric benefits, and so on. Some states go even beyond the mainstream types of benefits and require benefits for services such as infertility treatments (5 states).

Small business exemptions: Some states, such as Florida, Virginia and Washington, have innovative programs that exempt small businesses from certain mandatory offerings to reduce the cost of purchasing coverage. Private carriers are responding by providing bare-bones group health policies. Connecticut is experimenting with a program along the lines of the NAIC proposed model, by negotiating lower provider rates for small businesses and establishing risk pools for certain existing medical conditions.

Few states, however, *require* employers to provide their workers with health care benefits. There are two notable exceptions:

Hawaii: Hawaii's law requiring employers to provide employees with health care coverage has been in effect for 15 years. The law mandates hospitalization and basic medical coverage to employees who are paid 86.67% of the monthly minimum wage. Employers are required to pay at least half of the cost, with employees picking up the remainder, provided no employee pays more than 1.5% of his wages.

Massachusetts: Massachusetts was the first state to *guarantee* health insurance to all residents. The Massachusetts law was aimed at the 600,000 of its residents, both employed and unemployed, who lacked health care coverage.

Employers subject to the law include those with over five employees. A special program provides financial assistance to employers with six or fewer employees who wish to provide medical coverage. Employers with 50 or fewer employees are eligible for limited credits against state taxes, as well as assistance in securing affordable insurance.

Employer coverage is not mandatory, but failure to offer it is expensive. Beginning in 1992, employers will be required to pay the state a surcharge of 12% of the first $14,000 (indexed starting in 1993) of pay as their share of the costs of the state medical security trust fund. Those who already provide their employees with health care coverage, however, will be allowed to deduct the cost of that coverage from the surcharge—in effect largely exempting those employers who already provide coverage.

New York and Minnesota: These states have introduced programs to provide subsidized health care for children of families whose incomes fall below specified levels. These and similar programs are intended to fill in where Medicaid leaves off; Medicaid will cover children under the age of six whose family incomes fall below 133% of the poverty line. State programs will provide primary and preventive care such as doctors visits, prescription drugs and emergency room visits.

Rationing Care: Oregon and Medicaid Reform

Most Americans, more than 9 out of 10 according to a Louis Harris poll, believe that "everybody should have the right to the best possible health care—as good as the treatment a millionaire gets" even if the cost of an individual's care exceeded over $1 million. The spread of expensive technologies (in 1985, for example, there were 34 heart transplant centers; by 1988 there were 148), has increased the incidence of high cost procedures. It is no longer unusual to have programs of treatment, some of which may be regarded as experimental, running into the hundreds of thousands of dollars.

Some years ago, bioethicists began asking discomforting questions about traditional assumptions regarding health care availability. Does it make sense for society to underwrite the cost of all of these expensive procedures? Would we be better off if we channeled this money to other types of care which would provide valuable benefits to a wider range of people? Should there be formal mechanisms for weighing the benefits of various procedures against their costs, and cutting those off that do not meet specified cost/benefit standards?

The State of Oregon asked these questions about its Medicaid program. The joint federal/state program was costing Oregon some $70 million a year to help 130,000 of the state's low income residents. By cutting off high cost procedures that benefit relatively few residents, the state hopes to expand health coverage generally and provide at least some health care services to every resident living below the federal poverty level.

In public hearings held around the state, those attending supported preventive care services over costly life-saving procedures. Based upon the findings of these hearings, as well as a telephone survey, a "quality of well-being scale" was developed that ranked how an average person might feel after receiving treatment for a particular ailment. The scale takes into account the cost of a procedure and the number of years an average person might live after receiving the treatment. The final result is a cost-to-benefits ratio that allows each of the 1,600 procedures to be ranked, with those having the highest ratio given the best chance of Medicaid reimbursement, and those below certain cut-off figures denied reimbursement altogether.

The Oregon formula, which has already drawn protests from groups representing beneficiaries such as organ transplant recipients, must be approved by the federal government. If it is approved at all, the priority list will likely undergo many changes before it reaches its final form.

Conclusion

There is a growing consensus that government must be part of the solution to the twin problems of the growing numbers of uninsured and the growing burden of paying for those who are insured.

There appear to be two schools of thought as to how this might be done. One school's approach is to free up the private marketplace: reduce regulation and limit mandates. The second school favors increased government involvement in defining coverages, regulating rates, and managing funding. It appears that through efforts at both the state and federal levels, the next few years will find us committed to experimenting with both approaches at the same time.

Listing of Questions

Chapter 1 An Overview of Group Insurance

Q. 1:1	What are the various ways that individuals receive health insurance protection?	1
Q. 1:2	What is the major difference between group and individual insurance?	1
Q. 1:3	What are the advantages of group insurance over individual insurance?	2
Q. 1:4	How prevalent is group insurance in the United States?	2
Q. 1:5	Why do most employers provide group insurance?	3
Q. 1:6	What types of group protection do most employers provide?	3
Q. 1:7	What are the characteristics of group life insurance?	3
Q. 1:8	What are the characteristics of group AD&D insurance?	4
Q. 1:9	How does group disability insurance protect against loss of income?	4
Q. 1:10	What is included in the term "group health insurance"?	5
Q. 1:11	What are the characteristics of group health insurance?	5
Q. 1:12	What caused the rapid growth of group health insurance?	5
Q. 1:13	How important is group health insurance to employees?	6
Q. 1:14	What is the single most important factor affecting group health insurance in recent years?	6
Q. 1:15	Is group insurance available only to single employers?	7

Health Insurance Answer Book

Q. 1:16	What is a multiple employer trust?	7
Q. 1:17	How can a labor union provide group insurance?	7
Q. 1:18	What is an association plan?	8

Chapter 2 The Health Insurance Marketplace

Types of Insurance Professionals

Q. 2:1	Can an employer work directly with an insurance company?	9
Q. 2:2	What is a group health insurance underwriter?	10
Q. 2:3	What is risk?	10
Q. 2:4	What is adverse selection?	11
Q. 2:5	What is a group sales representative?	11
Q. 2:6	What is a client service representative?	11
Q. 2:7	What is an intermediary?	11
Q. 2:8	How do group sales representatives and intermediaries interact in the sale of a group health insurance plan?	12
Q. 2:9	What services do intermediaries provide prior to the purchase of a group health insurance plan?	12
Q. 2:10	What is an insurance broker?	12
Q. 2:11	What is the difference between an agent and a broker?	13
Q. 2:12	What is an employee benefits consultant?	13
Q. 2:13	How does an employer determine whether to use an agent, broker, or consultant?	13
Q. 2:14	What is a TPA?	14

Choosing and Compensating Intermediaries

| Q. 2:15 | How does an employer select a particular intermediary? | 14 |
| Q. 2:16 | Can an employer use a personal or business advisor as its group insurance intermediary? | 15 |

Listing of Questions

Q. 2:17	How are intermediaries compensated?	15
Q. 2:18	What are commission schedules?	15
Q. 2:19	What is vesting of commissions?	16
Q. 2:20	Are there laws that regulate the business practices of intermediaries?	16
Q. 2:21	If an employer wants to self-fund the plan, which type of insurance professional would it need?	17
Q. 2:22	Would an employer whose plan is fully insured use a TPA?	17
Q. 2:23	How does an employer decide whether to use a TPA or an insurance company to administer its plan?	17
Q. 2:24	If an employer has a TPA handle the administrative functions, would the employer's cost be decreased?	18
Q. 2:25	How are TPAs compensated?	18

HMOs, PPOs, and Health Care Coalitions

Q. 2:26	What is an HMO?	18
Q. 2:27	What is a PPO?	19
Q. 2:28	What is an employer health care coalition?	19

Chapter 3 Factors Influencing Insurance Plan Design

Legal Factors Affecting Design

Q. 3:1	Are employers required by federal law to purchase group insurance for their employees?	21
Q. 3:2	Are employers required by state law to purchase group insurance for their employees?	22
Q. 3:3	Are group health plans governed by federal laws or by state laws?	22
Q. 3:4	Do federal and state laws apply to self-insured group health plans?	23
Q. 3:5	When state and federal laws change, what are an employer's obligations regarding a group health insurance plan?	23

Health Insurance Answer Book

State Law

Q. 3:6	What are the responsibilities of the state insurance department?	24
Q. 3:7	What are the similarities among state laws governing group health insurance?	25
Q. 3:8	What is a mandated benefit?	25
Q. 3:9	Why are some benefits mandated by state law?	25
Q. 3:10	What is a mandated offering?	26
Q. 3:11	What is a right of direct payment?	26
Q. 3:12	What are the state requirements for employee participation in a group insurance plan?	26
Q. 3:13	What is the minimum number of employees allowed by state law to participate in a group health insurance plan?	26
Q. 3:14	Is there a maximum number of employees that may be covered under a group health insurance plan?	27

Workers' Compensation

Q. 3:15	What is Workers' Compensation?	27
Q. 3:16	What types of benefits does Workers' Compensation provide?	27
Q. 3:17	How is Workers' Compensation insurance made available?	28
Q. 3:18	May Workers' Compensation benefits be integrated with other employer benefits?	28
Q. 3:19	How are Workers' Compensation benefits taxed to employees?	28
Q. 3:20	Why is Workers' Compensation a growing concern for employers?	28
Q. 3:21	Why are Workers' Compensation costs rising?	29
Q. 3:22	What can employers do to control Workers' Compensation costs?	29

Federal Law

Q. 3:23	What federal laws affect group health insurance plans?	30
Q. 3:24	How does ADEA affect group health insurance plans?	31
Q. 3:25	Are employers required by federal law to cover retired employees under group health insurance plans?	32

Listing of Questions

Q. 3:26	What requirements does ERISA impose on group health insurance plans?	32
Q. 3:27	How are group health insurance plans affected by the HMO Act of 1973?	33

Pregnancy Discrimination Act

Q. 3:28	What is the Pregnancy Discrimination Act (PDA)?	34
Q. 3:29	What does the "same treatment for pregnancy related conditions" mean?	34
Q. 3:30	What employers are subject to the PDA?	34
Q. 3:31	Do the provisions of the Pregnancy Discrimination Act apply only to married employees?	35
Q. 3:32	Does the Pregnancy Discrimination Act extend to benefits for spouses of employees?	35
Q. 3:33	Does the Pregnancy Discrimination Act extend to other dependents?	35
Q. 3:34	Must abortions be covered by employer health plans?	35
Q. 3:35	Is mandatory maternity leave permitted under the PDA?	36
Q. 3:36	Must employees be allowed to return to their jobs following maternity leave?	37
Q. 3:37	Are state laws pre-empted by the Pregnancy Discrimination Act?	37
Q. 3:38	Does the PDA apply to "parental or family leave"?	37
Q. 3:39	Are there state laws governing parental or family leave?	38
Q. 3:40	Are there federal laws governing parental or family leave?	39
Q. 3:41	What is the difference between maternity leave and parental or family leave?	39
Q. 3:42	What features are commonly found in employer family leave policies?	40

Occupational Safety and Health Act

Q. 3:43	What is the Occupational Safety and Health Act (OSHA)?	41
Q. 3:44	What requirements apply to businesses?	41
Q. 3:45	What are the notification and recordkeeping requirements?	41

Health Insurance Answer Book

Q. 3:46	When does the Occupational Safety and Health Administration make inspections?	41
Q. 3:47	How can employers get more information on OSHA?	42

Americans with Disabilities Act

Q. 3:48	What is the Americans with Disabilities Act of 1990 (ADA)?	42
Q. 3:49	How does the law affect employers and their employees?	42
Q. 3:50	What size businesses must comply?	43
Q. 3:51	What is a qualified individual with a disability?	43
Q. 3:52	What is "reasonable accomodation"?	43
Q. 3:53	Will the ADA have an adverse effect on business?	43

Taxation of Group Health Plans

Q. 3:54	What state tax laws apply to group health insurance plans?	44
Q. 3:55	What is the federal tax status of group health insurance for employers?	44
Q. 3:56	Are employer contributions treated as taxable income to employees?	45
Q. 3:57	Are the benefits from a group health insurance plan taxable to employees?	45

Nonlegal Factors Affecting Design

Q. 3:58	Besides the legislative factors, what other issues must be addressed as part of the purchasing process?	45
Q. 3:59	Who is an eligible employee?	46
Q. 3:60	Can a single group health insurance plan meet the benefits needs of an employer's diverse workforce?	46

Restrictions on Coverage

Q. 3:61	For what reasons do employers typically exclude employees from group health insurance coverage?	47
Q. 3:62	Are there limitations on an employer's freedom to choose the employees it wants covered under a group health insurance plan?	47
Q. 3:63	Why would an employer offer benefits to which some employees already have access?	48

Listing of Questions

Q. 3:64 Do employers provide group health insurance to part-time and temporary employees?   48

Q. 3:65 Can an employer provide enhanced health care coverage for key employees?   49

Q. 3:66 Will an insurance carrier deny certain employees coverage under a group health insurance plan?   49

Q. 3:67 Can an employer require different service waiting periods?   50

Paying for Insurance

Q. 3:68 How much can an employer expect to pay annually for group health insurance?   51

Q. 3:69 Must employers pay the entire cost of group health insurance?   51

Q. 3:70 What factors should an employer consider when deciding whether its group health insurance plan should be contributory or noncontributory?   52

Q. 3:71 What legal constraints are imposed on the distribution of employer-employee costs for group health insurance?   53

Q. 3:72 Can an employer self-fund a group health insurance plan?   53

Q. 3:73 How common are self-funded plans?   53

Q. 3:74 What factors should a small employer consider when deciding whether to self-fund all or part of its health insurance plan?   53

Chapter 4 Types of Health Insurance Plans and Related Benefits

Medical Benefits

Q. 4:1 What types of group health insurance plans are available?   55

Q. 4:2 What is a base plus plan?   55

Q. 4:3 What is a comprehensive plan?   56

Q. 4:4 Are there advantages to a base plus plan?   57

Q. 4:5 What are the advantages of a comprehensive plan?   57

Q. 4:6 Do all insurers offer both types of group health insurance plans?   58

Health Insurance Answer Book

Blue Cross/Blue Shield Plans

Q. 4:7	What is Blue Cross/Blue Shield (BC/BS)?	58
Q. 4:8	Are BC/BS plans similar to those offered by private insurance companies?	59
Q. 4:9	Do most private insurers offer similar major medical supplements?	60
Q. 4:10	How are BC/BS premium rates different from those of private insurers?	60
Q. 4:11	Are expenses reimbursed at a more generous level by private insurers than by BC/BS?	60

Coverage

Q. 4:12	What types of services are generally covered by a group health insurance plan?	61
Q. 4:13	What types of services are generally not covered by a group health insurance plan?	62
Q. 4:14	What kinds of hospital charges are covered under a group health insurance plan?	62
Q. 4:15	How is surgery covered under a health insurance plan?	63
Q. 4:16	Why do some plans pay R&C charges and other schedule benefits?	64
Q. 4:17	If the physicians' charges exceed the R&C amount or the schedule amount, is the employee responsible for paying the balance?	64
Q. 4:18	How have hospital and surgical care changed recently?	64
Q. 4:19	How are nonsurgical physicians' services covered?	65

Outpatient Care, Extended Care, and HMOs/PPOs

Q. 4:20	What alternatives to hospital care are common today?	65
Q. 4:21	What kinds of hospital outpatient expenses are covered?	66
Q. 4:22	Does health insurance cover extended care facilities?	66
Q. 4:23	What other types of health care plans might an employer offer?	66

Deductibles, Copayments, and Reimbursements

Q. 4:24	What is a deductible?	67
Q. 4:25	What is a carryover deductible?	67

Listing of Questions

Q. 4:26	For insured employees with dependent coverage, does the deductible for each person have to be satisfied before reimbursement begins?	67
Q. 4:27	What is coinsurance?	68
Q. 4:28	What is a maximum out-of-pocket limit?	68
Q. 4:29	Is the deductible included in determining an OOP maximum?	69
Q. 4:30	Can medical expenses not covered by a health insurance plan be applied toward the deductible or OOP maximum?	69
Q. 4:31	What is a covered expense?	69
Q. 4:32	Are all covered expenses reimbursed?	69
Q. 4:33	How are covered expenses limited?	70
Q. 4:34	What is a reasonable and customary charge?	70
Q. 4:35	What is a schedule of insurance?	70
Q. 4:36	Do most policies include an overall limit to the amount reimbursable to one individual?	71

Dental Benefits

Q. 4:37	Do health insurance plans cover dental care?	71
Q. 4:38	Why is there growing interest in dental insurance?	71
Q. 4:39	How are dental benefits provided?	72
Q. 4:40	What is direct reimbursement for dental care?	72
Q. 4:41	What dental services are typically provided?	72
Q. 4:42	Are all types of dental services covered by insurance?	73
Q. 4:43	What cost-management features are built into dental plans?	73
Q. 4:44	Why is orthodontics often treated as a special coverage category?	74
Q. 4:45	Are there special cost-control considerations for dental plans?	74
Q. 4:46	What are dental plan incentives, and how do they work?	74
Q. 4:47	What is precertification?	75
Q. 4:48	Are some dental services excluded from coverage?	75

Vision and Hearing Benefits

Q. 4:49	How is vision care covered?	76

Health Insurance Answer Book

Q. 4:50 Is coverage available for hearing evaluations and hearing aids?   76

Prescription Drug Plans

Q. 4:51 Why are prescription drugs a growing concern for health insurance planners?   76
Q. 4:52 What other factors affect an employer's prescription drug costs?   77
Q. 4:53 Are all prescription drugs covered under health care plans?   77
Q. 4:54 Will some plans cover contraceptive prescription drugs?   77
Q. 4:55 Why would an employer have a separate prescription drug plan?   77
Q. 4:56 Why would an employer avoid a free-standing drug plan in favor of covering medication under a major medical or comprehensive health plan?   78
Q. 4:57 Are there different types of drug plans?   78
Q. 4:58 What is an open-panel drug plan?   78
Q. 4:59 What is a closed-panel drug plan?   78
Q. 4:60 What is a mail-order drug plan?   79
Q. 4:61 What is a prescription drug card plan?   79
Q. 4:62 How long have prescription drug card plans been in existence?   79
Q. 4:63 Is a prescription drug card plan better than regular reimbursement?   80
Q. 4:64 How can an employer decide whether to elect a prescription card plan?   80
Q. 4:65 Is prescription medication covered outside of these plans?   81
Q. 4:66 Who offers drug plans?   81

Mental Health Benefits

Q. 4:67 Are mental illnesses usually covered by health plans?   81
Q. 4:68 Why is there growing concern about mental health services?   82
Q. 4:69 What causes overutilization of inpatient mental health care?   82
Q. 4:70 Why has attention focused on mental health care issues?   82

Listing of Questions

Q. 4:71	What areas of mental health care are growing most rapidly?	83
Q. 4:72	Who is interested in controlling the cost of mental health care?	83
Q. 4:73	How can mental health services be better managed?	84

Mental Health Management

Q. 4:74	Why is managing dependent mental health care expenses important?	84
Q. 4:75	What methods for reducing these costs are employers considering?	85
Q. 4:76	Is there a downside to reducing benefits?	85
Q. 4:77	How does case management of mental health services work?	86
Q. 4:78	What is a prepaid mental health plan?	86

Life Insurance Benefits

Q. 4:79	Why would survivor benefits be included in a group health insurance program?	86
Q. 4:80	What form do these death benefits take?	87
Q. 4:81	How are these death benefits taxed?	87

Disability Benefits

Q. 4:82	How much of employers' payroll is used to pay disability benefits?	88
Q. 4:83	How pervasive are disabilities in the United States?	88
Q. 4:84	How do employees become disabled?	88
Q. 4:85	What programs are available to compensate employees for disability?	88
Q. 4:86	What is a short-term disability plan?	89
Q. 4:87	What is a long-term disability (LTD) plan?	89
Q. 4:88	How is disability defined?	89
Q. 4:89	What are other important components of an LTD plan?	90
Q. 4:90	How much do disabled workers receive from disability plans?	91
Q. 4:91	Are LTD plans expensive?	91
Q. 4:92	How are employees taxed on disability benefits?	91

Health Insurance Answer Book

Disability Management

Q. 4:93	How can employers achieve effective disability management?	92
Q. 4:94	How does an employer, union, or insurer put a disability prevention program in place?	92
Q. 4:95	How does rehabilitation fit into disability management?	93
Q. 4:96	What portion of the disabled can actually be rehabilitated?	93
Q. 4:97	Are some people better candidates than others for disability rehabilitation?	93
Q. 4:98	What ingredients go into a rehabilitation program?	93
Q. 4:99	Who staffs a rehabilitation team?	94
Q. 4:100	What is a return-to-work program?	94
Q. 4:101	What is an independent living program?	95

Chapter 5 Plan Rating and Funding

Q. 5:1	What does plan funding mean?	97

Fully Insured Plans

Q. 5:2	What are the components of the cost of a health insurance plan?	97
Q. 5:3	What are expected claims?	98
Q. 5:4	Why would claims be paid after the termination of the contract?	98
Q. 5:5	How does an insurer know what claims to expect?	99
Q. 5:6	What is a group health insurance actuary?	99
Q. 5:7	How does an actuary estimate which individuals will incur claims?	99
Q. 5:8	How does plan design affect the expected claims calculation?	100
Q. 5:9	How does the health plan's rate-guarantee period affect the rate?	100
Q. 5:10	How does the insurer project the cost of the medical services that are expected to be provided?	101
Q. 5:11	How is the expected cost of claims calculated for an employer with several locations?	101

Q. 5:12	How is a margin for higher than anticipated claims developed?	101
Q. 5:13	What is prospective rating?	102
Q. 5:14	What is retrospective rating?	103
Q. 5:15	How does a policyholder reimburse a deficit?	103
Q. 5:16	What are reserves?	104
Q. 5:17	How does an insurer determine what premium reserves are necessary?	104
Q. 5:18	How are expenses projected?	105
Q. 5:19	What percentage of the health insurance premium is generally an insurance company's profit?	105
Q. 5:20	What is credibility?	105
Q. 5:21	What is a manual rate?	106
Q. 5:22	What is a pool?	106
Q. 5:23	What is an experience rate?	107
Q. 5:24	How is an experience rate combined with a manual rate to produce a final premium rate?	107
Q. 5:25	Do all claims count toward an employer's claims experience, thus affecting the rate?	108
Q. 5:26	What is a pool charge?	108
Q. 5:27	What is retention?	109
Q. 5:28	How does an employer determine whether a premium rate is reasonable?	109
Q. 5:29	Are dependent rates developed separately from employee rates?	110
Q. 5:30	What is a loss ratio?	110
Q. 5:31	What is a tolerable loss ratio (TLR)?	110
Q. 5:32	Do TLRs vary from year to year and from employer to employer?	111
Q. 5:33	What is the difference between paid claims and incurred claims?	112
Q. 5:34	What is lag?	112
Q. 5:35	What is a lag study?	113

Alternatives to Fully Insured Plans

Q. 5:36	Are there alternatives to fully insured (conventionally funded) plans?	113
Q. 5:37	How do alternative funding methods differ from conventional funding methods?	114

Q. 5:38	For whom might an alternative method of plan funding be appropriate?	114
Q. 5:39	What size of employers typically seek funding alternatives?	115
Q. 5:40	Do some employers elect to insure the entire risk of a health insurance plan?	115

Stop-Loss Insurance

Q. 5:41	What is stop-loss insurance?	115
Q. 5:42	What is the difference between aggregate and specific stop-loss insurance?	116
Q. 5:43	From whom does an employer purchase stop-loss insurance?	116
Q. 5:44	What is the difference between pooling and stop-loss insurance?	116

Deferred Premium Arrangements

Q. 5:45	What is a deferred premium arrangement?	117
Q. 5:46	Why would an employer elect a deferred premium arrangement?	117
Q. 5:47	Why don't all employers elect deferred premium arrangements?	118

Shared Funding Arrangements

Q. 5:48	How does a shared funding arrangement differ from a conventionally funded plan?	118
Q. 5:49	Why would an employer elect a shared funding plan?	119
Q. 5:50	Why would an employer reject a shared funding plan as an alternative funding arrangement?	119
Q. 5:51	Why don't all employers elect shared funding arrangements?	120

Retrospective Premium Arrangements

Q. 5:52	What is a retrospective premium arrangement?	120
Q. 5:53	Why would an employer negotiate a retrospective premium arrangement?	121
Q. 5:54	What is a "deep cut" retro?	121
Q. 5:55	Why might an employer not negotiate a retrospective premium arrangement?	122
Q. 5:56	To whom are retrospective premium arrangements available?	122

Listing of Questions

Reserve Reduction Agreements

Q. 5:57	What is a reserve reduction agreement?	123
Q. 5:58	Why would reserves decrease if an insurer eliminates its liability after contract termination?	123
Q. 5:59	Why would an employer want to negotiate a reserve reduction?	123
Q. 5:60	Why might an employer not change the conventional reserve arrangement?	124
Q. 5:61	Do small employers typically implement reserve reduction agreements?	124

Minimum Premium Plans

Q. 5:62	What is a minimum premium plan (MPP)?	125
Q. 5:63	At what level does the insurer become responsible for benefits funding under an MPP?	125
Q. 5:64	If an individual incurs a shock claim (an unexpected claim of a high amount) under an MPP, does the full amount of that claim count toward the employer's trigger point?	127
Q. 5:65	How are claims paid with employer funds under an MPP?	127
Q. 5:66	Why would an employer benefit from establishing an MPP?	127
Q. 5:67	Why wouldn't an employer elect an MPP?	128
Q. 5:68	What employers typically elect MPPs?	129
Q. 5:69	How are third-party administrative services used in an MPP?	129

Voluntary Employee Benefit Associations (VEBAs)

Q. 5:70	What is a VEBA?	129
Q. 5:71	What tax benefits do VEBAs confer?	129
Q. 5:72	What "other benefits" can be provided through a VEBA?	130
Q. 5:73	What benefits cannot be provided through a VEBA?	130
Q. 5:74	What are the requirements for establishing a VEBA?	131
Q. 5:75	How does a VEBA obtain tax exempt status?	131
Q. 5:76	May a VEBA be established to benefit only one person?	131
Q. 5:77	May a VEBA benefit persons who are not employees?	132

Health Insurance Answer Book

Q. 5:78	Who is an employee for VEBA purposes?	132
Q. 5:79	What restrictions on membership are permissible?	132
Q. 5:80	Who controls a VEBA?	133
Q. 5:81	Is there a limit on deductible contributions to a VEBA?	133
Q. 5:82	What are the restrictions on funding for post-retirement benefits?	133
Q. 5:83	What are the special rules regarding contributions for key employees?	134
Q. 5:84	What is "unrelated business income"?	134
Q. 5:85	Are there non-discrimination requirements for VEBAs?	135

Chapter 6 Plan Implementation and Administration

Setting Up the Plan

Q. 6:1	After an employer selects a health insurance plan, what must be done to put the coverage into effect?	137
Q. 6:2	Is the coverage effective as soon as the insurer receives the application and enrollment material?	138
Q. 6:3	When might an underwriter not approve an application for coverage?	138
Q. 6:4	If an application is not approved by the underwriter, what happens?	138
Q. 6:5	Why does the insurance company require detailed coverage information before issuing the policy?	139
Q. 6:6	When an employer uses a third-party administrator, what services does the administrator provide?	139
Q. 6:7	Who provides the announcement materials necessary to inform employees about the plan?	140
Q. 6:8	What is a certificate of insurance?	140
Q. 6:9	What other materials are issued to employees?	140

Reporting and Disclosure

| Q. 6:10 | Are there reports that an employer must file with the state or federal government? | 141 |

Q. 6:11	How does the repeal of Section 89 affect welfare plan reporting and disclosure requirements?	142
Q. 6:12	When do the new reporting requirements become effective?	142
Q. 6:13	What is a summary plan description (SPD) and what information does it contain?	143
Q. 6:14	Should an employer rely on the SPD to explain plan benefits to employees?	143
Q. 6:15	What administrative material does the insurer initially provide to the employer?	144

Enrollment

Q. 6:16	Why is enrollment in the plan encouraged?	144
Q. 6:17	What information must individuals provide to enroll in the plan?	144
Q. 6:18	Must individuals enroll in a noncontributory plan?	145
Q. 6:19	Who enrolls the employees in the group health insurance plan?	145
Q. 6:20	How long do employees have to complete their enrollment forms?	145
Q. 6:21	Why would an employee who submits a late enrollment form not be allowed to participate as of the plan's effective date?	146
Q. 6:22	If an employee declines coverage initially, can he or she enroll at a later date?	146
Q. 6:23	Is any kind of reenrollment of employees in group health insurance plans necessary?	147

Billing

Q. 6:24	How are employers billed for group health insurance premiums?	147
Q. 6:25	Where can an employer get help in calculating premium payments?	148
Q. 6:26	If an employer's premium payment is late, does coverage lapse?	149
Q. 6:27	Does the insurer periodically audit employers that self-account?	149

Claims

Q. 6:28	How does an individual submit a claim for payment?	**150**
Q. 6:29	Can employees submit claims after the effective date of the plan but before they receive their certificates of insurance?	**151**
Q. 6:30	Do most individuals pay the health care provider for the service and receive reimbursement later from the plan?	**151**
Q. 6:31	What is assignment of benefits?	**151**
Q. 6:32	Where can an employee get help in completing a claims form?	**152**
Q. 6:33	Can employees determine whether a claim will be paid before they receive the medical care?	**152**
Q. 6:34	How quickly are insureds reimbursed for their claims expenses?	**152**
Q. 6:35	How rapidly should an employer or union expect claims to be processed?	**153**
Q. 6:36	Who receives the benefits check?	**153**
Q. 6:37	What is an explanation of benefits?	**153**
Q. 6:38	Why would an employee appeal a claims determination?	**154**
Q. 6:39	How does an employee appeal a claims determination?	**154**

Renewals, Changes, and Termination of Coverage

Q. 6:40	How does an employer renew its health insurance policy?	**154**
Q. 6:41	When can an employer change its coverage?	**155**
Q. 6:42	What kinds of changes do employers make at renewal?	**156**
Q. 6:43	When the policy is renewed, are all employees automatically covered?	**156**
Q. 6:44	If an employer believes that a renewal rate is too high, what options are available?	**156**
Q. 6:45	What kinds of plan changes might an employer want to make during the plan year?	**156**
Q. 6:46	Can an employer terminate coverage in the middle of a plan year?	**156**
Q. 6:47	If an employer terminates coverage, what protection do employees have against medical expenses?	**157**

Listing of Questions

Q. 6:48 If an employee is not actively at work on the date the new coverage takes effect, will he or she be covered? 157

Terminated Employees

Q. 6:49 If an employee terminates employment, what protection does he or she have against medical expenses? 157
Q. 6:50 What is a conversion privilege? 158
Q. 6:51 How does COBRA affect the group coverage conversion privilege? 158
Q. 6:52 What are the conversion requirements for other group plans? 158

COBRA

Q. 6:53 What is COBRA? 159
Q. 6:54 Where are the coverage continuation requirements incorporated into federal law? 159
Q. 6:55 What new terminology is added to the employee benefits lexicon? 160
Q. 6:56 What is COBRA continuation coverage? 161
Q. 6:57 What is the definition of employer? 161
Q. 6:58 What is a small employer plan? 162
Q. 6:59 How is a group health plan defined? 162
Q. 6:60 Are any group health plans excluded from COBRA? 163
Q. 6:61 What are qualifying events? 163
Q. 6:62 What is the definition of a COBRA covered employee? 164
Q. 6:63 Who is a qualified beneficiary? 165
Q. 6:64 What is core coverage? 166
Q. 6:65 What is noncore coverage? 166
Q. 6:66 Can a group health plan require a qualified beneficiary to elect continuation coverage? 166
Q. 6:67 What are the options available to a qualified beneficiary? 166
Q. 6:68 Can a qualified beneficiary choose to cover individuals who join the family on or after the date of the qualifying event? 166

Q. 6:69	What is the election period (that is, the maximum time period) in which a qualified beneficiary may decide to take COBRA continuation coverage?	167
Q. 6:70	Must a covered employee or other qualified beneficiary inform the employer or plan administrator when a qualifying event occurs?	168
Q. 6:71	Can each qualified beneficiary make his or her own election under the continuation-of-coverage provisions?	168
Q. 6:72	Who pays for COBRA continuation coverage?	169
Q. 6:73	How much does the qualified beneficiary pay?	169
Q. 6:74	Can the premium amount be increased?	169
Q. 6:75	Are installment payments permitted?	169
Q. 6:76	What deductibles apply to COBRA continuation coverage?	170
Q. 6:77	How long is coverage made available?	170
Q. 6:78	What happens upon the death of a retiree or surviving spouse?	171
Q. 6:79	How is continuation coverage handled in the event of disability?	171
Q. 6:80	When is the new disability provision effective?	172
Q. 6:81	Are there other factors that might result in an earlier termination of coverage?	172
Q. 6:82	Why did OBRA 89 change the duration of continuation coverage?	173
Q. 6:83	When does the new provision regarding other coverage take effect?	173
Q. 6:84	What is meant by timely payment?	173
Q. 6:85	Does a qualified beneficiary have the right to convert to an individual policy when COBRA continuation coverage ceases?	173
Q. 6:86	Can a qualified beneficiary defer coverage?	174
Q. 6:87	Does COBRA have a specific impact on flexible benefits programs?	174
Q. 6:88	Does COBRA supersede state continuation requirements?	174
Q. 6:89	Does state continuation extend the maximum COBRA continuation period?	175
Q. 6:90	What is the effective date for the COBRA requirements?	175
Q. 6:91	How is a collectively bargained plan defined?	175

Q. 6:92	What sanctions are imposed if a group health plan fails to comply with COBRA?	175
Q. 6:93	Are there any unresolved issues with regard to COBRA?	176

Computerized Administration

Q. 6:94	What role do computer systems play in managing health plans?	177
Q. 6:95	What role would a computer system play in performing nondiscrimination testing?	178
Q. 6:96	What sorts of features should a COBRA administration system have?	178
Q. 6:97	How would a computer help in administering flexible benefits plans?	179
Q. 6:98	What types of computer communications programs are available?	179
Q. 6:99	In buying or leasing an administrative computer system, what other features should a plan sponsor look for?	180

Chapter 7 Managing Health Insurance Costs

Q. 7:1	What factors are responsible for rising health insurance costs?	181
Q. 7:2	Why haven't private insurance companies limited reimbursements to control cost increases?	182
Q. 7:3	Do Medicare and Medicaid limit reimbursements to achieve cost control?	183
Q. 7:4	What is cost shifting?	183
Q. 7:5	How do higher claims affect health insurance costs?	184
Q. 7:6	Why do health care providers deliver unnecessary care?	184
Q. 7:7	Why haven't consumers purchased less care, as prices have increased?	184
Q. 7:8	How can a small employer manage health insurance costs?	185

Health Insurance Answer Book

| Q. 7:9 | How can employers determine what cost management is required? | 185 |
| Q. 7:10 | What plan features prevent illness and injury, thereby reducing costs in the long run? | 186 |

Health Care Data

Q. 7:11	Why have health data become an integral part of many employers' cost-management programs?	187
Q. 7:12	Why are employer-specific data helpful?	187
Q. 7:13	What kinds of data are useful to better manage health care costs?	188
Q. 7:14	Are there any resources available to assist employers in gathering and using data?	189
Q. 7:15	Who participates in health care coalitions?	189
Q. 7:16	How can existing health care coalitions be located?	189
Q. 7:17	What kinds of plan design features should employers implement, even without conclusive data on problems?	190

Cost-Sharing Strategies

Q. 7:18	How can a plan increase cost sharing by employees?	190
Q. 7:19	What are typical deductibles?	190
Q. 7:20	What are typical coinsurance percentages?	191
Q. 7:21	What effect do increased deductibles and coinsurance have on utilization?	192
Q. 7:22	What is a front-end deductible?	192
Q. 7:23	Do all comprehensive plans have front-end deductibles?	192
Q. 7:24	Would increases in required employee contributions toward premium help control costs?	192
Q. 7:25	Should employers that do not now require employee contributions for health care coverage introduce them?	193
Q. 7:26	How can health care plans be designed to encourage use of the most cost-effective care?	194

Listing of Questions

Coordination of Benefits

Q. 7:27	What is coordination of benefits (COB)?	194
Q. 7:28	How does COB help manage claims costs?	195
Q. 7:29	What is maintenance of benefits?	195
Q. 7:30	What is the birthday rule?	196
Q. 7:31	What has been the effect of the new birthday rule with respect to dependent children?	196
Q. 7:32	Have companies tried any other COB innovations?	196

Outpatient Surgery/Preadmission Testing

Q. 7:33	Does outpatient surgery coverage help control costs?	197
Q. 7:34	What is preadmission testing, and how does it control costs?	197

Second Surgical Opinions

Q. 7:35	What is a second surgical opinion (SSO) program?	198
Q. 7:36	Which procedures should require second opinions?	200
Q. 7:37	What is the difference between self-referral and referral by an SSO panel?	200
Q. 7:38	How do mandatory SSO programs work?	201

Utilization Review and Case Management

Q. 7:39	What is utilization review (UR)?	202
Q. 7:40	How does UR work?	202
Q. 7:41	Has UR grown in recent years?	202
Q. 7:42	What are the new kinds of utilization review and control?	203
Q. 7:43	What is individual case management (ICM)?	203
Q. 7:44	How does ICM work?	203
Q. 7:45	Is hospital discharge planning different from ICM?	204
Q. 7:46	How does preadmission certification work?	204
Q. 7:47	If hospital admissions are usually certified, why is UR necessary?	206

Q. 7:48	What happens during concurrent review?	206
Q. 7:49	How does retrospective review help manage claims costs?	206
Q. 7:50	Do the cost savings produced by UR justify the additional expense for the UR service?	207

Additional Cost-Management Strategies

Q. 7:51	Does coverage for extended care facilities and home health care help an employer manage health care costs?	207
Q. 7:52	Does the addition of a hospice care benefit help manage claims costs?	208
Q. 7:53	If an employer determines that plan design features alone will not manage costs sufficiently, what other options are available?	208
Q. 7:54	How does education contribute toward health care cost control?	208
Q. 7:55	What is a hospital bill audit?	209
Q. 7:56	How can negotiations with providers contribute toward cost management?	209
Q. 7:57	What are medical billing codes?	210
Q. 7:58	Why do providers engage in "code gaming"?	211
Q. 7:59	What kinds of code gaming are there?	211
Q. 7:60	What is a medical review organization?	211
Q. 7:61	Why do employers hire medical review organizations?	211
Q. 7:62	What kinds of services do medical review organizations provide?	212
Q. 7:63	How do medical cost–containment firms charge for their services?	212

Chapter 8 Alternative Health Care Systems: HMOs and PPOs

Q. 8:1	How has the traditional reimbursement system in this country contributed to the escalating cost of health care?	213

Listing of Questions

| Q. 8:2 | How are insurers and providers merging their services? | 214 |

Health Maintenance Organizations

Q. 8:3	What is an HMO?	214
Q. 8:4	When were HMOs developed?	214
Q. 8:5	Who develops and sponsors HMOs?	215
Q. 8:6	How prevalent are HMOs?	215
Q. 8:7	Do physicians own HMOs?	217
Q. 8:8	How are HMOs organized?	218
Q. 8:9	What are the differences among the various models?	218
Q. 8:10	How is a capitative payment structure different from a fee-for-service payment structure?	218
Q. 8:11	Don't employers prepay for health care services in traditional plans?	219
Q. 8:12	Do employees prepay for health care through their payroll deductions for traditional plans?	219
Q. 8:13	Does enrollment in an HMO entitle an individual to unlimited health care?	219
Q. 8:14	Do HMOs require a deductible that patients pay before care is provided?	220
Q. 8:15	What happens when an individual who is enrolled in an HMO needs to be hospitalized?	220
Q. 8:16	Is an employee reimbursed for care received outside the HMO area?	220
Q. 8:17	When can employees enroll in an HMO?	221
Q. 8:18	How does an employee choose whether to enroll in an HMO or in the traditional health plan?	221
Q. 8:19	Would an employee want to enroll in both a traditional plan and an HMO plan?	222
Q. 8:20	Are HMOs more cost-effective for employees?	222
Q. 8:21	How can an employer achieve 75% participation in its conventional plan if employees are allowed to enroll in HMOs?	222
Q. 8:22	Why has enrollment in HMOs increased during the health care cost crisis?	222
Q. 8:23	Why might employers experience lower costs with HMOs than with other health care plans?	223

Health Insurance Answer Book

Adverse Selection

Q. 8:24	Does adverse selection occur in the HMO setting?	224
Q. 8:25	Will the cost of an employer's conventional plan be affected by an HMO plan?	224
Q. 8:26	Why might HMOs attract younger, healthier persons?	224
Q. 8:27	Is the adverse selection obvious to employers?	225
Q. 8:28	What can be done about adverse selection?	225

Legal Standards

Q. 8:29	What is the Health Maintenance Act?	225
Q. 8:30	What standards must a federally qualified HMO meet?	226
Q. 8:31	How prevalent are federally qualified HMOs?	227
Q. 8:32	What is a community rating system?	227
Q. 8:33	What is the dual choice mandate?	227
Q. 8:34	Is an employer that self-insures subject to the dual choice mandate?	228
Q. 8:35	Does the HMO Act specify how much an employer is required to pay for HMO coverage for its employees?	228
Q. 8:36	What role has federal funding played in the development of HMOs?	229
Q. 8:37	Are HMOs subject to state regulations?	229
Q. 8:38	What is ERISA pre-emption?	230
Q. 8:39	Are state laws with respect to HMOs pre-empted by ERISA?	230

Evaluating HMOs

Q. 8:40	How can a company compare costs of health plans?	231
Q. 8:41	How does the quality of HMO care compare with that of conventionally insured medical care?	231
Q. 8:42	Why are some HMOs having financial difficulty?	232
Q. 8:43	How can a prospective HMO client get more information about the HMO?	232

Preferred Provider Organizations

Q. 8:44	What is a PPO?	235
Q. 8:45	How did the PPO concept develop?	235
Q. 8:46	How does a PPO differ from an HMO?	236

Q. 8:47	How is the PPO concept different from Blue Cross/Blue Shield and Medicare contracts with providers?	236
Q. 8:48	What is a preferred provider arrangement, and how is it different from a PPO?	237
Q. 8:49	What is an exclusive provider organization?	237
Q. 8:50	What services are offered by PPOs?	237
Q. 8:51	Who sponsors PPOs?	238
Q. 8:52	How prevalent are PPOs?	238
Q. 8:53	Who joins PPOs?	239
Q. 8:54	What is involved in establishing a PPO?	239
Q. 8:55	How are PPO providers selected?	240
Q. 8:56	What else is necessary for ensuring cost-effective treatment in a PPO?	241
Q. 8:57	What are the incentives for doctors and hospitals to be preferred providers?	241
Q. 8:58	Must a PPO include UR controls?	241
Q. 8:59	Are utilization controls important when using a PPO?	242
Q. 8:60	Who does the utilization review?	242
Q. 8:61	Are there federally qualified PPOs?	242
Q. 8:62	Do state PPO standards or laws exist?	242
Q. 8:63	What antitrust issues affect PPO development and negotiations?	243
Q. 8:64	What incentives do employers have to include PPOs in their health plans?	243
Q. 8:65	What kinds of employers can expect the largest discounts from a PPO health plan?	243
Q. 8:66	Is an employer that elects a plan with a PPO sacrificing quality care for low cost?	244
Q. 8:67	Can any employer include a PPO in its health care plan?	244
Q. 8:68	How can an employer or union evaluate a prospective PPO?	245
Q. 8:69	How should a PPO be incorporated into an existing program?	245
Q. 8:70	What types of discounts are available?	246
Q. 8:71	When incorporating a PPO into a health plan, what employee education is necessary?	247
Q. 8:72	What other kinds of health care delivery arrangements are available to employers?	247
Q. 8:73	What about hybrid HMO/PPO arrangements?	249
Q. 8:74	How prevalent are point-of-service HMOs?	249

Chapter 9 Flexible Benefits

Q. 9:1	What is a flexible benefits plan?	251
Q. 9:2	How does the Internal Revenue Code define a cafeteria plan?	252
Q. 9:3	What are qualified benefits?	252
Q. 9:4	What are the tax advantages of a cafeteria plan?	252
Q. 9:5	When were flexible benefits plans first introduced?	253
Q. 9:6	What is constructive receipt?	253
Q. 9:7	Why were flexible benefits plans developed?	254
Q. 9:8	How do flexible benefits help control costs?	254
Q. 9:9	How successful have flexible benefits plans been in controlling costs?	255
Q. 9:10	Are there different types of flexible plans?	256
Q. 9:11	What is a salary reduction premium conversion plan?	256
Q. 9:12	What is a flexible spending or reimbursement account?	256
Q. 9:13	What is a health care reimbursement account?	256
Q. 9:14	What is a dependent care reimbursement account?	257
Q. 9:15	How are these reimbursement accounts structured?	257
Q. 9:16	What happens if the benefits paid plus administrative costs are less than the total contributions plus interest earnings?	258
Q. 9:17	Are there any other special requirements for flexible spending arrangements?	259
Q. 9:18	Is the uniform reimbursement approach the only one permitted?	259
Q. 9:19	What new changes in family status permit participants to change their elections mid-year?	259
Q. 9:20	Are changes in the total cost of medical care options grounds for changing elections?	260
Q. 9:21	What is a modular plan?	261
Q. 9:22	What is a core plus plan?	261
Q. 9:23	What is a working spouse plan?	262
Q. 9:24	What is a full menu or total flexible benefits plan?	262
Q. 9:25	What types of benefits do cafeteria plans include?	262
Q. 9:26	What medical insurance options are available under a cafeteria plan?	263
Q. 9:27	Can a flexible plan include an HMO?	263

Listing of Questions

Q. 9:28	Can a flexible plan include a PPO?	264
Q. 9:29	Is all the insurance provided under a flexible plan provided by one insurer, or do insurers bid for pieces?	264
Q. 9:30	What are the advantages of using one carrier?	264
Q. 9:31	Does a cafeteria plan allow employees to select cash instead of benefits?	264
Q. 9:32	Can a 401(k) plan be integrated into a cafeteria plan?	265
Q. 9:33	What are the advantages of including a 401(k) plan in a flexible plan?	265
Q. 9:34	Why wouldn't all employees choose the plan options that offered the best coverage?	265
Q. 9:35	What nondiscrimination requirements must a cafeteria plan meet?	266
Q. 9:36	What are the requirements for qualified benefits?	266
Q. 9:37	What are the nondiscrimination requirements of IRC Section 125?	266
Q. 9:38	How are plans tested to assure compliance with nondiscrimination rules?	267
Q. 9:39	How are flexible benefits plans funded?	267
Q. 9:40	Must flexible benefits plans be contributory?	268
Q. 9:41	How does an employer determine its level of contribution to the flexible plan?	268
Q. 9:42	How are employee contribution levels determined?	268
Q. 9:43	How are employer and employee contributions made in a full flexible benefits plan?	269
Q. 9:44	Can small employers self-fund flexible benefits plans?	269
Q. 9:45	Is purchasing a flexible benefits plan similar to purchasing a traditional plan?	269
Q. 9:46	How does adverse selection affect flexible benefits plans?	270
Q. 9:47	What specific issues should an employer address in contemplating the purchase of a flexible benefits plan?	270
Q. 9:48	How can an employer determine what its employees' benefits needs are?	272
Q. 9:49	How are flexible benefits plans implemented?	272
Q. 9:50	How long does it take from the purchase of a flexible benefits plan until it can be implemented?	272

Q. 9:51	What kinds of employee communications are advisable in advance of enrollment?	273
Q. 9:52	How do employees enroll in a plan and select their benefits?	273
Q. 9:53	What is enrollment confirmation?	274
Q. 9:54	What kinds of changes may an employee make during the plan year?	274
Q. 9:55	How do the cost and pricing of a flexible benefits plan compare with those of a traditional employee benefits plan?	275
Q. 9:56	How does renewal of a flexible benefits plan compare with traditional employee benefits plan renewal?	276
Q. 9:57	What kinds of reports are necessary to ensure smooth implementation and administration of a flexible plan?	276
Q. 9:58	How does an employer decide who will administer the flexible benefits plan?	277
Q. 9:59	What type of billing arrangement is used—self-accounting or home office?	277
Q. 9:60	What assistance is available to an employer that wants to administer its own flexible benefits plan?	278

Chapter 10 Medicare

Q. 10:1	What is Medicare?	279
Q. 10:2	Who is eligible for Medicare coverage?	280
Q. 10:3	What services are covered under Part A?	280
Q. 10:4	What services are covered under Part B?	281
Q. 10:5	What types of care are not covered by Medicare?	281

Medicare Order of Benefit Determination

Q. 10:6	How are Medicare benefits integrated with employer-provided benefits for older active employees?	282
Q. 10:7	Except for treatment of end-stage renal disease, is Medicare the primary payor for disabled individuals who are less than age 65 and are not retired?	283

OBRA '89

Q. 10:8	How did OBRA 89 change the Medicare as secondary payer rules?	283

Listing of Questions

Q. 10:9	What information will the IRS and SSA provide?	284
Q. 10:10	Who is a "qualified employer"?	284
Q. 10:11	What does the HCFA do with the information from the IRS and SSA?	284
Q. 10:12	What are the penalties for failure to provide information?	285
Q. 10:13	How long are these provisions in effect?	285
Q. 10:14	What other changes were made to the Medicare secondary rules?	285
Q. 10:15	What are the implications of the new rules for the disabled?	286
Q. 10:16	Is this rule permanent?	286
Q. 10:17	Is there a penalty for failure to comply with this rule?	286
Q. 10:18	Are there any exceptions to the rule?	286
Q. 10:19	Who is considered disabled for Social Security purposes?	286
Q. 10:20	What special considerations apply to disabled individuals?	287
Q. 10:21	What is the absolute test?	287
Q. 10:22	What is the facts and circumstances test?	288
Q. 10:23	What other individuals are covered under the Medicare secondary rules?	288
Q. 10:24	What employer plans are subject to the Medicare order of benefit determination rules?	289

Medicare Cost Containment

Q. 10:25	What steps has Medicare taken to limit costs?	289
Q. 10:26	How are payments determined on the basis of diagnosis?	289
Q. 10:27	Are all Medicare claims paid on a DRG basis?	290
Q. 10:28	If the care delivered costs a hospital less than the DRG-allowed sum, does the hospital retain the difference?	290
Q. 10:29	Are DRGs reducing the delivery of expensive, unnecessary hospital care?	290
Q. 10:30	Is Medicare the only plan that uses the DRG reimbursement system?	291
Q. 10:31	How has the DRG system affected the insurance industry?	291
Q. 10:32	How did OBRA change the rules for Medicare physician reimbursement?	291

Q. 10:33	What is balance billing?	292
Q. 10:34	What are volume performance standards?	292
Q. 10:35	What is the RBVS pay system?	292
Q. 10:36	When will the RBVS system take effect?	293
Q. 10:37	What effect will RBVS have?	293
Q. 10:38	What happened to the Medicare Catastrophic Coverage Act?	294
Q. 10:39	What is the impact of the repeal of the Medicare Catastrophic Coverage Act on benefits in 1990?	294
Q. 10:40	What are the Part A hospital benefits in 1990?	294
Q. 10:41	What are the indexed coinsurance requirements for 1990?	294
Q. 10:42	Is there a maximum dollar out of pocket limit on the 20% co-insurance for Part B?	295
Q. 10:43	What are the Medicare premiums for 1990?	295
Q. 10:44	What happens to those who reduced or eliminated Medigap policies?	295

Chapter 11 Nondiscrimination Rules

Accident and Health Plans

Q. 11:1	Is discrimination in health plans permitted?	297
Q. 11:2	Which types of self-insured accident and health plans are not subject to discrimination testing?	298
Q. 11:3	What is a "highly compensated individual"?	298
Q. 11:4	What are the eligibility tests applicable to self-insured accident and health plans?	299
Q. 11:5	What employees are excluded in applying the eligibility tests?	299
Q. 11:6	What is the benefits test applicable to self-insured accident and health plans?	300
Q. 11:7	What is the penalty for discrimination, as to eligibility or benefits, in a self-insured accident and health plan?	300
Q. 11:8	How is the penalty determined?	300

Q. 11:9	Are all self-insured accident and health plans aggregated for the purpose of applying eligibility and benefits tests?	301
Q. 11:10	Are retiree plans subject to the same rules?	301

Group Term Life Plans

Q. 11:11	How does the repeal of Section 89 affect group term life plans?	301
Q. 11:12	Who is a key employee under IRC Section 416(i)?	301
Q. 11:13	What nondiscrimination tests are applicable to group term life insurance?	302
Q. 11:14	What are the eligibility tests applicable to group term life?	302
Q. 11:15	What employees may be excluded in performing these tests?	302
Q. 11:16	What is the benefits test?	303
Q. 11:17	Are all group term life insurance plans combined for testing purposes?	303
Q. 11:18	What is the penalty for discrimination?	303
Q. 11:19	Are dependent group term life benefits subject to nondiscrimination rules?	304
Q. 11:20	Are group term life benefits for retired and former employees subject to nondiscrimination rules?	304

Cafeteria Plans

Q. 11:21	What is the impact of the repeal of Section 89 on cafeteria plans?	304
Q. 11:22	Who is a highly compensated individual for the purpose of cafeteria plan nondiscrimination rules?	305
Q. 11:23	What is the eligibility test?	305
Q. 11:24	Which employees may be excluded for the purpose of the eligibility test?	305
Q. 11:25	What is the benefits test?	306
Q. 11:26	What is the concentration test?	306
Q. 11:27	What is the penalty for discrimination?	306
Q. 11:28	Does a plan that is part of a cafeteria plan have to satisfy more than one set of discrimination rules?	307

Dependent Care Assistance Plans

Q. 11:29 What is the impact of the repeal of Section 89 on Dependent Care Assistance Plans? — 307
Q. 11:30 What is the eligibility test? — 307
Q. 11:31 What is a highly compensated employee with respect to dependent care assistance plans? — 308
Q. 11:32 What employees are excluded for purposes of nondiscrimination testing? — 308
Q. 11:33 What is the benefits test? — 308
Q. 11:34 What is the concentration test? — 308
Q. 11:35 What is the average benefits test? — 309
Q. 11:36 What is the penalty for discrimination? — 309

Educational Assistance

Q. 11:37 What is an educational assistance plan? — 309
Q. 11:38 What are the nondiscrimination rules which apply to educational assistance plans? — 309
Q. 11:39 What is the penalty for failing the nondiscrimination tests? — 310

Group Legal Services Plans

Q. 11:40 What is a qualified group legal services plan? — 310
Q. 11:41 What are the nondiscrimination rules which apply to group legal services plans? — 310
Q. 11:42 What is the penalty for discrimination? — 311

VEBAs

Q. 11:43 What are the nondiscrimination requirements for VEBAs? — 311
Q. 11:44 Are there limits on compensation? — 312
Q. 11:45 What are the penalties for discrimination? — 312

Nondiscriminatory Classification

Q. 11:46 What is a nondiscriminatory classification of employees? — 312

Safe Harbor/Unsafe Harbor Chart

Q. 11:47 Which method is used after the repeal of Section 89?   314

Chapter 12 Benefits Trends

Substance Abuse Treatment

Q. 12:1 Is treatment for alcoholism and other types of substance abuse covered under typical health insurance plans?   317
Q. 12:2 How costly is substance abuse to companies and their employees?   317
Q. 12:3 What is the Drug-Free Workplace Act?   318
Q. 12:4 What coverage is provided for substance abuse?   318
Q. 12:5 Why should companies establish a drug testing program?   319
Q. 12:6 Why would a company not engage in testing for substance abuse?   319
Q. 12:7 What options are there for testing?   320
Q. 12:8 What should be included in a substance abuse policy?   321

Employee Assistance Programs

Q. 12:9 What is an employee assistance, program (EAP)?   322
Q. 12:10 Is EAP coverage expensive?   322
Q. 12:11 Do companies hire in-house counselors or use external resources?   323
Q. 12:12 What components are needed for an effective EAP?   324
Q. 12:13 Other than in-house or commercially, how else may EAP services be provided?   324

Health Promotion and Wellness

Q. 12:14 What is health promotion?   324
Q. 12:15 Why would an employer offer health promotion programs?   325

Health Insurance Answer Book

Q. 12:16 Are there advantages to offering health promotion programs at the worksite?   326
Q. 12:17 How does a company select a health promotion program?   326
Q. 12:18 What is the life-style cost index?   326
Q. 12:19 Why is interest in health promotion growing?   326
Q. 12:20 What is preventive care coverage?   327
Q. 12:21 What kinds of benefits does preventive care coverage provide when it is part of a health care plan?   327
Q. 12:22 How often are routine checkups usually covered under a preventive care plan?   327
Q. 12:23 What is the current trend with regard to routine physicals?   328
Q. 12:24 What has caused the move away from the traditional physical?   328
Q. 12:25 Are there any specific guidelines available for health screening for particular risk factors?   328
Q. 12:26 What is a wellness program?   328
Q. 12:27 In addition to behavioral modification and preventive programs, in what other ways can a company enhance health?   329
Q. 12:28 Why would an employer want to include preventive care or wellness programs in a group insurance plan?   329
Q. 12:29 Are wellness or health promotion programs usually insured?   329
Q. 12:30 What is a health risk appraisal (HRA)?   330
Q. 12:31 How does the HRA fit in with health promotion?   330
Q. 12:32 Would an employer use an HRA to determine the components of its group health insurance plan?   330
Q. 12:33 Are HRA results used to set the price for health insurance coverage?   331
Q. 12:34 Do insurance companies provide financial incentives to companies to adopt preventive care programs?   331

Retiree Health Benefits

Q. 12:35 Why has health care coverage for retirees become an issue?   331
Q. 12:36 How many employers provide health care benefits for their retirees?   332

Listing of Questions

Q. 12:37	How big is the retiree health care liability for U.S. corporations?	333
Q. 12:38	What are the proposed Financial Accounting Standards Board (FASB) accounting rules?	333
Q. 12:39	What effect would the proposed FASB rules have?	334
Q. 12:40	How should a company respond to the new accounting rules?	334
Q. 12:41	How can a company limit its retiree health care benefits liability?	335
Q. 12:42	Are there limitations on a company's ability to alter retiree benefits?	336
Q. 12:43	What options are available to an employer that wants to prefund for retiree health benefits?	336
Q. 12:44	What are the rules governing VEBAs?	336
Q. 12:45	What is a 401(h) account?	337
Q. 12:46	Are there any other approaches to financing retiree health care?	338

Long-Term Care

Q. 12:47	What is long-term care?	338
Q. 12:48	What are the special issues connected with long-term care?	339
Q. 12:49	What are the different levels of long-term care?	339
Q. 12:50	How expensive is long-term care?	340
Q. 12:51	What long-term care benefits does Medicare provide?	340
Q. 12:52	What long-term care services are covered by Medicaid?	340
Q. 12:53	What does a typical long-term care benefit cover?	340
Q. 12:54	Are benefits adjusted for inflation?	341
Q. 12:55	What is the tax status of custodial care?	341
Q. 12:56	Who provides long-term care insurance?	341
Q. 12:57	How much does long-term care insurance cost?	341
Q. 12:58	What considerations should be taken into account in evaluating long-term care insurance policies?	342

Impact of AIDS on Insurance

Q. 12:59	What is the impact of AIDS on health benefits and the use of medical resources?	343

Health Insurance Answer Book

Q. 12:60 Why will the medical costs be so high? 344
Q. 12:61 What other cost increases are associated with AIDS? 345
Q. 12:62 Are there restrictions on the information that may be requested to identify a person at risk for AIDS? 345
Q. 12:63 Would all forms of care for AIDS patients be covered under an employer's health insurance program? 346
Q. 12:64 What legal protections have been extended to persons with AIDS? 346
Q. 12:65 Is testing for AIDS permissible? 346
Q. 12:66 How should an employer respond to AIDS? 347

Introduction

Since the publication of the Second Edition of the Health Insurance Answer Book, there have been significant changes in the laws affecting health plans. Some of the major legislative changes discussed in this supplement include:

1. The repeal of welfare benefit plan nondiscrimination rules of Section 89 of the Internal Revenue Code. This puts welfare plan discrimination rules back to where they were prior to the Tax Reform Act of 1986.
2. The repeal of the Medicare Catastrophic Coverage Act.
3. The 1989 Omnibus Budget Reconciliation Act, which made changes to the COBRA continuation of coverage rules as well as to the rules governing Medicare as secondary payer.

These legislative changes are reflected by elimination of the affected sections from the last edition, and insertion of new ones. In addition, we have added some new material to expand topical coverage. This expansion includes information that impinges on employee health and safety such as the Occupational Safety and Health Act, the Pregnancy Discrimination Act, the Americans with Disabilities Act, workers' compensation, and the rules governing voluntary employees beneficiary associations. There is also a prefatory article that discusses the trends in health care reform that will be shaping the marketplace in the coming years.

Chapter 1

An Overview of Group Insurance

Group insurance is a technique for providing a group of people with protection against financial loss resulting from death, disability, or the expenses associated with illness or injury. This chapter describes the different types of group insurance available and the various ways in which employers purchase it.

Q. 1:1 What are the various ways that individuals receive health insurance protection?

Besides participating in group insurance plans, individuals may also be covered under federal and state government-sponsored programs such as Medicare and Medicaid, service-type plans such as Blue Cross/Blue Shield, or so-called alternative health care systems such as Health Maintenance Organizations (HMOs) and Preferred Provider Organizations (PPOs). Insurance may also be purchased privately on an individual basis, or through mass purchasing groups such as credit unions and professional or trade associations.

Q. 1:2 What is the major difference between group and individual insurance?

The major difference between group and individual insurance involves evidence of insurability. To purchase individual insurance, a person must generally answer a health questionnaire and undergo a medical examination to provide evidence of insurability to the insurance company. An insurer may decline coverage on the basis of the applicant's personal habits, health, medical history, age, income, or any other factors that bear on risk acceptance. Or the insurer may issue a policy with limitations on coverage.

Most group insurance, however, is issued without medical examination or other evidence of individual insurability because the insurer knows that it can cover enough individuals to balance those in poor health against those in good health. The risk of an insurer failing to achieve this balance is diminished as the size of the group increases, or as the insurer underwrites additional group policies and increases the total number of individuals covered. This is known as the "law of large numbers."

Q. 1:3 What are the advantages of group insurance over individual insurance?

For an employer that intends to provide insurance protection to its employees, the group approach ensures that all employees, regardless of health, can be covered. Those with known health problems, who might otherwise be unable to obtain individual insurance, can be covered automatically upon employment without evidence of insurability. Although some limits may be imposed on new hires for certain conditions that predate their enrollment in the plan, most employees can receive coverage as soon as they are eligible.

Group insurance offers a lower cost per unit of protection than individual insurance, because of the economies of scale resulting from selling, installing, and servicing one plan covering many individuals. In addition, group plans are typically more flexible and tend to provide more liberal benefits than individual coverage.

Q. 1:4 How prevalent is group insurance in the United States?

According to the U.S. Census Bureau's statistics, 85% of the population was covered by either government or private health insurance; 61% had coverage under a health plan related to the current employment of a family member.

A recent study by the Congressional Research Service concluded that 37 million Americans under the age of 65 are uninsured or underinsured.

Q. 1:5 Why do most employers provide group insurance?

Group insurance benefits have become a traditional and expected part of an employee's compensation and an integral part of an employer's total compensation strategy. A comprehensive benefits package allows employers to attract and retain quality employees. In markets in which certain skills are in short supply, employers often vie for labor by offering more attractive employee benefits plans than the competition.

In addition, group insurance is a concrete way for employers to show concern for their employees' welfare. For many employees, group protection is their only form of insurance protection; without it, they would be susceptible to financial catastrophe from the expenses associated with premature death, illness, or injury. By giving employees the peace of mind that comes from knowing that they and their families are protected against financial hardship, group insurance enhances employee morale. A formal benefits program, therefore, is effective from both an employer and an employee standpoint.

Insurance protection purchased by an employer is also more valuable to employees than equal cash compensation. Since the premiums and, to a large extent, the benefits from group insurance are not considered employee income, they are not taxable as such. (See the discussion of employer and employee taxation in Chapter 3.)

Q. 1:6 What types of group protection do most employers provide?

Although there are many variations of each, the four major types of insurance coverage provided by employers to their employees are life, accidental death and dismemberment (AD&D), disability, and health or medical. Some employers also provide additional coverages, including group legal, travel accident, and vision and dental care.

Q. 1:7 What are the characteristics of group life insurance?

Group life insurance provides cash benefits to the insured employee's designated beneficiary or beneficiaries in the event of the employee's death from any cause while covered under the group policy. Although group life insurance can take many forms, the most common is group term insurance. Term insurance has no cash value and will pay the face amount upon death. Some plans provide dependent life insurance, which pays the employee the face amount in the event of the death of a covered dependent.

In order to qualify for favorable tax treatment, a plan must meet the requirements for employer-provided group life insurance under Internal Revenue Code (IRC) Section 79. The law requires that the plan provide insurance under a formula that precludes individual selection. Also, in order to avoid income tax on the value of coverage (the first $50,000 of coverage would normally be tax-free to the covered employee), the plan must not discriminate in favor of key or highly paid employees. Chapter 11 provides details regarding the non-discrimination requirements applicable to various welfare benefit plans.

(Note: This discussion of group insurance pertains to those programs in which the employer bears all or most of the cost. An alternative is employer-sponsored individual insurance. Under this arrangement, employees may choose to buy individual policies for themselves under a program sponsored, but not paid for, by the employer. Costs and issue rules would still be somewhat more favorable than those available to an individual purchasing the insurance on his or her own.)

Q. 1:8 What are the characteristics of group AD&D insurance?

Accidental death and dismemberment (AD&D) insurance provides coverage for death or dismemberment that results directly from accidental causes within, generally, 90 to 180 days of the injury. A lump-sum cash benefit is paid to the designated beneficiary of an insured who dies as a result of an accident. The insured receives a smaller lump-sum cash benefit in the event of the accidental loss of a limb or eyesight.

Q. 1:9 How does group disability insurance protect against loss of income?

Group disability insurance provides cash payments to the insured for loss of income during a period of disability. The cash payments are often a percentage of the employee's weekly or monthly salary, or a fixed amount. Typically, benefits do not exceed 70% of the individual's salary and are reduced by disability benefits from other sources. Both short-term and long-term disability coverages are available. Short-term disability plans require a period of disability generally ranging from 1 to 30 days before benefits begin, and typically provide benefits for 13 to 26 weeks. Long-term disability plans typically pay benefits to age 65 (or longer) for disabilities that last longer than the duration of short-term benefits.

Q. 1:10 What is included in the term "group health insurance"?

Group health insurance is sometimes used as a comprehensive term that includes medical, dental, vision, and prescription coverages, as well as disability and AD&D. In this text, group health insurance usually refers to medical and dental insurance. Comments in this text apply equally to insured and self-funded plans, unless otherwise noted.

Q. 1:11 What are the characteristics of group health insurance?

Group health insurance provides full or partial reimbursement for various medical and dental expenses. Coverage almost always includes reimbursement for hospital and surgical expenses and for diagnostic x-rays, tests, and physicians' visits. The full extent of coverage depends on the master contract issued to the group. (For details on specific types of coverages, see Chapter 4.).

Q. 1:12 What caused the rapid growth of group health insurance?

A number of factors contributed to the rapid growth of group health insurance. Among the more important factors are:
- Industrialization and urbanization, which caused changes in the values of an increasingly affluent society, and lessened the family's responsibility for the health care of infirm family members; and
- Wage controls during World War II, which caused employers to

use rich employee benefits plans to attract employees during a period of short labor supply.

In addition, powerful labor unions demanded more and more benefits; favorable federal tax treatment made benefits a cost-effective way to increase employees' compensation. The rising demand for and cost of medical care made health insurance a necessity. Social legislation, together with refinements in the group insurance concept, led to more and different groups being covered and new benefits being added.

Q. 1:13 How important is group health insurance to employees?

For many employees, participation in a group health plan at work is their only means of acquiring health insurance coverage. Group health insurance has made it possible for hundreds of millions of Americans—who for various reasons (for example, inadequate income or uninsurability) would not otherwise be covered—to receive financial protection against major illness or injury.

Q. 1:14 What is the single most important factor affecting group health insurance in recent years?

The most significant factor affecting group health insurance in recent years has been the rapid escalation of health care costs. Increases in medical costs have exceeded the increases in the consumer price index. In addition, total health care spending (which includes both public and private expenditures for personal health care, medical research, construction of medical facilities, administrative and health insurance costs, and government-sponsored public health activities) increased at double-digit rates for several years, and now accounts for over 11% of the gross national product.

The increases in costs have led to greater sharing of costs with employees, new types of health care delivery systems, and greater emphasis on wellness and preventive medicine.

Q. 1:15 Is group insurance available only to single employers?

No. Although the plan sponsor or policyholder is most often a single employer (corporation, partnership, or sole proprietorship), it can also be an entity such as a union or a professional association. In addition, a single group program may be issued to cover employees of a number of different employers. These vehicles are often used to insure individuals who are employed by companies too small to offer group coverage on their own.

Q. 1:16 What is a multiple employer trust?

Under a multiple employer trust (MET), many small employers in the same or related industry participate in a group plan under a trust arrangement. The trust, rather than each participating employer, is the policyholder, and the master contract is issued to a trustee. Through mass purchasing, small employers can afford a level of insurance benefits that is normally available only to larger employers. METs are most common among employers with 10 or fewer employees, but some trusts also offer coverage to larger groups.

Q. 1:17 How can a labor union provide group insurance?

A labor union can provide group insurance for its members under a policy issued to the union. The union is the policyholder, just as the trust is the policyholder under a MET. A union may purchase a group policy for a large number of members who are employed by the same company, or for union members working for different companies. Group insurance purchased through a union is particularly advantageous in industries such as construction, where union members may work for many employers during a year.

Despite the opportunity for labor unions to purchase group insurance, few group contracts are issued to unions today. Organized labor more often obtains insurance benefits for its members through collective bargaining with employers. As a result, union members are usually covered under group insurance plans sponsored by one or more employers.

Q. 1:18 What is an association plan?

A professional or trade association can provide coverage for its members or member companies under a policy issued to the association. The association is the policyholder. Examples of association groups include the American Lung Association, state savings and loan associations, various professional and retail associations such as the American Medical Association, and chamber of commerce groups.

When compared with employer group plans, the percentage of eligible association members who actually enroll in these plans is usually small, because many association members have access to other insurance that may be less expensive or provide better coverage.

Chapter 2

The Health Insurance Marketplace

Because of limited resources and a lack of expertise, most small employers use an insurance professional—an agent, broker, or consultant—to assist in the design, purchase, and administration of a group health insurance plan. This chapter introduces the various types of professional organizations and the services they offer.

Types of Insurance Professionals

Q. 2:1 Can an employer work directly with an insurance company?

It is possible for an employer to deal directly with an insurer through a group sales representative (see below) to purchase group insurance. Premium rates and underwriting practices vary considerably from one insurer to another, however. In addition, the coverages provided are rarely identical. Comparison shopping is often beyond the capability of all but the most sophisticated purchaser, typically the very large company that has internal employee benefits expertise. For this reason, many group insurance purchasers do not deal directly with insurance company underwriters or group insurance representatives, preferring instead to deal with an intermediary.

Smaller employers need a qualified professional to act as intermediary because they lack the resources and expertise to handle their group insurance needs. An intermediary can help them define their needs and objectives, design a plan to meet those criteria, select the proper purchasing and funding vehicles, obtain competitive quotes from insurers, and service the plan.

Q. 2:2 What is a group health insurance underwriter?

A group health insurance underwriter is a risk evaluator, in that he or she analyzes each individual group to determine the financial risk it represents for the insurance company. To determine the acceptability of the risk a particular group represents, the underwriter examines the composition of the group as it relates to age, sex, prior claims experience, and the desired plan design.

A recent trend in risk evaluation is "life-style analysis." The underwriter may take into account the number of smokers in a group, for example. If the group is an "acceptable risk," the underwriter then determines what limits should be set on coverage for the group and what prices the group should be charged. A group will be deemed an acceptable risk if it has characteristics that the underwriter feels can be accurately priced to reflect the risk to the insurance company. This price, or "quote," is provided to the group representative for delivery to the prospective policyholder.

Q. 2:3 What is risk?

The risk an insurance company assumes when it agrees to cover a particular group is the possibility that claims will exceed the expected level. It is the chance of financial loss inherent in the group. Insurance companies use it to determine whether they will underwrite an insurance policy on a particular group.

The spread of risk is necessary not only because of the expected variations in a population's health but also because some policyholders—particularly very small groups—purchase group insurance to cover certain individuals with known health problems (see Question 2:4). This is a more costly way to obtain coverage for those high-risk individuals, but often the only way possible, given the evidence-of-insurability requirement for individual policies.

Q. 2:4 What is adverse selection?

Adverse selection, or antiselection, is the tendency for persons with known health problems to elect more insurance, or to incur significantly greater health care expenses, than healthy persons. Insuring a group that is heavily weighted with persons with high health risks is, therefore, more expensive than insuring a group of healthier individuals.

Q. 2:5 What is a group sales representative?

A group sales representative is an employee of an insurance company who sells group insurance for that particular company and performs a variety of services directly for the policyholder and in conjunction with the policyholder's intermediaries. The sales representative supplements the group insurance knowledge of the intermediary, especially with respect to the insurance company's products. Group sales representatives are often located in branch offices. They are compensated by the insurance carriers for whom they place business and service.

Q. 2:6 What is a client service representative?

Some insurance companies have specialized personnel in their field offices that are trained to deal with intermediaries and clients in the ongoing administration of the health insurance plan. This enables the insurer to deal with clients' questions locally and to visit clients, if necessary. Such specialized personnel are known as client service representatives.

Q. 2:7 What is an intermediary?

An intermediary is a knowledgeable benefits professional who helps employers and other groups to develop, design, purchase, and service benefits plans. An intermediary may be a broker, an agent, an employee benefits consultant or a Third Party Administrator (TPA).

Q. 2:8   Health Insurance Answer Book

Q. 2:8 How do group sales representatives and intermediaries interact in the sale of a group health insurance plan?

Group sales representatives of different insurance carriers approach intermediaries to explain their insurance products. In turn, intermediaries request quotes for plans to meet the needs of their clients. They may work together to determine the most appropriate plans and to discuss the premiums required for those plans. The intermediary represents his or her clients' interests; the group sales representative represents his or her company's products and services.

Q. 2:9 What services do intermediaries provide prior to the purchase of a group health insurance plan?

The services that intermediaries provide will depend, to a great extent, on (1) the employer's own employee benefits expertise and (2) the type of intermediary the employer chooses. For employers with little or no knowledge of health insurance, the intermediary can provide all of the following services:

- Designing the plan, including analyzing alternative programs from a cost standpoint;
- Determining how the plan should be funded;
- Providing necessary plan documents, including communications to employees;
- Selecting an insurance carrier, HMO, or other health care provider; and
- Servicing the plan, including claims analysis and preparation of annual reports.

Those employers that possess greater knowledge and resources, however, will likely play a more active role in the decision-making process. The type of intermediary the employer selects will also determine the extent of services provided.

Q. 2:10 What is an insurance broker?

An insurance broker is a representative of an employer who provides counsel on insurance-related issues and assistance in dealing with insurance companies. Brokers sell a variety of products and services, including business and group insurance, and market the products of many insurance companies.

Brokerage firms vary from the single broker operating independently to brokerage houses that employ thousands of professionals and operate offices nationally and internationally.

Q. 2:11 What is the difference between an agent and a broker?

The basic difference between an agent and a broker is that while the broker represents the employer, the agent is generally under contract with an insurance company to sell all of its products. That is, agents represent sellers (insurance companies) and brokers represent buyers (employers). Agents typically work with smaller single-employer groups.

If an agent's own company cannot meet the client's needs, the agent will deal with another insurance company, often through a broker; in this case, the distinction between an agent and a broker becomes blurred.

Q. 2:12 What is an employee benefits consultant?

Employee benefits consultants specialize in the analysis and design of an employer's entire noncash compensation program. They have an in-depth knowledge of a particular client's company, having often been hired to analyze that company's benefits objectives in detail. Their expertise may be especially useful to larger employers that elect to partially or totally self-fund their employee benefits plans. Some consultants act as administrators in providing continuing service to their clients. Some employers believe a consultant offers a more objective viewpoint, since consultants are compensated directly by the employer, usually on a fee-for-service basis.

Q. 2:13 How does an employer determine whether to use an agent, broker, or consultant?

Agents, brokers, and consultants provide many of the same services, and distinguishing among them is sometimes difficult. Generally, agents work with smaller companies that are less likely to require, or less able to afford, extensive analysis of their benefits strategies. Some brokers, especially those associated with large national brokerage houses, often provide some of the same services as consultants.

Q. 2:14 What is a TPA?

Third-party administrators (TPAs) are organizations hired to provide certain administrative services to group benefits plans. Their functions may include premium accounting, claims review and payment, claims utilization review, maintenance of employee eligibility records, and negotiations with insurers that provide stop-loss protection for large claims. Sometimes a TPA also fills the role of the consultant-broker, in which case the TPA would help design the benefits plan and recommend the appropriate purchasing and funding vehicles. However, TPAs are most commonly employed by association groups, trusts, and employers that self-fund, since many of their services would normally be provided by the carrier when benefits are purchased from an insurance company.

At the start of their business arrangement, the employer and TPA sign an agreement that outlines the services and authority of the TPA. If the employer's plan is only partially self-insured, most insurance companies reserve the right to approve the employer's TPA appointment.

Choosing and Compensating Intermediaries

Q. 2:15 How does an employer select a particular intermediary?

Most small employers select an intermediary just as they would hire any outside professional help. They consult friends, business associates, and authorities they respect. Based on this information, the employer can develop a list of potential candidates. It is generally advisable to speak with several candidates, because it is important that an employer trust the intermediary and feel comfortable doing business with that person. Many intermediaries, especially the larger ones, maintain client referral lists—lists of clients that have been satisfied with their services and have agreed to discuss their experience with prospective customers. Interviewing referred organizations similar in size and structure to one's own is a good way to determine whether the intermediary will meet one's needs.

Q. 2:16 Can an employer use a personal or business advisor as its group insurance intermediary?

Yes. The employer can use the broker or agent who handles the employer's business or personal insurance as an advisor, if the employer believes that this intermediary has the required degree of employee benefits expertise.

Q. 2:17 How are intermediaries compensated?

Agents and brokers typically receive a percentage of premiums—commissions—from the insurance companies with which they place business. Consultants generally charge either a fixed fee or an hourly rate to the employers for which they are providing services. In recent years, there has been a trend, especially among large brokerage houses, to negotiate a fee for services rendered. In addition, some individuals and firms will operate in either mode—commissions or fee for service.

Q. 2:18 What are commission schedules?

Commission schedules are a type of monetary incentive that insurance companies use to encourage agents and brokers to do business with their companies. The two most common types of commission schedules are the high-low schedule and the level schedule. Both reward agents and brokers by providing a percentage of the premium for the insurance that is sold.

The high-low commission schedule encourages group brokers and agents to place new business with a particular carrier, by providing commissions that are a higher percentage of premiums the first year of coverage and a lower percentage in renewal years.

The level commission schedule provides the same percentage of premium each year, assuming the premium is the same each year. This type of schedule encourages a group producer to keep business with a carrier, since there is no decrease in commissions after the first year. In theory, this commission schedule encourages the broker or agent to pay more attention to servicing existing clients rather than emphasizing sales of new business as the high-low schedule does.

Over time, the two types of schedules provide similar compensation. The following table compares them:

Commission Schedules

Annual Premium	High-Low Schedule Year 1	High-Low Schedule Years 2–10	Level Schedule First 10 Years
First $1,000	25.0%	6.5%	7.5%
Next $8,000	20.0	3.0	5.0
Next $5,000	15.0	2.0	3.5
Next $10,000	10.0	2.0	3.2
Next $10,000	7.5	2.0	2.8
Next $25,000	5.0	1.5	2.0
Next $100,000	2.5	1.0	1.5

Q. 2:19 What is vesting of commissions?

Vesting of commissions occurs when the insurer grants ownership of renewal commissions (commissions paid when coverage is renewed for another plan year) to the agent whether or not the agent continues to represent the policyholder. Although insurers differ in their vesting procedures, there is a general trend away from this concept, as it removes the agent's incentive to continue to provide services to the policyholder.

Q. 2:20 Are there laws that regulate the business practices of intermediaries?

Laws determining agent and broker licensing requirements vary from state to state and can require consultants to be licensed as well. Insurance companies monitor the licensure status of intermediaries that place business with them. Some states allow agents and brokers to operate in the state if they are licensed in another state.

Q. 2:21 If an employer wants to self-fund the plan, which type of insurance professional would it need?

An employer interested in partially or fully self-insuring its group insurance plan often works with an employee benefits consultant or a TPA. However, some brokers will have the expertise necessary to design and properly structure a self-funded plan. An insurance company may administer the plan even though it is not underwriting the entire risk.

Q. 2:22 Would an employer whose plan is fully insured use a TPA?

An employer with a fully insured plan may employ a TPA to handle the administrative functions of the plan, including claims payment, with the approval of the insurance company. However, insurance companies provide most fully insured employers with administrative services.

Q. 2:23 How does an employer decide whether to use a TPA or an insurance company to administer its plan?

Both insurance carriers and TPAs provide valuable administrative services, which an employer would find difficult to provide internally. The choice between a TPA and an insurer should be based on service, ease of administration, and cost.

The employer should determine what services are most important. Some employers believe that local claims service is advantageous. The two traditional components of claims service are claims turnaround time and resolution of problems associated with claims. These services are not necessarily handled any more expediently with local service. Some employers may prefer a single source for all their insurance dealings.

In addition to accurate claims payment, an important service

TPAs and insurance companies provide is giving the policyholder accurate information on benefits utilization. Examples of data reports should be requested from prospective administrators and compared. This is especially true for employers that have enough employees to be charged based on their own claims utilization.

Q. 2:24 If an employer has a TPA handle the administrative functions, would the employer's cost be decreased?

The expense portion of an employer's insurance premium would be decreased, since the insurance company's overhead costs are eliminated. However, the employer would be paying the TPA for the services. Depending on what those services are, their cost, and the efficiency of the TPA, the employer's overall cost could be higher or lower.

Q. 2:25 How are TPAs compensated?

Most TPAs charge for their consulting services on either a fixed fee or an hourly basis. All sorts of arrangements are made for administrative services, but most TPAs charge for administrative services on a monthly or per employee basis or as a fixed percentage of claims. Additional fees may be specified for installation, preparation of communication and enrollment materials, and other special services. The employer generally compensates the TPA directly. However, TPAs may also receive commissions from insurance products included in the program.

HMOs, PPOs, and Health Care Coalitions

Q. 2:26 What is an HMO?

A Health Maintenance Organization (HMO) is an organization that provides comprehensive health care to a voluntarily enrolled population at a predetermined price. Members pay fixed, periodic fees directly to the HMO and in return receive health care services as often as needed. HMOs are discussed in detail in Chapter 8.

Q. 2:27 What is a PPO?

A Preferred Provider Organization (PPO) is an association that contracts with a group of doctors, dentists, hospitals, or other health care service providers to provide care at prearranged rates or discounts. PPOs are discussed in detail in Chapter 8.

Q. 2:28 What is an employer health care coalition?

An employer health care coalition is an association of health care plan sponsors (employers) that pool resources, share ideas, and gather information on insurers and health care providers. Coalitions may serve as go-betweens to obtain information or to assemble data to provide standard price lists and fee schedules and comparative statistics. They may also negotiate with providers on behalf of coalition members. See the section on Health Care Data in Chapter 7 for additional information.

Chapter 3
Factors Influencing Plan Design

A variety of federal and state laws regulate the group health insurance market. These laws, as well as important social and financial considerations, will strongly influence an employer's decision-making process. This chapter covers both the external (legal) and internal (company environment) factors that affect the basic decisions concerning an employer's group health insurance plan.

Legal Factors Affecting Design

Q. 3:1 Are employers required by federal law to purchase group insurance for their employees?

Presently, no federal law requires employers to provide their employees with group insurance. There have been initiatives in Congress, however, that would require employers to provide specified minimum levels of health benefits. Although such proposals have so far failed to attract sufficient votes for enactment, mandatory health care is gathering support. There is every likelihood that some form of national standard will be legislated in the next few years.

(Note: Although federal law does not require an employer to offer health benefits, once the employer has decided to do so there are rules regarding how and to whom that coverage should be made available. See page 22.)

Q. 3:2 Are employers required by state law to purchase group insurance for their employees?

State laws generally do not demand coverage either, with two notable exceptions. Hawaii requires employees who work more than 20 hours a week to receive hospitalization and basic medical coverage. Massachusetts is phasing in a program that, in 1992, will give employers the option of either paying a surtax to the government to be used to fund a state medical care program or covering their employees themselves and offsetting the cost of their programs against the surtax (in effect, exempting from tax those employers that already provide coverage on their own).

New York, Rhode Island, California, New Jersey, and Hawaii have laws that mandate short-term disability coverage for all employees. Puerto Rico also requires such coverage.

As with federal law, if an employer elects to provide employees with other group insurance benefits, the plan must comply with additional requirements imposed by state laws.

Q. 3:3 Are group health plans governed by federal laws or by state laws?

Group health plans are governed by both. As employee benefits plans, or welfare plans, they are governed by federal laws that contain provisions pertaining to such things as nondiscriminatory participation requirements, reporting and disclosure, continuation of coverage for former employees, and taxation.

If the benefits are provided under an insurance contract, the contractual provisions are governed by state, rather than federal, law. This was provided for by the McCarran-Ferguson Act, which, as of 1948, provided that federal law will regulate insurance only when state law does not. Each state has its own laws governing contracts, including those for insurance, and most states have laws specifically covering group life and health insurance.

States usually have an appointed official who oversees the operations of insurers in that state, commonly either a Superintendent or Commissioner of Insurance. In addition, the National

Factors Influencing Insurance Plan Design   Q. 3:5

Association of Insurance Commissioners (NAIC), a voluntary organization of state insurance officials with influence but no legislative authority, has developed standard model bills and procedures that are designed to provide some consistency from state to state. Although there has been general acceptance of model laws on a number of issues, leading to substantial uniformity, there are other issues on which the various states have chosen to pursue their own distinct policies. For this reason, before conducting business in a new state, it is advisable to contact that state's insurance commissioner.

Q. 3:4 Do federal and state laws apply to self-insured group health plans?

Most federal laws that govern group health insurance plans apply to all welfare plans, and as such apply to self-insured plans. State insurance laws do not apply, however, and the Employee Retirement Income Security Act (ERISA) supersedes any state laws governing self-insured plans. (ERISA's breadth with relation to state law has been tested in the courts, most notably in the area of spousal rights. The upshot has been that there are a limited number of areas where state laws were not preempted.)

Q. 3:5 When state and federal laws change, what are an employer's obligations regarding a group health insurance plan?

Although it is the employer's responsibility to see that its plan complies with applicable laws, the complexity of these laws makes reliance on assistance from insurers and/or intermediaries essential. Insurers are required by law to write legally acceptable benefits plans and, therefore, take the responsibility for helping employers comply with the laws. Insurers generally take responsibility for informing employers about legislative developments. The insurer, with the intermediary, will explain exactly how the new law affects the employer and will outline how and when the employer's plan must change to comply with the new law.

Groups that self-fund must comply with laws that affect self-funded plans. Generally, the intermediary, third-party administrator (TPA), or insurance company, if it is administering the plan, will take responsibility for informing the employer about legislative developments.

Changes to laws that affect group health insurance plans usually fall into one of three categories: (1) laws that affect only policies issued after the effective date of the law, (2) laws that not only affect newly issued policies but also require compliance at the next renewal date of an already existing policy, and (3) laws that require compliance at any upcoming change to an existing policy, but at least at the next anniversary date of the policy. Some laws simply require that policyholders be offered the opportunity to purchase a new benefit. In that situation, the employer has the right to refuse to change the existing benefits plan.

Plans that are offered pursuant to a collective bargaining agreement will generally not be required to make legislated changes until the expiration of that agreement.

State Law

Q. 3:6 What are the responsibilities of the state insurance department?

The state insurance department is the administrative agency that supervises the insurance companies doing business in that state. The insurance department is assigned the task of making sure that carriers obey the insurance laws. Areas of responsibility include licensing companies and agents, issuing regulations, conducting examinations of companies, making legislative recommendations, monitoring fees and rates, handling customer complaints, developing model bills, and performing any other duty that will ensure that state insurance laws are kept up-to-date and adequately enforced. Insurance contracts must be filed with and approved by the insurance commissioner before being offered for sale within that state.

Q. 3:7 What are the similarities among state laws governing group health insurance?

Most states, having adopted NAIC model bills, have similar programs that govern each of the following: minimum participation, eligibility, certificates to insureds, payment of premiums, grace periods, claims processing, the appeals process, and the coordination of health insurance benefits among insureds' plans. Despite these somewhat standard provisions, laws governing specific required benefits vary considerably from state to state. These mandatory state programs generally fall into three categories: mandated benefits or coverage, mandated offerings of benefits, and right of direct payment. According to a study by the Blue Cross and Blue Shield Association, as of the end of 1986 every state had at least one such requirement, and a number of states had more than 20.

Q. 3:8 What is a mandated benefit?

A mandated benefit is a specific coverage that an insurer is required to include in its contract under state law. For example, most states require that coverage for substance-abuse treatment be provided. Other kinds of coverage that are mandated in some states include coverage for newborn children, mental and nervous disorders, and hospice care.

States may differ in the way they require the insurer to provide the mandated benefits. Some states require that benefits be provided on the same basis as for any other illness; others require that an insurer provide a minimum specified benefit (for example, an annual dollar amount or number of visits for each individual for claims relating to certain types of care).

Q. 3:9 Why are some benefits mandated by state law?

Some states mandate benefits because it is felt that there is a need that is not being covered satisfactorily. Benefits that are mandated are usually intended to promote a widely recognized social goal, while limiting state expenditures for that type of care.

Q. 3:10 What is a mandated offering?

A mandated offering is coverage that must be made available to each policyholder. The coverage is extended to the employer as an additional price option; the employer is not required to purchase it. Unlike a mandated benefit, a mandated offering is not required to be part of every group insurance policy.

Q. 3:11 What is a right of direct payment?

A right of direct payment requires a plan to pay for services from certain categories of providers that are not prescribed or referred by a licensed physician. Examples of such providers include home nurse practitioners, midwives, marriage counselors, and social workers.

Q. 3:12 What are the state requirements for employee participation in a group insurance plan?

State laws require that insurance companies set participation percentages to ensure against adverse selection, which could jeopardize the insurer's solvency. In most states, the participation requirement is 75%. This means that at least 75% of an employer's eligible employees must participate in a group health insurance plan.

Q. 3:13 What is the minimum number of employees allowed by state law to participate in a group health insurance plan?

Most states require that an employer enroll a minimum number of employees (generally 10, though fewer in some states) for coverage in order to purchase and maintain a group health insurance plan. This minimum size requirement reduces the potential for adverse selection. Employers with fewer than 10 enrolled employees often participate in a group insurance trust, such as a multiple employer trust (MET).

Q. 3:14 Is there a maximum number of employees that may be covered under a group health insurance plan?

There is no legal limit to the number of employees that may be covered under a group health insurance plan. Some plans cover tens of thousands of employees.

Workers' Compensation

Q. 3:15 What is Workers' Compensation?

State workers compensation laws require employers to carry insurance protecting employees and their dependents against financial loss resulting from death, disability, or injury that occurs during the course of employment. The intent of the laws was:

- To make financial compensation readily available to workers without the need for protracted litigation, and
- To place limits on employer liability so as to make costs predictable and manageable.

Q. 3:16 What types of benefits does Workers' Compensation provide?

Workers' compensation benefits include:

- Income replacement benefits for permanent and temporary disabilities and death;
- Medical care to treat on-the-job illnesses and injuries;
- Rehabilitative services to restore employability; and
- Survivor benefits for dependents in the case of the employee's death.

Q. 3:17   Health Insurance Answer Book

Q. 3:17   How is Workers' Compensation insurance made available?

Depending upon state law, employers may purchase the insurance either through a state insurance fund or through an authorized commercial insurer, or they may elect to self-insure.

Q. 3:18   May Workers' Compensation benefits be integrated with other employer benefits?

Until Tax Reform eliminated it, there was a provision of the Internal Revenue Code that permitted pension plan benefits to offset income replacement benefits provided by workers' compensation. A recent statement by the IRS said that this may still be permissible, provided the arrangement does not discriminate in favor of highly compensated employees. In comparing benefits, workers' compensation benefits cannot be treated as employer-provided benefits. Regulations are expected to explain just how the non-discrimination test operates.

Charges incurred as a result of a work-related injury or illness are generally excluded from covered expenses provided by group health insurance plans. Disability plans typically offset workers' compensation benefits in determining the net benefit payable.

Q. 3:19   How are Workers' Compensation benefits taxed to employees?

Workers' compensation payments are excludible from gross income under IRC Section 104.

Q.3:20   Why is Workers' Compensation a growing concern for employers?

Costs attributable with workplace injuries—including costs associated with health care, liability, and workers' compensation—totalled an estimated $47.1 billion in 1988, up 35% from the $34.8 billion estimated for 1986, according to the National Safety

Council. Workers' compensation costs themselves have risen twice as fast as the general rate of inflation, accounting for over 3 cents of every payroll dollar, up from less than 2 cents a decade ago.

Q.3:21 Why are Workers' Compensation costs rising?

Some of the increase is the result of the increasing cost of health care services generally. The rest is caused by:
- More workplace accidents. Between 1987 and 1988, the number of work-related permanent disabilities rose from 60,000 to 70,000, an increase of 16%. The number of recordable injuries per 100 full time employees was 8.6 in 1988, up from 7.9 in 1986, while the number of lost workdays increased from 65.8 to 76.1.
- Broader definitions of disability. While originally aimed at physical diabilities such as loss of limbs, etc., workers' compensation laws are written and construed broadly enough to include stress and accompanying ailments such as headaches and backaches. The difficulty of contesting these claims routinely leads insurers to settle out of court. Many states are now revising their workers' compensation laws to be more specific about what constitutes a compensable disability.
- Incidental costs. According to the Workers' Compensation Research Institute, litigation costs associated with those claims which insurers did contest increased nearly 6 times in a 10-year period. As legal costs are often covered by workers' compensation insurance, there is little incentive for employees not to sue on the slightest pretext.

Q. 3:22 What can employers do to control Workers' Compensation costs?

Beyond promoting workplace safety, employers can employ many of the same cost containment techniques with regard to workers' compensation claims as they do with health care costs. However, there are some key differences:

- Employers who operate in more than one state must have a program that is flexible enough to meet the standards of up to 51 different workers' compensation laws.
- Cost-sharing with employees is one key strategy that will not work with workers' compensation, as employees cannot be required to contribute to their own treatment. The plus side of this is that discussions regarding payments involve only the health care provider and the employer/insurer, providing more latitude for challenges of provider charges.
- Most workers' compensation claims emanate from relatively few categories of ailments. There are, for example, large numbers of back and neck ailments, which makes a focussed utilization review program very effective.
- A significant number of disabling *injuries* can be attrributed to falls (16%), and hitting or being hit by an object (26%). Workplace safety programs can make a big difference in the frequency of these accidents.
- Workers compensation costs, like disability costs generally, are especially susceptible to savings from return-to-work programs. The Washington Business Group on Health estimates that companies can expect a return of $8-10 for every dollar invested in return-to-work programs.

Federal Law

Q. 3:23 What federal laws affect group health insurance plans?

Federal law has a pervasive influence on the design and operation of group health plans. The laws may be categorized as follows:

1. Laws enacted primarily to protect employees from discrimination in employment. Although these laws do not specifically address group health insurance issues, they do contain relevant regulations. The most important of these laws are the Age Discrimination in Employment Act of 1967 (ADEA),

as amended in 1978, and Title VII of the Civil Rights Act of 1964, as amended; the Pregnancy Discrimination Act and the Americans with Disabilities Act.

2. Laws addressing specific health insurance issues. The most important of these include the 1965 amendment to the Old Age, Survivors' and Disability Insurance Act (OASDI), which established Medicare, effective July 1966 ; the HMO Act of 1973, as amended in 1988, which governs the terms on which HMO coverage is offered to employees; and the Consolidated Omnibus Budget Reconciliation Act of 1985 (COBRA), which requires that health care coverage continue to be made available to former employees and their dependents.

3. Laws that set general standards for the operation of employee benefits plans. Most prominent of these is the Employee Retirement Income Security Act of 1974 (ERISA), which makes federal law preeminent regarding employee benefits plans, establishes standards for fiduciaries charged with administering these plans, and imposes standards for reporting and disclosure.

4. Laws governing the tax consequences of group health plans as they affect employers, employees, and the plans themselves. These rules, including standards that must be met to qualify for employer tax deductions and exclusion from employee income, are found in the Internal Revenue Code (IRC), Treasury regulations and IRS rulings, and periodic amendments to the law itself, such as the Tax Equity and Fiscal Responsibility Act of 1982 (TEFRA), the Deficit Reduction Act of 1984 (DEFRA) and the Technical and Miscellaneous Revenue Act of 1988 (TAMRA).

5. Laws that affect employee health and safety in the workplace such as the Occupational Safety and Health Act (OSHA).

Q. 3:24 How does ADEA affect group health insurance plans?

The Age Discrimination in Employment Act (ADEA) prohibits discrimination in employment against individuals aged 40 and older (until January 1, 1987, the maximum age was 70 under TEFRA). Although the main intent of this law is to prohibit mandatory retirement (with certain exceptions), related provisions of the law apply to health insurance. ADEA, as amended in 1986, requires employers with 20 or more employees to offer all active employees and their spouses, regardless of age or eligibility for Medicare, the same coverage. ADEA does not permit cost-justified reductions for health insurance, although such reductions are permitted for life and disability insurance.

Q. 3:25 Are employers required by federal law to cover retired employees under group health insurance plans?

No. Employment law generally applies to active employees. The decision to cover retirees is a human resources issue, rather than a legal requirement. The employer should examine its employee benefits objectives to decide whether to cover retirees. Many companies are encouraging early retirement to manage expenses and avoid layoffs; for them, it might be in their best interests to provide health insurance coverage to retirees. Most retirees aged 65 and older have access to health insurance through Medicare, so coverage through an employer's plan would be supplemental. The cost of retiree coverage is high in spite of the share paid by Medicare. Recent court rulings have prohibited employers from changing existing retirees' promised coverage. Therefore, employers should evaluate the pros and cons carefully before implementing retiree coverage.

A related issue is the right of employers to discontinue retiree health care once it has been made available. Attempts to do so have generally been challenged in court, with mixed results. (For more on this, see the discussion of retiree health care at Questions 11:31–11:42.)

Q. 3:26 What requirements does ERISA impose on group health insurance plans?

ERISA was enacted primarily to effect pension equity, but it also protects the interests of welfare benefit plan participants and

Factors Influencing Insurance Plan Design   Q. 3:27

beneficiaries. Under ERISA, group health insurance plans must be established pursuant to a written instrument that describes the benefits provided under the plan, names the persons responsible for the operation of the plan, and spells out the arrangements for funding and amending the plan.

ERISA established a reporting procedure that requires that a summary plan description (SPD) be filed with the Department of Labor, and an annual financial report be filed with the Internal Revenue Service. Plan participants must be given copies of the SPD and the summary annual report (SAR). Simplified reporting requirements apply to plans with fewer than 100 participants because Congress considered the reporting requirements too burdensome for small employers. (See Chapter 6.)

Q. 3:27   How are group health insurance plans affected by the HMO Act of 1973?

The provision of the HMO Act that has the most significant effect on group health insurance plans is the "dual choice option." This provision requires that employers with 25 or more employees in a health maintenance organization (HMO) service area include HMO coverage as an alternative to the employer's regular health plan if requested by an HMO to do so. The law requires that at least one group-practice and one individual-practice HMO be offered to employees if the employer receives a request for inclusion by each type. HMOs are responsible for requesting inclusion by employers as alternative health plans, and are subject to certain federal requirements in order for employers to be required to recognize them.

Employers must make contributions on behalf of their employees to an HMO sufficient to ensure that HMO enrollees are not discriminated against; that is, the contributions must be reasonable and assure a fair choice among competing health plans. This can mean equal dollars, equal percentage of premiums, equal contributions for demographic groups, or negotiated rates between employer and HMO.

This dual choice option (which, under a "sunset" provision included in HMO amendments passed in 1988, is scheduled to expire in 1995) was established to encourage individuals to consider coverage under an HMO instead of under their employer's traditional plan. (HMOs are discussed in detail in Chapter 8.)

The Pregnancy Discrimination Act

Q. 3:28   What is the Pregnancy Discrimination Act?

The Pregnancy Discrimination Act (PDA) is an amendment to Title VII of the Civil Rights Act of 1964. It requires employers to regard disabilities or medical conditions associated with pregnancy and childbirth the same as other disabilities or medical conditions. That means that these conditions receive the same treatment as is afforded to similarly situated individuals who have not experienced pregnancy or childbirth. Similar treatment extends to:

- Disability benefits,
- Health insurance benefits,
- Short-term sick leave, and
- Employment policies including seniority, leave extensions, and reinstatement.

Q. 3:29   What does "the same" treatment for pregnancy-related medical conditions mean?

It means that where employees are offered a choice among several different health care plans, pregnancy related coverage must be available in all of them, and that there may be no distinction made in the applicability of such items as:

- Terms of reimbursement, including maximum reimbursable amounts;
- Deductibles, copayments, and out-of-pocket maximums;
- Preexisting conditions; and
- Choice of physician and hospitals.

Q. 3:30   What employers are subject to the law?

Title VII of the Civil Rights Act applies to all private employers who employ 15 or more employees each working day for 20 or more weeks in the current or the preceding calendar year. Court decisions have interpreted coverage standards very broadly, to include part-time employees, independent contractors, successor corporations, parent-subsidiary groups, and other groups of employers who are affiliated or under common control.

Q. 3:31   Do the provisions of the Pregnancy Discrimination Act apply only to married employees.?

No. Pregnancy-related disability benefits may not be restricted to married employees, *unless* all disability benefits are so restricted.

Q. 3:32   Does the Pregnancy Discrimination Act extend to benefits for spouses of employees?

Yes. According to the Supreme Court (Newport News Shipbuilding & Dry Dock v EEOC, 462 US 669, 1983), *if* the employer provides health insurance coverage for dependents, benefits for pregnancy-related conditions of employees' spouses must be the same as those for non-pregnant spouses and the spouses of female employees.

Q. 3:33   Does the Pregnancy Discrimination Act extend to other dependents?

Health insurance plans need not cover the pregnancy-related conditions of employees' daughters and other dependents, provided the pregnancy-related conditions of male and female employees' dependents are excluded on an equal basis. (Note: complications of pregnancy for dependent daughters are usually required to be treated as any other illness under most state provisions.)

Q. 3:34   Must abortions be covered by employer health plans under the Pregnancy Discrimination Act?

No, the Act specifically states that employer plans are not required to provide for abortions, unless the mother's life would be endangered by carrying the fetus to term, or there are medical complications that have arisen from an abortion.

This does not prevent employers from choosing to provide abortion benefits, and most insurance carriers provide options regarding this coverage. Under EEOC guidelines, however, those employers who choose to provide abortion benefits must do so in the same manner and at the same level as for benefits for other medical conditions.

Q. 3:35 Is mandatory maternity leave permitted under the Pregnancy Discrimination Act?

No. Employers cannot require pregnant employees to take leave unless there is a similar requirement for other non-pregnant employees with disabilities that could impair their performance. Employees mandatory leave dates must take into consideration the individual's ability to continue performing their duties, and should not be determined by administrative convenience. Pregnant employees must be permitted to work at all times, so long as they are able to perform their jobs.

Mandatory leave has been upheld, however, where there was clear business necessity, such as where flight attendants would be unable to assist passengers in an emergency, should an unexpected pregnancy-related problem occur.

[Note: The issue of mandatory leave, or reassignment away from duties that might be hazardous to the public or to women who are either pregnant or of childbearing years, continues to present problems that must be resolved by the courts. While some level of special treatment or consideration has been widely accepted, drawing the line between permitted and prohibited discrimination is very difficult and must be determined on a case-by-case basis. Generally, the more arbitrary the policy, the less it is supported by business necessity and medical evidence, and the smaller the threat to employee or public safety, the greater chance the chance that the policy is unlawful.]

Q. 3:36 Must employees be allowed to return to their jobs following maternity leave?

Yes, on the same basis as any other employee returning after a period of sick or disability leave. That means that return cannot be conditioned upon position vacancy or employer discretion, if those standards are not applied to other forms of disability leave. An employer was upheld, however, who conditioned return on the employee's prior notice of an intent to return because this policy was applied to all employees returning from all forms of disability leave.

Q. 3:37 Are state laws pre-empted by the Pregnancy Discrimination Act?

Not necessarily. Where the provisions of those laws are more restrictive than those of the PDA, they are invalid since they run counter to the requirement that pregnancy-related benefits be the same as non-pregnancy related benefits. State laws which require more generous benefits than those required by the PDA, however, have generally been upheld.

Some state laws, such as that of California, extend the PDA mandates to employers who are not covered by Title VII.

Many states have maternity provisions, which are modelled on the New York state provision, that requires employers to provide benefits for "complicated maternities" on the same basis as for any other illness. These complications include caesarean delivery, therapeutic abortion, miscarriage, toxemia, and other defined conditions. Benefits for dependent children, in addition to employees and spouses, are mandated as well.

Q. 3:38 Does the Pregnancy Discrimination Act apply to "parental or family leave?"

No. The Act protects those taking pregnancy leave. Additional time off, for males or females, to care for newborn children, newly adopted children, or children who are ill, is not protected by the act. Nor is it considered a welfare benefit or payroll practice covered or exempted (respectively) by ERISA.

Where federal law is concerned, therefore, parental leave is considered to be part of an employer's general leave policy. These leave policies, however, are governed by a number of federal prohibitions against sex discrimination, so they should be drafted with care. A recent federal court decision, *Shafer v. Pittsburg Board of Education*, concluded that it would be a violation of the Civil Rights Act to extend family or parental leave only to female employees and not to male employees as well.

The case involved a schoolteacher who was denied a one-year unpaid leave to take care of his son. His union contract had provided for such leave, but that provision had thus far only been applied to women. The Appeals Court found this to be a violation of the ban on sex discrimination of Title VII of the Civil Rights Act. The decision affirmed the lower court's theory that preferential treatment for women who have recently given birth to a child does not violate Title VII, provided there is a showing that it is tied to a continuing disability related to the pregnancy or delivery. But that would be for *pregnancy disability leave*; Mr. Schafer's case involved "childrearing" leave, which is something different, and must be provided equally to employees of both sexes.

▶ **Planning Pointer:** The decision is only immediately applicable to the Third Circuit's jurisdiction (Pennsylvania, New Jersey, Delaware and the Virgin islands) although it is likely to be influential in similar cases elsewhere. Also, this decision *does not require* employers to offer childrearing leave; it only mandates that if they do so, the leave be granted on a nondiscriminatory basis.

Q.3:39 Are there state laws governing parental or family leave?

Yes. Almost half of the states have enacted legislation that requires employers to permit natural or adoptive parents to take unpaid leave to care for a child. While the laws vary considerably from one jurisdiction to another, they generally provide that employers with a minimum number of employees (at least 25, although a number of states specify higher numbers such as 50 or 100) must allow employees (usually permanent employees: those who have been with the employer for a year or more) to take leave of from 6 weeks to 12 months within a specified period (12 to 24 months, usually commencing with the child's birth or adoption). The laws also govern matters such as notice of intent to return, reinstatement procedures, continuation of benefits, compensation and penalties for failure to comply. A number of states have broader family leave laws. Still others are considering legislation.

Q. 3:40 Are there federal laws governing family leave?

No. The Family and Medical Leave Act, which would have required employers with 50 or more employees to grant leave of up to 12 weeks of unpaid leave in conjunction with the birth or adoption of an employee's child, or the illness of a child or parent, was vetoed by President Bush. Many companies have adopted such policies anyway and states are becoming more active in promulgating family leave laws of their own.

Q. 3:41 What is the difference between maternity leave and parental or family leave?

Maternity leave stems from the characterization of pregnancy as a "disability". Pregnancy disability laws, both federal and state [see the discussion of the Pregnancy Disability Act below], refers only to females and are in effect only as long as the attendant disability persists (or is legally presumed to persist). Family leave, on the other hand, is not conditioned upon the physical health of the employee or anyone else.

Family leave policies generally apply to both sexes.

A recent federal case makes that distinction. In that case, the Third Circuit Court of Appeals ruled that firms with 15 or more workers must provide males with child-rearing leave if they provide such benefits to female workers. [Schafer v. Board of Public Education of the School District of Pittsburgh, Pa.].

The PDA protects those taking pregnancy leave. Additional time off, for males or females, to care for newborn children, newly adopted children, or children who are ill, is not protected by the Act. Nor is it considered a welfare benefit or payroll practice covered or exempted (respectively) by ERISA.

Where federal law is concerned, therefore, (barring resurrection of the Family and Medical Leave Act) parental leave is considered to be part of an employer's general leave policy. [These leave policies, however, are governed by a number of federal prohibitions against sex discrimination, so they should be drafted with care.]

Q. 3:42 What features are typically found in employer family leave policies?

Many companies have policies regarding time off for expectant or new mothers, fathers, or other employees who need to look after a close relative.

Common features of such leave policies include:

- Paid maternity leave, combining prenatal and postnatal time off, usually totalling up to 8 weeks;
- Unpaid leave for care of a newborn or newly adopted child for periods of 3 months up to 3 years;
- Continuation of some or all employee benefits during the period of absence;
- Reinstatement provisions which guarantee reinstatement to the employee's original job if he or she returns to work within a specified period of time, usually not more than 6 months;
- Reinstatement to a comparable job if return to work occurs after a stated period (say 6 months), and/or
- A best effort to place the employee in a job consistent with the employee's training, experience and other qualifications if the period of leave exceeds a certain number of months.

Occupational Safety and Health Act

Q.3:43 What is the Occupational Safety and Health Act (OSHA)?

The Occupational Safety and Health Act of 1970 was enacted to establish workplace safety standards and to reduce the number of job-related injuries and illnesses stemming from unsafe working conditions.

Q. 3:44 What OSHA requirements apply to businesses?

OSHA requirements vary from industry to industry. Regulations impose stricter operating standards on companies whose workers are exposed to toxic substances than on financial and retail firms.

Firms with 10 employees or less are exempt from many of the OSHA requirements.

Q. 3:45 What are the notification and recordkeeping requirements under OSHA?

OSHA requires employers to post permanent notices to employees regarding job safety. A second notice must advise employees of the rights of those who have raised objections to working under unsafe conditions.

Covered employers must maintain a log (Federal Form 200) of all workplace illnesses and injuries. At the end of each year this information is summarized. A supplemental record (Federal Form 101) must be kept for each injury or illness. All of these records must be on file and available for inspection for 5 years.

Q. 3:46 Does the Occupational Safety and Health Administration make inspections?

Yes, OSHA makes safety inspections and health inspections. To determine which companies will be inspected, it compiles a county by county list, grouping companies according to their Standard Industrial Classification (SIC) listing and ranking them by size. For safety inspections it ranks industries according to lost workday injury rates. For health inspections, it ranks industries based upon potential exposure to hazardous substances. Companies that pose the greatest health risk to the greatest number of workers are targeted for inspection first.

Q. 3:47 How can employers get more information on OSHA?

The following booklets are available from local OSHA offices or from the Department of Labor, OSHA Publication Office, Room N-3101, 200 Constitution Avenue, N.W., Washington, DC 20210.

What Every Employer Needs to Know About OSHA

OSHA: Employee Workplace Rights

Recordkeeping Requirements Under The Occupational Safety and Health Act

Americans with Disabilities Act

Q. 3:48 What is the Americans with Disabilities Act of 1990 (ADA)?

The ADA bars discrimination against persons with disabilities in transportation, public facilities and employment.

Q. 3:49 How does the ADA affect employers and their employees?

The law prohibits discrimination against any "qualified individual with a disability" (see Question 3:51) in areas relating to hiring, firing, pay, promotion, training and other terms and conditions of employment.

Q. 3:50 What size businesses are affected?

Employers with 25 or more workers must change their personnel policies to comply with law within two years; employers with 15-24 employees have 4 years to comply. Employers who can demonstrate that the required changes may be too costly or disruptive would be exempt.

Q. 3:51 Who is a qualified individual with a disability?

An individual who can perform the essential functions of a job, with or without reasonable accommodation is considered "a qualified individual with a disability" under the ADA.

Q. 3:52 What is "reasonable accommodation"?

Reasonable accommodation includes:
- Converting existing facilities to make them accessible and usable by disabled persons;
- Use of part-time or otherwise modified work schedules;
- Restructuring the job or reassigning the individual;
- Acquiring or modifying equipment or devices used in the job;
- Restructuring training and support, including providing readers or interpreters.

Q. 3:53 Will the ADA have an adverse effect on business?

Supporters of the ADA contend that the cost of compliance will be small, and that most necessary modifications will cost $500 to $5000 for most small businesses.

Critics of the Act, however, complain that it imposes too heavy a burden on businesses. The Act's definitions of disability could sweep in as many as 43 million Americans, which could have serious repercussions for compensation and benefit programs (such as employer sponsored disability plans, workers compensation). Even supporters admit that much depends on the character of the implementing regulations, due out within the next 18 months, and the degree to which courts extend the disability concepts to other areas of employment law.

Taxation of Group Health Plans

Q. 3:54 What state tax laws apply to group health insurance plans?

All states tax the premiums that group insurance policyholders pay to insurers based on the residence of covered employees. These taxes range from 1% to 3.3% of premiums. The cost of the tax to insurance companies is passed along to the policyholder. Depending on the state, certain costs associated with self-funded plans are also taxed.

Self-employed individuals (those who own any part of an unincorporated business) are treated differently. They may deduct 25% of their health insurance premiums from their taxable incomes. As we went to press, this provision was scheduled to expire in September of 1990.

Q. 3:55 What is the federal tax status of group health insurance for employers?

Under IRC Section 162, an employer's contributions to a group health insurance plan are deductible as ordinary and necessary business expenses. There is no limit on the amount that can be deducted for current expenses, as long as the contributions qualify as additional reasonable compensation to the insured and the benefits are payable to the employees, not the employer. No deduction is available, however, if the plan fails to comply with the COBRA continuation of coverage requirements for former employees and dependents (see Chapter 6). [Ref.: IRC Section 162(k)]

An exception to the general rule on deductions concerns

Factors Influencing Insurance Plan Design   Q. 3:58

group insurance plans funded through voluntary employees' beneficiary associations (VEBAs), also known as 501(c)(9) trusts. VEBAs that establish a reserve fund for the payment of future benefits are subject to special deduction limits under IRC Sections 419 and 419A. Failure to comply with all of the requirements of these sections can result in loss of deduction, unrelated business income tax on excess reserves (IRC Section 512), and/or excise tax on "disqualified" (discriminatory) benefits (IRC Section 4976). (See Chapter 5.)

Q. 3:56 Are employer contributions treated as taxable income to employees?

No. Under IRC Section 106, contributions by an employer to a health insurance plan are not considered part of an employee's taxable income. Plans of employers with 20 or more employees that do not meet the COBRA continuation of coverage requirements (IRC Section 162(k)) will not enjoy this employee income exclusion.

In addition, the value of a discriminatory benefit (see Chapter 11) attributable to employer contributions may be taxable to highly compensated employees of the Section 89 nondiscrimination rules.)

Q. 3:57 Are the benefits from a group health insurance plan taxable to employees?

No. Generally, payments of an employee's or employee's dependents' medical expenses by a group health plan are not includible in the employee's taxable income. [Ref.: IRC Section 105]

Nonlegal Factors Affecting Design

Q. 3:58 Besides the legislative factors, what other issues must be addressed as part of the purchasing process?

To some extent, general economic conditions will determine what type of plan an employer can select. For example, if the economy is depressed or the outlook for the employer's industry is poor, the employer may not be in a position to offer a generous benefits plan. However, the employer must simultaneously determine what role the group health insurance plan will play in its hiring strategy. Should the employer set up a "rich" plan in order to gain a recruiting advantage over competitors by providing employees and prospective employees with a more attractive benefits package, or will it settle for a less competitive plan?

Company demographics will also be a factor. If the majority of a company's employees are young and, therefore, would value certain types of benefits more than a predominantly older employee population would, the benefits plan can be structured to meet those needs. In addition, the employer will have to determine how its corporate culture should be manifested in the plan (for example, a traditionally employee-oriented company will want a benefits plan that reflects that orientation). Some employees may already have insurance from other sources.

Q. 3:59 Who is an eligible employee?

An eligible employee is any employee who meets the definition in the plan for participation. Definitions of eligible employee vary widely from employer to employer, though they may be influenced by:

- Legal considerations. For example, those employees who are not considered for purposes of nondiscrimination testing those who are covered by a collective bargaining agreement) may be excluded.
- Company structure. Eligible employee may be defined to exclude employees from different operating units, different geographical areas, or different employment categories (for example, salaried versus hourly).

Q. 3:60 Can a single group health insurance plan meet the benefits needs of an employer's diverse workforce?

Most group health insurance plans are comprehensive enough to cover a wide range of medical expenses. They provide coverage to protect even those in the employer's workforce with the greatest need for health insurance. Ironically, the comprehensive nature of today's group benefits plans has created two new problems: duplication of benefits and coverage levels not needed by many of today's workers. Because today's workforce contains a growing number of two-wage-earner families—with both earners entitled to health coverage from their own employers—the potential for duplication of benefits is great.

Restrictions on Coverage

Q. 3:61 For what reasons do employers typically exclude employees from group health insurance coverage?

There are a number of reasons that employers may exclude certain employees from coverage. For example:

- Union employees who have coverage that was negotiated as part of a collective bargaining agreement would be excluded.
- An employer may choose to cover employees working in different locations under different plans.
- A subsidiary of an employer may be in a different industry, with different benefits needs; the subsidiary could be excluded and covered under a different plan.
- An employer may want to give extra benefits to a special class of higher-paid employees and would, therefore, exclude all other employees from the extra coverage.
- The expense of covering part-time and temporary employees may be too great for the employer to consider covering them.

Q. 3:62 Are there limitations on an employer's freedom to choose the employees it wants covered under a group health insurance plan?

An employer may choose to cover only certain classes of employees under a group health insurance plan, as long as applicable employment laws are not violated and the insurer approves the classification as one that precludes individual selection. Federal laws prohibit discrimination on the basis of age, sex, or race, so these criteria cannot be used as the basis for exclusion from an employer's health plan. In addition, failure to include a significant percentage of employees, especially if those excluded represent a disproportionate share of lower-paid employees, may cause certain types of plans to be deemed discriminatory. This can result in tax penalties to certain highly compensated employees. (See Chapter 11 for a comprehensive discussion of nondiscrimination rules.) Therefore, an employer must weigh the cost of covering or making similar coverage available on a broad basis against the value of tax-free benefits for highly paid employees.

Q. 3:63 Why would an employer offer benefits to which some employees already have access?

Health coverage has become an expected part of an employee's total compensation package, and if an employer hopes to attract and retain quality employees, medical coverage is among the first types of noncash compensation the employer should consider. A group plan allows all employees to participate without evidence of insurability. This is a valuable commodity to employees and their dependents who have health problems and are unable to purchase individual protection.

Although most employees have access to individual coverage, many do not elect it, usually due to the cost. Other employees may have "known" health conditions that either prevent them from obtaining individual coverage altogether or make the cost of that coverage so expensive that they cannot afford it. Employees who receive coverage from a spouse's plan are dependent on the continued employment of that spouse for health insurance. In addition, receiving dependent coverage through a spouse is generally more expensive for the employee's family than for that employee to be covered in a group plan where he or she works.

Q. 3:64 Do employers provide group health insurance to part-time and temporary employees?

Many employers do not cover part-time and temporary employees under their group health plans. Part-time employees are defined most often as those who work less than either 20 or 30 hours per week, depending on the industry. In general, employers believe that although these workers provide a valuable service, they do not justify the considerable expense associated with health benefits, particularly when they may be working for the company only a short time, or may already have coverage through another employer.

Some employers do cover part-time and temporary employees, although it is often difficult to find a carrier that will include these workers in a group health insurance plan. However, due to changes in the tax law and in employment practices—such as job sharing among employees who choose to work part time while raising families—more coverage is being made available to part-time employees.

Q. 3:65 Can an employer provide enhanced health care coverage for key employees?

Under current tax law, different benefits can be provided to different classes of employees based on a condition of employment (for example, salaried versus hourly employees). However, discriminatory medical reimbursement plans (which typically cover any expense not reimbursed by the regular medical benefits plan for select employees), must be insured and exhibit risk shifting in order to avoid imputed income for selected employees covered under such a plan. [Ref.: IRC. 105(h)]

Q. 3:66 Will an insurance carrier deny certain employees coverage under a group health insurance plan?

Generally, insurers will not deny coverage to any full-time employee. Inherent in the principle of group insurance is the understanding that all employees can be covered. Most carriers, however, require an employee to be actively at work on the day the employer-provided coverage becomes effective, and to have enrolled in a contributory plan within the time required.

Rather than deny certain employees insurance, most insurers reduce the chance of adverse selection by (1) requiring evidence of insurability if an employee wishes to enroll late or (2) placing restrictions on the coverage. The most common restriction is the preexisting-condition limitation. It is intended to limit payments of expenses resulting directly from a condition for which the employee received medical treatment or care within a specified period of time, prior to the date he or she becomes insured. The coverage may provide only a limited benefit for the preexisting condition, such as $1,000 for the first year the coverage is in effect. Some policies provide a more generous benefit; the amount the insurer will pay can range from no payment to as much as $10,000 in the first year. Some policies require a waiting period for coverage of a preexisting condition, which can vary in length from three months to two years. This preexisting-condition restriction is usually not applicable after the individual has been insured under the plan for twelve months. Certain states prohibit the inclusion of limits for preexisting conditions or specify permitted limitations. For example, accident and health policies issued in New York that cover 300 employees or more may not include a preexisting-condition limitation.

Q. 3:67 Can an employer require different service waiting periods?

Because employers use employee benefits to attract quality employees, it may make good business sense in some cases to cover all new hires under the group health insurance plan from the first day on the job. Some employers provide immediate health benefits only for certain job grades or levels, specifically indicating those individuals for whom the employer uses benefits as a recruiting tool. The other new hires are subject to a service waiting period—typically between one and three months for life and medical insurance and as much as one year for dental insurance—before their enrollment in the plan becomes effective.

A waiting period is advantageous to companies that suffer from significant turnover, because the administration involved in adding new employees to the plan and the risk associated with many short-term insureds is reduced considerably. Employees who are subject to a waiting period may purchase individual health policies to provide temporary insurance until they are eligible under the group health plan or, if they were previously covered by another employer's plan, elect to continue that plan under COBRA by paying the required cost. Rather than adjusting the waiting period, many employers reimburse select individuals for the cost of COBRA continuation under the prior employer's plan.

Paying for Insurance

Q. 3:68 How much can an employer expect to pay annually for group health insurance?

An A. Foster Higgins, Inc. survey of 1943 public and private employers with 12.5 million workers found that the average per-employee cost of medical care, including indemnity coverage, HMOs and dental coverage was $2748 in 1989, up 20.4% from a year earlier.

These employers may be the fortunate ones, however. According to the latest figures available from the U.S. Chamber of Commerce, the per employee costs in 1987 were $2820 for salaried employees and $3059 for hourly ones.

Q. 3:69 Must employers pay the entire cost of group health insurance?

No. Group health insurance plans can be noncontributory or contributory. Under a noncontributory plan, the employer pays the entire cost of the plan. Employees are automatically covered as soon as they become eligible for insurance coverage. Noncontributory plans have 100% participation.

Under a contributory plan, the employee shares in the cost of the plan. Once employees are eligible to participate in a contributory group health plan, they have 30 days in which to enroll. This is the enrollment period, and employees who elect coverage during this period do not have to submit medical evidence of insurability. If an employee does not elect coverage during the enrollment period, he or she may enroll at another time, but coverage will be subject to medical evidence of insurability. Enrollment periods are limited to specific times of the year, usually beginning January 1 and July 1.

Q. 3:70 What factors should an employer consider when deciding whether its group health insurance plan should be contributory or noncontributory?

The decision depends primarily on how competitive the job marketplace is, what the competitors in the marketplace are doing, and the amount of money the employer can afford. Many employers want their employees to share in the cost of health coverage to make them aware of and responsive to its cost. Today, when more than half of all two-adult families are also two-paycheck families, contributions encourage employees to avoid duplicating coverage. The trend in health insurance is to place greater financial responsibility on the insureds for premiums and expenses, thereby helping to ensure that employees use their plans as efficiently as possible.

The U.S. Department of Labor reports that the proportion of employees whose health coverage is fully employer paid dropped sharply in 1986: 54% received fully paid individual coverage (down from 61% in 1985), and only 35% received fully paid coverage for their families (down from 42% in 1985).

As more and more employers introduce contributions, those that retain noncontributory plans will pay more for insurance as a result of higher claims. Employees covered by contributory plans, whose spouses have noncontributory dependent coverage, will drop their employer plans and receive full benefits under their spouses' plans.

The following table illustrates how businesses typically distribute the cost of group health insurance:

Employee Coverage	Dependent Coverage
Company A 100% noncontributory	100% noncontributory
Company B 100% noncontributory	50% contributory

Factors Influencing Insurance Plan Design   Q. 3:74

Company C   10% contributory   50% contributory

Company D   25% contributory   25% contributory

Q. 3:71 What legal constraints are imposed on the distribution of employer-employee costs for group health insurance?

There are no legal requirements for employer-employee cost sharing with respect to medical and dental (and other health) insurance, although many states have provisions concerning employee contributions for life and disability insurance.

Q. 3:72 Can an employer self-fund a group health insurance plan?

Yes. Companies with more than 200 employees often self-fund all or part of their group health insurance plans. The employer's objectives are to improve cash flow, save premium taxes, eliminate the insurer's risk charge, and benefit from better than expected claims experience.

Q. 3:73 How common are self-funded plans?

Self-funded plans are the rule among larger employers. The U.S. Department of Labor reported that 45% of plan participants in medium-sized and large plans were covered by self-funded arrangements in 1986.

Q. 3:74 What factors should a small employer consider when deciding whether to self-fund all or part of its health insurance plan?

A small employer must decide whether it can accept the total risk. If not, an insurer must be found to assume part of it, and the employer must decide whether possible savings are worth the added risk of highly fluctuating claims levels. If protection is purchased to eliminate that risk, the employer must determine its cost.

Depending on what technique is used, the employer must decide whether added administrative costs would wipe out any savings that might result from partial self-funding. There are alternative funding techniques, such as extended grace periods (see Chapter 5) and retrospective premium payment arrangements (see Questions 5:52–5:56), that provide similar cash-flow advantages at reasonable cost and risk.

Chapter 4

Types of Health Insurance Plans and Related Benefits

With hundreds of insurance companies offering group health insurance plans, it is often difficult for smaller employers to determine exactly which plan will best meet their business objectives and their employees' health care needs. This chapter examines the different types of group health plans available and the forms of benefits they can provide. It also examines related benefits such as life insurance and disability income.

Medical Benefits

Q. 4:1 What types of group health insurance plans are available?

There are generally two types of group health insurance plans available to smaller employers: a basic medical plus major medical plan, commonly referred to as a "base plus" or "first dollar" plan, and a comprehensive medical plan, called simply "comprehensive." Because it is believed to be more cost-effective, the trend in plan design is clearly toward the comprehensive plan.

Q. 4:2 What is a base plus plan?

A base plus plan is a two-part health insurance plan. Basic medical coverage—for such expenses as hospitalization, surgery, physicians' visits, and diagnostic laboratory tests and x-rays—is provided under the first part. There may be limits on these expenses, such as a limited number of hospital days and a surgical schedule, but no deductible or coinsurance applies to the covered expenses. The employee is reimbursed starting with the first dollar of expenses.

The second, or major medical, part of the plan covers other health expenses. The coverage is broad, with fewer limits; however, a deductible is required before the employee is reimbursed for expenses. Coinsurance, usually 80%/20%, is applied until the maximum employee out-of-pocket expense is reached. Further covered expenses are reimbursed in full. (See the chart at Question 4:3.)

This two-part plan is the result of the historical development of health insurance. When first offered, group health insurance extended only basic hospital and later surgical coverage. This was followed years later by broader coverage for more catastrophic illness. (Deductibles and coinsurance are discussed at Questions 4:24–4:27.)

Q. 4:3 What is a comprehensive plan?

A comprehensive plan provides coverage for most medical services using one reimbursement formula. In a pure comprehensive plan, a deductible must be met before reimbursement for any covered expenses begins, and coinsurance applies to all covered expenses until the maximum employee out-of-pocket expense limit is reached. Additional covered expenses are paid in full. There have been many modifications to the pure comprehensive design to meet various market needs. For example, some employers have comprehensive plans with hospital expenses fully covered, with no deductible or coinsurance requirements. This form was first used by employers that wanted to move gradually away from base plus plans.

Types of Health Insurance Plans

The chart below shows the difference in design between base plus and comprehensive plans.

Base Plus Plan	Comprehensive Plan
100% of balance to maximum	100% of balance to maximum
80% Coinsurance 20% Deductible	80% Coinsurance 20% Deductible
Basic plan benefits (hospital, surgical, other medical, or Blue Cross/Blue Shield)	

Q. 4:4 Are there advantages to a base plus plan?

Base plus plans have been in existence longer than comprehensive plans; thus, many employers have had experience and feel comfortable working with them. From the employee's point of view, base plus plans appear to provide more generous benefits because of the lack of deductibles and coinsurance in the basic medical part. Also, although it is generally not true, the major medical coverage gives employees the impression that they are receiving supplemental coverage that pays for everything the basic medical coverage does not.

Q. 4:5 What are the advantages of a comprehensive plan?

Because employees share from the beginning in the cost of their medical expenses when they are incurred, a comprehensive plan encourages them to use more cost-effective health care. For example, if an individual's physician recommends surgery and a hospital admission, the base plus plan would not require a deductible or coinsurance. The patient who pays nothing for health care is less inclined to question the cost of it or to ask about alternatives. An individual covered by a comprehensive plan must satisfy a deductible and pay coinsurance on all expenses. This patient is more likely to be cost-conscious and to seek out more cost-effective health care services and providers. Furthermore, the higher the deductible, the greater the influence on employees' utilization of medical services.

The cost-sharing feature of comprehensive plans makes them generally less expensive to employers, with price differentials ranging from 5% to 12% less than base plus plans. In addition, one reimbursement formula is applied to all covered expenses, making it easier for employees to understand their benefits.

Q. 4:6 Do all insurers offer both types of group health insurance plans?

Most private insurers offer both base plus and comprehensive plans, although recently some insurers have decided not to market base plus plans due to the greater simplicity and cost control provided by comprehensive plans. Blue Cross/Blue Shield (BC/BS) recently started offering a comprehensive plan as an alternative to its traditional base plus plan.

Although most insurers are similar in that they offer the two plan types, the actual benefits and the specific plan features vary by insurer.

Blue Cross/Blue Shield Plans

Q. 4:7 What is Blue Cross/Blue Shield (BC/BS)?

BC/BS has different relationships with the providers of health care than do private health insurance companies. "The Blues"

Types of Health Insurance Plans   Q. 4:8

also use different reimbursement structures and determine premium rates on a different basis.

BC/BS contracts directly with physicians and hospitals to establish the level of charges it will pay for services rendered to its subscribers. When an insured incurs a covered health care expense, the health care provider—a participating hospital or physician—bills BC/BS directly. Payment is made to the provider based on the prearranged payment schedule, which is often accepted as payment in full.

This unique payment system between health care providers and the BC/BS network is an extension of the historically close relationship the Blues have maintained with the U.S. medical community over the years. This association dates back to the 1930s, when Blue Cross was established under the auspices of the American Hospital Association; Blue Shield was established by the American Medical Association in the 1940s. Blue Cross promised hospitals prompt payment and first-dollar reimbursement, thus guaranteeing that a patient's bill would be paid in full. In return, the hospitals gave Blue Cross a discount on hospital services for Blue Cross subscribers. The ability to obtain large discounts from hospitals has given the Blues a significant competitive edge over private insurers, and in some areas of the country, BC/BS has gained a large share of the third-party reimbursement market.

Q. 4:8 Are BC/BS plans similar to those offered by private insurance companies?

Yes. BC/BS plans have traditionally been similar to private insurance company base plus plans. BC/BS usually offers both a base plan and a supplemental major medical plan, but some employers purchase only the base plan from the Blues. This is because the Blue Cross base plan in some areas is less expensive than private insurance; the Blue Cross hospital discounts can be significant. An employer may elect a private insurer's major medical plan as a supplement, however, due to better price, coverage, or service.

Q. 4:9 Do most private insurers offer major medical supplements?

Generally, major medical plans offered by private insurance companies to supplement a Blue Cross base plan fall into two categories: supplemental major medical and wraparound major medical. The difference between the two is that the wraparound plan covers some basic expenses, such as surgery, and also covers major medical expenses, whereas the supplemental plan provides only major medical coverage. In the latter case, the surgical and doctors' charges would usually be covered by Blue Shield, which may or may not be operating jointly with Blue Cross.

Employers that like the Blue Cross hospital coverage but want a different plan for all their surgical coverage often elect wraparound plans.

Q. 4:10 How are BC/BS premium rates different from those of private insurers?

The negotiated hospital discounts arranged through BC/BS plans sometimes allow BC/BS to offer lower rates to employers. Also, BC/BS is a nonprofit organization in most states and as such pays no premium tax to the state.

A few Blue Cross plans are able to offer lower expense levels by not paying sales commissions, although a majority of Blues plans have begun to compensate brokers.

(Note: Although the Blues pioneered discounted, prenegotiated fees, newer health care delivery systems such as PPOs can now offer similar arrangements. See the discussion of alternative health care delivery systems in Chapter 8.)

Q. 4:11 Are expenses reimbursed at a more generous level by private insurers than by BC/BS?

Today, employers can choose from a variety of plans from BC/BS or private companies. Thus, it is the plan itself that dictates reimbursement, not the insurer. Both Blue Cross and commercial insurance company plans usually fully reimburse individuals for semiprivate room expenses, and there is no balance billing for the insured unless a private room is used.

Coverage

Q. 4:12 What types of services are generally covered by a group health insurance plan?

Base plus and comprehensive plans vary by insurer but generally cover the same kinds of services. These include:

- Professional services of doctors of medicine and osteopathy and other recognized medical practitioners;
- Hospital charges for semiprivate room and board and other necessary services and supplies;
- Surgical charges;
- Services of registered nurses and, in some cases, licensed practical nurses;
- Home health care;
- Physiotherapy;
- Anesthetics and their administration;
- X-rays and other diagnostic laboratory procedures;
- X-ray or radium treatment;
- Oxygen and other gases and their administration;
- Blood transfusions, including the cost of blood when charged;
- Drugs and medicines requiring a prescription;
- Specified ambulance services;
- Rental of durable mechanical equipment required for therapeutic use;
- Artificial limbs and other prosthetic appliances, except replacement of such appliances;
- Casts, splints, trusses, braces, and crutches; and
- Rental of a wheelchair or hospital-type bed.

Q. 4:13 What types of services are generally not covered by a group health insurance plan?

Services that are generally not covered include those associated with procedures that are not medically necessary (for example, elective cosmetic surgery) and those that do not contribute materially to the treatment of an illness or injury, such as a hospital telephone or television. Also, in order to avoid duplicate payments, benefits that are available to an employee from another source, such as workers' compensation, are generally not covered.

Coverages that would create a substantial risk to the insurer are also excluded. For example, coverage for long-term nursing care has traditionally been excluded because of the unpredictability of the extent of the need for care and the resulting inability of insurers to price the coverage. In addition, care required as a result of war and care that would normally be provided without charge, such as care in certain state or federal hospitals, are not covered. Expenses for transportation are not covered, except for specified ambulance services.

Until recently, routine physicals and other preventive care procedures have not been covered, but some insurers now include a preventive care benefit.

Q. 4:14 What kinds of hospital charges are covered under a group health insurance plan?

Group health insurance plans typically cover a variety of inpatient and outpatient charges. Inpatient covered charges include room, board, and necessary services and supplies.

Room and board charges are covered on a per-day basis up to either a maximum dollar amount each day or the most common semiprivate room and board charges of the particular hospital. Private rooms are generally not covered. Base plans cover hospital stays up to a certain number of days, such as 120 or 365 days per calendar year. The major medical plan covers days exceeding the base plan limit. Comprehensive plans typically cover all hospital days at a percentage of the semiprivate room rate.

Hospital services and supplies include items such as drugs and use of the operating room. Some base plans allow maximum dollar amounts for these expenses, but most plans cover them in full when room and board charges are covered. Comprehensive plans cover the same services the base plus major medical plans do but require a deductible and coinsurance. Of course, supplemental major medical also requires a deductible and coinsurance.

Intensive care is usually covered up to two or three times the room and board allowances for a semiprivate room. Some plans cover intensive care at the reasonable and customary (R&C) charge for the service.

Q. 4:15 How is surgery covered under a health insurance plan?

Surgical expense benefits are provided on a scheduled or nonscheduled basis. Scheduled plans specify an allowance for each kind of surgery, either in dollar terms or relative to other procedures listed. Nonscheduled plans cover surgical expenses on a reasonable and customary basis. Basic plans have traditionally provided for surgery in conjunction with hospitalization. Today, base plus plans cover surgery wherever performed, to discourage unnecessary hospitalization. The plan benefits include payment for the surgeon, assistant surgeon, and anesthesiologist. Charges associated with the surgery, such as blood products, are also covered under the plan, although sometimes only up to a maximum amount, whereupon the major medical plan takes over.

Some employers purchase a plan that does not treat surgical expenses differently from nonsurgical expenses. They purchase a wraparound major medical plan that covers surgery in addition to the standard major medical features. Comprehensive plans cover surgery after the insured satisfies a deductible. Coinsurance usually applies, but some plans encourage outpatient (as opposed to hospital) surgery by waiving the coinsurance provision in an effort to manage medical care costs.

Q. 4:16   Why do some plans pay R&C charges and others schedule benefits?

These differences are due in part to the evolution of health insurance benefits coverage. The earliest plans used schedules paying limited and controlled amounts for the procedures covered. As plans were expanded, R&C fees replaced schedule amounts (usually for surgery) to meet the market demand for full payment for expenses incurred. As charges increased, reimbursement automatically increased.

Some employers would like to return to schedules, because without them, their premiums increase significantly as physicians increase their R&C charges. This change would be difficult to implement. Employees would perceive it as a reduction in benefits, due to the more generous payment expectations today under the R&C system. This situation may change as more charges are based on Diagnostic Related Groups (DRGs).

Q. 4:17   If the physicians' charges exceed the R&C amount or the schedule amount, is the employee responsible for paying the balance?

Yes. An insured is responsible for any charge that exceeds the R&C or schedule amount.

Q. 4:18   How have hospital and surgical care changed recently?

The number of hospital procedures has decreased considerably, and patients who do enter hospitals for care are released more quickly. In addition, procedures once considered unsafe on an outpatient basis are now performed that way routinely. These changes have resulted from improved technology, increased competition in the health care market among different kinds of providers and facilities, and the growing concern about rising health care costs.

Q. 4:19 How are nonsurgical physicians' services covered?

Under a base plus plan, the basic medical part often covers physicians' fees to hospital patients up to a specified maximum, and for a duration that normally coincides with the duration of the hospital benefits. Base plans usually also provide for limited home or alternative care facility physicians' visits directly related to recuperation after a hospital discharge. In addition, "office" visits are usually covered but are limited to a dollar amount per visit or per illness, or to a maximum number of visits per calendar year. Major medical plans pick up the coverage for physicians' visits where the base plan coverage leaves off.

Comprehensive plans cover physicians' services in the hospital, at alternative care facilities, at home, or in the office. Deductibles and coinsurance apply.

Not all physicians' services are covered by group health insurance plans. For example, physicians' services for dental treatments or examinations and for the prescription or fitting of eyeglasses or hearing aids are commonly excluded.

Outpatient Care, Extended Care, and HMOs/PPOs

Q. 4:20 What alternatives to hospital care are common today?

The most common alternative is the free-standing care center, also known as a "surgicenter" or "quick clinic." Some of these centers offer outpatient surgery under general anesthesia and some offer only routine, noninvasive care. Other alternatives are skilled nursing facilities. Patients discharged from acute care facilities find less expensive, more appropriate care at these extended care facilities during their convalescence. (See Question 4:22.)

Q. 4:21 What kinds of hospital outpatient expenses are covered?

Three kinds of hospital outpatient care are covered: emergency treatment, surgery, and services rendered in the outpatient lab or x-ray department. Some comprehensive plans encourage the use of outpatient services (when appropriate) by covering them at a more generous level than hospitalization.

Q. 4:22 Does health insurance cover extended care facilities?

Extended care facilities offer one of three types of care: skilled nursing care, intermediate care, or custodial care. Most health plans cover skilled care facilities for a maximum number of days per calendar year per patient, or specify a dollar amount per day that will be covered. Usually, a patient must have been hospitalized within 7 to 14 days before entering a skilled nursing facility in order to be eligible for benefits. Health insurance plans do not cover custodial nursing care, and intermediate care may or may not be covered.

Under base plans, stays in skilled nursing facilities are covered similarly to hospital expenses—a maximum benefit per day, to a maximum number of days in a calendar year. Major medical plans supplement this by providing additional days of care and by covering expenses associated with the care, all subject to deductible and coinsurance provisions until the maximum out-of-pocket (OOP) is reached. Comprehensive plans usually pay for a specific number of days of care, subject to deductible and coinsurance provisions until the OOP maximum is reached, whereupon the plan pays 100% of the R&C charges, as long as the care remains eligible, up to the limits of the policy.

Q. 4:23 What other types of health care plans might an employer offer?

Some employers may offer a health maintenance organization (HMO) as an option in their group health insurance plans, and some of their employees may choose to participate. In addition, in recent years, medical care providers and medical care insurers have been working together to establish preferred provider organizations (PPOs) to build relationships similar to those that the Blues have with providers. HMOs and PPOs are explained in detail in Chapter 8.

Deductibles, Copayments, and Reimbursements

Q. 4:24 What is a deductible?

A deductible is a specific dollar amount that an individual must pay (or "satisfy") before reimbursement for expenses begins. The primary purpose of the deductible is to encourage employees to use health care services only when necessary, and to discourage submission of small claims to the insurance company because of the administrative expense involved. Deductibles typically range from $50 to $1,000. The higher the deductible, the lower the cost of the health insurance plan.

Q. 4:25 What is a carryover deductible?

A carryover deductible allows covered expenses incurred in the last three months of the prior calendar year to be carried over to the new year and counted toward satisfying the new year's deductible. This provision is included to avoid the financial hardship to an insured of having to pay a deductible in the last quarter of one year and another in January of the next year. The trend is to eliminate the carryover provision and require each individual to pay an annual deductible, regardless of the timing of the claim, which is often within the control of the claimant.

Q. 4:26 For insured employees with dependent coverage, does the deductible for each person have to be satisfied before reimbursement begins?

Each person covered under a group health insurance plan must meet a deductible before expenses will be covered. However, plans usually include some type of family deductible in order to limit a family's exposure for health care expenses.

The family deductible is usually some multiple of the individual deductible, generally two or three. For the family deductible to be satisfied, the combined expenses of covered family members are accumulated. Some plans require, however, that at least one family member satisfy the full individual deductible before the family deductible can be met.

Q. 4:27 What is coinsurance?

Coinsurance is a feature found in most group health insurance plans. It sets forth the percentage of covered expenses that the employees and the health insurance plan will pay. Under a base plus plan, no coinsurance is involved for basic medical coverage. For supplemental major medical and for comprehensive plans, a coinsurance provision applies. The most common coinsurance level is one in which the employee pays 20% of the expenses and the insurer pays 80%. This is called 80% coinsurance.

Q. 4:28 What is a maximum out-of-pocket limit?

A maximum out-of-pocket (OOP) limit is the maximum amount of coinsurance that an insured employee will have to pay for expenses covered under the plan. The most common OOP maximum is $1,000, or 20% of $5,000. Like the deductible, OOP maximums are increasing because greater cost sharing by employees is a tool for controlling benefits utilization. Most covered expenses in excess of the OOP maximum are paid by the insurer without coinsurance, that is, at 100%. This is true even in cases in which an employee's coinsurance obligation would exceed the OOP maximum. For example, assume 80% coinsurance and a $1,000 OOP maximum. The employee (after satisfying the deductible) has a $20,000 bill for expenses covered under the plan. With 80% coinsurance, the employee apparently would have to pay $4,000 (20%), and the insurer $16,000 (80%). With a $1,000 OOP maximum, however, the employee's total expense would be limited to $1,000. Thus, a maximum OOP puts a cap on the cost of a catastrophic illness, at least for covered expenses under the plan.

Q. 4:29 Is the deductible included in determining an OOP maximum?

Some group health insurance plans do not include the deductible in their OOP limits. In such situations, the insured employee would be responsible for paying the sum of the deductible and the OOP maximum. Other plans do include the deductible as part of the OOP maximum.

Q. 4:30 Can medical expenses not covered by a health insurance plan be applied toward the deductible or OOP maximum?

No. Expenses incurred by the insured employee must be covered expenses under the health insurance plan to be applied toward the deductible or OOP maximum.

Q. 4:31 What is a covered expense?

A covered expense is an eligible expense under a group health insurance plan. A covered expense is an expense incurred by a covered individual that will be reimbursed in whole or in part under the group health insurance plan. For example, under most health insurance plans, doctors' visits are a covered expense. That is, a doctor's fee up to the amount provided by the plan will be reimbursed by the insurer.

Q. 4:32 Are all covered expenses reimbursed?

No. The fact that an expense is covered does not mean that the coverage is unlimited. Both base plus and comprehensive plans have limits on the expenses for which they will reimburse. In addition, as described above, some form of deductible and coinsurance is often applicable.

Q. 4:33 How are covered expenses limited?

Insurers limit covered expenses in a variety of ways. One way is to cap allowable payments for a certain procedure or service. A common example of this type of limit would be a surgical schedule. Insurers also restrict covered expenses by limiting the number of visits or days for home health care or skilled nursing care, or by establishing a reasonable and customary charge.

Q. 4:34 What is a reasonable and customary charge?

A reasonable and customary (R&C) charge, also called a usual, customary, and reasonable charge (UCR), is the maximum amount that an insurer will consider eligible for reimbursement for a medical care expense covered under the group health insurance plan. These amounts are usually determined from a database that identifies the cost of each procedure or service in various regions of the country. For example, to determine at what level to reimburse a surgeon's fee for a certain type of operation, an insurance company will examine the fees of all surgeons located within a certain geographic area. An R&C could be set so that some percentage, such as 90% of all surgeons' fees, would be covered. That is, if 1,000 surgeons' fees are reviewed, and 10% of the surgeons charge more than $5,000 and 90% charge less, the maximum covered charge would be $5,000 for that surgical procedure. That portion of the surgeon's charges over the R&C amount would not be considered a covered expense under the plan. R&C charges are adjusted periodically.

Q. 4:35 What is a schedule of insurance?

A schedule of insurance sets forth a specific maximum amount an insurer will pay for each procedure, such as surgery or dental procedures. Schedules are sometimes denominated in units, rather than in dollars. These are called relative value schedules; a factor that reflects the level of charges in a geographic area multiplied by the number of units provided for each procedure determines the maximum amount the plan will pay.

Q. 4:36 Do most policies include an overall limit to the amount reimbursable to one individual?

Many policies have an overall lifetime limit. This is usually $1 million or $2 million. Some policies do not include an overall limit. Limits may be based on a calendar year or per illness or injury.

Most policies have a "reinstatement" provision that reinstates, or adds back, dollar amounts that have been counted toward the lifetime maximum limit each year, usually on January 1. Most plans automatically reinstate a small amount, such as $1,000. Higher reinstatement requests must be approved by the insurance carrier after reviewing current health status.

Dental Benefits

Q. 4:37 Do health insurance plans cover dental care?

Proper dental care has been considered a budgetable expense, so traditionally it has not been included in group health insurance plans. In the 1970s, as its cost increased, dental care was added to employee benefits plans. Some plans include dental coverage as part of the medical plan; others include dental coverage as a separate plan. However, many health insurance plans do provide coverage for noncosmetic dental work necessary as the result of an accident. Some plans include limited coverage for hospital room and board expenses related to dental procedures, such as removal of impacted wisdom teeth, performed in a hospital.

Q. 4:38 Why is there growing interest in dental insurance?

Dental benefits are the fastest growing of all employee benefits, not only health-related benefits. Dental services are a priority item with employee unions, and they are popular with employees. There are several reasons for this popularity. Many women have moved into the workforce, and women traditionally use dental services more than men. The better educated use dental services more often than those with less education, and, of course, the population is becoming more educated. In addition, young people use more dental services, and women in the workforce influence this utilization through their children.

Q. 4:39 How are dental benefits provided?

Dental benefits plans grew rapidly in the 1980s. In 1979, only half of the employees of medium and large companies enjoyed such coverage according to the Bureau of Labor Statistics; by 1985, 76% of the workers in those firms were covered. Of the 100 million persons with dental coverage in that year (according to the Health Insurance Association of America), 62 million were covered by commercial insurers, 17 million were covered by dental service organizations, and 14 million were covered by Blue Cross/Blue Shield plans.

Self-insured plans have been most prevalent among larger companies, which frequently have administrative services only (ASO) contracts with commercial carriers for claims processing and review. Dental coverage through HMOs and PPOs is also available. (See Chapter 8.)

Q. 4:40 What is direct reimbursement for dental care?

Direct reimbursement is a noninsured dental program in which an employer agrees to pay for a specified percentage or amount of receipted dental expenses. It has been used by smaller employers as a way of avoiding both the costs associated with an insured plan and the administrative complexity that often accompanies insurance company programs. And, since dental expenses are more predictable than medical expenses—seldom involving emergencies or catastrophic expenses—the risk to employers is considerably smaller.

Q. 4:41 What dental services are typically provided?

Dental services fall into a number of categories:

- Diagnostic;
- Preventive;
- Restorative;
- Oral surgery;
- Endodontic;
- Periodontic;
- Prosthodontic; and
- Orthodontic.

Q. 4:42 Are all types of dental services covered by insurance?

Usually not. Dental services are often divided into different coverage levels. Level I services include semiannual examinations, semiannual cleaning, x-rays, and diagnosis. Most plans cover at least preventive and diagnostic care. Level II (basic services) includes simple restoration (fillings), crowns and jackets, repair of crowns, extractions, and endodontics (root canals and internal pulp treatment). Level III (major services) includes dentures, bridges, and replacement of bridges and dentures. In order to emphasize prevention, many plans cover the Level I services at higher reimbursement levels than Level II or III services.

Q. 4:43 What cost-management features are built into dental plans?

Dental plans in general tend to have more cost-effectiveness built into their design. The reason is that the insurance industry learned a lot from its experience with medical plans. Dental plans had the benefit of this experience and have cost management as an integral part of plan design. Cost-effective features include precertification and an emphasis on prevention as well as deductibles and copayments. There may also be maximum limits on outlays for services during a year, including separate maximums for orthodontic benefits, and the exclusion of orthodontic benefits altogether for persons over a certain age, such as 19.

Q. 4:44   Health Insurance Answer Book

The trend is away from R&C reimbursement toward scheduled allowances to protect plan costs from the effects of inflation. Benefits remain fixed until the employer decides to increase the allowances.

Q. 4:44 Why is orthodontics often treated as a special coverage category?

Orthodontic problems are usually not the result of a disease, generally involve no acute symptoms, and are often more a matter of aesthetics (akin to cosmetic surgery). Some form of malocclusion (faulty spacing or meeting of teeth) occurs in large numbers of people. To provide all of these people with time-consuming and costly orthodontic corrections would be prohibitive for most plans. Since these problems can rarely be categorized as emergencies, orthodontics is well suited to controls such as special dollar limits and prospective review.

Q. 4:45 Are there special cost-control considerations for dental plans?

Yes. Because dental expenses tend to be more predictable and less costly than other forms of medical care, participants can better estimate likely expenses and compare them with the costs of joining the plan. For this reason, contributory dental plans may be more prone to adverse selection (that is, more likely to attract those with known dental problems) than noncontributory ones.

Also, high deductibles and coinsurance may discourage routine maintenance and early diagnosis and prompt participants to defer regular dental care. This can result in the need for more expensive treatment later on, thereby increasing costs rather than lowering them.

Q. 4:46 What are dental plan incentives, and how do they work?

Briefly, plan incentives are designed to encourage cost-effective benefits utilization. They are geared toward preventive services that are less costly and that will preclude the need for more costly services. For example, a plan may specify that Level I services will be reimbursed at 100%, while Level II services will be reimbursed at only 80%. Level III services, such as bridges, may be limited to 50% of their usual and customary charges. (See Question 4:42 for a more detailed explanation of Level I, II, and III services.)

Q. 4:47 What is precertification?

Dental plans have used precertification or predetermination for years. Precertification or preauthorization of services involves three steps:

1. The dentist examines the patient and proposes a course of treatment;
2. A precertification form is completed by the dentist and the patient, and the form is submitted to the insurer or self-insured plan administrator for review prior to commencement of treatment; and
3. The insurer considers the proposed treatment plan and approves it, denies it, or approves it with some modification.

Usually the precertification requirement applies to any amount over a specified level—often $100, $150, or $200. Thus, excess paper work is not generated for minor or low-cost items. This allows the employee to reconsider or prepare to pay for nonapproved treatment.

Q. 4:48 Are some dental services excluded from coverage?

Yes. Many plans exclude all cosmetic services. Plans also may not cover work in progress that is not completed within a specified period (say 60 to 90 days) of termination of coverage. Other plans limit costs by excluding adult orthodontia or any orthodontia. Another area of controversy involves temporomandibular joint syndrome (TMJ). Many plans limit the benefits for TMJ and periodontia.

Vision and Hearing Benefits

Q. 4:49 How is vision care covered?

Most health insurance plans provide coverage for medical care related to eye injury or disease but do not cover the costs of periodic eye examinations or corrective lenses. Like dental care, vision care is a relatively new employee benefit, offered by employers that can afford to expand their employee benefits plans to include additional fringe benefits previously considered budgetable. Vision care is most often covered on a scheduled basis that pays a fixed dollar amount for examinations, lenses, and frames. Vision care is almost universally noncontributory due to the potential for biased selection.

Q. 4:50 Is coverage available for hearing evaluations and hearing aids?

Like vision care, most health insurance plans provide coverage for medical care related to diseases or injury to the hearing mechanisms. They do not cover the cost of hearing evaluations or hearing aids to restore a person's ability to hear.

Prescription Drug Plans

Q. 4:51 Why are prescription drugs a growing concern for health insurance planners?

The increase in both the cost and utilization of prescription drugs has grown significantly in the past decade and is expected to continue to do so. Bureau of Labor Statistics figures show that prescription drug price increases outpaced consumer price index increases by about two to one from 1981 to 1987. Because older workers use more prescription drugs and incur greater prescription drug expenses, an aging workforce will mean higher prescription drug outlays. Finally, the need for and availability of specialized wonder drugs (such as AZT used in the treatment of AIDS) will raise the average costs for prescription drug plans.

Q. 4:52 What other factors affect an employer's prescription drug costs?

Other factors that determine how much employers and employee participants will spend for drugs are:
- Ingredient pricing, including the markup from average wholesale price;
- Generic drug dispensing rate—the higher the dispensing rate of less expensive generic drugs, the lower the average cost of drugs to the plan;
- Dispensing fees and administration costs; and
- Waste and overutilization, including fraud by employees and pharmacies, errors in dispensing, and drug abuse.

Q. 4:53 Are all prescription drugs covered under health care plans?

Generally, only prescription drugs that are for treatment of an illness or injury are covered, subject to applicable deductibles and coinsurance. Many plans do not cover contraceptive prescription drugs, for example, or nicotine chewing gum prescribed for smokers who are trying to quit.

Q. 4:54 Will some plans cover contraceptive prescription drugs?

Yes. In fact, most prescription drug plans offer plans "with or without contraceptives."

Q. 4:55 Why would an employer have a separate prescription drug plan?

There are several reasons for having separate plans:
- Employees may not realize that their medical plan covers medications;
- High deductibles may preclude reimbursement for medication because many people do not meet the deductible;

- The use of a card (see Questions 4:61–4:66) eliminates claim forms; and
- Year-end claims submission is reduced, which facilitates processing by the insurer.

Q. 4:56 Why would an employer avoid a free-standing drug plan in favor of covering medication under a major medical or comprehensive health plan?

Quite simply, a free-standing plan encourages greater utilization of the benefit. At a time when cost management is so important, emphasis is on covering long-term care, catastrophic illness, and other big-ticket items rather than budgetable items such as medications. Moreover, abuse of the benefit as well as overutilization have occurred under the card approach to prescription drugs. (See Questions 4:61–4:66.)

Q. 4:57 Are there different types of drug plans?

There are a number of variations, but the principal types of prescription medication plans are open panel, closed panel, mail order, and prescription drug card plans.

Q. 4:58 What is an open-panel drug plan?

An open-panel drug plan allows the employee or covered dependent to go to the pharmacist of his or her choice. The employee completes a claim form, which is sent to the insurer, company, or union for retrospective reimbursement.

Q. 4:59 What is a closed-panel drug plan?

A closed-panel plan contracts with a fixed number of pharmacies that dispense medication to members at agreed-upon prices. The employee/dependent pays only a small deductible. The pharmacist bills the insurer directly for the medication, often at cost plus a dispensing fee.

Q. 4:60 What is a mail-order drug plan?

Under the mail-order approach, a participant sends the prescription to a designated mail-order supply house that dispenses medications to many members in large volume. Discounts are made possible by economies of scale. This approach works especially well for maintenance drugs for circulatory problems, high blood pressure, or diabetes, and in general for all but about 20% of medications requiring emergency dispensation.

One problem associated with such plans is the high volume of drugs they dispense—sometimes 60- or 90-day supplies. This may promote overuse and wastefulness.

Q. 4:61 What is a prescription drug card plan?

Instead of reimbursing individuals for their drug purchases using the standard retrospective reimbursement process (involving claims forms), some employers elect a prescription service plan. All covered individuals are issued prescription drug cards that allow them to "charge" their drug purchases. The plan sets a deductible amount that must be paid by the insured every time the card is used to purchase a prescription. Typically, this deductible is between $1 and $5. The pharmacy collects the deductible, completes the charge slip, and dispenses the drug. The pharmacy bills the prescription drug card company for the drug plus administrative expenses, and the prescription card company bills the insurance company (usually monthly) for the batch of prescriptions provided to its insureds. A third-party administrator enrolls and reimburses pharmacies, bills sponsors, provides statistical data, and develops claims control strategies.

Q. 4:62 How long have prescription drug card plans been in existence?

The first prescription drug plans (also known as prescription medication plans) began in 1964. They were initiated to encourage patients to comply with drug therapy.

Q. 4:63 Is a prescription drug card plan better than regular reimbursement?

Individuals like prescription drug cards because claims forms are eliminated. Health plans without prescription drug card programs require that the calendar-year deductible be satisfied before drug expenses are reimbursable. Many individuals do not meet the deductible, and thus get no reimbursement for various antibiotics or analgesics routinely prescribed for minor illnesses or injuries. Further, for those who do meet the deductible, coinsurance still applies to drug expenses.

Insurers like drug card plans because the drug card administrators assume the administrative responsibilities of claims processing and control. Insurance companies without card programs process claims and cut reimbursement checks for individuals' drug expenses—an expensive process, due to the volume of claims. Prescription card administrators streamline the claims process through standardized forms and procedures and a network of participating pharmacies that follow these procedures and make batch claims processing possible. A few insurers have developed their own drug card administration to further control costs by eliminating the middleman prescription card company.

Q. 4:64 How can an employer decide whether to elect a prescription card plan?

Employees and dependents generally like the convenience of the card plan. The determining factors for employers are usually cost and administration. Depending on the per-prescription deductible elected and the calendar-year deductible and coinsurance level of the health plan, a prescription card plan may be more expensive than standard reimbursement procedures.

The employer must also consider the card distribution and recovery issue. For a company with a great deal of turnover, the claims liability involved when cards are not recovered from terminated individuals may make a card plan more expensive than it looks at first glance. (Claims submitted by a terminated individual who has retained the card will be paid by a card administrator if it has no record of employee termination.) There are also other loopholes for erroneous claims payment.

A third hidden cost is the elimination of coordination of benefits (COB) savings. The insured with the drug card will always be considered primary for coverage of family members.

The ease and convenience of card plans may promote overuse, higher utilization, lower rates of generic substitution, and use of marginally effective drugs.

Q. 4:65 Is prescription medication covered outside of these plans?

Yes. Most major medical plans cover prescription medication.

Q. 4:66 Who offers drug plans?

Prescription medication plans originate through many sources, including commercial insurance carriers, Blue Cross/Blue Shield plans, unions, HMOs, and, in some instances, self-funded employers or other organizations.

Mental Health Benefits

Q. 4:67 Are mental illnesses usually covered by health plans?

Group health insurance plans generally limit coverage for mental illnesses, because of a lack of understanding and agreement among health care professionals about the nature and causes of mental illnesses. It is difficult for insurers to make judgments and thus calculate benefits payments and costs—as they do for surgery, for example—without defined criteria for what is appropriate medical treatment. Thus, they prevent excessive utilization of the mental illness benefit and limit their financial risk by limiting the coverage available in any given calendar year.

Q. 4:68 Why is there growing concern about mental health services?

Several factors have contributed to a growing concern with both the provision and the cost of mental health services. These factors include a lack of adequate coverage, particularly for outpatient services; a growing demand for services by increasingly sophisticated consumers; overutilization of inpatient psychiatric care; and high benefits costs.

Coverage is typically very limited, especially for outpatient services. Company plans often limit payment to some arbitrary level annually—frequently $500 or $1,000. Many of these same plans will pay for inpatient care at the same level as for other medical services. Other plans limit inpatient care as well, resulting in a gap in needed coverage. The demand is present and growing, but adequate controls and definitions of appropriate care are missing from the process.

Q. 4:69 What causes overutilization of inpatient mental health care?

The availability of payment for inpatient mental health care and the lack of payment for outpatient services is a big factor. Overutilization takes several forms: Unnecessary utilization occurs when someone who could be treated as an outpatient is admitted to a hospital. Intensity of care is another problem—for example, the duration of treatment (that is, overly long length of stay or excess treatment). Finally, the cost of inpatient care for mental illness is often substantially higher than for a comparable stay for physical illness.

Q. 4:70 Why has attention focused on mental health care issues?

One reason for the sudden interest is the recent availability of data on both benefits utilization and costs. Many employers have initiated benefits redesign as one technique for managing health costs. These redesign efforts include flexible benefits programs and other sophisticated approaches that have focused attention on particular problem areas. Moreover, the use of data is coming into its own as a decision support mechanism. As hard data on benefits usage and costs become available to employers and unions responsible for cost-management decisions, they are better able to pinpoint specific areas in need of attention. One of these areas is mental health services.

Another reason for the growing concern is the realization that mental health and behavioral disorders are taking a substantial toll on quality and productivity.

Q. 4:71 What areas of mental health care are growing most rapidly?

The fastest growing areas of mental health care are treatment of mood disorders such as depression and anxiety, and childhood and adolescent disorders. Problems among young dependents are becoming especially troublesome. According to the American Psychiatric Association, in any six-month period, 7.5 million persons under the age of 18 will experience some form of psychiatric illness. The National Center for Health Statistics reported that the number of Americans between 10 and 19 discharged from psychiatric units grew 43%, from 126,000 in 1980 to 180,000 in 1987. The National Association of Private Psychiatric Hospitals estimates that 12% of children under the age of 18 need mental health care services.

Not only is the incidence of adolescent mental health problems high, but treatment costs are high as well. Young persons often have longer stays in psychiatric care facilities. Overall, costs for adolescent mental health care can account for 50% of the total program cost.

Q. 4:72 Who is interested in controlling the cost of mental health care?

Several groups in the health care system are showing increasing interest in managing the cost of mental health benefits. They include HMOs that are providing comprehensive packages of services; employers that see their benefits costs escalating; self-insured unions and employers that have to actively manage benefits utilization; insurers that are answerable to their clients; and health care providers that are being subjected to growing pressure to do something about health care cost and quality.

Q. 4:73 How can mental health services be better managed?

There are a number of ways that an informed employer, union, or insurer can get a handle on mental health services. One way is to improve outpatient services so that only those individuals in need of hospitalization will be admitted. For example, a typical outpatient visit might cost $75, while a day in a psychiatric hospital might cost $600. In some cases, people really need to be hospitalized; other patients may be hospitalized unnecessarily because their companies' benefits packages pay for inpatient care but provide inadequate coverage for outpatient services.

Case management is another effective cost-control technique. Stated simply, case management involves professional review of proposed services by an independent organization that specializes in this field. This independent review checks the diagnosis, prognosis, proposed treatment plan, and other variables in order to determine the most effective treatment.

Mental Health Management

Q. 4:74 Why is managing dependent mental health care expenses important?

Dependent care costs, especially those associated with mental health and substance abuse, are a major area of employer health care cost inflation. A survey by Northwestern National Life Insurance Company found that the average cost of health care in 1989 was $1,172 for individuals compared with $3,000 for families, and that 47 cents of every health care dollar went for dependent health care expenses. A 1986 survey by the National Association of Addiction Treatment Providers found that average charges for persons under the age of 20 were 46% higher per admission than charges for adults, and that adolescents' average length of stay was 30.2 days vs. 22.1 days for adults.

Q. 4:75 What methods for reducing these costs are employers considering?

Many plans are either raising the employer share of dependent costs or reducing the level of benefits, especially for mental health and substance abuse treatment, which are heavily frequented by dependent adolescents.

Some popular cost-cutting approaches include:

1. *Limiting the length of stay.* While normal hospitalization has no set limitations, many plans have limitations on the length of time they will cover inpatient mental health or substance abuse treatment. Limits of 30 to 60 days are becoming more common.
2. *Limiting the size of payment.* There may be caps on the per diem rate for inpatient care (such as $1,000), annual caps (such as $20,000 per year), or lifetime caps (such as a lifetime maximum reimbursement of $50,000).
3. *Increasing the copayment level.* Some plans demand copayments of 50% for mental and substance abuse treatment, as opposed to 20% or less for other types of health care. There may also be no cap on out-of-pocket expenditures.
4. *Increasing premiums.* Some plans are shifting some (or even all) of the additional costs for dependents to employees.
5. *Substituting outpatient care or partial hospitalization.* This may be effective for the short term, but outpatient costs are rising as well, and less intensive care may be required for a longer period of time.

Q. 4:76 Is there a downside to reducing benefits?

Some studies have found that arbitrary cutoffs of benefits, such as limits on lengths of stay, can ultimately cost more. By limiting the length of time that is reimbursable, or the size of the reimbursement, patients may be deprived of the care they need. By denying the necessary extra days, the patient may be discharged before treatment is complete. Ultimately that may mean additional costs over a longer period of time.

Q. 4:77 How does case management of mental health services work?

In most instances, prior approval is needed before treatment commences. In an emergency situation, review takes place as soon as possible. Briefly, the professional representative of the review organization, usually either a psychologist or psychiatrist, contacts the mental health practitioner who is going to treat the patient and discusses the case. This discussion is designed to determine the relevant facts in the case, including diagnosis, clinical condition, severity, proposed treatment, medications, goals of treatment, discharge plans, reasons for admission (if hospitalization is proposed), and alternative treatment possibilities. The independent professional makes an assessment of the case and, if necessary, makes alternative recommendations. When necessary, ongoing monitoring also takes place.

Q. 4:78 What is a prepaid mental health plan?

Prepaid mental health plans offer care through a prescreened panel of mental health care providers who offer their services through discounted negotiated fees. Fees are set in advance, and the plan assumes the risk of providing the benefits for program beneficiaries. These plans may be offered through mental health PPOs, mental health carve-outs, or capitated mental health plans.

Life Insurance Benefits

Q. 4:79 Why would survivor benefits be included in a group health insurance program?

Small group health insurance policies offered by many insurers carry an option to provide life insurance benefits. Some companies require such coverage as a condition for issue of a group health policy.

Q. 4:80 What form do these death benefits take?

Under IRC Section 79, group term life insurance benefits must be offered to a group of employees on the basis of factors that preclude individual selection. This means that coverage is based on such things as age, years of service, compensation, and position.

The coverage may not discriminate in favor of key employees. Common nondiscriminatory formulas include flat benefits, with all covered employees entitled to identical death benefits, and earnings-based benefits, with each employee covered up to some multiple of compensation, commonly 1, 1½, or 2 times pay. Another formula, the position schedule, provides different levels of coverage to different classes of employees, with senior employees typically receiving the greatest benefits. This arrangement is most likely to produce discriminatory benefits and additional taxable income.

Q. 4:81 How are these death benefits taxed?

Under IRC Section 79, the cost of providing the first $50,000 of these benefits is tax-free to non-key employees. Key employees receiving "discriminatory benefits" also pay tax on the value of the first $50,000 of benefit. Amounts in excess of $50,000 result in taxable income to all employees. The value of imputed income is determined as the greater of actual cost or IRS Table I cost. Taxable life insurance benefits are also subject to FICA withholding.

Death benefits under an insured group term or AD&D (Accidental Death and Dismemberment) program are not taxable income to the beneficiary. Self-insured death benefits in excess of $5,000 would be treated as ordinary income to the beneficiary.

Q. 4:82   Health Insurance Answer Book

Disability Benefits

Q. 4:82   How much of employers' payroll is used to pay disability benefits?

Although the cost varies by region of the country and by industry, disability benefits add up to about 4% of payroll. This includes long-term disability, weekly indemnity plans, workers' compensation costs, disability-related absenteeism, and that portion of the Social Security (FICA) contribution that is allocated to the disability insurance trust fund.

Q. 4:83   How pervasive are disabilities in the United States?

A 1986 report by the U.S. Census Bureau revealed that 14% of the population aged 16–64 had difficulty performing one or more fundamental physical activities. Moreover, 12% of the population, or 18 million people, had a disability that affected their work; 8 million were unable to work.

Q. 4:84   How do employees become disabled?

Accidents account for more than 300,000 disabilities annually. Lower back injuries account for one out of five compensable disabilities and one-third of the total costs. Somewhere between 6% and 12% of any given employee population are alcohol or substance abusers. One-fourth of the entire population suffers some form of emotional distress. The costs in lost productivity, disability, health care, and related morale or performance problems are astronomical.

Q. 4:85   What programs are available to compensate employees for disability?

There are a number of public and private programs. Public programs include Social Security, workers' compensation at the state level, and nonoccupational temporary disability plans in some states. Private programs include individual disability plans, short-term disability (STD), long-term disability (LTD), accidental death and dismemberment (AD&D), and disability pension benefits.

Q. 4:86   What is a short-term disability plan?

Short-term disability (STD) plans are designed to provide income to employees during temporary periods of disability. Although this period may extend up to two years, the most common period is six months. An STD program may be made up of two types of plans:

1. A sick pay plan that pays employees according to their credited sick days, which are accrued ratably over the employee's period of service; and
2. An accident and sickness plan that provides for full or partial replacement of income following a waiting period of a specified number of weeks, generally ranging from 13 to 52, at which time LTD benefits would commence.

Sick pay plan payments are generally made from general company accounts; accident and sickness plan payments are usually insured or self-insured.

Q. 4:87   What is a long-term disability plan?

A long-term disability (LTD) plan is a program that provides income to employees who are disabled for significant periods of time, generally from six months to life.

Q. 4:88   How is disability defined?

LTD plans may define disability as the inability to perform the duties of any occupation, or the inability to perform the duties associated with one's own occupation. Some plans use the latter definition for the first two or three years to allow time to adapt to a new occupation, after which the first definition becomes operative. Still other definitions tie disability income payments to the inability to perform the duties (or "any," "every," or "material" duties) of one's own occupation (or any other occupation for which one is qualified by education, training, or experience) and a loss of some income. Partial disability benefit payments could be payable if the employee is unable to perform some functions of his or her job and has experienced a loss of some portion (e.g., 20%) of his or her income.

Q. 4:89 What are other important components of an LTD plan?

LTD plans have the following components:

- Eligibility period. Employees may be required to complete a minimum period of service with the company, which may be as much as a year but is generally less.
- Preexisting conditions. Disability benefits may not be payable if the disability results from a condition the employee suffered or for which he or she was receiving treatment during a specified period (e.g., 3 to 12 months) preceding coverage. When benefits for such a disability are payable, they may be contingent upon a continuous period of coverage, for example, a full year.
- Elimination period. LTD benefits become payable a specified number of months after the disability commences, usually 6 to 12. STD payments are usually payable in the interim.
- Integration with other benefits. To prevent pyramiding of disability income payments, LTD plan benefits are generally offset by payments from other sources such as pension plans and Social Security.
- Payment period. Although some plans provide lifetime disability income payments, most are payable up to age 65 or 70, at which time payments from other sources, such as pension plans and Social Security, would commence. In order to comply with the Age Discrimination in Employment Act, payment durations may be tied to age at the time

the disability commences—equal premium costs translating to shorter payment periods for older workers.
- Cost-of-living adjustments (COLAs). COLAs may be either a fixed percentage or a floating percentage tied to an index such as the consumer price index.

Q. 4:90 How much do disabled workers receive from disability plans?

Typically, an STD plan will pay anywhere from 50% to 100% of salary, with 50% to 67% of salary being the most common. LTD plans generally provide from 50% to 67%, with 70% at the high end.

Q. 4:91 Are LTD plans expensive?

Not when compared with medical insurance. LTD coverage may cost as little as one-half of 1% of pay per employee, compared with $2,000 or more per worker for medical insurance.

Q. 4:92 How are employees taxed on disability benefits?

Employer contributions to accident or health plans are not includable in employee income under IRC Section 106. Benefits received by employees from a noncontributory employer plan are generally taxable, except for those unrelated to absence from work that constitute payment for loss of a bodily function or permanent disfigurement. [Ref.: IRC Section 105] Other accident and health insurance payments (i.e., those attributable to employee contributions, or employer contributions that were included in the employee's income) are not part of an employee's taxable income. [Ref.: IRC Section 104]

Individuals under age 65 with limited incomes who are retired due to permanent and total disability (that is, inability to engage in any substantial gainful activity by reason of a medically determined physical or mental impairment that can be expected to result in death or that has lasted or can be expected to last for at least 12 continuous months) are entitled to a tax credit. The credit is 15% of an "initial amount" ranging from $3,750 to $7,500 (depending on the tax filing status of the recipient) and adjusted for pension, Social Security, veterans, or other disability payments; and 50% of adjusted gross income in excess of specified levels (ranging from $5,000 to $10,000, again depending on tax filing status). [Ref.: IRC Section 22]

Disability Management

Q. 4:93 How can employers achieve effective disability management?

There are two fundamental approaches to disability management: prevention/wellness and rehabilitation.

Q. 4:94 How does an employer, union, or insurer put a disability prevention program in place?

There are nine steps in effective disability prevention:

1. Collect adequate data;
2. When appropriate, use preemployment physicals;
3. Screen employees and prospective employees for health risks;
4. Correct on-the-job health hazards;
5. Educate employees and prospective employees about health risks;
6. Educate employees regarding job-related health hazards;
7. Develop employee assistance programs (see Questions 11:5–11:9);
8. Identify and treat lifestyle-related problems with education and behavioral modification programs; and
9. Optimize employee health benefits design.

Q. 4:95 How does rehabilitation fit into disability management?

Many disabled employees are able to return to work, and even more are able to return to work sooner than they normally would have. The key to reducing the ranks of the disabled is introducing an effective return-to-work program.

Q. 4:96 What portion of the disabled can actually be rehabilitated?

Most of the disabled can and do return to work, and certain groups are more likely to return than others. For example, one study showed that those at higher income levels and with more education are most likely to return. Income, education level, and head-of-household status are factors in the likelihood of a disabled employee returning to work.

Q. 4:97 Are some people better candidates than others for disability rehabilitation?

Yes. It may help to ask the following questions as part of the disability assessment process:

1. Is the disabled employee motivated to come back to work?
2. Does the company want the employee back?
3. How close is the employee to retirement?
4. Was this a good, bad, or excellent employee before the disability?
5. Can the job be modified if necessary?
6. Is there a potential for a gradual return to work?

Q. 4:98 What ingredients go into a rehabilitation program?

The following six ingredients have proven to help program success:

1. Specific program objectives;
2. Use of a team approach;
3. Rapid disability assessment;
4. Professional evaluation of return-to-work potential;
5. Flexibility with regard to treatment and job functions; and
6. Well-informed management.

Q. 4:99 Who staffs a rehabilitation team?

The following seven people need to be involved:
1. Rehabilitation coordinator;
2. Registered nurse;
3. Vocational specialist;
4. Claims adjustor;
5. Company health and safety manager;
6. Treating physician; and
7. Supervisor.

Q. 4:100 What is a return-to-work program?

A return-to-work program actively involves the employer in finding ways for the employee to get back on the job as soon as possible. The program usually consists of:

- A monitoring system that keeps a current list of disabled employees, their treatment, condition, and estimated return-to-work date;
- A rehabilitation program that offers physical and psychological therapy; and
- A job accommodation program that tailors work to the abilities of the employee as much as possible, including special arrangements for light duty, modified low-stress work, or a new job altogether.

Q. 4:101 What is an independent living program?

An independent living program (ILP) helps disabled persons live as independently as possible. Often run or managed by disabled persons themselves, ILPs develop job training programs, teach job skills, provide housing assistance, and coordinate worksite modifications. They also provide assistance to disabled workers who are returning to work, or workers who are helping to care for a disabled person.

Chapter 5

Plan Rating and Funding

Plan rating and funding are important aspects of group health insurance. The approach used is the basis on which the cost of the plan to the employer is determined. This chapter covers plan rating and funding techniques, including conventional funding, shared funding plans, deferred premium, retrospective premium arrangements, reserve reduction arrangements, minimum premium, pooling, experience rating, stop-loss insurance, and self-funding.

Q. 5:1 What does plan funding mean?

Plan funding refers to the way claims liabilities and administrative costs will be financed. The fully insured insurance contract represents the most common method of financing claims: The policyholder pays a monthly premium to an insurance company that is responsible for administering and paying claims for covered expenses. For most small employers, this is the conventional and most appropriate approach to funding the costs of a health care plan.

Fully Insured Plans

Q. 5:2 What are the components of the cost of a health insurance plan?

No matter what funding vehicle is used, the cost components of a plan are similar. They are:

- Expected claims;
- Margin for higher claims than expected;
- Reserves for future claims;
- Expenses; and
- The insurer's profit charge.

Q. 5:3 What are expected claims?

The amount of claims that will be incurred during the policy year is estimated by the insurer. The estimate includes claims payments that are expected to be made during that policy year as well as claims payments for expenses incurred during that year, but not reported until after the end of the year. Thus, expected claims are composed of:

- Claims expected to be reported and paid in the policy year;
- Claims incurred during the year but not paid in that year; and
- Claims for which the insurer is liable after the contract terminates, such as extensions for disabled individuals.

Although claims that will be paid after termination of the contract are also typically included in this "expected claims" projection, exactly what claims an insurer is liable for varies from contract to contract.

Q. 5:4 Why would claims be paid after the termination of the contract?

The insurer usually guarantees certain benefits after the termination of an insurance contract. For example, consider a situation in which an expense was incurred in April, but the claim was not submitted to the insurer until May; the employer has terminated coverage with the insurer as of April 30. The insurer is typically liable for paying the claim, since the expense was incurred while the coverage was in force, even if the employer has signed a contract with a new insurance company. In addition, under most policies, the insurer is liable for "extended benefits" for employees who are disabled when an insurance contract terminates. Policies vary, but these benefits often cover expenses for a year or more after termination.

Q. 5:5 How does an insurer know what claims to expect?

Insurance actuaries base expected claims estimates on their past experience with large numbers of insureds, as well as on published statistical information regarding (1) the probability that individuals will incur medical expenses, (2) the plan design (what expenses are covered), and (3) the probable cost of those expenses. Deviations between "expected" and "actual" claims are very common on a policy-by-policy basis. An insurer hopes to accurately estimate expected claims for its entire block of business, thus collecting enough premium to pay claims overall.

Q. 5:6 What is a group health insurance actuary?

A group health insurance actuary is an accredited insurance mathematician who analyzes health care providers' costs associated with delivering health care and insurance companies' costs associated with insuring against the risk of incurring health care expenses. Traditionally, actuaries have focused on group morbidity and mortality and insurance administrative expenses to develop premium rate structures for health coverage.

Q. 5:7 How does an actuary estimate which individuals will incur claims?

Actuarial data that reflect claims probabilities for individuals and groups of individuals, according to certain characteristics, are continuously compiled and updated. These data are available to actuaries through various insurance industry channels. The probability of incurring a medical expense is based primarily on age and sex, but some actuaries also consider the effects of income and occupation or industry.

For example, expected claims for an architectural firm where the average age is 35 and 80% of the employees are male would usually be lower than for a retail store where the average age is 45 and only 40% of the employees are male. This is because younger people are generally healthier, and women generally incur more claims than men, especially during their childbearing years.

Actuarial statistics show that the incidence of claims is often higher for employees who change jobs frequently; they use health care coverage when they have it, for fear that they may not have it at some point in the near future. And because better health is generally tied to higher socioeconomic status, all else being equal, insurers expect fewer claims, but higher claims dollars, from professionals, as compared with other employees.

Q. 5:8 How does plan design affect the expected claims calculation?

If the plan is a base plus major medical plan, claims will be higher than for a comprehensive major medical plan, due to a plan design that not only increases the actual dollar benefit for each hospital stay but also promotes expensive inpatient care. The lower the deductible, the higher the claims expenses for the insurer, since many small claims are submitted.

For any plan, the amount of the deductible and the coinsurance percentage are the key factors that determine the cost. Today, many plans cover similar expenses, but the cost-sharing provisions vary. If the employer decides to include utilization review in the plan, hospital admissions and lengths of stay are expected to be lower than for a plan without this cost-management feature. Other cost-controlling features are discussed in Chapter 7.

Q. 5:9 How does the health plan's rate-guarantee period affect the rate?

Monthly premium rates are guaranteed to remain fixed for a specified period, such as one year. The longer the rate guarantee, the higher the rate. This is because of the difficulty of projecting the cost of health care in the future and the expectation that health care costs will continue to rise at least as fast as the consumer price index.

When an employer's own claims experience is the basis for setting premium rates, the older those data, the more "trend" or projected cost increase is built in. Trend is typically calculated from the midpoint of the experience period to the midpoint of the rate guarantee period.

Q. 5:10 How does the insurer project the cost of the medical services that are expected to be provided?

The two major components of claims cost projections are (1) geographic location and (2) medical care inflation trend. Health care costs more, as do other goods and services, in certain areas of the country. Historically, "trend" has been a component of every insurer's rate structure. It is a measure of the annual inflation rate of medical care goods and services and the effects of increased technology and utilization of services. Medical care costs have been rising much faster than the costs of other items; the trend component of most insurers' rates in 1989 was about 27%. That is, the insurer estimated that prices would rise during the year the contract was effective; thus, the rates were set initially at a point to cover those expected increases.

Q. 5:11 How is the expected cost of claims calculated for an employer with several locations?

The costs in each location are analyzed to develop claims projections. If there are large numbers of employees in more than one location, there may be separate rates for each location.

Q. 5:12 How is a margin for higher than anticipated claims developed?

Insurance company actuaries project how much fluctuation is likely in their expected claims estimates, based on their experi-

Q. 5:13

ence with rate setting and the volatility of the medical care climate at the time a group rate is set. The margin that is added to the expected claims figure is based on the probable stability of the group, which varies with the size of the group and, for larger groups, is based on the past experience of the group. Margin is a potential cost for retrospectively rated groups and a guaranteed cost for prospectively rated groups. (Purists hold that margin is not applicable to prospectively rated groups, but the practice of most carriers today is to illustrate and include a provision for margin in all but the smallest groups.)

Q. 5:13 What is prospective rating?

Prospective rating is a term applied to groups whose premium constitutes both the minimum and maximum cost for a plan year. (This used to be known as a "pooled" group, but the terminology became confused with high-amount (major medical) claims pooling.)

Prospectively rated groups do not "participate" directly in the financial results of the plan; if the premium exceeds claims plus expenses, the surplus supports the carrier's pool and is not returned to the policyholder as a dividend. If the premium is insufficient, the group is supported by the carrier's pool and the policyholder is not responsible for the shortfall or deficit.

Prospective rating is appropriate for smaller groups whose claims levels are not stable. It is also preferred by some larger groups that would rather have a fixed cost, known in advance, for the policy period. At one time, a group had to be large enough to be fully "credible" (see Question 5:20) in order to participate. Today, many carriers offer some degree of participation down to 100 employees.

Groups may be experience rated prospectively. That is, their premium rates are based to some degree on their own experience, but set in advance and guaranteed, so the decision to shift the entire risk does not mean that an employer must forgo the advantages of credibility (see Question 5:20). Many products are available that permit limited participation. That is, in return for some additional margin (potential cost), a corresponding level of surplus premium, if any, would be returned. This hybrid of prospective and retrospective rating preserves the budgetability and maximum cost guarantees associated with prospective rating, with only a small, manageable upside risk. The addition of margin results in a reduction in the carrier's risk charges to reflect the transfer of risk to the policyholder.

Q. 5:14 What is retrospective rating?

Retrospective rating means that the cost of a plan is established at the end of a policy year, rather than fixed in advance as under prospective rating. The policyholder pays an estimated premium throughout the year. Claims plus expenses are reconciled with the premium at year end and a settlement or dividend calculation is produced. If the result is positive, the policyholder receives a dividend; if the result is negative, the policyholder must reimburse the carrier for the deficit. Therefore, it is only retrospectively, after the settlement process is complete, that the net cost for a plan year is known.

Q. 5:15 How does a policyholder reimburse a deficit?

There are several basic approaches to reimburse a deficit, but policyholders may negotiate a settlement that combines attributes of more than one method. These methods are:

1. Paying in a lump sum, single payment, or installment, with interest charged from the midpoint of the policy year;
2. Transferring surplus developed from another line of coverage (some carriers insist on this);
3. Building deficit recoup into subsequent years' estimated premium by increasing the margin;
4. Placing the deficit into an agreement (between policyholder and insurance company) to pay upon contract termination, in exchange for lower or no interest payment on the deficit, or
5. Drawing down a special reserve, called a premium stabilization reserve, that was accumulated out of previous surplus

not received as a dividend. (Note: The combination of all reserves, including incurred but not reported reserves, cannot exceed DEFRA safe-harbor limits unless actuarially certified.)

Q. 5:16 What are reserves?

In broad terms, reserves are a measure of an insurance company's liability for future claims. Insurers establish a dollar amount for each group they insure that is an estimation of the amount of money they will need to fund claims payments, for which they may be liable after policy termination. This reserve estimate is added to the claims estimate developed for the claims incurred in the present plan year to get an "expected claims" projection for a group. Since the carrier, rather than the employer, is responsible for claims payments under insured plans, reserves are legally required to prevent insolvency.

Q. 5:17 How does an insurer determine what premium reserves are necessary?

Insurance company actuaries develop projections of future claims liability for their entire pool of insured groups. They base their projections on the past experience of similar groups, and they factor in the expected cost increases for medical care and expected changes in utilization.

For smaller employers, an average percentage of premiums is usually used to estimate the expected incurred claims and set the premium reserves.

The insurance company underwriting a new contract on a larger employer typically reviews the incurred but not reported, or "run-out," claims of prior years to get an idea of the reserves that should be established for future liability. As a result of claims run-outs, "lag studies" are generated for underwriters to analyze (see Question 5:35).

Q. 5:18 How are expenses projected?

The expense components of premium include:
- The insurer's initial underwriting work;
- Issue of the contract and the plan materials, such as employee booklets;
- Ongoing plan administration (for example, billing, the cost of paying claims, and underwriting work for plan changes and renewals);
- Premium taxes;
- Broker and agent commissions; and
- Contribution to the insurance company's overhead.

For small employers, average expenses are used, but for large employers, expenses are often itemized. For example, a charge for each claim paid could be agreed to by the policyholder and the insurer at the beginning of the plan year.

Q. 5:19 What percentage of the health insurance premium is generally an insurance company's profit?

Generalizations regarding insurer profits are difficult to make. One reason for this is that profit charges, like expense charges and methods of calculating expected claims, vary by insurer (most states, however, place some kind of maximum on insurer profits). Part of the reason for the variation is the role that different accounting methodologies can play in profit reporting. Finally, the sharp rise in provider costs and utilization has had a marked effect on insurer profits as well as on premiums, as insurers race to raise their charges to shore up battered bottom lines.

Q. 5:20 What is credibility?

Credibility refers to belief in past claims experience as an indication of future claims experience. Each insurer interprets claims history differently, and each has a certain credibility formula that applies to groups that are large enough to be experience rated. The basis for the formula is the size of the employer in terms of both covered employees and plan design. Since credibility increases with predictability, the more claims available for projection purposes, the higher the credibility.

For example, an employer with 100 covered employees and a wraparound major medical plan (with Blue Cross for hospitalization) would be less credible than the same group with a comprehensive major medical plan where all claims are included in the analysis. However, a group of 250 covered employees with a wraparound plan would be as credible as a 100-employee comprehensive plan.

The greater the frequency of claims, the higher the credibility as well. Dental claims are more predictable than medical claims, because of greater frequency and lower potential claims costs. Hospitalization—less frequent than nonhospital treatment—is also less predictable and often given less credibility for purposes of projecting claims.

Q. 5:21 What is a manual rate?

A manual rate is the rate generally charged to groups with too few employees to create credible claims experience. It is a combination of the expected claims factor with margin for higher than anticipated claims, expenses, and profit. All four components are based on actuarial formulas that produce an approximation of expected "average" claims and "average" expenses, given the size and demographics of the group based on the experience of the insurance carrier's entire pool of business. Manual rates are occasionally referred to as "pooled rates."

Q. 5:22 What is a pool?

The term "pool" refers to a large number of small groups that are analyzed as a single large group. Claims projections for a group of policyholders can be more accurately estimated than for small policyholders individually—thus, the term "pooled rates." (See also Question 5:26.)

Plan Rating and Funding   Q. 5:24

Q. 5:23 What is an experience rate?

An experience rate is a combination of the employer's specific expected claims estimation with margin for higher than anticipated claims, expenses, and profit.

For groups of 50 or more employees, the insurer will use past claims experience to project future claims experience. However, for groups with fewer than 200 employees, the insurer will not give full credibility to the past claims history as a basis for projecting the future.

Small employers have rates that are at least partially manual (see Question 5:21)—that is, based only partially on experience. Employers with several hundred employees are typically fully experience rated.

Q. 5:24 How is an experience rate combined with a manual rate to produce a final premium rate?

For a case that is 50% credible, half of the experience rate and half of the manual rate would combine to form the final rate. Each carrier follows a different credibility formula based on size and available claims experience. For example, Blue Cross typically uses low credibility and bases most of the premium rate on company average, even for larger clients. Therefore, groups with poor experience may obtain lower rates from Blue Cross than from commercial carriers that use higher credibility formulas.

Small groups, which ordinarily would not benefit from good claims experience with carriers whose formula is based on size, may obtain partial credibility from carriers that use a "life years" formula. For example, if a carrier would consider a "500 life year" group fully credible, an employer with 100 employees and three years available experience data would be considered the same as a group of 300 employees (3 years times 100 employees) and be 60% credible (300 divided by 500). Therefore, 60% of the premium rate would be a function of claims and 40% would be a function of company average or manual. The "life year" approach typically incorporates weighting in order to give more credibility to recent claims than to prior years' claims, given the expectation

107

that the group is more like the group that incurred the most recent claims.

Q. 5:25 Do all claims count toward an employer's claims experience, thus affecting the rate?

Arrangements are usually made for insurers to "pool" claims over a certain dollar limit so that large, infrequent claims do not adversely affect the employer's claims/loss ratio. The employer pays a premium to the insurer for this protection, which keeps large claims amounts out of the experience analysis, so rates will not increase solely as a result of occasional unpredictable claims. However, employers with large claimants often find the carrier increasing the pooling level (less of the claim is forgiven) or increasing the charges for pooling protection. The higher the pooling point, the less risk to the insurer that such a claim will occur, and the lower the pool charge.

Many large employers (5,000 employees and up) forgo individual claims pooling entirely because their own "pool" is large enough to absorb such claims. Smaller employers are wise to purchase protection, usually set at 5% to 25% of expected claims.

Q. 5:26 What is a pool charge?

Some risks are excluded from an employer's experience, such as very large claims that are "pooled" rather than counted as part of the employer's claims experience for rate setting. The fee for this protection is called a pool charge.

Small group rates include provision for the risk of large claims, which is not negotiable. Larger employers, on the other hand, may choose to pool claims at a certain dollar level, based on the risk the employer wants to assume. Claims included in an employer's experience analysis will cause premium rates to fluctuate. A large employer must decide whether it is a better financial decision to pay a larger pool charge to be protected against claims, or to pay a smaller pool charge but be less protected from large claims risk. The decision is based on the potential cost of a large claim versus the guaranteed cost of a fixed premium charge for shifting the risk.

Q. 5:27 What is retention?

An insurance company's retention is the premium charged for expenses and profit. Retention is generally an average charge for small employers, based on how much administration is typically required, the risk assumption involved, and the insurance company's profit margin. It is expressed as a percentage of premium. For small groups, the term "retention" is not generally used to refer to expenses and profit. since the entire premium is retained by the carrier.

For larger employers or for policies that have alternative funding arrangements, the term "retention" is used and is usually a negotiated percentage of premium, ranging from 6% to 20%, based on the services and risk assumption the employer requires from the insurer.

Q. 5:28 How does an employer determine whether a premium rate is reasonable?

It is difficult for employers to determine the reasonableness of rates because it is difficult to make "apples to apples" comparisons among various plan quotes by insurance companies. Coverage provisions vary among insurers.

For employers whose rates are manual, the intermediary typically offers "spreadsheet" quotes from several carriers. Rate comparisons can be made, but differences in benefits must be carefully reviewed. Rate alone is not a good basis for choosing a plan.

For employers whose rates are partially or fully experience rated, the intermediary obtains quotes from several insurers, but because the quotes are based on more subjective information, which each insurer analyzes somewhat differently, there will be more rate negotiation than on smaller policies. One significant variation is in the amount of credibility the insurer assigns to a particular employer's past claims experience.

Q. 5:29 Are dependent rates developed separately from employee rates?

No. Dependent rates are artificial and are based on company-average relationships between employee and dependent loss ratios. Usually, spouses' actual ages are not required; the assumption is made that spouses' ages will average out to be the same as employees' ages. For the experience portion of a premium rate, the employer's loss ratio is reviewed as a whole, rather than by employee and dependent. Thus, even if only dependent claims were resulting in high loss ratios, employee rates as well as dependent rates would reflect these high losses. Although rates quoted to the employer are separate, all premiums—both employee and dependent—are combined, as are claims.

With the increase in employee contribution requirements, many carriers are adjusting the historical relationship between employee and dependent rates, increasing the employee rate and decreasing the dependent rate in order to obtain sufficient premium if contributory dependent coverage is waived. Employers should obtain separate rates that are more nearly "self-supporting" for the purpose of determining employee contributions.

Q. 5:30 What is a loss ratio?

An employer's loss ratio is an expression of claims compared with premium. A low ratio indicates "good" claims experience—the premium collected was more than required to fund the actual claims. A high loss ratio indicates that claims exceeded premium.

Q. 5:31 What is a tolerable loss ratio?

A tolerable loss ratio (TLR), or acceptable loss ratio (ALR), is the loss ratio the insurer can tolerate without losing money on the group. The insurer projects what claims are expected for a certain group. Premium rates are set based on that projection of claims, plus the charges necessary to cover the insurer's expenses. A typical small employer's premium might be 82% for expected claims payments and 18% for expenses—underwriting, issue, administration, claims processing, commissions, overhead, and profit. The amount of claims that is "tolerable" in this case—the TLR—would be 82% of premium. A loss ratio of over 82% for this employer group indicates that the insurer did not accurately project claims.

The insurer has a TLR for its block of cases as a whole, as well as a target TLR for each policy. If the overall loss ratio exceeds the TLR, profits may be reduced or eliminated.

If an insurance carrier has set rates properly and the loss ratio is exactly at the tolerable level, at renewal the rate will still be increased by 20% to 30% to anticipate "trend." Rates will be continued or decrease only if the carrier charged too much in the year prior to the renewal.

Q. 5:32 Do TLRs vary from year to year and from employer to employer?

TLRs vary annually because expected claims and expenses vary from year to year. Expenses vary with the size of a group and with the plan design elected by the employer. Expected claims vary by group and plan design, and they also vary considerably from the first year of coverage to later years.

For the first year in which an insurance company underwrites an employee group, the claims actually paid are expected to be less than 80% of premium. Typically, first-year paid claims are estimated to be between 45% and 60% of premium. This is because claims that were incurred in the prior year under another insurance contract are usually paid by the prior insurer. Thus, the prior insurance company is liable for claims incurred but not reported (IBNR) instead of the present insurer.

The premiums charged by the new insurance company may appear, at first glance, to be much too high, based on the expected paid claims for that first year the contract is in force. However, since the new insurer will be liable for all claims incurred during the period, even though they may not be reported

Q. 5:33

and paid until later, it is necessary for it to collect premiums to fund the claims that will be paid at a later date. These premiums are known as "reserves." (See Question 5:16.)

Q. 5:33 What is the difference between paid claims and incurred claims?

Paid claims are claims actually paid in a defined period. Incurred claims are a combination of claims that are actually paid, claims that have been incurred but have not yet been submitted for payment, and claims for which an insurer will be liable after termination of the contract. When an insurer develops a premium rate, incurred claims are used to set the rates, since the incurred claims estimate represents the insurer's liability.

Q. 5:34 What is lag?

Lag is the time between claim incurrence and claim payment. Lag varies by type of service and amount of claim. For example, hospital bills are usually submitted directly by the provider within a short period of time. However, routine medical expenses that do not represent a substantial out-of-pocket expense may be accumulated by the employee for weeks or months before being submitted, while large bills such as for surgery are likely to be submitted within a moderate period of time. The average lag, weighted for dollars, is determined and expressed as a number of months, a percentage of claims, or, in the first year, a percentage of premium. If the average lag is expected to be three months, a 25% (3 divided by 12) reserve for incurred but not reported claims is necessary. (The full reserve will be higher than the lag estimate, since the reserve must also cover claims for disability extensions after contract termination.)

Lag for basic hospital expenses is usually 2 1/2 to 3 months, due in part to the need for large claims to be reviewed. Dental lag is similar. Major medical lag, however, can be 5 or 6 months. For comprehensive plans, the combination of hospital and non-hospital lag typically ranges between 4 and 4 1/2 months, depending on the mix of claims and the deductible level.

Q. 5:35 What is a lag study?

A lag study is an analysis of the historical timing patterns of claims submissions. The results are used to estimate claims expected to be submitted after the end of the policy period. Lag studies are rarely done for employers with fewer than 2,000 employees, because of the high volume of claims necessary to make the studies believable projections. However, actuaries compile lag studies for their entire case block to establish reserve requirements for the expected total run-out liability on their entire block of business, and apply formula reserve requirements based on these studies.

Alternatives to Fully Insured Plans

Q. 5:36 Are there alternatives to fully insured (conventionally funded) plans?

Alternative funding vehicles allow the employer to absorb some of the risk that the insurer assumes under a conventionally funded insurance plan. The alternatives can be divided into those that increase cash flow:

- Deferred premium (extended grace period);
- Retrospective premium arrangements;
- Reserve reduction agreements; and
- Minimum premium plans (MPPs); and those that increase employer risk:
- Shared or split funding (high self-insured deductibles (HSIDs)); and
- Self-funding or administrative services only (ASO) plans.

Employers that elect alternative funding can be either partially self-funded or fully self-funded.

Q. 5:37 How do alternative funding methods differ from conventional funding methods?

The fundamental differences between conventional and alternative funding methods are the split of risk between insurer and policyholder and the expenses associated with the alternative funding arrangement. The split of risk changes the insurer's liability for claims during the plan year as well as after contract termination. For example, the employer may elect to be responsible for "run-out" claims (claims submitted after plan termination). By assuming additional risk, the employer can reduce its premium to the insurer. Expenses payable to the insurer vary, depending on what risks and services the insurer retains responsibility for. For instance, premium taxes are reduced to the extent premium is reduced when the employer assumes more risk, as are risk charges.

Q. 5:38 For whom might an alternative method of plan funding be appropriate?

The rising cost of health care has resulted in increased interest in funding alternatives by many employers that want to:

- Improve their cash flow;
- Reduce premium taxes and insurance company charges;
- Eliminate or reduce services provided in conventionally insured plans; or
- Enjoy exemption from state mandated benefits.

An employer can achieve any of these objectives by assuming some of the risk the insurer traditionally assumes. Whether a particular employer should attempt to do this depends on the size of the employer, the past claims experience of the group, the current health status of the employees, the risk attitude of the employer, and the willingness of an insurer to provide the employer with protection against whatever share of the risk the employer is unwilling to assume.

Q. 5:39 What size of employers typically seek funding alternatives?

The majority of employers with fewer than 250 employees do not elect an alternative funding arrangement; however, employers with as few as 100 covered employees are sometimes candidates for nonconventional funding. Some insurers have special funding products for employers with as few as 50 employees.

Employers with fewer than 500 employees rarely fully self-fund. Even those that do, almost always have stop-loss insurance as protection against very large individual claims or substantial variations from the employer's expected claims level.

Q. 5:40 Do some employers elect to insure the entire risk of a health insurance plan?

Some very large employers may elect to fully self-fund. Depending on their risk capacity, even these employers may purchase some form of stop-loss insurance. When an employer elects to fully self-fund a plan but have an insurer administer it, a contract for administrative services only (ASO) may be arranged. Self-funded plans typically retain the less expensive claims payment services of a third-party administrator (TPA).

Stop-Loss Insurance

Q. 5:41 What is stop-loss insurance?

Employers that partially or fully self-fund, usually purchase stop-loss insurance to avoid unbudgetable risks and large losses. The coverage reimburses the employer for claims that exceed a certain limit. Two types of stop-loss insurance are available: specific and aggregate.

Q. 5:42 What is the difference between aggregate and specific stop-loss insurance?

Specific stop-loss insurance limits the employer's liability to a predetermined amount for any single claimant during a certain time period. For example, the specific stop-loss level for a single claimant might be set at 10% to 15% of expected claims per policy year. Typically, claims are determined on a paid, rather than incurred, basis. That is, claims actually paid during the policy year will count toward the stop-loss maximum for that year and will not be carried over into subsequent policy years.

Aggregate stop-loss insurance limits the employer's liability to a predetermined amount for the entire insured group during a certain time period. For example, the aggregate stop-loss limit might be set at 125% to 135% of expected claims.

Employers may purchase either specific or aggregate stop-loss insurance, both, or, in the case of very large employers, neither.

Q. 5:43 From whom does an employer purchase stop-loss insurance?

Most often, the employer arranges stop-loss coverage with the insurer for the plan. This typically does not require an additional contract, but would be a part of the master contract.

Q. 5:44 What is the difference between pooling and stop-loss insurance?

Both pooling and stop-loss insurance involve the same concept: protection for the employer against large losses in set time periods. Pooling is used to exclude large claims from an employer's claims experience so that when renewal rates are developed, fluctuations are not counted. Employers pay a pool charge to avoid this fluctuation and the resulting fluctuation in rates. Without pooling, the insurer would pay the claims and would also apply them toward the employer's loss ratio.

Stop-loss insurance is a term used in many different contexts; it is also used as a synonym for out-of-pocket maximum by some insurers. However, technically, it refers to a contractual agreement involved in most alternative funding arrangements. The protection requires the insurer to pay for claims in excess of predetermined limits. Without stop-loss insurance, the employer would have to pay for all claims.

Deferred Premium Arrangements

Q. 5:45 What is a deferred premium arrangement?

A deferred premium arrangement is the simplest of all alternative funding arrangements. Conventionally funded plans allow the employer a 31-day grace period, during which premium for the current month is overdue but payable without allowing the policy to lapse. Insurers will defer premium receipt for certain employers by an additional 30 or 60 days, thus extending the grace period to 60 or 90 days. This enables the employer to retain funds for an extended period, thereby allowing investment income on those funds to accrue to the employer rather than to the insurer. It also permits the policy to remain intact without payment of premium.

Since 90 days worth of premium is typically equivalent to the reserves required by the insurer, this deferred premium arrangement effectively eliminates the cash reserve usually held by the insurer. If the policy terminates, then all of the deferred premium is typically due as of the date of termination.

Q. 5:46 Why would an employer elect a deferred premium arrangement?

The employer's cash flow is improved because the employer is able to use the premium deferred in either that business or elsewhere.

An employer must compare its use-of-money cost to the interest charged by the insurance carrier on what is effectively a loan. Several factors must be taken into account:

Q. 5:47   Health Insurance Answer Book

1. Whether or not the carrier charges interest. If so, at what rate?
2. When is the interest compounded. From the first day premium is due? From the thirty-first day?
3. What cost, if any, does the company incur from borrowing the same dollars through normal commercial channels?

The insurer profits depend significantly on cash flow. Therefore, there will be a charge to the company; if there is no direct interest charge, there may be an increase in retention (see Question 5:27).

Since carrier interest charges are typically set annually and rarely float (although some carriers index and adjust the rates monthly), it may be possible to achieve positive cash flow in periods of rising interest. When interest rates fall, however, the carrier's rate is likely to be much higher, and the arrangement should be terminated.

Q. 5:47   Why don't all employers elect deferred premium arrangements?

Insurers do not provide deferred premium arrangements for most employers. This practice is essentially an extension of credit, and insurers are not inclined to underwrite that risk without protection, such as a letter of credit. In addition, the insurer charges a fee for its loss of income when premiums are deferred. The combination of the costs of determining and ensuring the employer's credit worth, plus the loss of investment income to the insurer, results in an increased expense for the insurer and may produce a very small net saving for the employer.

Shared Funding Arrangements

Q. 5:48   How does a shared funding arrangement differ from a conventionally funded plan?

Shared funding (also called high self-insured deductible (HSID) plans) allows the employer to self-fund all of an individual's covered expenses for health care up to a specific limit. The employer chooses the "employer deductible" level, such as $2,000, and pays covered expenses for anyone who incurs claims, up to that maximum. The insurance company typically provides eligibility review, claims processing, and assumption of the risk above $2,000 per individual.

Basically, shared funding is a minimum premium plan (MPP) for small employers. Most carriers will not offer MPPs to employers under a certain size due to underwriting or state filing limitations. Certain carriers specializing in small groups adapted the concept for their clients.

Q. 5:49 Why would an employer elect a shared funding plan?

Shared funding requires less premium to the insurer for both current and future claims. The employer retains funds that would usually be paid to the insurance company, thereby improving its cash-flow position. The employer must fund current claims up to the employer deductible level, but may be able to pay funds out less quickly than if the plan had been totally insured, depending on the timing of the claims. Also, if claims are less than would normally be expected, the employer will come out ahead. This is because the insurance company would have set premiums at a level to fund "expected claims"; thus, if the plan experiences lower than expected claims, the employer will spend less. Conversely, the timing and claims level may result in a greater cost. That is the risk inherent in these types of plans.

The employer may also save money because it will pay the insurer no premium tax on the self-insured part of the plan. Therefore, even if the employer self-funds claims that are nearly equal to what the insurer would have expected, it will still save money by avoiding the premium tax.

Q. 5:50 Why would an employer reject a shared funding plan as an alternative funding arrangement?

An employer with a shared funding arrangement could pay out more than for a conventionally funded plan in some years. Also, additional administration is involved and budgetability is virtually impossible for smaller groups.

The employer could pay more, in total, for the shared funding plan than for a conventionally insured plan when:

- Claims for which the employer is liable exceed expected levels. In which case fully insured premiums would have been a better investment, based on the fact that an insurer that accepts a fixed premium is not entitled to additional premium to fund higher than expected claims;
- The employer assumes liability upon contract termination, and run-out claims liabilities for claims up to the employer deductible are excessive; or
- The employer uses a third-party administrator (TPA) to administer claims and perform other services the insurer usually performs, and the combination of the TPA expenses plus the insurer's expenses is higher than the expenses would have been under a conventionally insured plan. This sometimes happens due to the split of services and extra coordination work done by the TPA and employer that traditionally is done by the insurer.

Q. 5:51 Why don't all employers elect shared funding arrangements?

Only employers that have 50 or more covered employees and are willing to absorb a piece of the risk usually taken by the insurer are the logical candidates for shared funding arrangements. The employer must be able to absorb peaks of outgoing cash flow over months and years.

Employers with more than 500 covered employees typically elect other funding alternatives that have the potential for greater savings.

Retrospective Premium Arrangements

Q. 5:52 What is a retrospective premium arrangement?

Under a retrospective ("retro") premium agreement, the insurer agrees to collect less than the conventional premium from the employer. At the end of the year, the insurer has the right to collect additional premium from the employer if the actual loss ratio exceeds the loss ratio agreed to at the beginning of the retro agreement period. Typically, the initial premium reduction is equal to the margin built into the rate. The maximum additional premium payable is capped; it is agreed to at the beginning of the policy year and may raise the total premium to more than would have been paid in the absence of the retro agreement.

In effect, the insurer is agreeing to collect premiums at the expected claims level, collecting no premium for fluctuation. If claims exceed the expected level, some or all of the retro may be "called."

Q. 5:53 Why would an employer negotiate a retrospective premium arrangement?

Retrospective premium arrangements were originally known as "advance dividends." The margin in excess of expected claims was presumed to be the dividend payable if claims were as anticipated. Rather than wait until the close of the policy year plus three months to perform the settlement calculation, the "dividend" is "paid" in advance and available to the policyholder throughout the year.

The employer retains funds it ordinarily would remit to the insurer during the year, thus improving its cash-flow position. The employer assumes some additional risk if the retro agreement states that more than the conventional premium can be collected if claims exceed a set level, but this risk is limited because a maximum retro is agreed on at the beginning of the policy year.

Q. 5:54 What is a "deep cut" retro?

Typically, only the margin is placed in a retro. Some carriers, however, especially Blue Cross, allow retrospective arrangements for as much as 20% of expected premium. This includes not only margin, but a portion of the reserves—the piece attributable to the increase in reserves that will accrue by the end of the policy year.

Deep cut retros can be negotiated when the reserve change is expected to be negative (for example, when there is a reduction

Q. 5:55 Health Insurance Answer Book

in covered persons, a plan change that reduces expected benefits, or significantly improved claims levels).

Q. 5:55 Why might an employer not negotiate a retrospective premium arrangement?

An employer that implements a retro arrangement may find that the savings are minimal, due to the insurance company's increased retention charges. These include an interest charge for the loss of the use of money during the policy year and a charge for assuming the credit risk of the employer. The employer may be required to pay additional premium at policy year end. If the retro agreement specifies that the collectible additional premium is capped, but at a level that makes the total potential premium higher than the conventional premium would have been, the employer can pay more than under a conventional plan. In order to guarantee payment of the retro, the insurer may require a letter of credit. This will result in a bank fee, usually 1% of the retro amount, which together with the carrier's interest charges might exceed a policyholder's cash flow.

Q. 5:56 To whom are retrospective premium arrangements available?

Insurers are unwilling to provide retrospective premium plans to employers with fewer than 50 covered employees and, in fact, rarely allow retro plans for employers with fewer than 150 employees. Retrospective premium arrangements are most often arranged for employers with between 200 and 500 employees whose past experience requires rates that the employer and intermediary believe are too high. They may negotiate a lower premium rate with the insurer by agreeing to pay a retro, but only if claims do accumulate to the insurer's original projections. To ensure that the retro will be paid if it is called, insurers will confirm the creditworthiness of the employer requesting a retrospective arrangement.

Some insurers offer retrospective premium arrangements to small employers whose experience is habitually better than the manual pool. These employers, whose rates are based partially on experience and partially on manual rates, are becoming more willing to assume some of the risk the insurer has traditionally assumed. Rate increases may be necessary in general, due to increasing claims costs, but for small employers whose claims experience is better than average, a modified retro agreement may be available.

Reserve Reduction Agreements

Q. 5:57 What is a reserve reduction agreement?

Reserve reduction agreements take two forms: (1) an upfront amendment to the insurance policy, which eliminates the insurer's liability after contract termination, and (2) an agreement between employer and insurer that the employer will retain the reserves traditionally paid to the insurer, but the insurer will be liable for benefits after termination and the employer must return the reserves to the insurer. Both arrangements result in decreased premiums payable to the insurer.

Q. 5:58 Why would reserves decrease if an insurer eliminates its liability after contract termination?

Traditionally, the insurer is liable after contract termination for extended benefits for disabled employees and for claims incurred but unreported prior to termination. Some employers are willing to assume this liability, thereby eliminating the reserves held by the insurer.

Q. 5:59 Why would an employer want to negotiate a reserve reduction?

Premiums decrease for employers that modify benefits payable upon contract termination or hold the reserves traditionally held by the insurer. This is especially true in the first year, when the insurer typically establishes reserves with a percentage of the initial premium.

Q. 5:60 Why might an employer not change the conventional reserve arrangement?

When an employer holds the reserves usually paid to the insurer, the insurance company still typically retains liability for certain claims payments after contract termination. Therefore, the insurer must have access to the funds, and the employer may be required to provide them at a most inconvenient time. The insurer also typically requires some form of arrangement to protect its credit risk, such as a letter of credit from a bank, for which there is a charge. This may be in addition to the maintenance of the minimum balance in an account where the reserves or a portion of the reserves will be held.

Some arrangements require the employer to invest the funds (the amount of the conventional reserve requirement) in certain accessible securities; the employer may not be allowed to use the captured reserves as working capital in the business, because of the risk of loss and the inaccessibility of funds. This arrangement is agreed to by employer and insurer, and although the funds are the employer's property, the insurer has the contractual right to withdraw money to fund obligations after contract termination.

The administration required for these arrangements can be cumbersome. Furthermore, an insurer may be unwilling to allow the employer to retain reserves, based on an assessment of the employer's creditworthiness and the practical effectiveness of letters of credit.

The reserve level must be adjusted annually and carried on the employer's books if a hold-harmless agreement has been executed. If the carrier retains liability, interest charges will be accumulated and charged in the carrier's retention.

Q. 5:61 Do small employers typically implement reserve reduction agreements?

The release of reserves is rarely available to smaller employers. The additional administration involved requires that a significant reserve amount be involved in order for the employer to net savings. Generally, the smaller the employer, the less the benefits expertise. Administration of the banking arrangements requires a knowledgeable employer and intermediary.

Minimum Premium Plans

Q. 5:62 What is a minimum premium plan?

Minimum premium plans (MPPs) are fully insured plans in which the employer agrees to fund expected claims; the insurance carrier funds claims in excess of the employer's aggregate claims liability and claims in excess of a specific high-amount claim per individual. It is fully insured, however, because the insurance carrier is ultimately liable for all benefits due under the terms of the plan, including those incurred but not reported at termination.

Two kinds of MPP are available:

1. The insurer holds reserves similar to those required under a conventionally insured plan; or
2. The employer is permitted to hold reserves to fund this liability.

The insurance carrier, in both cases, is responsible for benefit obligations after termination of the contract.

Q. 5:63 At what level does the insurer become responsible for benefits funding under an MPP?

The employer and insurer establish a "trigger point" beyond which the insurer is liable. This liability can be set on a monthly cumulative basis or on an annual basis. The trigger is negotiated between each employer and insurer, based on expected claims. A trigger point of 125% of expected claims is one example.

Under a monthly cumulative arrangement, the employer is protected against fluctuation in claims from month to month. If cumulative claims exceed the monthly trigger point, the insurer pays claims from its own funds. In a subsequent month, if claims are below the trigger point, the insurer is usually allowed to recoup the amount from the employer to cover the payments made in the month when claims exceeded the trigger point. For example:

Month	Employer Obligation	Claims	Employer Pays	Insurer Pays	Unexpended Employer Funds
1	$ 100	$ 60	$ 60	$ 0	$40
2	200	70	70	0	70
3	300	120	120	0	50
4	400	150	150	0	0
5	500	100	100	0	0
6	600	110	100	10	0
7	700	40	40	−10	50
8	800	100	100	0	50
9	900	130	130	0	20
10	1,000	50	50	0	70
11	1,100	180	170	10	0
12	1,200	140	100	40	0

Under an annual arrangement, the employer funds all claims until the annual trigger point is reached. For example:

Month	Employer Obligation	Claims	Employer Pays	Insurer Pays	Unexpended Employer Funds
1	$1,200	$ 60	$ 60	$ 0	$ 1,140
2	1,200	70	70	0	1,070
3	1,200	120	120	0	950
4	1,200	150	150	0	800
5	1,200	100	100	0	700
6	1,200	110	110	0	590
7	1,200	40	40	0	550
8	1,200	100	100	0	450
9	1,200	130	130	0	320
10	1,200	50	50	0	270
11	1,200	180	180	0	90
12	1,200	140	90	50	0

The insurer's and employer's obligations for funding under both arrangements are the same, in amounts, by the end of the year. The only difference is the timing.

Q. 5:64 If an individual incurs a shock claim (an unexpected claim of a high amount) under an MPP, does the full amount of that claim count toward the employer's trigger point?

Whether or not the full amount will count towards the trigger point depends on whether an arrangement has been made to "stop the employer's losses" at a certain point per claimant per policy year (specific pooling or stop loss). Some employers elect to buy individual high-amount claim pooling and pay a pool charge as part of the "minimum premium."

Q. 5:65 How are claims paid with employer funds under an MPP?

The employer establishes a bank account to which the insurer has access to pay claims. The account is funded as claims are submitted for payment. However, three days to two weeks worth of expected claims, called an "imprest balance," are required to be maintained in the account. Claims analysis is typically performed by the insurer, although some employers use third-party administrators instead, who would have access to the funds, just as the insurer would if it were the administrator.

Q. 5:66 Why would an employer benefit from establishing an MPP?

The employer retains significant funds under an MPP, paying the insurer a "minimum premium," which consists of administrative expenses, reserves (unless the employer holds the reserves), and predetermined premium for stop loss to fund claims above the trigger point. In the first year, when the insurer establishes reserves, premium could be as much as 35% of the conventionally insured premium, but in later years, premium could be as little as 7% of the conventionally insured level, covering only administration, change in reserves due to change in claims levels, and excess claims premium.

Premium tax is usually not payable for the employer-funded portion of the plan; in some states, however, an insurance company's obligations to pay premium tax are not changed for MPPs. In this case, the employer pays premium tax to the insurer, which, in turn, remits it to the state insurance department. Usually, an agreement for this contingency is reached initially. Most insurers require a "hold-harmless" agreement that relieves the insurer of any obligation to pay taxes a state might assess in the future. (Hold-harmless agreements are also used when insurers need assurance that an employer will release reserves t has been holding in various funding arrangements.)

Employers that were previously fully retrospectively rated will have the same claims cost under conventional and MPP funding. Thus, the savings are usually realized not from positive claims experience but from decreased premium taxes and from investment income on reserves.

Q. 5:67 Why wouldn't an employer elect an MPP?

Properly structured, MPP arrangements expose employers to no more of the risk than they assume under conventional, retrospectively rated plans. However, the administrative work required to establish and maintain the banking arrangements requires expertise and effort too burdensome for some employers.

The insurer's risk charges may be substantial for some employers whose creditworthiness is questionable, especially if a letter of credit is used, which is expensive to arrange.

If the carrier (or the state) does not permit the release of the reserves, MPP savings may be minimal. Without the interest gain on the reserves (approximately 20% of conventional premium), the premium tax savings (as low as 0.5% to 1% in most states; up to 2% or 2.5% in some states) may be offset to a large degree by banking expenses and additional internal administration.

The same level of retention savings (but not premium tax savings) can be obtained in a conventionally insured plan with a 90-day premium deferral.

Q. 5:68 What employers typically elect MPPs?

Employers with MPPs usually have at least 200 employees enrolled in the health plan. Insurers also require some protection against the credit risk an MPP represents. Thus, if an employer cannot supply a letter of credit or excellent financials, an MPP may not be an option. MPPs are not available in every state.

Q. 5:69 How are third-party administrative services used in an MPP?

An employer may elect to have administration, including claims determination, performed by a source other than the insurer, if the service the third-party administrator (TPA) can provide is better or less expensive. In this situation, the insurer only assumes risk; the TPA provides documentation to the insurer for claims payments for which the insurer is liable over the trigger point. The TPA must be approved by the insurer, and not all insurers are willing to engage in such arrangements.

Voluntary Employee Benefit Associations (VEBAs)

Q. 5:70 What is a VEBA?

A voluntary employees' beneficiary association (VEBA) is an association established for the purpose of providing "life, sick, accident or other benefits" (IRC Section 501(c)(9)) to employees, their dependents, and beneficiaries. It is the primary self-funding method for establishing reserves to pay for these benefits.

Q. 5:71 What tax benefits do VEBAs confer?

Provided the VEBA complies with the requirements of IRC Sections 501(c)(9), 505 and 419A, employer contributions to VEBAs are tax-deductible, the VEBA pays no tax on earnings, and income is not taxable to association members.

Q. 5:72 What "other benefits" can be provided through a VEBA?

VEBAs may be used to provide benefits similar to life, sick or accident benefits that are intended to safeguard or improve the health of a member or beneficiary, or protect against a contingency that would reduce a member's income. Such benefits include:

- Vacation benefits and facilities,
- Recreational activities such as sports leagues,
- Child care facilities,
- Supplemental unemployment benefits,
- Severance benefits,
- Education or training benefits,
- Workers' compensation,
- Legal service benefits,
- Emergency loans, and
- Job readjustment and economic dislocation payments.

Q. 5:73 What benefits cannot be provided by a VEBA?

VEBAs may *not* be used to provide:

- Deferred compensation benefits, or any other form of compensation that is dependent upon the passage of time rather than the occurance of an unanticipated event. This prohibition extends to pensions, savings plans, stock bonus plans, and the like,
- Accident or homeowners insurance,
- Non-emergency loans,
- Malpractice insurance, or
- Miscellaneous employment expenses such as commuting costs.

Q. 5:74 What are the requirements for establishing a tax-exempt VEBA?

The requirements for establishing a VEBA are as follows:

1. The organization must be an employees' association, which means it must be an entity such as a trust or corporation which is independent of the employer or its employees;
2. Membership must be voluntary, which means that it involves some sort of affirmative act on the part of the employee, or that it is required as a result of a collective bargaining agreement, or that it is conferred as a result of employment provided there is no detriment to employees (such as a mandatory contribution);
3. Substantially all of its operations must be devoted to providing life, sick or accident benefits to employees and their beneficiaries, and
4. No part of the organization's net earnings may inure to the benefit of any private shareholder or individual, except for the payment of life, sick and accident benefits.

Q. 5:75 How does a VEBA obtain tax-exempt status?

A VEBA gives notice to the IRS that it is applying for tax-exempt status as a VEBA by submitting Form 1024, "Application for Recognition of Exemption under Section 501(a) or for Determination under Section 120". The application must be filed within 15 months (plus extensions) of the end of the month in which the association was organized.

Q. 5:76 May a VEBA be established to benefit only one person?

No. It must be for the benefit of a group of employees.

Q. 5:77 May a VEBA benefit persons who are not employees?

Yes, provided they share an employee-related common bond. Employee-related common bond means that they are employees of a single employer, employees of several employers who are members of a controlled group or and affiliated service group as defined by IRC Section 414, members of a collective bargaining group, or employees of several companies in the same type of business in the same geographical area.

Membership may be extended beyond actual employees to other individuals who are not employees, but otherwise share the common bond, such as owners of a business whose employees are VEBA members. Where the VEBA benefits such individuals, it will still be considered to be an "employees'" association, provided 90% of the total membership of the association (on one day of each quarter) consists of employees.

Q. 5:78 Who is an employee for VEBA purposes?

An individual is considered to be an employee for VEBA purposes if he is an employee for employment tax purposes or under a collective bargaining agreement. Temporary, part-time and retired employees, surviving spouses and dependents also qualify.

Q. 5:79 What restrictions on VEBA membership are permissible?

Membership may be restricted on the basis of employment-related criteria such as geographical area, length of service, maximum compensation, full-time employment status, or reasonable classification of workers. In addition, VEBAs may exclude individuals who are members of another employer-funded association that provides comparable benefits, employees who are subject to a collective bargaining agreement or those who refuse to make required contributions, those who do not meet a reasonable standard for health condition.

Q. 5:80 Who controls a VEBA?

In order for the organization to be considered a voluntary association of employees, the employees' interests must be represented by:

- Member employees,
- An independent trustee such as a bank, or
- Trustees, at least some of whom are designated by or on behalf of the member employees.

Q. 5:81 Is there a limit on deductible contributions to a VEBA?

The amount which may be set aside for an exempt purpose in a VEBA may not exceed the qualified direct costs determined under IRC Section 419, plus certain additional amounts for reserves determined under IRC Section 419A.

Qualified direct costs are the amounts that the employer could have deducted if the benefits were provided as direct cash payments to employees.

IRC Section 419A sets limits on additional assets that may be "set aside" to provide future disability, medical, supplemental unemployment or severance or life insurance benefits. The basic limits are:

1. The amount reasonably and actuarially necessary to fund the cost of claims that have been incurred but unpaid, plus the administrative cost of processing those claims; and
2. Certain limited additions to reserves for the payment of post-retirement medical and life insurance benefits.

Q. 5:82 What are the restrictions on funding for post-retirement medical and life insurance benefits?

The maximum funding limits are:

- The level annual contribution, spread over the working lives of the covered employees, that are necessary to fully fund such benefits upon retirement, using reasonable actuarial assumptions, or

- A nonactuarially calculated safe harbor of 35% of the preceding year's medical costs, not including insurance premiums.

Each year's limit must be determined on the basis of current medical costs; projected inflation may not be taken into account.

Q. 5:83 What are the special rules regarding VEBA contributions for key employees?

Contributions made on behalf of "key employees" as defined in IRC Section 416 must be made to a separate account, and key employee benefits must be paid from that account. These contributions are treated as annual additions to a defined contribution pension plan for purposes of applying the overall limits on annual pension contributions.

▶ **Planning Pointer:** Though the contribution to the postretirement medical benefits reserve is deductible, the income on that reserve constitutes "unrelated business income."

Q. 5:84 What is "unrelated business income"?

Certain VEBA income is deemed to be unrelated business income (under IRC Section 512), which means it is not entitled to exemption from tax and is taxed at corporate rates. Amounts set aside and used for purposes other than for providing benefits are unrelated business income. The earnings on reserves for postretirement medical benefits are also unrelated business income. Some VEBAs circumvent this problem by investing in tax-deferred investment vehicles such as annuities.

Q. 5:85 Are there special non-discrimination rules for VEBA's?

Yes. See Chapter 11 for a complete discussion of the non-discrimination rules applicable to VEBAs.

Chapter 6

Plan Implementation and Administration

Proper administration of a health insurance plan is essential if both employer and employee are to receive maximum value. Plan administration begins before the effective date of the plan and continues throughout the plan year. This chapter examines plan administration and implementation and covers such topics as setting up the plan, employee enrollment, claims filing, billing procedures, the renewal process, terminating employees, COBRA administraton, discrimination testing, and the use of computers in plan administration.

Setting Up the Plan

Q. 6:1 After an employer selects a health insurance plan, what must be done to put the coverage into effect?

After reviewing proposals and selecting the plan, the employer makes written application and pays a binder that approximates the first month's premium to the selected insurer. A worksheet usually accompanies the application. It provides a precise explanation of all the information required for smooth operation of the plan. This includes, but is not limited to, the legal name of the policyholder and the locations of employees who will be insured, classes of employees eligible for coverage, the effective date of the plan, details of the coverage requested, the amount of

Q. 6:2   **Health Insurance Answer Book**

employee contributions and policyholder premium payment, the claims payment method, and the intermediary involved.

In addition, enrollment of employees must take place before the underwriter will approve coverage (accept the group as a risk) and issue final premium rates. Changes in enrollment from estimates on which the proposal was based can significantly affect the cost of the plan. Thus, the employees are told about the new coverage and required to enroll prior to final approval by the insurer.

Q. 6:2 Is the coverage effective as soon as the insurer receives the application and enrollment material?

No. The enrollment forms accompany the application materials to the insurance company's home office, where the underwriter reviews the enrollment and the final coverage requested. This preissue work typically occurs during the month prior to the effective date of the coverage, although the extra preparation required for implementation of some plans, such as flexible benefits plans, must be done several months earlier. Only after the final review and approval by the insurer is the coverage effective.

Q. 6:3 When might an underwriter not approve an application for coverage?

There are two general reasons that an underwriter would not approve an application: The coverage details are substantially different from the plan the underwriter had originally agreed to, thus materially changing the risk; or the group's enrollment produces a substantially different final group than expected.

Q. 6:4 If an application is not approved by the underwriter, what happens?

Usually, the intermediary and group representative work together to make changes to the plan or the premium that make the group an acceptable risk for the underwriter.

Q. 6:5 Why does the insurance company require detailed coverage information before issuing the policy?

It is important that the master contract reflect precisely the coverage desired, because claims are paid on the basis of the contract. Although the underwriter may have a detailed record of what coverage is desired and who is likely to participate based on the materials submitted for the initial quote, the final master contract must be developed from current information.

Another reason for requiring detailed coverage information is that some insurers allow policies with fewer than 100 participants to be "field underwritten." This means that the initial quote is developed by a field sales representative. As a result, the home office may have no prior knowledge of the employee group, and the application and enrollment forms may be the first information the underwriter receives.

Q. 6:6 When an employer uses a third-party administrator, what services does the administrator provide?

The third-party administrator (TPA) or a service bureau may take care of changes in enrollment, premium payment, claims determination, and reporting functions. When the TPA also acts as an intermediary, plan change and renewal administration would be included. Depending on how much of the plan is self-funded, the TPA will perform various services that the insurer performs for a conventionally insured plan. Typically, when an employer self-funds, one of the reasons is to unbundle administrative services and eliminate duplicate carrier administration, which adds unnecessarily to the cost of the program. Therefore, even though TPAs offer most services available from insurance carriers, many self-funded employers perform as many tasks as possible in-house and buy any necessary adjuncts from one or more third parties.

Q. 6:7 Who provides the announcement materials necessary to inform employees about the plan?

Typically, a concise letter from the employer to employees explains what benefits the new plan will provide, who is eligible to enroll, how much an employee's monthly contribution will be (if the plan is contributory), and when the coverage will become effective. An insurance company representative may provide form letters to the policyholder that can be customized to meet the employer's needs. When substantial changes are being made or the plan is complex, professionals may be retained to provide special communications.

Q. 6:8 What is a certificate of insurance?

Once the plan becomes effective, a certificate of insurance is given to each employee. This may or may not be mandatory; certificates are not required in all states. The certificates provide employees with a summary of coverage, just as the master contract does for the employer. (However, the "cert" does not constitute a contract between the employee and the insurer.)

Insurers typically provide covered employees with booklets that describe coverage in less technical language than the master contract. These booklets are not filed with the state insurance department as certificates are usually required to be. Booklets explain coverage in readable language and are becoming increasingly common, due in part to state "readability" laws. It is also common for insurers to provide "booklet certs" that include both a technical coverage explanation and a layperson's explanation under one cover. Neither the booklet nor the certificate automatically satisfies the summary plan description (SPD) requirement of ERISA. Special wording must be added to standard insurance company-provided material in order to meet ERISA requirements.

Q. 6:9 What other materials are issued to employees?

Many plans include identification cards so that each employee has a wallet-sized card to refer to when questioned by a provider or when filing a claim. Many employers purchase hospital guarantee cards from their insurers as part of their plans instead of ID cards. The guarantee card typically ensures that a hospital will accept a patient even if the hospital cannot reach the insurance company to verify coverage. Cards usually guarantee coverage for 72 hours, and are meant to serve as temporary coverage confirmation on weekends and holidays when a provider would not be able to contact the insurer. Cards may be provided to covered dependents as well as employees.

Other materials involve preferred provider organizations (PPOs). In order for an employee to visit a preferred provider, he or she must know who those providers are. The insurance company or TPA publishes a list of the preferred providers periodically, because additions and deletions are made during the year.

If the health care plan includes a prescription drug card plan, employees are issued cards as soon as possible after the effective date of the policy. The prescription drug administrator produces the cards and often ships them directly to the employer. The employer can specify that it wants cards for employees only or cards for both covered dependents and employees. A guide to participating pharmacies that will accept the card is necessary with such plans.

Various other materials are distributed, especially when a new policy provision is being added. If new limitations are being placed on coverage or if expansions are being made to coverage, employers and insurers want to communicate the changes so that employees understand what benefits will be payable. For example, if utilization review (UR) is added to the health plan, employees will need to understand when they must contact the UR organization, where to call or write, and what the ramifications will be if they do not follow the UR procedures.

Reporting and Disclosure

Q. 6:10 Are there reports that an employer must file with the state or federal government?

Yes. Generally, employers/plan sponsors must file plan descriptions and annual reports.

Q. 6:11   Health Insurance Answer Book

Plan Descriptions: Employers with 100 or more covered employees must file a summary plan description (SPD) with the U.S. Department of Labor and distribute the SPD to employees within 120 days after the plan is initiated. The plan administrator (usually the policyholder) is responsible for this action. (See Question 6:13) If changes are made to the plan that affect the information in the SPD or materially affect the plan, a filing called a summary of material modification (SMM) must be made within 210 days after the close of the plan year in which the modification was made. The SMM or a revised SPD must be distributed to employees within the same time frame.

Annual Reports: Plan administrators must also file annual reports. These reports, known as 5500 Series Annual Return/Reports, are due within seven months following the close of the plan year, unless an extension has been requested. Large plans must file a Form 5500 each year. Smaller plans—those with fewer than 100 participants—file a simpler 5500-C/R. Failure to comply with ERISA reporting requirements can result in fines of up to $1,000 a day for each day of noncompliance.

Q. 6:11   How does the repeal of Section 89 affect welfare plan reporting and disclosure requirements?

In place of the plan documentation requirements of Section 89(k), ERISA Section 402, which requires plans to be in writing as well as requiring other reporting and disclosure items, is restored.

In addition to restoring plan-specific nondiscrimination rules, the repeal of Section 89 also restored the separate reporting and disclosure requirements of cafeteria plans, dependent care assistance plans, educational assistance plans, and group legal services plans.

Q. 6:12   When do the new reporting requirements become effective?

New rules require medical plans and group term life plans as well as cafeteria and dependent care assistance plans to report highly compensated employee data beginning with the Form 5500 for the 1989 plan year. However, Treasury had prohibited the IRS from enforcing the new requirements until September 30, 1990.

It was recently announced that the expanded 5500 reporting and the newly required highly compensated information are delayed until further guidance is provided by the IRS.

Q. 6:13 What is a summary plan description, and what information does it contain?

A summary plan description (SPD) furnishes the Department of Labor with specific information about the health plan. It includes the name and address of the policyholder; the type of benefits plan; the name, address, and telephone number of the plan administrator; the name and address of the person designated as agent for service of legal process; and the names and addresses of the plan trustees, if any. It also includes eligibility requirements, contribution requirements, claims processing procedures, benefits denial guidelines, and an explanation of the appeals process. Each plan participant, as well as the Department of Labor, is provided with an SPD.

Q. 6:14 Should an employer rely on the SPD to explain plan benefits to employees?

The SPD is a legal document with a specified format the employer must follow. It is not an especially good vehicle for communicating with employees. Therefore, it is helpful to supplement the SPD with some down-to-earth employee communications materials. Ongoing education of employees will lead to more effective use of the health care system, along with better quality of care and improved health cost management. It will also maximize the employee relations value of providing benefits.

Q. 6:15 What administrative material does the insurer initially provide to the employer?

The employer is usually given a supply of enrollment forms, certificates, and booklets for additional enrollees; premium reporting forms; claims forms; the master contract; a final employee roster or listing; an administrative manual; and all forms required to administer changes (additions and deletions), including conversions and COBRA.

Enrollment

Q. 6:16 Why is enrollment in the plan encouraged?

The employer is attempting to meet its employees' coverage needs by providing a health care plan. If employees are not educated about the plan and encouraged to enroll, the employer will not have achieved that objective. Further, because a larger insured group sometimes results in a better spread of risk, the rates may be better as enrollment increases. Administrative charges by the insurer also may reflect economies of scale in the rates.

Q. 6:17 What information must individuals provide to enroll in the plan?

Enrollment forms ask enrollees to provide some or all of the following information:
- Name;
- Sex;
- Age;
- Social Security number;
- Salary;
- Occupation (rarely required for health care coverage);
- Election or rejection of coverage (if contributory);
- Marital status and election or rejection of dependent coverage (if contributory);

- Dependents to be covered (more and more plans require this);
- Selection of coverage if there is more than one offered;
- The employee's beneficiary for life insurance (usually an accompaniment to health coverage); and
- Authorization for payroll deductions (for contributory plans).

This information is more detailed and up-to-date than the census data provided to the insurer for the initial quote.

Q. 6:18 Must individuals enroll in a noncontributory plan?

Yes. Although the employer knows that everyone will be covered, demographic information and beneficiary designation (for life insurance coverage) is necessary for the insurer to develop a final premium rate and, for some plans, to establish the employee records needed to pay claims.

Q. 6:19 Who enrolls the employees in the group health insurance plan?

The company's employee benefits administrator, with or without the assistance of the intermediary or insurance representative, enrolls employees. Small employers may not need help because of the limited number of employees. Employee meetings to explain the new plan and distribute the enrollment forms are conducted by the employee benefits administrator, but may include representatives of insurance companies and HMOs.

Q. 6:20 How long do employees have to complete their enrollment forms?

Because the enrollment forms must be submitted to the insurance company before the effective date of the plan, employees are encouraged to return them as quickly as possible. An arbitrary time period for form return, such as a week, is typically established by the employer. Employees who submit forms late may or may not be allowed to participate in the plan as of the effective date of the plan.

Q. 6:21 Why would an employee who submits a late enrollment form not be allowed to participate as of the plan's effective date?

Insurance companies have established rules regarding late enrollment in order to ensure consistent, accurate premium and coverage records, and to protect the plan against adverse selection. Whether the employee obtains coverage as of the plan's effective date depends on how late the form is submitted. If the insurer does not have the form before the effective date, the employee is typically added to the plan on the date the form is received, if it is received within 31 days of the effective date. If the employee does not enroll within 31 days of becoming eligible, it is assumed that he or she has declined coverage. Insurers try to have employees return enrollment forms that note if they are actually declining coverage in order to protect themselves, and to ensure that no employee is inadvertently excluded from enrollment in the plan.

Q. 6:22 If an employee declines coverage initially, can he or she enroll at a later date?

For contributory plans, an employee who initially declines coverage, whether as of the initial effective date of the plan or as of his or her initial eligibility date (a new hire or an employee who becomes part of an eligible class after the initial plan effective date), must supply evidence of insurability in order to enroll in the plan later. Otherwise an employee could elect health care coverage only after he or she has been injured or becomes ill. This is known as adverse selection (or antiselection), and can significantly increase the cost of the medical plan beyond the anticipated levels. Even if an individual presents evidence of insurability that is acceptable to the insurer, most plans for smaller employers limit coverage for conditions that existed before the individual's enrollment date. Many states prohibit preexisting condition exclusions in plans beyond a certain size (in

New York, 300 employees) or specify a limited benefit for preexisting conditions, such as $5,000 in the first 12 months of coverage.

An exception is often negotiated to allow employees who originally declined contributory coverage due to other insurance through a spouse's employer to enroll without evidence of insurability within 31 days of involuntary loss of such coverage.

Q. 6:23 Is any kind of reenrollment of employees in group health insurance plans necessary?

Periodic reenrollment is desirable—even necessary. The employer's list of eligible participants needs regular updating, or the employer will be paying benefits for ineligible people. Employees come and go; dependent status changes; employees marry, divorce, and have children. All of these changes require updating of eligibility lists. A regularly scheduled reenrollment will minimize the chances of paying health benefits for someone who is ineligible or no longer eligible.

Other reasons for reenrollment include:

- Change of carrier;
- Change in benefits or cost to employees (required to reauthorize employee contributions);
- Annual HMO "crossover" (required); and
- Annual flexible benefit elections.

Even in noncontributory plans, periodic updates of employee and dependent information is advisable to assure continued eligibility and correct claims determination.

Billing

Q. 6:24 How are employers billed for group health insurance premiums?

There are two kinds of billing arrangements between employers and insurers for group health insurance premiums: self-accounting and home-office billing.

Self-accounting billing allows the employer to calculate premium due based on changes that have occurred since the last premium due date, such as employee additions and terminations. The insurer receives only a summary of the changes, rather than an itemized listing. Some insurers generate reminder bills for self-accounting employers, but these typically provide only a recap of the prior period's changes and premium.

Most large employers are required to use self-accounting billing because of the significant number of changes that are likely to occur from month to month. The insurer prefers not to keep track of employee additions, terminations, and status changes (e.g., addition of dependents). Further, most large companies have sophisticated payroll systems that can produce monthly reports with changes automatically translated into changes in premium, making it unnecessary for the insurer to do this work.

Smaller employers that elect home-office accounting (also known as roster or list billing) are required to submit individual changes in insured status to the insurer so that accurate bills can be generated from the insurance company's home office. For example, when a new employee is hired and completes an enrollment form, the form is submitted to the insurer, and the insurer establishes a file on that employee, thereby increasing the required monthly premium. A bill reflecting that will be produced for the coming period. The initial enrollment forms provide the insurer with the information required for computerized claims payment and billing.

As employers' electronic data-processing systems become more sophisticated, less billing will be done on paper. Compatible systems allow the employer to enter enrollment changes electronically by means of a modem. Employers can also transfer premium over the phone from the employer's bank account to the insurer or claims administrator.

Q. 6:25 Where can an employer get help in calculating premium payments?

A service representative of the insurance company located in one of the insurer's field offices can be contacted by phone.

Some insurers provide their policyholders with the name of their billing representative in the home office.

Q. 6:26 If an employer's premium payment is late, does coverage lapse?

Generally, policyholders have 31 days from the premium due date to remit the premium. However, if the insurer does not receive the premium by that date, the coverage usually is not canceled immediately. Instead, the insurer attempts to collect the premium by sending late notices and then a formal cancellation notice, assuming, until proven otherwise, that the employer wants to maintain coverage. Insurance companies have different time requirements and procedures regarding late premium payment.

Usually the employer pays the late premium, and the policy remains in force. If the insurer has made it clear when the premium must be paid to avoid policy termination, and the employer still does not remit the premium, the policy will be terminated.

Reinstatement of a terminated policy is not automatic upon payment of the late premium; an insurer may offer revised premium rates as a condition of reinstatement or may want to ascertain whether large life or health claims have been incurred. The insurer may refuse to reinstate coverage.

Q. 6:27 Does the insurer periodically audit employers that self-account?

Yes. Audits are done randomly or for employers that have requested help to solve a significant billing problem. The audits are performed in order to ensure that the employer is adhering to the administrative requirements of the plan, especially with respect to enrollment of employees and premium payment.

Proper enrollment of employees is crucial to claims payment. The administrator must understand when employees can be enrolled with and without evidence of insurability, when coverage becomes effective, and when premium payments must start in order to ensure coverage. Audits help the insurer understand what needs to be more clearly explained to administrators and identifies employers that may be having problems.

Claims

Q. 6:28 How does an individual submit a claim for payment?

Certain information regarding the medical expense must be provided to the insurer or the third-party administrator (TPA) for review. This can be communicated on a claims form or electronically, depending on the provider's and insurer's or administrator's procedures. The majority of private insurers require that the insured obtain a claims form from the employer, have the provider complete information about the care provided, and then submit it for payment. This is known as a "direct claim" because the employer does not become involved in certifying eligibility; the claim goes directly from employee to insurer/administrator. Of course, the insurer/administrator must be continually updated regarding enrollment changes.

Some employers require that an insured request a form from the benefits administrator, who certifies eligibility by signing the form before it is provided to the employee. The insurer does not ascertain eligibility for these insureds, since the employer has already done so. Few employers today use the "policyholder cert" approach, although it is effective in limiting claims by ineligible individuals.

Some plans require no claims forms for employees. For example, an employee may present a card to the health care provider. The provider submits charges directly to the insurer/administrator for services rendered. Usually, the card shows what coverage the employee has, and the provider knows what fees/services are eligible. Sometimes services for which there is only partial coverage are provided. In that case, the insured is billed for the balance.

Plan Implementation and Administration   Q. 6:31

Q. 6:29 Can employees submit claims after the effective date of the plan but before they receive their certificates of insurance?

Yes. Claims for medical care received after the plan effective date (other than those resulting from a preexisting condition not covered by the plan) can be submitted and paid as soon as the underwriter approves the policy and the enrollment information is filed at the home office of the insurer.

Q. 6:30 Do most individuals pay the health care provider for the service and receive reimbursement later from the plan?

Individuals either pay providers at the time of service and receive reimbursement later or "assign benefits" to the provider, thus avoiding payment at the time of service. (The practice of assigning benefits originated to assure payment for services rendered; some insureds requested reimbursement from the insurer but did not pay the provider with the money they received, thus creating cash-flow and bad-debt problems for the providers.)

Today, hospitals usually accept assignment upon the showing of evidence of coverage, but it is becoming rare for physicians and other health care professionals to do so. Most individual providers require payment by the insured at the time of service. This eliminates bookkeeping for the provider because the claims forms are submitted by the insured, although the insured must usually get an explanation of the service rendered and a signature from the provider in order for the claim to be paid by the insurer. It also improves the provider's cash flow.

Q. 6:31 What is assignment of benefits?

The insured authorizes the insurance company to pay any benefits directly to the provider of medical care, rather than to the insured.

Q. 6:32   Where can an employee get help in completing a claims form?

The employer's benefits administrator can usually help employees, but many insurers can also provide assistance. A toll-free number is sometimes provided by the insurer for benefits questions.

Q. 6:33   Can employees determine whether a claim will be paid before they receive the medical care?

This is a prudent practice, and one that is becoming more widespread due to changes in benefits programs that leave some expenses uncovered.

Although a preclaims review is an excellent idea, employees are always cautioned by the insurer that the actual claim determines what will finally be paid. General statements regarding coverage can be made, but until the actual claim is submitted, eligibility is ascertained, and the claim circumstances are reviewed, neither the insurer nor the insured can be absolutely sure that certain expenses will be covered.

One of the advantages of utilization review programs is that the employee is informed, prior to incurring an expense, how many days of hospital confinement (if any) will be covered and whether elective surgery will be considered medically necessary and eligible for reimbursement.

Most insurers/administrators will give information regarding eligibility, but will not provide estimates of "reasonable and customary" charges.

Q. 6:34   How quickly are insureds reimbursed for their claims expenses?

Claims turnaround time varies by insurer from several days to several months. The information an insurer requires in order to determine reimbursement is sometimes detailed and comes from various sources. Providers are sometimes asked to provide addi-

Plan Implementation and Administration Q. 6:37

tional information when the claims form is completed improperly or the reasons for the procedures and charges are unclear. If benefits are to be coordinated with other insurance programs, information from other insurers must be requested in order to determine each insurer's payment.

Q. 6:35 How rapidly should an employer or union expect claims to be processed?

Processing time can vary considerably, but a good rule of thumb is that about 90% of claims should be turned around within 10 working days. Some claims will be delayed due to processing difficulties; some will require investigation or additional information from the provider; others will be incomplete. Nevertheless, about 98% of all claims should be processed within 30 calendar days.

For cash-flow purposes, slower turnaround can be desirable. This can be accommodated under self-funded arrangements, but generally not under insured programs.

Q. 6:36 Who receives the benefits check?

The employee normally receives the payment. If reimbursement is for a service received by a dependent, the insured (the employee) still receives the payment unless it has been assigned. Some employers prefer to receive the checks from the insurer and distribute them to employees. If the employee has assigned benefits to a provider, the provider is paid directly. An explanation of benefits (EOB) accompanies the check.

Q. 6:37 What is an explanation of benefits?

An explanation of benefits (EOB) summarizes how a reimbursement was determined. It usually includes the services provided, the providers involved, the date of the care, and an explanation of what services were covered or not covered. If payment is made directly to a provider, a facsimile of the check is often provided to the insured, with an EOB. Due to improvements in claims systems, EOBs now provide year-to-date information regarding deductibles, maximums, and coordination of benefits "bank" amounts. Many administrators include the name of the person who processed the claim to improve customer service. Typically, the EOB material also explains how the claims appeal process works. ERISA requires this explanation whenever a claim is denied.

Q. 6:38 Why would an employee appeal a claims determination?

An employee may disagree with all or part of the payment calculation or the denial of certain charges as covered expenses.

Q. 6:39 How does an employee appeal a claims determination?

ERISA regulations establish and define the appeal process for both insurer and employee. Generally, by law, the claimant can be required to complete reasonable forms for the insurer. Claimants have at least 60 days to appeal claims, and the insurer or plan administrator must answer the appeal within 60 days. If a claim is denied, the insured must be provided with a written explanation of the reasons for the denial and references to the policy provision on which the denial is based. This procedure is followed for initial claims denial as well as for an appeal denial.

Renewals, Changes, and Termination of Coverage

Q. 6:40 How does an employer renew its health insurance policy?

The insurer assumes that the policyholder wants to renew its policy and maintain the same plan design unless it hears differently from the employer's intermediary. Thus, policy renewal can be as simple as the insurer rerating the group to determine a premium rate for the coming policy period (typically a year) and sending the notice of the renewal rate to the policyholder or intermediary.

Small employers whose policies are manually rated have little or no opportunity to negotiate premium. Unless they request a plan change, such as an increase in deductible or the addition of utilization review service, the coverage will remain in force as it has been, although the rate may change. If the insurer does not have an up-to-date employee census, the employer will be asked to submit one three months before the policy anniversary date, so that a new policy rate may be calculated. A notice must be sent to the policyholder before the policy anniversary date, based on the contractual agreement regarding the timing required for premium changes.

For employers with more than 50 covered employees, the renewal process usually involves an analysis of the policy period's claims in order to develop the experience-rated portion of the rate. For more complicated policies, such as collectively bargained groups and flexible benefits, the renewal process involves more negotiation on benefits and rates, and the process must start earlier.

Q. 6:41 When can an employer change its coverage?

Plan changes can be made at any time, given the insurer's approval. The employer discusses needs with the intermediary, and a request is made to the insurer for the change in premium that would result from a change in coverage.

The insurer can make plan changes for the employer at any time, but the most common point is coincident with renewal. Typically, the underwriter develops a renewal rate based on the in-force plan, and then calculates a different rate based on the proposed changes. Often, the request for a plan change follows an underwriter's premium rate change notice. In recent years, the rates for most policies have increased, even when claims experience has been good, because of the trend component. Thus, employers have been looking for plan changes that will decrease their rates.

Q. 6:42 What kinds of changes do employers make at renewal?

Recently, the most common changes have been changes from a base plus plan to a comprehensive plan, increases in deductibles and coinsurance, and the implementation of other cost-management provisions. (See Chapter 7.)

Q. 6:43 When the policy is renewed, are all employees automatically covered?

Only employees who have previously enrolled are automatically covered. Others, known as "late enrollees," have to submit evidence of insurability.

Q. 6:44 If an employer believes that a renewal rate is too high, what options are available?

The intermediary can attempt to negotiate a decrease in the renewal rate or get quotes from other carriers.

Q. 6:45 What kinds of plan changes might an employer want to make during the plan year?

An employer might want to implement cost-management provisions in the middle of a plan year due to concern that the renewal rate will call for a large increase. Employers that are going through significant organizational changes or experiencing economic difficulties may choose to make changes immediately, rather than waiting for renewal.

Q. 6:46 Can an employer terminate coverage in the middle of a plan year?

Yes, but the employer will be held responsible for all premiums due and unpaid up to the official termination date. The request for termination must be in writing and dated prior to the requested termination date. Some Blue Cross contracts permit termination only upon anniversary.

Q. 6:47 If an employer terminates coverage, what protection do employees have against medical expenses?

Normally, there is no gap in coverage for employees. If an employer terminates coverage, another insurer has usually been lined up to pick up the protection as of the minute the other coverage is terminated.

Q. 6:48 If an employee is not actively at work on the date the new coverage takes effect, will he or she be covered?

Employees who are on vacation or who are on a leave of absence are usually covered administratively, but this provision varies by insurer. Protection for employees who are not at work because they are disabled varies by state and by insurer. Some states require that the new insurer guarantee coverage for employees who were insured under a prior plan. Some insurers provide continuation of coverage for disabled employees even if the employer's state (situs of the policy) does not require this. "Continuity of coverage" and "preexisting conditions limitations" provisions should be carefully reviewed before changing insurance carriers.

Terminated Employees

Q. 6:49 If an employee terminates employment, what protection does he or she have against medical expenses?

Some states require continuation of coverage for a certain period. Otherwise, those who terminate employment, either involuntarily or voluntarily, become insured under a new employer's plan, elect a conversion policy from the previous employer's insurer, or elect to continue coverage under COBRA.

Q. 6:50 What is a conversion privilege?

Individuals insured under a group plan (in most policies, they must have been insured for at least three months) can convert to an individual policy without evidence of insurability. Individuals eligible for similar group coverage under another plan offered by the same employer and those aged 65 or older are typically not allowed to convert. Coverage is available to the employee as well as to his or her dependents.

The individual often has several plans to choose from, but rarely do these options include a plan that provides benefits similar to those of the group plan. The actual plans available are those normally issued by an insurer in the state in which the terminated employee resides. Most states require specific benefits offerings and policy forms.

For an additional premium, self-funded employers may purchase the conversion privilege from either the life insurance carrier or the carrier that provides stop-loss insurance. Fully self-funded plans with no stop-loss insurance are not required to offer conversion, since they are not subject to state insurance laws.

Q. 6:51 How does COBRA affect the group coverage conversion privilege?

Many employees and their dependents are eligible for COBRA continuation coverage and elect this rather than a traditional conversion policy, which is probably more expensive and offers less coverage (see below). Nevertheless, some people will not be eligible for COBRA, and some conversion policies will continue to be necessary.

Q. 6:52 What are the conversion requirements for other group plans?

Similar to group health plans and depending on the state of issue, life insurance plans are required to offer conversion options upon termination of coverage. Many long-term disability and accidental death plans offer conversion privileges as well.

Continuation of Coverage: COBRA

Q. 6:53 What is COBRA?

The Consolidated Omnibus Budget Reconciliation Act of 1985 (COBRA) is a federal budget measure that includes a requirement for mandatory continuation of health benefits coverage for certain employees and their dependents who would otherwise lose their group health plan eligibility. Briefly, COBRA requires employers to make health care plans available to former employees and qualifying family members. These plans are to be made available for periods ranging from 18 to 36 months. The legislation specifies rates, coverage, qualifying events, eligible individuals, notification requirements, and payment terms.

The law has since been amended for technical corrections by the Tax Reform Act of 1986 (TRA '86), the Omnibus Budget Reconciliation Act of 1986 (OBRA), the Technical and Miscellaneous Revenue Act of 1988 (TAMRA) and most recently by the Omnibus Budget Reconciliation Act of 1989 (OBRA '89). Proposed Treasury regulations relating to COBRA were released on June 15, 1987.

Q. 6:54 Where are the coverage continuation requirements incorporated into federal law?

COBRA added Section 162(k) to the Internal Revenue Code and amended the Employee Retirement Income Security Act of 1974 (ERISA) and the Public Health Service Act, which covers state and local employees. Although many of the provisions discussed in the questions that follow also apply to public employers, answers are intended to address the issues from the perspective of private employers.

Q. 6:55 What new terminology is added to the employee benefits lexicon?

Understanding the following terms should help in understanding COBRA:

- *COBRA continuation coverage.* Group health plan coverage that must be offered to an employee or dependent of that employee in the event of a qualifying event, such as termination of employment or divorce.
- *Qualified beneficiary.* Any individual who, on the day before the qualifying event, is covered under the group health plan maintained by the employer of a covered employee. Covered individuals include a covered employee, the spouse of a covered employee, and the dependent child of a covered employee.
- *Qualifying event.* An event that triggers protection under the provisions of COBRA. These events include death of the employee, termination of employment, reduction of work hours, divorce, legal separation, or a dependent child ceasing to meet dependency requirements.
- *Section 162(k).* Refers to the applicable section of the Internal Revenue Code that was established by this legislation.
- *Core coverage.* All of the health coverage that a qualified individual was receiving immediately before a qualifying event (other than dental or vision care).
- *Noncore coverage.* Dental and vision care.
- *Applicable premium.* The premium that the qualified beneficiary must pay. The law merely requires that the continuation coverage be made available at the same benefits level as of the day before the qualifying event, and on the same basis as available to other employees. The rate cannot exceed 102% of the "cost."
- *Notification statements.* The employer and plan administrator must notify qualified beneficiaries of their eligibility. These notification statements must be disseminated when a plan becomes subject to COBRA (for example, a new plan), when an employee becomes eligible, or when a qualified beneficiary becomes eligible because of a qualifying event.

- *Notification period.* There are different notification rules for different qualifying events. If the event is death, termination of employment, or reduction in hours worked, the employer must notify the plan administrator within 30 days. If the event is legal separation, divorce, or a dependent child ceasing to be eligible, the employee must notify the plan administrator within 60 days. The plan administrator in turn must notify the qualified beneficiary within 14 days. The individual has 60 days in which to elect continuation coverage or forfeit eligibility. In the event that notification is late, the individual has 60 days from the date of the notice.

Q. 6:56 What is COBRA continuation coverage?

When a designated qualifying event occurs, qualified beneficiaries must be offered the opportunity to continue with the same core group health coverage that they had immediately before the qualifying event. This coverage must be available at no higher than 102% of what the employer group plan costs. This provision does not apply to qualified beneficiaries for whom the qualifying event will not result in any immediate or deferred loss of coverage.

The coverage must not differ in any way from the benefits offered immediately prior to the qualifying event. If the coverage differs, the plan is not in compliance with COBRA regulations. In addition, the continuation coverage must not have an evidence-of-insurability condition.

Q. 6:57 What is the definition of employer?

For all practical purposes, any employing entity is an employer under COBRA, except businesses with fewer than 20 employees. (See Internal Revenue Code Sections 414(b), 414(c), 414(m), and 414(o) for more information on the definition of employer.)

Q. 6:58 What is a small employer plan?

A small employer plan is a group health plan maintained by one or more employers that normally employed fewer than 20 employees during the preceding calendar year. Each employer maintaining the plan will, in combination with all other employing entities under common control with that employer, be considered a single employer. This latter provision discourages organizational ploys to get around the COBRA provisions. With regard to the limits on the number of employees, an employer is considered to have normally employed fewer than 20 employees if it had fewer than that number working at least 50% of its working days.

For purposes of the small-employer exception, growth and acquisitions are treated differently. For example, if one employer acquires another, resulting in more than 20 employees, COBRA applies immediately. In the case of normal growth, COBRA applies on the first day of the calendar year following the one in which the company no longer meets the size requirement. Specifically, if an employer ceases to meet the definition of small employer because the business acquires a company with 20 or more employees (according to the law's definition), the plan is no longer exempt from COBRA, and Section 162(k) becomes effective right away. On the other hand, if a company ceases to be a small employer because it adds employees and no longer meets the size exclusion, COBRA also applies, but not until the beginning of the next calendar year.

Q. 6:59 How is a group health plan defined?

Any medical plan maintained by an employer to provide care to the company's employees, former employees, or their family members is a group health plan. This definition applies whether the services are provided through insurance, directly provided, or directly reimbursed; it also applies to cafeteria or flexible benefits plans. Insurance includes group insurance or individual policies that are arrangements to provide medical care to two or more employees.

The definition of medical care includes the diagnosis, cure, treatment, mitigation, or prevention of disease or related undertakings, and covers transportation primarily for and essential to medical care. Anything that is merely beneficial to general health or well-being is excluded. Some examples may help clarify this point. In general, wellness and health promotion programs are excluded, and medical treatment is included. Employee fitness programs are excluded, while employee assistance programs (EAPs) meet the medical definition and are included. Swimming pools and fitness and exercise facilities may further good health generally, but they do not relieve or alleviate medical problems; therefore, they do not constitute medical care. Moreover, they are available to all employees, regardless of health. In-house medical facilities and EAPs address particular medical problems and are considered group health plans for purposes of this law, but first-aid facilities are excluded.

Q. 6:60 Are any group health plans excluded from COBRA?

Three specific group health plans are excluded from the provisions of COBRA: (1) small employer plans, (2) church plans, and (3) federal government plans. Some government plans are controlled by similar requirements added to the Public Health Service Act by COBRA. These provisions are administered by the federal Department of Health and Human Services.

Q. 6:61 What are qualifying events?

The following are qualifying events:

- Death of a covered employee;
- Termination or reduction in hours of a covered employee (other than for gross misconduct);
- Divorce or legal separation of a covered employee from the employee's spouse; and
- A dependent child ceasing to be dependent under plan provisions.

The Omnibus Budget Reconciliation Act of 1986 (OBRA) added employer bankruptcy as a qualifying event for COBRA continuation coverage.

Basically, an event that causes a qualified beneficiary (employee, spouse, or dependent child) to lose coverage under the plan is a qualifying event. Coverage cannot be reduced or eliminated in anticipation of a qualifying event. If it is, this change is disregarded in deciding whether the event causes a loss of coverage.

A voluntary termination of employment remains a qualifying event. With the exception of gross misconduct, the circumstances connected with a termination or reduction in work hours are irrelevant. It does not matter whether the employee was discharged or left voluntarily. Layoffs, strikes, and walkouts are all qualifying events if they result in a loss of coverage. The only restrictions are that the plan must be subject to COBRA, and the event cannot occur before the effective dates of the IRC Section 162 regulations.

Q. 6:62 What is the definition of a COBRA covered employee?

A COBRA covered employee is any individual who is (or was formerly) covered under a group health plan subject to COBRA on the date of a qualifying event. For example, a retiree or former employee covered under a plan is considered a covered employee for COBRA purposes if the original coverage was the result of that employment relationship. The individual actually has to be covered—not merely eligible for coverage.

There are other categories of COBRA covered employees: self-employed individuals defined under IRC Section 401(c), agents and independent contractors, and directors of the company. Here again, they have to be covered under the group health plan as a result of their relationship with the employer, and the plan or some other plan of the employer has to cover common-law employees of the employer.

OBRA 1989 provided clarification of the definition of a covered employee and includes any one who was covered under an employer's plan as a result of "performance of services . . . for one or more persons maintaining the plan." Contractors and consultants would be entitled to continuation coverage for plan years beginning in 1990.

Q. 6:63 Who is a qualified beneficiary?

Any individual who, on the day before a qualifying event, is covered under the group health plan maintained by the employer of a covered employee is a qualified beneficiary. Covered individuals include a covered employee, the spouse of a covered employee, and the dependent child of a covered employee.

An individual is not a qualified beneficiary if, on the day before a qualifying event, he or she:

1. Is covered under the group health plan through someone else's election of COBRA continuation coverage and is not a qualified beneficiary himself or herself by reason of a prior qualifying event; or
2. Is entitled to Medicare benefits under Title XVIII of the Social Security Act.

Moreover, an individual is not a qualified beneficiary if he or she obtains what would normally be qualifying status at a later date. This provision applies to newborn children, adopted children, and spouses who later join the family of a qualified individual.

OBRA expanded COBRA's definition of qualified beneficiary by including any covered employee who retired at any time before he or she suffered a substantial elimination of coverage attributable to the employer's bankruptcy (retiree) and, in the case of a retiree who died prior to the commencement of bankruptcy proceedings, his or her surviving spouse, if the surviving spouse was a beneficiary under the plan on the day before bankruptcy proceedings commenced (qualifying surviving spouse).

Q. 6:64   What is core coverage?

Core coverage is all the group health coverage that a qualified beneficiary was receiving under the group health plan immediately before a qualifying event, except for dental and vision care.

Q. 6:65   What is noncore coverage?

Coverage for dental and vision care is noncore coverage.

Q. 6:66   Can a group health plan require a qualified beneficiary to elect continuation coverage?

The individual always has the right to elect or decline coverage. Moreover, a qualified beneficiary who wishes to receive continuation coverage does not have to elect all of the continuation coverage if core and noncore coverage are offered separately.

Q. 6:67   What are the options available to a qualified beneficiary?

Each qualified beneficiary (employee, former employee, spouse, or dependent child) may elect core coverage, noncore coverage, or no coverage at all. If a plan provides noncore coverage but no core coverage, then the individual must be offered the opportunity to continue the noncore plan.

In cases in which the applicable premium for core coverage would be at least 95% of the applicable premium for core and noncore coverage, the plan may include dental and vision care in core coverage. In those instances, COBRA requires employees to take the entire coverage (or none at all).

Q. 6:68   Can a qualified beneficiary choose to cover individuals who join the family on or after the date of the qualifying event?

If the plan covering the qualified beneficiary provides that such new family members (newborns, adopted children, or new spouses) of active employees can be covered before the next open-enrollment period, then the same right must be extended to the new family members of a qualified beneficiary.

A retiree who is eligible for continuation due to employer bankruptcy may elect continued coverage for himself or herself as well as a spouse and any dependent children, provided the spouse and dependent children were beneficiaries under the plan on the day before bankruptcy proceedings commenced.

Q. 6:69 What is the election period (that is, the minimum time period) in which a qualified beneficiary may decide to take COBRA continuation coverage?

Separate notification rules apply for different qualifying events. In the event of death, termination of employment, reduction in hours of work, or Medicare eligibility, the employer must notify the plan administrator within 30 days. In the event of legal separation, divorce, or a dependent child losing eligibility, the employee must notify the plan administrator within 60 days. The plan administrator must, in turn, notify the individual within 14 days. The qualified beneficiary has 60 days to elect continuation coverage or forfeit eligibility. If the notification process is late, then the individual has 60 days from the date of actual notification.

If coverage normally continues after termination (many plans continue coverage until the end of the month or longer), then the individual has 60 days from the end of the coverage period. Separate notification must be given to the spouses of employees. (Notice to the employee is not considered adequate notification to the spouse or child.) Notice to the spouse is considered to be adequate notice to all qualified beneficiaries who live with the spouse. Notice must be given in writing and sent to the qualified beneficiary's last known address. The election period must begin on or before the date that the qualified beneficiary would lose coverage because of the qualifying event.

OBRA 1989 permits employers, at their option, to commence the time periods for notification and coverage duration on the date employer coverage ends if it is later than the actual date of the qualifying event.

Q. 6:70 Must a covered employee or other qualified beneficiary inform the employer or plan administrator when a qualifying event occurs?

Both the employer/plan administrator and the employee/qualified beneficiary have responsibilities under the COBRA provisions. Generally, the employer or benefits plan administrator must determine when a qualifying event occurs. On the other hand, each qualified beneficiary is responsible for notifying the employer/administrator of certain qualifying events, which include: a dependent child ceasing to be dependent, divorce, or legal separation. If appropriate notice is not sent, the otherwise qualified beneficiary would lose coverage. Notice must be sent within 60 days after the date of the qualifying event or 60 days after the date that the eligible person would lose coverage.

Multi-employer plans may extend the notification periods beyond what is required by COBRA as part of the plan itself. Further, the plan administrator may make the determination that a qualifying event has occurred without notice from the employer in the case of reduction of work hours or termination of employment.

Q. 6:71 Can each qualified beneficiary make his or her own election under the continuation-of-coverage provisions?

Each qualified beneficiary must be offered the opportunity to make an independent election to receive continuation coverage and, if applicable, an election to receive only core coverage or to switch to another group health plan during an open-enrollment period.

There is an exception to this provision. If any qualified beneficiary makes an election to provide another qualified beneficiary with continuation coverage, that election is binding. Examples include an election on behalf of a minor child by a parent or legal guardian, or an election made on behalf of a qualified beneficiary who is incapacitated or who dies before making an election (in which cases, election can be made by the legal

Plan Implementation and Administration   Q. 6:75

representative of the individual or the estate, under applicable state law, or by the spouse of the qualified beneficiary).

Q. 6:72 Who pays for COBRA continuation coverage?

The qualified beneficiary pays for coverage. COBRA is not free coverage or a new government benefit. Rather, it is an opportunity to continue health care coverage at group rates instead of prohibitively expensive individual rates. COBRA is also a bridge benefit that helps individuals through a transitional period.

Q. 6:73 How much does the qualified beneficiary pay?

During any initial period of continuation coverage, a group health plan can require a qualified beneficiary to pay an amount that does not exceed 102% of the applicable premium. The applicable premium is essentially the cost of the plan. The extra 2% is to cover administrative expenses.

Premiums for extended continuation coverage during total disability may be increased from 102% of cost to 150% of cost for the period of coverage following the initial 18-month period.

Q. 6:74 Can the premium amount be increased?

The payment can be increased if the applicable premium increases. However, the applicable premium must be fixed for each "determination period" before the period begins. A determination period is any 12-month period selected by the plan, as long as that period is applied consistently from year to year.

Q. 6:75 Are installment payments permitted?

The group health plan must allow a qualified beneficiary to pay for continuation coverage in monthly installments. The individual can be given the option of paying less frequently—

quarterly, semiannually, or annually—but a monthly payment option must be available.

Q. 6:76 What deductibles apply to COBRA continuation coverage?

Qualified beneficiaries electing continuation coverage under COBRA are generally subject to the same deductibles as active employees. For individuals whose continuation coverage begins before the end of a deductible period, credit for expenses already incurred is retained.

Example: An employee who is covered on a calendar-year basis has accumulated $75 toward a $150 annual deductible by June. She leaves the company and becomes eligible for COBRA continuation coverage. Later in the year, after electing to continue coverage under COBRA provisions, this person incurs another $75 in covered services. At this point, the person has satisfied the deductible.

If the plan deductible is calculated separately for each individual receiving coverage, each person's remaining deductible on the date continuation coverage begins is carried forward—that is, credit toward deductibles is retained. In general, deductibles must be handled in a manner consistent with the principles set forth in the federal regulations.

Aside from the deductibles, other plan limits apply in the same way to continuation coverage. This rule applies to limits such as number of hospital days, dollar amounts, copayments, and out-of-pocket catastrophic limits. It includes both annual and lifetime limits.

Q. 6:77 How long is coverage made available?

The COBRA continuation coverage provisions are designed to be a bridge benefit until the employee or family member can obtain other coverage or employment. Consequently, employers are required to make continuation coverage available for a specified period of time. Except in cases where the beneficiary is totally disabled on the day of the qualifying event, the maximum period of coverage is 18 months for employee termination or reduction in hours and 36 months for all other qualifying events (divorce, legal separation, death, the covered and minor children's change in status).

A retiree or qualifying surviving spouse is entitled to continued coverage until the earliest of:

- The retiree's or qualifying surviving spouse's death;
- The retiree's or qualifying spouse's failure to make timely premium payments; or
- The employer's ceasing to provide any group health plan to any employee.

Eligibility for Medicare coverage does not terminate entitlement to continued coverage in this situation.

A retiree, spouse, surviving spouse, or dependent child who is entitled to continued coverage and who becomes covered under another plan ceases to be entitled to continued coverage.

Q. 6:78 What happens upon the death of a retiree or surviving spouse?

If a retiree (see Question 6:91) dies after bankruptcy proceedings have commenced, his or her surviving spouse and dependent children are entitled to 36 months of continued coverage under COBRA's general rules (see Question 6:77).

Q. 6:79 How is continuation coverage handled in the event of disability?

OBRA 1989 extended the duration of continuation coverage from 18 months to up to 29 months for beneficiaries who are totally disabled, within the meaning of Social Security, on the day of the qualifying event.

Application for the extension must be made to the plan administrator during the initial continuation period. The beneficiary is responsible to apply to the Social Security Administration for disability determination and must inform the plan administrator of the response within 60 days of receipt. Coverage may be continued during an appeal of the Social Security determination of disability but terminates on the first of the month following 30 days after final Social Security denial of total disability.

Q. 6:80 When is the new disability provision effective?

The provision is effective for plan years beginning on or after November 22, 1989. Therefore, a disabled beneficiary whose initial continuation coverage commenced in a prior plan year could apply for extension as long as the notice to the plan administrator was provided after the new provision became effective but before the end of the initial 18-month continuation period.

Q. 6:81 Are there other factors that might result in an earlier termination of coverage?

Yes. There are several disqualifying events that can result in an earlier termination of coverage. The dates of these events include:
- The first day for which timely premium payment is not made;
- The date on which the employer ceases to maintain any group health plan (including any successor plan);
- The first date after the date of election on which the qualified beneficiary is covered under any other group health plan not maintained by the employer, even if that coverage is less valuable except that OBRA 1989 provides that coverage will not terminate if the new plan contains a pre-existing condition limitation; and
- The date that the qualified beneficiary is entitled to Medicare coverage.

Q. 6:82 Why did OBRA 1989 change the duration of continuation coverage?

Originally, continuation coverage ended when a beneficiary became covered under another employer's plan, as an employee or otherwise. This caused serious inequities and recently resulted in a court decision that an employee who was covered by his spouse's employer's plan when he terminated employment was nevertheless entitled to COBRA continuation (*Oakley v. City of Longmont*).

Q. 6:83 When did the new provision regarding other coverage take effect?

This provision is generally effective for qualifying events which occur after December 31, 1989. However, the rule applies to those who first elected COBRA coverage after December 31, 1988 "for the period for which the required premium was paid or was attempted to be paid but was rejected as such."

Q. 6:84 What is meant by timely payment?

A timely payment is made to the plan within 45 days of the date of election. OBRA 1989 provided the clarification that the 45 day period begins on the date of the initial election, not the qualification or notification date. For ongoing coverage, payment must be made within 30 days of the due date.

Q. 6:85 Does a qualified beneficiary have the right to convert to an individual policy when COBRA continuation coverage ceases?

If such a conversion option is available to active employees, the same option must be made available to qualified beneficiaries within a 180-day period ending on the last day of the maximum continuation period (18 or 36 months). If continuation coverage ceases for any reason other than the expiration of the maximum continuation period, conversion need not be offered.

Q. 6:86 Can a qualified beneficiary defer coverage?

No. The individual has 60 days from the date of losing coverage to inform the plan administrator that he or she wants to continue coverage. Payment applies to the period beginning with the date of eligibility (the first day after coverage would have been lost under the employer's group plan because of a qualifying event).

Q. 6:87 Does COBRA have a specific impact on flexible benefits programs?

Yes. COBRA requirements apply only to medical benefits that an individual has actually chosen to receive. Although the provision of medical care through a Section 125 cafeteria plan or other flexible benefits plan is subject to COBRA standards and does constitute a group health plan, continuation coverage is required only if the covered individual has actually selected some form of coverage.

> **Example:** Employee A has selected an HMO, Employee B has selected an indemnity plan, and Employee C has not elected health care coverage. Each of them would be offered continuation coverage consistent with his or her choice. For Employees A and B, if there is an open-enrollment period during the continuation period, they would also have the option of changing coverage just as if they were active employees.
>
> This means that A could switch from the HMO to the indemnity plan or stay with the HMO. Employee B could stay with the indemnity plan or switch to the HMO. Employee C would continue to be ineligible.

Q. 6:88 Does COBRA supersede state continuation requirements?

No. State continuation requirements may be met by means of COBRA coverage, but when state requirements are more generous, the most generous coverage must be offered.

Q. 6:89 Does state continuation extend the maximum COBRA continuation period?

No. The two periods are considered to run concurrently. However, COBRA continuation may terminate before the state requirement is satisfied, in which case the longer period is observed.

Q. 6:90 What is the effective date for the COBRA requirements?

For noncollectively bargained plans that are not excepted (i.e., that are not small employer plans, church plans, or certain government plans), the provisions apply on the first day of the first plan year beginning on or after July 1, 1986.

For nonexcepted collectively bargained plans, the provisions apply as of the first day of the first plan year beginning on the later of January 1, 1987, or the date on which the last collective bargaining agreement terminates.

Q. 6:91 How is a collectively bargained plan defined?

A collectively bargained group health plan is one covering employees and former employees and their families who are subject to a collective bargaining agreement entered into between employee representatives and one or more employers. If an arrangement that would otherwise be a single plan covers individuals under a collective bargaining agreement as well as individuals not subject to the agreement, the plan is treated as two separate plans for the sake of effective dates.

Q. 6:92 What sanctions are imposed if a group health plan fails to comply with COBRA?

Originally, COBRA penalized companies that failed to comply by disallowing certain company tax deductions and the income exclusion for certain highly compensated employees. TAMRA amendments in 1988 substantially revised COBRA penalties.

In general, effective on the first day of an employer's tax year, failure to satisfy the requirements of COBRA results in an excise tax of $100 a day for each day of noncompliance, assessed separately with respect to each qualified beneficiary. The penalty is limited to $200 a day when a violation applies to several members of an immediate family.

The noncompliance period begins on the date COBRA failure first occurs and ends on the earlier of the date the failure is corrected or six months after the last date the employer could have been required to provide COBRA coverage to the qualified beneficiary (assuming required premiums were paid).

For plans other than multiemployer plans, except in cases of willful neglect, the maximum excise tax penalty for all failures during a tax year is the lesser of (1) $500,000 or (2) 10% of the employer's liability for group health plans during the preceding tax year.

The noncompliance period will not start on the first day of COBRA failure under the following special circumstances:

- *Inadvertent failure.* IRS must be satisfied that the employer, exercising reasonable diligence, did not know or would not have known that a failure took place. The noncompliance period commences when a person responsible for COBRA knows, or should have known, of the failure. (The person is deemed to know the law.)
- *30-day grace period.* If a COBRA failure is due to reasonable cause and not willful neglect and is corrected within 30 days of the failure, the excise tax will generally not apply.

Q. 6:93 Are there any unresolved issues with regard to COBRA?

Yes, IRS has yet to issue a methodology for calculating the "applicable premium." There are numerous ways to determine the premium, and even the term "premium" is a misnomer for many plans that are self-insured.

More seriously, OBRA 1989 apparently erred with respect to the maximum period of continuation coverage in the event of multiple qualifying events. Previously, the maximum period of coverage for all qualifying events was 36 months from the date of the initial qualifying event (except for retirees in the event of bankruptcy). In what is believed to be an error, OBRA 1989 *adds* 36 months for dependents of an employee who becomes eligible for Medicare subsequent to another qualifying event i.e., termination of employment.

Computerized Administration

Q. 6:94 What role do computer systems play in managing health plans?

Even when significant portions of the administrative job are performed by insurers or third-party administrators, computers are still extremely useful in helping the employer perform those functions that it must do, or those that it elects to do. These functions include:

- Gathering data;
- Performing nondiscrimination tests;
- Tracking flexible benefits credits;
- Administering COBRA benefits;
- Tracking costs and utilization;
- Preparing management reports;
- Preparing employee statements; and
- Providing interactive communication with employees.

The ultimate responsibility for assembling most of the necessary data (the "input") for almost all of these administrative functions falls on the employer. This includes personal data on the employee and dependents, eligibility data, compensation, contributions, plan option choices, and claims filed.

Q. 6:95 What role would a computer system play in performing nondiscrimination testing?

Actually performing the nondiscrimination tests (see Chapter 11) is difficult enough; getting ready to do so can be even more demanding. One of the most difficult aspects of nondiscrimination testing is "categorizing." Employees must be categorized and tracked according to their status. Categories include:

- Highly compensated versus nonhighly compensated, and key versus nonkey employees;
- Ineligible, eligible, and participating employees; and
- Employees in separate lines of business.

Nor are these categories static. An employee who falls into one category one year may fall into another in another year, either because the definitions change (e.g., a cost-of-living adjustment in compensation criteria for highly compensated employees) or because the employee's circumstances change.

For employers with significant numbers of employees and/or plan options, the only way of keeping all this information current and accurate is by means of a system that accepts data from the personnel recordkeeping system and has been programmed to assign everyone to the proper slots.

Q. 6:96 What sorts of features should a COBRA administration system have?

A system for administering COBRA should be able to:

- Produce notices and form letters for qualified beneficiares;
- Calculate premium amounts and prepare billing notices;
- Keep track of qualified beneficiaries, their payment records, and status;
- Keep track of all transactions, producing an auditable report; and
- Generate management reports.

It should also be accompanied by a manual that summarizes

Plan Implementation and Administration   Q. 6:98

COBRA rules for ready reference, keying legal requirements to menu items in the system.

Q. 6:97 How would a computer help in administering flexible benefits plans?

The more options available in a flexible benefits plan—including the option to change one's mind from time to time—the more data that has to be managed. A computer flex system can:

- Determine and communicate costs of various options to the employee and the company;
- Calculate premiums due to insurers;
- Monitor individual accounts, including contributions or credits, and charges against those accounts;
- Prepare employee statements of account balances; and
- Monitor the nondiscrimination requirements that apply to flex plans, with respect to both overall requirements and each underlying benefit.

A listing of flex systems is available from the Employers Council on Flexible Compensation.

Q. 6:98 What types of computer communications programs are available?

There are several types of communications programs available:

1. Statements and correspondence systems. These can be used to provide customized employee benefits statements and letters that incorporate individualized employee information in a more standardized format. Although such systems are often subroutines of broader administrative systems, stand-alone systems are also available.
2. Financial projection systems. These assist the employee in selecting options by providing summaries of other benefits for which he or she is eligible.

3. Interactive programs. These can tap into plan and compensation databases to provide an employee with information on his or her current status and benefits eligibility, project future benefits/costs, and permit the employee to engage in "what if" scenarios. Although these systems are generally more common in financial security-type plans (e.g., pensions), as compensation and benefits decisions become more closely interwoven (especially with flexible benefits plans), they may become more important in making welfare benefit decisions as well.

Q. 6:99 In buying or leasing an administrative computer system, what other features should a plan sponsor look for?

All systems arrive with potential, but that is no guarantee that the user will derive any value from them. To avoid a costly mistake, potential systems buyers should look for:

1. A free trial period or money-back guarantee;
2. A formal training period for personnel;
3. Systems and software support, especially when the system must interact with other systems—someone must be sure they are all properly connected;
4. A complete set of user documentation (i.e., a manual);
5. Phone support for answers to questions; and
6. An ongoing service contract that provides for updates as laws or any other external factors that influence the system's operation change.

Prior to purchase, a visit to a seasoned user of the system to gauge user friendliness, as well as the quality of the support, is advised.

Chapter 7

Managing Health Insurance Costs

As health insurance costs have increased in recent years, insurers and plan sponsors have redesigned their plans to include cost-containment features. This chapter explores the reasons behind rising health care costs and explains some of these cost-containment features and how they work.

Q. 7:1 What factors are responsible for rising health insurance costs?

There are two broad interrelated factors that have resulted in rising health insurance costs: the rising cost of health care services and an increase in the frequency of claims. The proliferation of new medical technologies, inappropriate use of medical services, an oversupply of medical professionals and facilities, high malpractice insurance rates, overall inflation, a payment system that insulates individuals from the true cost of care, and programs such as Medicare and Medicaid that require the private sector to pick up more than its true share of the cost of health care (known as "cost shifting") have all contributed to rising health care costs and increased utilization. Thus, the problem is widespread, and each party involved in the delivery of, consumption of, and payment for health care has contributed significantly to unbridled cost increases.

Health care providers—physicians, allied health practitioners, and health care facilities—deliver a great deal of excellent, necessary medical care. They also provide unnecessary care, and they have been allowed to price the care after it has been purchased.

Until fairly recently, consumers have been insulated from the costs of medical care. Insurance encouraged people to "buy" care without regard for its price. Many believed they were entitled to the best medical care available, whatever the cost. Many people felt that they did not have to take responsibility for their health, and simply looked toward the doctors as experts.

Insurance arrangements through private insurers, Blue Cross/Blue Shield (BC/BS), government programs, and employers' self-funded plans insulated individuals from the cost of care. Expanding reimbursement parameters were demanded by powerful employee groups such as organized labor, and filtered to employees everywhere. Insurance companies, anxious to meet employers' and unions' demands, traditionally delivered coverage with few cost controls. Of course, this situation has changed quite dramatically over the past decade. Employees have begun to shoulder more of the cost burden, and society as a whole is beginning to take more responsibility for personal health.

Q. 7:2 Why haven't private insurance companies limited reimbursements to control cost increases?

When insurance companies have tried to limit reimbursement, individuals have been intolerant. For example, years ago, most health care plans covered a limited number of days of hospital care; patients with additional expenses were financially burdened. The demand for additional coverage was met by adding a major medical plan. More recently, an individual whose plan allowed only a specific dollar allowance for a certain surgical procedure was unhappy when the surgeon's charge exceeded that limit. Insurers responded to the demand for increased coverage by providing reasonable and customary (R&C) surgical reimbursement.

Attempts by insurers to market increased deductibles, coinsurance, and other benefits limitations have met with little positive response until recently. The demand has been for expanded coverage rather than for limits. Slowly, however, more limitations are being implemented by insurers, as a result of employers' demands for health insurance cost control.

Q. 7:3 Do Medicare and Medicaid limit reimbursements to achieve cost control?

Both programs have more limitations than private insurance or BC/BS coverage. Two kinds of reimbursement limitations—benefits restrictions and provider reimbursement restrictions—were intended to control costs, but have not.

The benefits restrictions limit the kinds of care and services that are covered. These are explained to insured individuals in their benefits booklets. The reimbursement restrictions are rules concerning the costs of care that Medicare and Medicaid will not recognize. That is, although coverage for an insured's hospital stay is provided by law, the hospital's charge for care cannot include the costs of:

- Bad debt and charity costs incurred in tracking patients who do not pay their bills;
- Some equity capital requirements associated with replacement and addition of facilities and equipment; and
- Teaching and research programs within the hospital.

The government did add a 2% load on the allowable charges to compensate for some of the reimbursement exclusions.

These government insurance programs also specify "reasonable" costs, similar to private insurers' R&C allowances, but the Medicare and Medicaid limits have become more conservative.

Q. 7:4 What is cost shifting?

Cost shifting is the term used to describe how one patient's health care is subsidized by the charges made to another for the same services. It occurs when the first patient's insurer has an arrangement, established by law or negotiation, that allows for reimbursement at less than the normal full charge. Medicare and

Medicaid are examples of cost-shifting arrangements created by law. Hospitals and physicians are faced with what they believe is less than adequate reimbursement for a large number of patients, which must be made up elsewhere. The providers shift costs to other patients, thus inflating the charges for the care delivered. BC/BS plans have created a similar situation through negotiation.

Q. 7:5 How do higher claims affect health insurance costs?

Health insurance premiums are based in part on the expected number and cost of claims that will be filed during a plan year. If the actual number and cost of claims exceed the expected level, the insurer will probably increase future premiums to reflect the higher claims experience.

Q. 7:6 Why do health care providers deliver unnecessary care?

Most physicians and other practitioners do not set out to provide unnecessary care to their patients. However, they—as well as the facilities they practice in—are encouraged to do so, because:

- Demand for care is not driven by price;
- Patients traditionally do not question treatment; and
- Care deemed unnecessary by one physician may be deemed appropriate by another.

It should not be surprising that when no one questions the price or the quantity of care provided, and the quality of care is subjective, more care, rather than less, is "bought" and "sold." In any market, increased demand increases price. In the health care market, price increases have not, until recently, resulted in a corresponding decrease in demand for services.

Q. 7:7 Why haven't consumers purchased less care, as prices have increased?

Insurance companies reimburse individuals for health care expenses with relatively few restrictions on the price of the care received. Although, in reality, consumers are the payors, they fail to see it that way because they continue to receive care while sharing little in the cost. Further, consumers feel entitled to medical care. An increase in price, even if passed directly to consumers, does not result in the same relative decrease in demand that occurs in simpler markets.

Q. 7:8 How can a small employer manage health insurance costs?

Many factors affecting the rising cost of health care are beyond the scope of the small employer. However, small employers can manage their health insurance costs in several ways:

- Work-site programs that encourage employees to improve their health and educate them on prudent and effective use of health care;
- Benefits plan designs that encourage cost-effective consumption of health care; and
- Arrangements with health care providers, generally through an insurer, that control the price and quantity of care provided.

Combining cost-management techniques is usually necessary. For example, if an educational program encourages employees to obtain periodic physical examinations, the health insurance plan should be adjusted to reimburse individuals for that. Arranging for physicals and tests to be provided at an agreed-upon price by a certain provider is one way to control the cost of this preventive care benefit.

Q. 7:9 How can employers determine what cost management is required?

To determine the appropriate cost-management programs, the employer must ascertain the specific problems that are causing the company's costs to rise. This involves analyzing the internal situation—an employer's own claims experience—as well as the external situation—the price and quality of care delivered by providers in the local area.

Insurers have developed management information systems and reporting and analysis services that can provide employers with many of these cost data. These automated systems also provide the information that will allow insurers to suggest plan redesign and work with employers for direct intervention with physicians and hospitals.

Q. 7:10 What plan features prevent illness and injury, thereby reducing costs in the long run?

Preventive care programs that pay for routine physical examinations and screening tests can help detect symptoms of illness early and prevent its progression. Individuals who take advantage of covered physicals and tests may learn to take better care of themselves, as their physicians educate them on proper wellness care or preventive care strategies.

Other wellness programs, such as lower back care and nutrition workshops, can prevent injury and illness or improve an already existing condition. Programs for weight control, substance abuse, and smoking cessation can significantly affect employees' health and the eventual cost of the employer's health care plan. Wellness features such as fitness courses (on site or at a local facility) or health club memberships are gaining popularity.

Many employers provide their employees with periodic health risk appraisals (HRAs) to help increase awareness and, over the long term, change employees' health-related behaviors in the hope that healthier employees (and their dependents) will result in higher morale and lower claims costs. (HRAs are explained more fully at Questions 11:26–11:29.)

Employers subsidize, in whole or in part, the cost of such programs either directly (cash payment) or indirectly by waiving deductibles or reducing premium contributions. The net cost of providing a wellness program is generally minimal. The view is that gains from increased productivity, reduced absenteeism, and reduced utilization of medical care will, in the long run, offset the cost if not exceed it. Although many employers make this claim, there are very few hard data to support it. Nevertheless, such programs are an essential component of a long-term cost-management program.

Health Care Data

Q. 7:11 Why have health data become an integral part of many employers' cost-management programs?

Health cost management is highly complex. There are many alternative cost-containment solutions, and employers are trying to sort out the most effective approaches from among many competing options. Hard data provide a decision support framework. Specifically, good data can help pinpoint the problem areas and the extent of the problems. In essence, managers have an opportunity to focus their efforts. Rather than trying to implement several solutions without any idea which are most needed and will have the greatest impact, they can predict with some certainty the likely results of particular health cost management programs.

Q. 7:12 Why are employer-specific data helpful?

Employer-specific data can help a company focus its cost-management strategies. For example, data may reveal the need for a smoking cessation program at one plant and an employee assistance program (EAP) at another. Both programs may not be needed at both plants. Or data may indicate that an HMO is working well at one plant while it is causing a problem with adverse selection at another. Comparisons of hospital admission rates among divisions may spur local managers to greater action than a general call for action at the corporate level.

A corporation can use health utilization and cost data to determine plan design modification needs, develop collective bargaining positions, select the right level of deductible and/or copayment, understand the operation of the health care system, educate employees and managers, evaluate insurance carriers and other plan administrators, evaluate the impact of plan changes

Q. 7:13 Health Insurance Answer Book

and cost-control measures, select HMOs and PPOs, and identify the need for particular wellness programs.

Q. 7:13 What kinds of data are useful to better manage health care costs?

Useful data include several years of claims experience, presenting such detail as charges and allowed payments, broken down by diagnosis and health care provider. However, unless an employer's claims volume is very high for specific conditions and for specific providers, conclusions may be inaccurate. Employers with fewer than 100 employees cannot rely on claims experience to indicate conclusively what type of cost management is appropriate. This is why insurers offer many standard cost-controlling plan design features, even if specific claims problems are not clear.

For employers with fewer than 500 employees, conclusions about providers based on just their own claims analysis can also be dangerous. Additional data regarding provider practice patterns are necessary. These can be obtained from the employer's insurer, third-party administrator (TPA), or local employer coalition.

Historically, insurance carriers have furnished companies with two types of data: reports on claims experience and employee coverage information. More recently, interest has developed with regard to claims cost and benefits utilization levels. The following utilization indicators are very helpful:

- Hospital inpatient days per year per 1,000 employees and dependents;
- Hospital admission rate;
- Average length of hospital stay;
- Number of inpatient and outpatient surgeries; and
- Number of outpatient visits per year per person.

In addition, the following cost measures are relevant:

- Total annual payments;

- Average annual cost per employee;
- Total charges;
- Total payments after adjustments;
- Total hospital inpatient payments;
- Total surgical payments; and
- Total out-of-hospital payments.

Q. 7:14 Are there any resources available to assist employers in gathering and using data?

Employer coalitions are groups of employers that have joined together primarily for purposes of gathering and sharing data on health care. Although the establishment of a useful health care database was initially the chief priority, coalitions have been instrumental in applying pressure to gain the release of data historically withheld by providers and HMOs.

Today, coalitions in 42 states and the District of Columbia are actively addressing issues in health care such as mandated benefits, quality assurance, and delivery systems.

Q. 7:15 Who participates in health care coalitions?

Although primarily made up of local business firms, coalitions include as members and advisors various provider representatives (medical society, hospital association), consumer organizations, health systems agencies, and insurers. Most function on a county or regional basis, although a dozen large cities are serviced by their own coalitions. All provide member education through publications, workshops, and seminars.

Q. 7:16 How can existing health care coalitions be located?

The American Hospital Association, Office of Health Coalitions and Private Sector Initiatives, publishes The Directory of Health Care Coalitions in the United States. Contact:

Q. 7:17   Health Insurance Answer Book

> American Hospital Association
> 840 North Lake Shore Drive
> Chicago, Illinois 60611
> 312-280-6000

Q. 7:17 What kinds of plan design features should employers implement, even without conclusive data on problems?

Several specific actions can be taken to help manage costs, such as implementing plan features that:

- Prevent illness and injury;
- Increase cost sharing by employees; and
- Encourage utilization of the most cost-effective care.

Cost-Sharing Strategies

Q. 7:18 How can a plan increase cost sharing by employees?

A cost-sharing increase does not, as used in this question, refer to an increase in the employees' contributions to premium, although some employers have found this necessary in recent years. Here, cost sharing refers to increases in the individual's cost when he or she consumes health care.

The simplest cost sharing is achieved through implementation of or increases in deductibles and coinsurance percentages. For example, base–plus plans may be changed to comprehensive plans to implement deductibles and coinsurance on all health care expenses. Employers can implement deductible amounts ranging from $100 to $1,000 (or even higher) per individual per calendar year. Special deductibles for certain kinds of care, or for care related to one illness or injury, may also be applied, and deductibles may be based on employees' earnings.

Q. 7:19 What are typical deductibles?

According to the U.S. Department of Labor, the most common deductible is between $100 and $149 per individual per year.

Surveys of nonunion employees, however, indicate that deductibles of $200 or more are widespread. Many employers have increased deductible amounts and/or added separate deductibles for specific services, such as inpatient hospital confinements. For example, an employer that wants employees to stay out of the hospital whenever possible may require that a hospital-admission deductible be added to the plan. This may be in addition to the regular $200 deductible.

An employer that adds a preventive care benefit to the plan may waive the regular annual deductible on that care to encourage employees to use it. The deductible may also be waived on outpatient services such as surgery and home health care to provide a financial incentive for their use. Conversely, an additional deductible may be required for unnecessary emergency room visits.

Deductibles based on earnings may be achieved by use of a schedule or a formula percentage amount. For example, employees earning less than $20,000 a year may be subject to a $200 deductible; employees earning $20,000 to $40,000 a year, $300; and employees earning more than $40,000, $400. Or each employee may have his or her own deductible, figured as 1% or 1 1/2% of salary, to a maximum of $600. This adds complexity to the plan, and may cause dissatisfaction among the more highly paid employees. However, it does provide an equitable way to control costs that takes into account an individual's ability to pay.

Q. 7:20 What are typical coinsurance percentages?

Coinsurance percentages on both major medical and comprehensive plans are usually 20% for the employee, 80% for the employer. Some have changed to a 25%/75% split, or have decreased the employee's share when certain kinds of care are received. For example, a visit to an outpatient surgical center may be paid at 90% by the insurance company, while a hospital visit would be paid at 80%. Most plans limit the amount of coinsurance or out-of-pocket cost to an employee, typically $1,000 to $2,000 (20% of $5,000 and $10,000) per individual and twice the amount per family.

Q. 7:21 What effect do increased deductibles and coinsurance have on utilization?

A now famous study by the Rand Corporation demonstrated that although increased cost sharing decreased both inpatient and outpatient utilization, it did not prevent anyone, except the very poor, from seeking necessary care. And, except for the very poor, it had no impact on health.

Q. 7:22 What is a front-end deductible?

A front-end deductible is a deductible that must be satisfied before any covered health insurance expense will be reimbursed. It is also commonly called a first-dollar deductible and is included in a "purely" comprehensive health insurance plan.

Q. 7:23 Do all comprehensive plans have front-end deductibles?

Some comprehensive plans do not require a front-end deductible for all covered health care expenses. Such plans most often have a full-pay hospital provision under which no deductible is required for reimbursement of hospital expenses. The employee, however, would have to satisfy the deductible before being reimbursed for any other covered health care expenses.

This type of plan design can encourage unnecessary hospitalization because care as an inpatient is financially advantageous. However, this can be controlled by also including a preauthorization review feature for all hospital confinements.

Q. 7:24 Would increases in required employee contributions toward premium help control costs?

There is a school of thought that believes employees who are asked to contribute more to health care coverage will feel more entitled to care, and may be less likely to be concerned about the cost and the quantity of care they purchase. However, if an increase in employee contributions is suggested to employees as a likelihood (if costs are not controlled soon), employees may be more responsive to benefit redesign as the alternative.

Some employers have not increased required employee contributions *per se*, but have offered employees choices in coverage by giving them a certain amount of benefits money to "spend" in order to purchase various insurance benefits. These plans, called cafeteria plans or flexible benefits plans, usually result in employees being more aware of the costs of care, because they themselves have made the decision about where to spend their benefits dollars and have elected medical coverage with increased deductibles and coinsurances. Further, some employers include a medical reimbursement account in their cafeteria plans. These accounts allow individuals to place money into the account through payroll deductions (on a pretax basis) to be used for medical care not covered by the health insurance plan. The money is perceived as their own money, and they usually spend it more wisely. It serves as a cushion that makes employees more comfortable with the idea of selecting a medical care plan with a higher deductible. (See Chapter 9 for a more detailed discussion of flexible benefits.)

Q. 7:25 Should employers that do not now require employee contributions for health care coverage introduce them?

Yes. The majority of two-adult households are also two wage-earner households, with nearly universal access to health coverage through employment. A husband and wife with both a contributory and a noncontributory health plan available to them will certainly opt for the plan that does not cost them to join. Therefore, claims that would have been submitted to the other employer now become the full liability of the employer with the noncontributory plan. Such plans allow other employers to shift costs, and the only solution is to act defensively by structuring plans to balance or reverse the situation. Some employers "give" employees the money to make the contribution, since the intent is not to collect from employees, but to prevent selection.

Despite contributions, employees may choose to be covered by both available plans, resulting in overinsurance and, in all likelihood, overutilization as well. The level of contributions as well as reduced combined payments under the alternative coordination of benefits approach described at Question 7:29 should act as disincentives to overinsurance.

Q. 7:26 How can health care plans be designed to encourage use of the most cost-effective care?

Traditionally, coinsurance provisions have been the only incentive for individuals to seek less expensive care. However, their effectiveness is limited. Many individuals equate expensive care with quality care, and more care with better care. Physicians have encouraged "Cadillac" care because there was no incentive for them to recommend otherwise, for patients with insurance. As costs have increased, more effective cost-management features have been developed, including coordination of benefits, outpatient surgery coverage, preadmission testing, second surgical opinion programs, extended care facility coverage, home health care, hospital bill audit, and hospice care.

Coordination of Benefits

Q. 7:27 What is coordination of benefits?

Coordination of benefits (COB) provisions were developed during the 1950s to eliminate the potential for employees to obtain dual reimbursement for medical expenses when they had multiple coverage. Without COB, an individual might receive more than 100% of the cost for medical care. For example, assume that an employee has an 80/20 copay plan, and her spouse also has an 80/20 copay plan. She has a claim, and her employer pays 80% of the bill. She might collect another 80% under her husband's plan if there were no coordination provision. This results in a 60% profit on the medical service. At a time of high health care costs, this kind of windfall is no longer affordable.

Q. 7:28 How does COB help manage claims costs?

COB is a process by which insurers that cover the same individual for similar kinds of health care expenses coordinate their payments so that the insured is reimbursed for no more than the amount of the expense. When a claim is submitted and the insured is entitled to benefits for the same expense from more than one source, the benefits are coordinated among insurers. The employee usually cannot receive coverage for more than 100% of health care expenses. COB was initiated years ago, due to the rapid increase in overinsurance. COB saves between 4% and 9% in claims costs. Standard COB provisions are included automatically in almost all group health care plans.

Q. 7:29 What is maintenance of benefits?

Many employers are using a new COB approach called maintenance of benefits (MOB), which limits the total reimbursement from all sources to the amount one plan would have paid in the absence of other coverage. The objective is to pay in total only what the most generous of the plans would normally pay.

Under this approach, employees with coverage under two plans do not receive 100% reimbursement. For example, if an employee has an 80/20 copay plan and his spouse has a similar plan with her employer, he could collect the 80% from his employer but not an additional 20% from his wife's company plan as he would be able to do under COB. Using another example, if the spousal plan had a 90/10 copay, and the employee's plan had an 80/20 copay feature, he could collect 80% from his plan and another 10% from the spouse's plan.

MOB, also called "nonduplication," is approved by the National Association of Insurance Commissioners (NAIC) and is included in most self-funded plans. It is becoming the norm in COB administration in insured plans as well, because it discourages duplicate coverage.

Q. 7:30 What is the birthday rule?

Some changes over the last couple of years have been made in the male/female rule with respect to payment for dependent children. Historically, the plan of the father was considered primary. However, with a new awareness of fairness and a climate of nondiscrimination, NAIC has developed guidelines to eliminate any appearance of discrimination. When a child is covered by both parents under either the same company plan or two different company plans, the primary plan will be the plan of the parent whose birthdate falls earlier in the year.

Q. 7:31 What has been the effect of the new birthday rule with respect to dependent children?

Although the intention was to distribute the cost of providing coverage for dependent children, companies with high female populations will see costs rise as much as 25%, with a corresponding decrease in heavily male groups. This has resulted in a movement toward self-funding by groups such as hospitals, which have traditionally preferred less risk. By self-funding in certain states, the gender rule for determining order of benefits payment can be retained.

Q. 7:32 Have companies tried any other COB innovations?

As health cost management becomes increasingly important, companies are experimenting with all sorts of innovative approaches. Some companies are requiring COB against a spousal plan even if the spouse does not participate in the plan. Mere eligibility for the plan triggers coordination. This is called coordination with a "phantom plan," prohibited in many states.

When the wife and husband work for the same employer, the company might not pay both an employee benefit and a spousal benefit. Each can collect as an employee, but cannot collect in both capacities.

In an effort to avoid duplicate coverage, J. C. Penney went all the way to the U.S. Supreme Court to win the right to deny dependent coverage to an employee who was not the head of household or the highest paid earner in a family. Other employers have conditioned dependent coverage on lack of availability of any other group coverage.

Outpatient Surgery/Preadmission Testing

Q. 7:33 Does outpatient surgery coverage help control costs?

Outpatient surgery coverage helps reduce hospital admissions for procedures that can be performed safely in the outpatient department, in a freestanding surgicenter, or even in a doctor's office. These alternatives usually cost less. To encourage use of such alternatives, some plans provide better payment for outpatient surgery than they do for inpatient care. For example, the plan may waive the deductible for a surgicenter procedure or pay the bill at 100% instead of 80%. It is ironic that base–plus major medical plans have made payment on exactly the opposite basis for years.

As more and more plans implement hospital preauthorization programs, differentials in benefits levels for inpatient and outpatient surgery become unnecessary, since utilization management, not benefits incentives, determines the most cost-efficient setting for care.

When a utilization review (UR) program is in place that directs employees to use outpatient facilities when appropriate, it is not cost-effective to reimburse such expenses at a higher coinsurance level, since it is not optional. The plan will not pay for unnecessary inpatient care, but pays regular plan benefits for appropriate alternatives. Therefore, previous plan design must be considered when adding UR.

Q. 7:34 What is preadmission testing and how does it control costs?

Preadmission testing (PAT) results in shorter hospital stays. X-rays, lab tests, and examinations are done before the individual's hospital admission. Reimbursement is sometimes made on a more generous basis, such as at 100% payment or with no deductible, to encourage PAT.

Previously, health insurance encouraged hospital admission for diagnostic tests by covering the days needed to perform the tests. Patients supposedly could become acclimated to the hospital before treatment, and doctors, as well as patients, sometimes found early admission more convenient; hospitals also wanted to keep their beds filled. But times have changed. Technological advances have made testing safe and efficient on an outpatient basis; people are becoming accustomed to treatment without acclimation; and the costs involved in longer-than-necessary stays are of more concern than the convenience. Preauthorization programs require outpatient PAT, and as more and more states move to diagnosis-related group (DRG) reimbursement, the hospitals themselves have incentives to shorten stays by testing prior to admission.

When a UR program is in place, PAT on an outpatient basis is mandatory. In DRG states, such as New York, New Jersey, Connecticut, and Maryland, PAT is demanded by the hospitals themselves to keep the length of stay and charges below the DRG limits.

Second Surgical Opinions

Q. 7:35 What is a second surgical opinion program?

Second surgical opinion (SSO) programs encourage individuals to have a second evaluation of a medical condition for which elective surgery has been recommended. The kinds of surgery for which SSOs are especially suggested, because there is evidence they are often performed unnecessarily, include:

- Adenoidectomy—removal of adenoids;
- Bunionectomy—removal of bunion (on the foot);
- Cataract extraction—removal of lens from eye;
- Cholecystectomy—removal of gallbladder;

- Coronary bypass—open-heart surgery;
- Excision of neuroma—removal of tumor of nerve fibers;
- Gastrectomy—removal of a portion of the stomach;
- Hemorrhoidectomy—removal of hemorrhoid;
- Herniorrhaphy—repair of hernia;
- Hip surgery;
- Hysterectomy—removal of uterus;
- Knee surgery;
- Laminectomy—removal of intervertebral disc of spine;
- Ligation and stripping of varicose veins—tying and removal of varicose veins of leg;
- Mammaplasty—plastic surgery on breasts;
- Menisectomy—removal of semilunar cartilage of knee joint;
- Myringotomy—incision into tympanic membrane of ear to drain fluid;
- Ocular muscle surgery for strabismus;
- Oophorectomy—removal of ovaries;
- Prostatectomy—removal of prostate;
- Reattachment of retina;
- Submucous resection—removal of submucous membrane from nasal septum;
- Thyroidectomy—removal of thyroid gland;
- Tonsillectomy—removal of tonsils; and
- Tympanoplasty—surgical repair of eardrum.

The decision to elect or reject surgery still remains with the patient.

Insurance reimbursement for an SSO has been available through many plans for years, but it has only been in the last several years that the coverage has been highlighted. Some plans provide SSO coverage and require no deductible or coinsurance for an SSO, or even a third surgical opinion, if the first two disagree.

Q. 7:36 Which procedures should require second opinions?

Each insurance carrier or UR vendor uses a list, called a "focus list," of procedures that it considers to be the most appropriate. The lists vary by region due to different physician practice patterns.

Since most plans pay for the required second opinion (and related tests) in full, the cost of the program may outweigh the demonstrable savings from surgery avoided (although resulting in better medical care). With the widespread inclusion of UR programs, the need for focused lists has been questioned. The most cost-efficient programs now require a second opinion only when the clinical information suggests the probability of nonconfirmation. The UR vendor decides when an opinion is necessary, saving employees' time and the plan's resources.

Q. 7:37 What is the difference between self-referral and referral by an SSO panel?

Self-referral means that the original physician who recommended surgery refers the patient to another physician for the required second opinion. There are no restrictions on who can perform the second opinion consultation; for example, it can be the first physician's associate, someone in another specialty, or the assistant surgeon. Such self-referral programs are ineffective in achieving the goals of an SSO program and may actually add to plan costs.

Panel referral is the only method that will achieve both objectives of an SSO program—cost-effectiveness and quality medical care. With panel referral, the second opinion must be obtained from a select group of specialists who have agreed (1) to fixed fees for the consultation, (2) not to perform additional tests unless strictly necessary, and (3) not to perform the surgery. The patient is given a list of three or four physicians from which to choose, and the administrator of the panel (carrier or UR vendor) arranges the appointment and the reporting of the results

Q. 7:38 How do mandatory SSO programs work?

There are two types of mandatory SSO programs. The first requires only that an employee obtain a second opinion in order to receive regular plan benefits. Failure to obtain an opinion when required results in benefits reduction. Benefits may be reduced as little as 10%, or payment may be denied altogether, with a 50% cutback the norm. If the opinion does not confirm the need for surgery, the employee may still proceed without penalty.

The second type is called "mandatory-affirming" and requires that a second opinion (or third opinion, called a "tiebreaker") affirm the need for surgery. If no affirming opinion is obtained and surgery is elected, penalties apply.

When used in conjunction with preauthorization programs, second opinions are required on a case-by-case basis only when the clinical information suggests the probability of nonconfirmation. This approach is more cost-effective than spending $150 to $500 (including additional testing) to review all surgery on a certain list.

Some employers are uncomfortable with programs that inhibit their employees' free choice or penalize them for choosing a certain type of care. Certain states, such as New York, do not permit programs that reduce benefits unless a confirming opinion is obtained, although reduction is permitted for failure to obtain a second opinion. Studies have shown that second opinion programs that leave the choice of physician for the second opinion entirely up to employees are not as effective as programs that require employees to choose a consultant from a list of physicians provided by an SSO panel (see Question 7:37). The panel approach, combined with a preauthorization program that determines necessity for a second opinion, is the acknowledged state of the art today.

Utilization Review and Case Management

Q. 7:39 What is utilization review?

A process called utilization review (UR) has been implemented by some insurers and employers in recent years. It evaluates the appropriateness, necessity, and quality of health care provided at various stages in its delivery. Although this feature is technically a part of health insurance plan design, it is different in that it analyzes whether the care prescribed and delivered is justifiable and appropriate. Other cost-management plan design features encourage cost-effective use of care, rather than try to manage care on an individual basis.

Q. 7:40 How does UR work?

UR offers some control over providers' decisions on what care to provide, and allows for retrospective review of care provided to uncover aberrant practice patterns among physicians. For years, insurance companies have retrospectively reviewed claims in order to catch charges or services that were inappropriate. UR is peer review—doctors analyzing other doctors' care—and some of it is done before or during delivery of care.

Employers can obtain UR services directly from a UR organization, through a broker or TPA, or through the insurer. Numerous review companies are available to choose from, but their services are similar. The services usually focus on hospital review, but some UR agencies provide review of outpatient surgery, treatment of mental illness, and long-term care. The hospital review services usually consist of:

- Preadmission certification;
- Concurrent review with discharge planning; and
- Retrospective review.

Q. 7:41 Has UR grown in recent years?

Yes. New forms of UR have appeared, and more employers, unions, and insurers have introduced UR as an important part of their cost-management and quality-improvement efforts. Utilization control is usually used in conjunction with utilization review.

Q. 7:42 What are the new kinds of utilization review and control?

There are several techniques in use, including:
- Individual case management;
- Preadmission certification;
- Second opinions—medical and surgical;
- Hospital discharge planning;
- Retrospective review and audit; and
- Specialized review for specific services (mental health, podiatric, chiropractic).

Q. 7:43 What is individual case management?

Individual case management (ICM) is a special form of utilization control used with high-cost cases. These cases include:
- Cardiovascular disease;
- Cancer;
- Strokes;
- AIDS;
- Severe traumatic injury;
- Degenerative neurological disease; and
- Long-term psychiatric cases.

Early involvement in any potentially high-cost case is essential to achieve loss control and optimum treatment for the patient. This is the essence of ICM—early involvement by specially trained utilization reviewers or case managers.

Q. 7:44 How does ICM work?

Trained reviewers, usually registered nurses with extensive discharge planning experience and specialized clinical experience, monitor catastrophic cases during the acute hospitalization phase. At a very early stage, they begin to develop a long-term treatment plan to achieve the most efficient use of medical resources and the best patient outcome. These case workers may recommend alternatives to lengthy hospitalization such as home care, hospice care, rehabilitation services, skilled nursing facilities, or other options; they may also contact the employer regarding early return to work or required job modification. Family counseling may be involved. The process involves flexibility geared toward what is best for the patient and what will be the most efficient use of resources.

Q. 7:45 Is hospital discharge planning different from ICM?

Yes. Discharge planning may be used with any hospitalization rather than with only catastrophic cases. Discharge planning is used to ensure that the patient stays in the hospital only as long as is medically necessary, and that once the patient is discharged, any ongoing care is appropriate. The process may include a recommendation that the patient leave the hospital for home care, nursing home care, skilled nursing facility care, rehabilitation services, or other treatment.

Q. 7:46 How does preadmission certification work?

An employer that elects UR for its health plan explains to employees and their dependents that before any nonemergency hospital admission, the individual will be expected to contact the UR organization, or the medical care review agent, to obtain preadmission certification. The medical review agent will analyze the situation prior to the prescribed surgery or hospital stay. This watchdog function stimulates the attending physician to prescribe necessary, cost-efficient care and, when questioned, to justify surgical procedures or hospital stays with clear evidence of patient need. Failure by the insured to initiate the process usually results in reduced payment for treatment even if it would have been certified if reviewed. Emergency admissions are to be reported for review usually within 48 hours of admission.

This idea is not new: In the 1950s, several unions asked medical societies to help them conserve dollars in their health and welfare funds by reviewing health care services received by their members. Medicare spawned foundations for medical care (FMCs) in the early 1960s, and later, 200 professional standards review organizations (PSROs) were created to provide review of all federally financed patient care in acute care hospitals, with plans to extend review to long-term care and ambulatory care services in later years. Recently, private insurers have incorporated UR into their benefits services.

An individual contemplating a hospital admission may not have any contact with the medical review agent after the first call or letter. The agent often deals directly with the attending physician in order to get a clear understanding of the reasons for the admission. The agent confirms the need for the admission; suggests an alternative setting, such as an outpatient facility; or suggests that the surgery or treatment is inappropriate, and that an alternative be explored. A second surgical opinion may be requested. In any situation in which an intake nurse reviews the plan of care and does not agree with it, he or she passes the case to a doctor, who then attempts to reach an agreement with the attending physician as to the appropriate care. If the two physicians disagree, usually a second UR physician reviews the plan of care. If the UR organization still disagrees with the patient's physician after that second review, and the patient goes ahead with the admission, the employer's insurer will either pay the claim as usual or reduce the benefit percentage. The course of action depends on the arrangement agreed upon when UR is implemented as part of the insurance plan. Employees receive materials explaining the claims payment implication involved before the UR process takes effect.

The review process is fully documented, and the information is provided to the insurer as well as the attending physician and the patient. Most often, the hospital admission is approved and the person is admitted as planned. The review process then continues with concurrent review.

Q. 7:47 If hospital admissions are usually certified, why is UR necessary?

Although it is difficult to prove, it appears that UR has a sentinel effect on physicians. That is, physicians who are told by their patients that the hospital admission must be precertified are more likely to suggest an alternative to hospitalization if there is one. Except in states where hospital payments are based on DRGs, the length of stay is often shorter with UR.

Q. 7:48 What happens during concurrent review?

Patients' care is monitored while they are in the hospital. The UR organization may send a nurse on site or communicate with the physician or physician's assistant by telephone to keep abreast of the length of the stay. Less frequently, other procedures and services are audited. Concurrent review is aimed at getting the patient out of the hospital as quickly as possible, with due regard to patient safety.

Patients are often kept an extra day or two even though they can be discharged safely if home care or extended care at a more appropriate facility can be arranged. Concurrent review allows the discharge planning process to begin as soon as possible after the patient is admitted. Some hospitals have been slow to discharge privately insured patients because they subsidize other patients' hospital stays. It has also been easier for a physician to decide to keep a patient than to risk the repercussions if a patient is sent home too early. Malpractice suits remind physicians to practice conservatively.

Q. 7:49 How does retrospective review help manage claims costs?

The UR organization typically provides the insurer (or large employer) with periodic reports on physicians' practice patterns and hospitals' length-of-stay averages. In areas where there are several providers to choose from, the providers that consistently deliver cost-effective care can be identified, and insureds can be channeled to them. In regions with only one hospital and a handful of doctors, discussions can at least be opened with that institution and those physicians to review patterns of care. Information that will help alter practice patterns may be a sensitive issue, but such discussions are being held frequently, as insurers and employers pursue cost management.

Q. 7:50 Do the cost savings produced by UR justify the additional expense for the UR service?

Experience of plans that have had UR in effect long enough to evaluate indicates that savings exceed the cost, resulting in a 3% to 10% reduction in overall premium. Actual cost savings depend on the state (DRG states typically have control of length of stay; UR savings are attributable only to admission avoidance) and the degree of hospital overutilization that exists. Careful analysis of utilization data is necessary to determine the potential savings.

Without a special communication effort, employees will not use the program as intended and savings will inadvertently result from penalties. A review of the source of UR savings is essential in determining the effectiveness of the program.

Additional Cost-Management Strategies

Q. 7:51 Does coverage for extended care facilities and home health care help an employer manage health care costs?

The average cost for a day in a hospital varies from region to region and hospital to hospital, but it is almost always higher than for a day in an extended care facility. Many individuals can recuperate just as quickly and safely at a skilled nursing center.

Home health care can be even less expensive. In addition, some patients find that recuperation at home is more comfortable and faster than in a hospital. Further, the possibility of contracting an infectious disease while in the hospital makes extended stays riskier than most people are aware of.

Q. 7:52 Does the addition of a hospice care benefit help manage claims costs?

Hospice care is palliative, intended to relieve pain or symptoms rather than actually cure disease. It is provided to individuals with diseases that are incurable or have progressed to untreatable stages. Most hospice care benefits pay for additional home care, hospice facility care, palliative drugs and therapy, family counseling, and respite for family members caring for the patient.

This care has been shown to cost much less than confinement in an acute care hospital, where many chronically ill individuals spend much of their last several months. Traditional health care plans cover expenses for necessary medical care, aimed at curing illness or injury. Technically speaking, hospice care does not cure disease; therefore, clear-cut contractual coverage for palliative care is necessary in order for insurers to cover hospice care expenses.

Q. 7:53 If an employer determines that plan design features alone will not manage costs sufficiently, what other options are available?

A wide variety of techniques other than plan design features have been implemented to reduce the cost of health insurance plans. The most common of these are educational programs, hospital audits, negotiated arrangements with health care providers, UR, and some form of self-funding.

Q. 7:54 How does education contribute toward health care cost control?

Some employers have undertaken massive communication campaigns to educate their employees on the prudent purchase of medical care. Insurers often provide educational material to help employees understand their health insurance plans, and sometimes they help run educational meetings. The message for cost control comes best from the employer; employees will not respond as well to an insurer that suggests they purchase less or less expensive health care when it is more appropriate. However, a plea by the president of a company may fall on receptive ears. Messages can be communicated quickly and effectively to smaller groups, and confusion can be dealt with immediately.

Q. 7:55 What is a hospital bill audit?

Hospital bill audits take two forms: audits done by an insurer or a professional bill review organization hired by the insurer, and audits by patients themselves. Professional bill audits involve retrospective review of all charges billed by a hospital, to ascertain whether all services for which charges are billed were delivered, and whether the charges are reasonable. Many hospital bills have errors, and insurers have found significant cost savings in questioning them. Audits are generally performed on larger bills, and the claimant and the hospital are put on notice that an audit is being performed, so that late payment is not an insured's problem.

Employee bill audits have been implemented recently at some companies. Employees are encouraged to review their own hospital bills, just as they would review car repair bills, before they pay them or submit them to their insurer for payment. Financial incentives help; some insurance companies will pay the person who discovers an error half of the amount of the billing error, up to a maximum amount per year. These programs may be worthwhile not only in helping insurance companies find billing errors, but also in educating individuals on the substantial costs of care.

Q. 7:56 How can negotiations with providers contribute toward cost management?

A more complex approach to cost management involves negotiations between insurance companies and health care providers. Large self-insured employers may become directly involved with providers, but most employers work through their insurers.

Preferred provider organizations (PPOs) are groups of health care providers—doctors, allied health practitioners, and hospitals—that contract with insurers (or large employers) to provide specified health care, sometimes at discount rates and always with strict utilization review. This contrasts with traditional insurance arrangements in which insurers did not negotiate prices with the providers; they simply paid the charges for the services performed in accordance with the contract. As has been discussed previously, both Blue Cross/Blue Shield (BC/BS) and Medicare/Medicaid negotiate price, to a degree, with providers. Recently, private insurers have also become involved with PPOs.

Typically, employers looking for cost management purchase a health care plan that gives employees an unlimited choice of health care providers, but when individuals use a "preferred provider," they are reimbursed at a more generous rate than they would have been had they been treated by a nonpreferred provider. Health care costs are managed for the employer in two ways: (1) the price for a plan that includes preferred providers is less expensive than one without, because the health care prices have been discounted; and (2) the preferred providers are contractually bound to give appropriate care. Utilization review is an integral part of preferred provider arrangements. (PPOs are discussed in detail in Chapter 8.

Billing Codes

Q. 7:57 What are medical billing codes?

Medical billing codes are complex billing systems required by Medicare and private insurers that assign a code number to each specific medical procedure.

One prominent coding system, Current Procedural Technology (CPT) was developed by the American Medical Association to categorize 7000 different medical procedures, each of which is represented by a 5-digit code.

The complexity of billing codes leads to incorrect billings, either as a result of ignorance of the correct code to apply, or as a result of deliberate manipulation of the coding system, or "code gaming".

Q. 7:58 Why do providers engage in code gaming?

Incorrect codes are deliberately used in billings generally either to increase the provider's income, or to qualify a patient for reimbursement for which he would be ineligible if the correct code were used.

Q. 7:59 What kinds of code gaming are there?

- *Upcoding (also known as "code creep").* This involves reclassifying or redefining a procedure so that it falls into a category which qualifies for a higher rate of reimbursement.
- *Exploding.* Itemizing a group of tests performed on the same specimen as individual procedures.
- *Unbundling.* Itemizing each step of a procedure and billing each separately, such as billing for the surgical incision as a procedure separate from an appendectomy.
- *Visit Churning.* Charging for the same visit more than once. For example, a doctor who meets a patient in the emergency room and accompanies him when he is admitted may bill the emergency room visit and inpatient time as separate visits.

Q. 7:60 What is a medical review organization?

A medical review organization assists in various claims management functions related to health care, disability workers compensation plans.

Q. 7:61 Why do employers hire medical review organizations?

Employers hire professional review organizations to:
- Control costs by managing the size of health care bills;
- Reduce the amount of work time lost through monitoring of treatment and return-to-work programs for the disabled; and
- Spread the liability for claims of bad faith in controlling the availbility of health care.

While some firms make promises as to the level of savings, there are rarely solid guarantees. Employers should require savings on the order of some multiple of expected charges for the services provided that is not less than $2 to $4 in savings for each dollar in fees. In order to establish the value of specific services rendered, comparisons of claims experience before and after professional review is critical.

Q. 7:62 What kinds of services do medical review organizations provide?

A full-service cost containment firm would be able to offer provider bill audits, utilization review, individual case management, and oversight of return-to-work programs. It should also maintain a claims experience data base to assist clients in determining utilization norms and costs per case norms.

Q. 7:63 How do medical cost-containment firms charge for their services?

While some services are provided on a time and expense basis, other billing arrangements may be tied to the actual amount of work performed, such as charge per line item audited, charge per bill audited or percentage of billings reviewed.

(These are discussed in more detail in Chapter 8.)

Chapter 8

Managed Health Care Systems: HMOs and PPOs

In the past decade, employers and other health care plan sponsors have experimented with a variety of methods to manage health care costs. One cost-management option available to employers is to completely reorganize the way in which their employees' health care services are provided and paid for. This chapter discusses managed health care delivery systems such as HMOs and PPOs.

Q. 8:1 How has the traditional reimbursement system in this country contributed to the escalating cost of health care?

Retrospective reimbursement guarantees revenue to doctors and hospitals. There are few financial incentives for providers to reduce the amount of care or to deliver it more efficiently; in most plans, payment and reimbursement are on a fee-for-service basis. More care generally means more revenue. Patients have allowed this to occur because they have been insulated from the cost of care through their insurance plans. There are minimal financial barriers to getting as much care as desired.

Broad insurance coverage encourages employees to use medical care with little regard for price. Demand for care does not drop as price increases, and insurance companies have passed along the costs of increased utilization and cost of care to employers in the form of premium rate increases.

Q. 8:2 How are insurers and providers merging their services?

Employers and their insurers—the government, Blue Cross/Blue Shield, and private insurers—all agree that too much money is being spent on health care. Insurers cannot simply restrict reimbursement and shift costs to insureds in order to reduce costs. Furthermore, providers—particularly hospitals—are experiencing decreasing demand for their services due to alternative care facilities and insurance plans that channel patients to the least expensive care sites. As a result, insurers have begun working with providers to reorganize the delivery of care. Providers and insurers are exchanging roles. Insurers are becoming involved in defining reimbursable health care, and providers are entering into risk-sharing and profit-sharing arrangements with insurance companies. Two well-defined models of integrated delivery systems are health maintenance organizations (HMOs) and preferred provider organizations (PPOs).

Health Maintenance Organizations

Q. 8:3 What is an HMO?

An HMO is an organization that provides comprehensive health care to a voluntarily enrolled population at a predetermined price. Members pay fixed, periodic (usually monthly) fees directly to the HMO and in return receive health care service as often as needed. This payment structure is known as "capitation."

HMO revenues increase only when enrollment increases, not when services increase. If monthly payments from members exceed the funds the HMO expends on care, the HMO profits. If revenues are less than the cost of care, the HMO loses.

Q. 8:4 When were HMOs developed?

Although HMOs have existed since 1929, the real impetus to their development came in 1970. It was then that the federal government, as part of its continual evaluation of the health care

Managed Health Care Systems: HMOs and PPOs Q. 8:6

delivery system, recognized that the concept of prepaid health plans might correct structural, inflationary problems with fee-for-service health care.

The government was impressed with the health care plan created by the Kaiser Aluminum Company. The plan was a combination insurer-provider for workers building the Grand Coulee Dam. The government was interested in the approach because Kaiser was providing its workers with quality health care for considerably less than it cost under traditional plans. The reduced costs were attributable in part to a decrease in utilization. The rate of hospitalization at that time was 349 days per 1,000 members per year, compared with a national average of 1,149 days per 1,000. The plan's emphasis on preventive care and its prepayment basis concept, which the government believed would encourage physicians to be more cost-conscious in their delivery of care, seemed to be working.

Congress later passed the HMO Act of 1973 to encourage the development of HMOs. It set requirements for federal qualification and provided for grants and loan guarantees for planning, development, and initial operating costs for those HMOs that met the qualifying standards. The Act also encouraged enrollment among a skeptical public by establishing criteria for HMOs seeking federal qualification. Only federally qualified HMOs are eligible for federal funding.

Q. 8:5 Who develops and sponsors HMOs?

HMOs have several different types of sponsors. Some have been developed and sponsored by employers and/or labor unions. Others have been started by medical schools, hospitals, or medical clinics. Some insurance companies have also been involved in establishing their own HMOs or have invested capital or in-kind expertise in existing or developing organizations.

Q. 8:6 How prevalent are HMOs?

According to InterStudy, there were 575 HMOs serving 33 million individuals at the beginning of 1990. Enrollment in

HMOs now accounts for about 14% of the health care market. Arthur D. Little, Inc., predicts that by 1995, HMO market share will increase to 25%–30% or more. Although membership and market share continue to increase, the actual number of HMOs continues to decrease. The number of terminating plans remained stable, but the number of new start-ups declined, resulting in a net loss. See the tables that follow for statistics on the number of HMO plans by state (top 10), the top 10 HMOs by size, and HMO enrollment and penetration by state (top 10 states).

HMO Plans: Top 10 States

State	Number of Plans
California	79
Texas	46
Florida	42
Ohio	41
Wisconsin	35
New York	34
Illinois	33
Pennsylvania	26
Colorado	24
Arizona	22

Source: American Medical Care and Review Association (AMCRA) Directory of HMOs (5410 Grosvenor Lane, Bethesda, MD 20814).

Top 10 HMOs by Size

Name	Enrollment	Age
Kaiser Foundation Health Plan/Northern California	2.2M	43
Kaiser Foundation Health Plan/Southern California	1.9M	43
Health Insurance Plan of Greater New York	870,000	41
HealthNet	630,000	9
HMO of Pennsylvania	510,000	12
Health Alliance Plan of Michigan	390,000	28
Harvard Community Health Plan	390,000	19
CIGNA Healthplans of California	380,000	59
Group Health Cooperative of Puget Sound	350,000	42
Kaiser Foundation Health Plan/Northwest	340,000	43

Source: InterStudy Edge, Volume II, 1989 (InterStudy, P.O. Box 458, Excelsior, MN 55331).

HMO Enrollment: Top 10 States

State	Enrollment
California	8.1M
New York	2.5M
Illinois	1.6M
Massachusetts	1.4M
Michigan	1.4M
Ohio	1.3M
Texas	1.2M
Florida	1.2M
Pennsylvania	1.2M
Wisconsin	1.0M

HMO Penetration: Top 10 States

State	% of Population in HMOs
District of Columbia	65.6
Guam	43.8
California	28.6
Massachusetts	24.0
Wisconsin	21.5
Oregon	21.3
Rhode Island	21.1
Hawaii	20.5
Colorado	19.1
Connecticut	19.1

Source: InterStudy Edge, Volume II, 1989 (InterStudy, P.O. Box 458, Excelsior, MN 55331).

Q. 8:7 Do physicians own HMOs?

Most HMOs require too much development and working capital to be owned exclusively by physicians. HMOs are owned by major employers (such as John Deere, which developed an HMO primarily for its own employees), private insurance companies, hospitals, and various investors. Physicians typically have "pieces of the pie" under profit-sharing arrangements or partial ownership of the corporations. Therefore, they are inclined to provide the most cost-effective care. This contrasts with physicians in the traditional fee-for-service delivery system, who can increase their income by delivering more care.

Q. 8:8 How are HMOs organized?

HMOs are organized on a physician basis. There are four basic organizations of HMO physicians:

1. The group model;
2. The staff model;
3. The network model; and
4. The independent practice association (IPA) model.

Q. 8:9 What are the differences among the various models?

InterStudy, the leading HMO analysis organization, provides the following definitions:

Group model. An HMO that contracts with one independent group practice to provide health services. Care is usually billed to the HMO on a fee-for-service basis.

Staff model. An HMO that delivers health services through a physician group that is controlled by the HMO. The physicians, in effect, are employed and paid by the HMO.

Network model. An HMO that contracts with two or more independent group practices (no solo practices) to provide health services.

IPA model. An HMO that contracts with physicians from various settings (individual physicians, or a mixture of solo and group practices) to provide health services.

Q. 8:10 How is a capitative payment structure different from a fee-for-service payment structure?

Health care providers—which include both individuals (e.g., medical doctors, dentists, osteopaths, psychiatric social workers, physical therapists, and chiropractors) and institutions (hospitals, clinics, surgicenters, skilled nursing care facilities, and hospices)—have historically been compensated on a fee-for-service basis. For each unit of service provided, an associated fee is billed. A doctor examines a patient complaining of back pain and is compensated for that examination. A hospital provides emergency room care to a heart attack victim and is paid for the treatment provided.

A capitative payment structure, however, is one in which services are paid for in advance for treatment of an enrolled person before it is known which services (if any) will be required. This prepaid arrangement is analogous to a person buying an annual maintenance warranty without knowing whether the washing machine will ever need repair.

Q. 8:11 Don't employers prepay for health care services in traditional plans?

In a sense, employers prepay for expenses their employees will incur by agreeing to pay fixed monthly health care premiums to an insurer. Although premiums are prepaid, providers are still paid on a fee-for-service basis. This means that the risk is assumed by an intermediary, the insurer. With HMOs, it is the care provider itself that assumes the risk.

Q. 8:12 Do employees prepay for health care through their payroll deductions for traditional plans?

To a degree, employees do prepay for their medical care. Many employees perceive their health care costs to be on a prepaid basis, because their monthly contributions are fixed payroll deductions. However, in most plans, employees do share in the cost of each service as it is provided (through deductibles and coinsurance), in addition to the monthly premiums paid. HMOs typically require much smaller copayments.

Q. 8:13 Does enrollment in an HMO entitle an individual to unlimited health care?

Care under HMO plans is very comprehensive and includes both physician and hospital services. Enrollment in an HMO entitles the individual to as much future health care service as the HMO physician deems necessary and appropriate. There are limitations, just as there are restrictions on the care allowable under other health plans. For example, cosmetic surgery would generally not be covered by an HMO plan unless required to correct a congenital condition or in connection with accidental injury.

Q. 8:14 Do HMOs require a deductible that patients pay before care is provided?

Typically, HMOs require a small per-visit deductible or a charge for certain services, such as maternity, in addition to the membership payments.

Q. 8:15 What happens when an individual who is enrolled in an HMO needs to be hospitalized?

Some HMOs lease or own hospitals to provide care to their members. Others simply negotiate arrangements with hospitals to provide the HMO members with hospital services. The patient must be admitted to a hospital with which the HMO has such arrangements in order for the care to be covered.

Q. 8:16 Is an employee reimbursed for care received outside the HMO area?

If an HMO member receives emergency care from a non-HMO provider, usually the member's HMO will pay the cost of that emergency care. If an individual elects to receive nonemergency care from a non-HMO provider, the cost of this care is not reimbursable.

Under the 1988 amendments to the HMO Act, however, HMOs have the option of developing benefit offerings that reimburse fee-for-service care from physicians who are not part of the HMO panel. The amount of out-of-panel care that can be reimbursed under the "self-referral option" is limited to 10% of all basic health services, and such services can be subject to traditional deductibles and coinsurance typically found in indemnity plans.

Forty-eight "open-ended HMOs," which provide coverage for out-of-panel services, now account for 7.5% of total annual enrollment—nearly half a million members. Due to competition from PPOs, this is likely to be the fastest growing segment of the HMO industry.

Q. 8:17 When can employees enroll in an HMO?

Employees can enroll in an HMO immediately upon employment instead of enrolling in the employer's plan. Otherwise, they must wait until the specified period of open enrollment or "crossover" required under the dual choice mandate (see Question 8:33). The mandate specifies that once a year employees are allowed their choice of enrolling in either a federally qualified HMO or the conventional insurance plan without providing evidence of insurability.

Q. 8:18 How does an employee choose whether to enroll in an HMO or in the traditional health plan?

When deciding whether to choose an HMO or a conventional health care plan, employees weigh the advantages and disadvantages of both. Generally, employees who join HMOs do so for one or more of the following reasons:

- The credentials and quality of care are well-established;
- The selection of doctors is broad enough to meet their needs;
- The HMO is located near home or work;
- The HMO's office hours include late evenings and holidays, and it offers a 24-hour emergency on-call service;
- The individuals are agreeable to being treated for some conditions by a paraprofessional (e.g., a nurse practitioner or other nonmedical doctor, whom some HMOs rely on heavily);
- HMO specialists to whom patients are referred are of high quality;
- HMOs require no claims forms; and

Q. 8:19   **Health Insurance Answer Book**

- The price is comparable to or less than the price of the regular group plan.

Q. 8:19 Would an employee want to enroll in both a traditional plan and an HMO plan?

No. Enrolling in two plans would provide duplicate coverage, and the employee would pay premium/membership fees under two plans. Further, most insurers do not allow employees enrolled in an HMO to enroll in a traditional health plan as well.

Q. 8:20 Are HMOs more cost-effective for employees?

Yes and no. Employees usually pay less for care once they are enrolled in the HMO, because there are few or no copayments or deductibles required. However, if employees receive care from non-HMO providers, neither the employer nor the HMO is required to pay their expenses. The HMO physicians determine medically appropriate care, and if a member does not agree with that determination and wishes to receive unauthorized care, he or she must pay for all the expenses associated with that care. (See Question 8:16 regarding reimbursement of some non-HMO care.)

Q. 8:21 How can an employer achieve 75% participation in its conventional plan if employees are allowed to enroll in HMOs?

The 75% enrollment required by most insurers uses eligible individuals as a basis. Employees enrolled in an HMO generally are not eligible to participate in the employer's plan.

Q. 8:22 Why has enrollment in HMOs increased during the health care cost crisis?

Some employers are encouraging their employees to enroll in an HMO in their area if the cost of the HMO would be less than what the employer is currently spending on conventional plans or if the annual increase in membership payments is likely to be lower than the expected increase in insurance premiums. In addition, HMOs are increasingly attractive to employees who must pay for part of their health care costs. Since employers are increasing deductibles and coinsurance, some employees have found HMOs more attractive. (Although HMOs have cost-sharing provisions, they are generally far less significant than conventional deductible and coinsurance amounts.)

Q. 8:23 Why might employers experience lower costs with HMOs than with other health care plans?

HMOs emphasize preventive care, and they minimize hospitalization by treating patients on an outpatient basis whenever possible. The financial structure of HMOs rewards physicians for providing the most cost-effective care. This strategy helps control the rate of hospital admissions and the length of hospital stays.

On average, the number of inpatient days per 1,000 individuals per year is considerably lower in HMOs than under traditional health care plans. Various studies have shown that HMOs' inpatient days per 1,000 members range from 50% to 75% of those of traditional fee-for-service group health plans. Since hospital costs make up a large part of health care costs, HMO costs have tended to be lower, in aggregate, than those under traditional health care plans. In addition, there is evidence that HMOs attract younger and perhaps healthier people who would require, on average, less medical care than older persons.

However, as traditional health plans have changed to provide for cost management, rates of hospitalization and lengths of stay have begun to decrease under those plans as well. Costs of HMOs versus those of other providers may become comparable as additional efficiency is introduced into the traditional health care delivery system, as HMOs cover a broader cross section of the population, and as financially troubled HMOs are forced to accelerate the rate of fee increases.

Adverse Selection

Q. 8:24 Does adverse selection occur in the HMO setting?

Yes. In fact, employers sponsoring HMOs are becoming increasingly concerned about the potential impact of adverse selection. Frequently, healthier or younger employees gravitate toward HMOs, leaving sicker or older workers in the insured or self-insured indemnity plan. This adverse selection drives up the cost of the indemnity plan.

Q. 8:25 Will the cost of an employer's conventional plan be affected by an HMO plan?

If an employer loses half of its employees to an HMO, the employer's rates on a conventional plan may be higher than if all employees were enrolled. There is some evidence that suggests that younger, healthier employees are more inclined to enroll in HMOs than their older, less healthy counterparts (see Question 8:26). Premium rates charged by insurance companies reflect the characteristics of a group. The size, "average" sex, and average age of the group will be affected when certain employees join an HMO. So, for example, if the group is older because young employees enrolled in the HMO, the premium rates would be higher.

Q. 8:26 Why might HMOs attract younger, healthier persons?

One reason may be that HMOs require members to receive care from a limited group of physicians. Younger persons are generally less likely to be attached to one doctor. Also, younger persons tend to be less concerned than their elder counterparts about experiencing serious illness, and their choice of medical plans may reflect this attitude. Younger persons may also be more willing to try new types of health care plans. The HMO care model is a relatively new concept, and older persons may question the quality of care. However, HMOs have begun to enroll more older members since Medicare began allowing its insureds the option of belonging to an HMO.

Q. 8:27 Is the adverse selection obvious to employers?

No. Many employers assume that the HMO is a good deal because the cost is sometimes lower than the cost or premium of the indemnity plan (although this cost difference is rapidly disappearing as HMO costs rise). What they fail to realize is that the adverse selection factor is pushing up the cost of the indemnity plan. In order to truly measure costs, the company must have adequate data to compare the various plans it offers to employees.

Q. 8:28 What can be done about adverse selection?

A company experiencing adverse selection can negotiate a lower rate with the HMO based on actual HMO utilization. Another option is to bring younger, healthier employees back into the indemnity plan by offering certain attractive benefits such as health club membership, dental care, or prescription drug cards in conjunction with the indemnity plan. Another alternative might be to change the contribution levels so that they are more equitable, based on the actual experience with each plan, or by employee age bracket. Current amendments to the HMO Act specifically authorize adjustments based on utilization experience, geographic variation, and employee demographics.

Legal Standards

Q. 8:29 What is the Health Maintenance Act?

The Health Maintenance Act of 1973 was intended to encourage the spread of HMOs. In addition to establishing standards for federally qualified HMOs, it required employers to make HMOs available to their employees under certain circumstances (the "dual choice" requirement). Affected employers are those that are subject to the minimum wage standards of the Fair Labor Standards Act, employ 25 or more full- or part-time employees in the calendar quarter, and offer a health benefits plan.

The Health Maintenance Organization Amendments of 1988 were signed into law October 24, 1988. The amendments eliminate the dual choice requirement effective October 24, 1995; revise employer contribution requirements; permit rates to be set on the basis of employer experience; impose stricter financial requirements for federal qualification; and permit greater flexibility in benefits offerings.

Q. 8:30 What standards must a federally qualified HMO meet?

To be federally qualified, an HMO must be organized and operated according to the law and provide health services as prescribed by the law. These include certain "basic health services," such as:

- Physician services (including consultant and referral services by a physician);
- Inpatient and outpatient hospital services;
- Medically necessary emergency health services;
- Short-term (maximum 20 visits) outpatient evaluative and crisis intervention mental health services;
- Medical treatment and referral services (including referral services to appropriate ancillary services) for the abuse of or addiction to alcohol and drugs;
- Diagnostic laboratory services and diagnostic and therapeutic radiological services;
- Home health services; and
- Preventive health services, including immunizations, child care from birth, periodic health evaluations for adults, voluntary family planning services, infertility services, and children's eye and ear examinations to assess the need for vision and hearing correction.

A qualified HMO may also make available "supplemental health services" as specified in the law, including:

- Services or facilities for intermediate and long-term care;
- Vision care not included as a basic health service;
- Dental care not included as a basic health service;
- Mental health care not included as a basic health service;

- Long-term physical medicine and rehabilitative services (including physical therapy);
- Prescription drugs prescribed in the course of the provision by the HMO of a basic health service, or of one of the preceding supplemental health services; and
- Other health services, not included as basic health services, that have been approved by the Secretary of the Department of Health and Human Services.

Q. 8:31 How prevalent are federally qualified HMOs?

According to the National Association of Employers on Health Care Action (NAEHCA), 58% of HMOs were federally qualified in 1988. However, many of the newer HMOs did not seek federal qualification in order to be flexible and competitive with respect to benefits offerings and rate structure.

Q. 8:32 What is a community rating system?

Under a community rating system, one average premium rate is determined on the basis of the entire membership's characteristics and past claims experience. This is different from rate setting on private insurance plans, where a particular group's rates can be partially or fully based on that group's risk characteristics (age, sex, industry) and past claims experience. However, 1988 amendments to the HMO Act allow "adjusted community rating." Although HMOs are still not permitted to return surplus or dividends to employers, they are now permitted to prospectively establish specific employer rates based on utilization of services. For groups of less than 100 employees, the adjusted rates cannot be more than 10% higher than community rates.

Q. 8:33 What is the dual choice mandate?

Under the HMO Act of 1973, employers (1) with 25 or more employees employed within the service area of a federally qualified HMO, (2) paying minimum wage, and (3) offering a health benefits plan to employees are required to offer HMO coverage if requested to do so in accordance with specific procedures. An employer that receives such a request must offer its employees a federally qualified HMO as an alternative to the conventional health plan. The HMO must make a formal written application to the employer, explaining the details of the HMO plan, at least 180 days before the anniversary date of the existing health plan (and at least 90 days before the expiration of a collective bargaining agreement). The employer is required to offer only one IPA and one group or staff model, even if more than one of each applies for recognition. The employer is not obligated to offer the specific HMO that requested the mandated offering, as long as an HMO of that type is offered.

The dual choice requirement will be repealed October 24, 1995, under the Health Maintenance Organization Amendments of 1988. Note that several states, including Connecticut, New York, Michigan, Ohio, Rhode Island, Tennessee, Washington, and West Virginia, have similar dual choice requirements for state-certified HMOs that are not affected by changes in the federal law.

Q. 8:34 Is an employer that self-insures subject to the dual choice mandate?

Yes, as long as the three criteria described at Question 8:33 are met. Self-funded plans are included as health benefits plans, which are defined as "any arrangement for the provision of, or payment for, any of the basic and supplemental health benefits specified in the law and towards which the employer makes a contribution that is offered to eligible employees and their eligible dependents, by or on behalf of an employing entity." (Retirees eligible for health benefits do not have to be counted toward the 25-employee minimum.) For a plan that is self-insured, the 180-day requirement (see Question 8:33) applies to the budget year.

Q. 8:35 Does the HMO Act specify how much an employer is required to pay for HMO coverage for its employees?

Prior to the 1988 amendments, the law required that the employer contribute at least the same dollar amount for an employee who joined an HMO as would be paid for that employee to enroll in the employer's conventional health plan. If the HMO was more expensive, the employee could be required to pay the difference, although there are various employer approaches to this situation.

The new law substitutes a requirement that the employer contribution to a federally qualified HMO under a mandate not financially discriminate against an employee enrolling in such HMO. The method for determining the employer contribution must be "reasonable and assure employees a fair choice among health benefit plans." A variety of methods, including equal dollar amount, class rates for both HMO and indemnity plans, equal percentage, or any mutually acceptable arrangement between employer and HMO, is permitted by existing HMO regulations.

Q. 8:36 What role has federal funding played in the development of HMOs?

Early HMO development, propelled by substantial federal funding, was relatively rapid, although growth slowed during the period 1976–1982. With the recent increased emphasis on cost management and changes in delivery systems, enrollment in HMOs is increasing at record levels despite reduced federal funding and some HMOs' near insolvencies.

Q. 8:37 Are HMOs subject to state regulations?

Many states have laws meant to promote HMO development while ensuring the quality of care the HMO delivers. These laws also provide for grievance procedures for enrollees and allow for some form of enrollee participation in the HMO's policy-making body. Also, some states have established financial reserve requirements for HMOs that are similar to those required by insurance companies, or they require state approval of an HMO's rates. These laws vary from state to state. Minnesota law, for example, includes a provision that all companies with 100 or more employees who reside in Minnesota must offer HMO coverage to those employees even if the employer does not offer an existing health plan.

The model National Association of Insurance Commissioners (NAIC) HMO law is being reviewed with the expectation that changes will be made that would:

- Make becoming a licensed HMO more difficult;
- Tighten financial reserve conditions;
- Hold enrollees harmless for HMO debts; and
- Offer membership in new HMOs to enrollees of failed HMOs at their old rates.

Q. 8:38 What is ERISA pre-emption?

Pre-emption refers to ERISA's restriction of a state's ability to make laws relating to employee welfare benefit plans. State's are still permitted to regulate insurance and are thus "saved" from pre-emption in this area. However, state's are not permitted to "deem" an employee welfare benefit plan to be an insurance company in an attenpt to regulate those plans.

Q. 8:39 Are state laws with respect to HMOs pre-empted by ERISA?

Certain laws which regulate the HMO's themselves are not pre-empted by ERISA. However, there is growing evidence that dual choice requirements of certain states (not the Federal dual choice requirement that is due to expire in 1995) is pre-empted by ERISA. A California court case involving Hewlett-Packard found such requirements pre-empted becuase they sought to regulate employee welfare benefit plans as insurance companies. The court relied on a letter from an official at the U.S. Department of Labor stating his opinion that the California HMO dual choice provisions were pre-empted by ERISA.

Although the California decision sets a precedent, it is not binding in other jurisdictions. However, an employer seeking to avoid a dual choice mandate may be able dissuade an agressive HMO from taking expensive legal action to enforce the mandate. Alternatively, with the assistance of counsel, an advisory opinion letter could be requested from the U.S. Department of Labor. If an employer does business in more than one state, the request should specify all business locations.

Evaluating HMOs

Q. 8:40 How can a company compare costs of health plans?

A company must accumulate the demographic information for each plan population in order to analyze the age and sex composition of the employees and dependents in the indemnity plan and those in the HMOs. Next, the company can obtain claims experience data from its insurance carrier and HMOs in order to find out the true cost of each plan and each demographic category. By weighting the relative participation in each plan and comparing the "cost" to the premiums paid for coverage, the company will know whether there is adverse selection and, if so, the extent of it. Then it can elect to take action to bring things back into balance.

Q. 8:41 How does the quality of HMO care compare with that of conventionally insured medical care?

Although HMO members see their doctors more frequently than conventionally insured individuals (an average of 4.4 physician encounters versus 2.7 in the general population per year), and are admitted to hospitals less often (449 bed days per 1,000 covered persons per year versus 889 nationally), no conclusion concerning the quality of care can be drawn. Less care does not necessarily mean poorer quality care, and more care does not suggest better care. Surveys have shown regular conflicts between HMOs and employee assistance program (EAP) personnel regarding access to and length of stay in mental health and substance abuse treatment programs. Other complaints involve physician compensation arrangements, especially those that divide unspent treatment funds among participating physicians. This practice may provide too strong an incentive for doctors to withhold needed care.

Several states, including New York and Kansas, now require periodic on-site quality assessments. Employers that are concerned about HMO quality should carefully review the financial incentives for physicians and be wary of those arrangements that discourage referral to specialists or inpatient hospital confinement.

Q. 8:42 Why are some HMOs having financial difficulty?

HMO failures during the early 1980s were generally the result of undercapitalization, severe inflation leading to high medical care costs, slow membership enrollment, and inexperienced management. Without a sufficient spread of risk—number of members—a period of uncontrolled inflation can wreak havoc for insurers and health care providers. The HMO, a unique combination of medical care and risk management, is extremely difficult to manage successfully.

Part of the problem stems from the relative newness of HMOs. Some analysts feel that it takes four years for an HMO to become profitable; almost half of the HMOs in existence were established since 1985. Financial woes exist among older HMOs as well, however. According to a GHAA survey in December 1988, only 57% of HMOs surveyed projected a surplus; 38% projected a loss. This situation may be easing, however, as HMOs respond to losses with sharp increases in fees, and by combining with other organizations.

The spate of mergers, acquisitions, and closings (232 HMOs have been acquired since 1981 and 186 since 1986) has resulted in legislative activity to prevent HMO insolvencies. Over a dozen states now require reserves or set "minimum worth" standards or mandate successor provisions for the protection of HMO members.

Q. 8:43 How can a prospective HMO client get more information about the HMO?

Information on HMOs can be obtained from:
- The HMO itself, its annual reports, and, for public corporations, SEC filings;

Managed Health Care Systems: HMOs and PPOs Q. 8:43

- Employer health care coalitions;
- State insurance commisioners and health departments;
- Accrediting organizations such as the American Association of Ambulatory Health Centers; and
- The U.S. Health Care Financing Administration's Office of Prepaid Health Care.

HMO Evaluation Checklist

Evaluating an HMO is a complex undertaking. The following is a listing of some of the things to consider in making an assessment.

Structure and Organization

☐ Type: group, staff, IPA, or network?
☐ Ownership: insurer, BC/BS, HMO chain?
☐ If owned by a larger entity, how much local autonomy?
☐ What is management structure?
☐ Is it federally qualified?
☐ How many members (enrollees, employers)?
☐ How are medical personnel and hospitals recruited and compensated?
☐ Is the HMO accredited with organizations such as the Joint Commission for the Accreditation of Health Care Organizations?
☐ Are all providers contracted by the HMO fully licensed or accredited, and supervised by the HMO?

Benefits and Services

☐ Basic services: Do they include mental health, dental, and prescription drugs?
☐ Are other services, such as substance abuse treatment, and preventive care (smoking cessation, stress management) provided?
☐ How is coverage provided outside the HMO area; is it nationwide; international?
☐ What is HMO's policy regarding nonaffiliated doctors and hospitals?

Q. 8:43   Health Insurance Answer Book

- ☐ What sort of marketing support does it provide?
- ☐ What other services does it provide (e.g., COBRA administration)?
- ☐ Is there a single account representative for the employer to deal with for questions and resolution of problems?

Rates

- ☐ Will the group be rated by its own experience, community rated, or community rated by class?
- ☐ Can rates be negotiated?
- ☐ What additional charges are there for supplemental services?
- ☐ What charges will enrollees pay in the form of deductibles or per-visit fees?

Financial Status

- ☐ Is it nonprofit or for profit?
- ☐ What is its past profitability, and what are projections for the future?
- ☐ Are enrollees protected from creditors in the event of insolvency?

Data

- ☐ What sorts of reports are provided?
- ☐ Are reports available on a customized basis to employers, or on a standardized basis such as that of the Group Health Association of America?

Quality

- ☐ Has the HMO been cited for noncompliance by state or federal regulators?
- ☐ Has it been a defendant in any lawsuits?
- ☐ What sorts of reviews or surveys have been conducted that would indicate enrollee satisfaction?
- ☐ Has there been a significant drop or increase in enrollment? If so, why?

Preferred Provider Organizations (PPOs)

Q. 8:44 What is a PPO?

A PPO is an organization that arranges contracts between a select group of health care providers (hospitals, physicians) and purchasers of health care (employers, union trust funds), but is itself neither a provider nor a purchaser. Typically, provider fees are negotiated in advance and providers offer discounts in return for rapid reimbursement and potential increase in market share. Payment is on a fee-for-service rather than a capitated basis. Strict utilization controls are combined with flexibility in benefits design and freedom of choice with respect to providers.

Q. 8:45 How did the PPO concept develop?

The preferred provider approach developed initially out of negotiated fee arrangements such as those pioneered in connection with workers' compensation laws in 1911 in the states of Washington and Oregon. In the 1930s, an organization called the California Physicians' Service offered discounted fees and participating physician payment-in-full benefits, which became the basis for the modern-day Blue Cross/Blue Shield. Various "foundations for medical care" (FMCs) proliferated throughout the 1950s, and the concept was adopted by Medicare and Medicaid in 1966.

Modern PPOs—the second generation—combined provider selectivity with discounts for the first time in the early 1980s in California and Colorado. The 1982 revisions to Medi-Cal established contractual arrangements with cost-efficient hospitals for Medi-Cal beneficiaries, and the state of California passed laws permitting selective provider contracting. The West continues to lead the PPO field; almost 33% of employees there participate in PPOs, compared with only 1% in the Northeast. Although many states have enacted PPO enabling legislation or revised laws to permit PPOs (such as California, Florida, Illinois, Indiana, Kansas, Louisiana, Maryland, Michigan, Nebraska, North Carolina, Utah, Virginia, Wisconsin, and Wyoming), the majority of states have laws that limit or prohibit PPO development.

Q. 8:46 How does a PPO differ from an HMO?

An HMO is an alternative to a traditional health plan and is separate. PPOs exist within the traditional plan structure and are integrated.

An HMO requires that services be rendered by participating providers in order to be covered. Integrated plans such as PPOs typically reimburse services by nonpreferred providers at a lower rate than participating providers, but cover, to some extent, all medically necessary services.

HMOs assume risk. It assumes the possibility that the cost of services required by members could exceed revenues generated by capitation. PPOs assume no risk and reimburse on a fee-for-service basis; the risk continues to be assumed by the employer, union trust fund, or insurance carrier.

HMOs are strictly regulated by federal HMO and various state laws; PPOs remain largely unregulated.

An HMO delivers health care; a PPO facilitates the delivery of cost-effective health care, but is not itself a provider. Rather, it is more of a manager or broker.

Q. 8:47 How is the PPO concept different from Blue Cross/Blue Shield and Medicare contracts with providers?

With respect to discounting charges, the PPO concept is not very different. For years, individuals covered under the Blue Cross/Blue Shield (BC/BS) plans have had the option of receiving care from a participating or a nonparticipating physician or hospital. Charges of participating providers are covered more fully because of agreements between the providers and BC/BS and Medicare. Commercial insurers have only recently entered this negotiated price and service arena, in the form of PPOs.

PPOs, however, focus less on price discounts than on managed care. One significant weakness in BC/BS provider-insurer contracts has been the lack of utilization review (UR) and case maement. Prices for care were discounted to BC/BS, but the amount of care was not managed. Thus, providers sometimes sought to make up for the agreed-to discounts by providing more care, on a fee-for-service basis, than might have been necessary. PPOs, however, include stringent utilization controls, agreed to by the providers and monitored by the insurance company or other party to the agreement.

Q. 8:48 What is a preferred provider arrangement, and how is it different from a PPO?

A preferred provider arrangement (PPA) is an agreement between health care providers and another entity or group of entities (insurance companies, employers, TPAs) to provide medical care services at negotiated fees to certain groups in return for prompt payment and increased patient volume. A PPO typically indicates an actual organization of providers, while a PPA suggests simply that a contractual agreement has been made, but there is no other legal entity formed as a result of the agreement. The providers enter into a contract directly with the insurer, employer, or TPA. (The term PPA can be used to describe a PPO arrangement itself, and is sometimes used interchangeably with the term PPO. This text uses PPO as the generic term.)

Q. 8:49 What is an exclusive provider organization?

An exclusive provider organization (EPO) closely resembles an HMO and is a type of PPO that requires individuals to use only designated preferred providers. Payment to providers, however, is on a fee-for-service basis.

Q. 8:50 What services are offered by PPOs?

There are two basic types of PPOs: (1) comprehensive PPOs and (2) limited PPOs. The comprehensive variety typically includes a broad range of physicians in every specialty as well as general and specialty hospitals and support services such as home health care agencies.

It is not uncommon, however, for a PPO to include only hospitals or only physicians. Also in the limited category are specialty PPOs that provide dental, mental health, or substance abuse services, cardiac care, maternity care, vision services, and prescriptions.

In arranging a plan of benefits, one or more specialty PPOs may be more cost-effective in addressing particular utilization concerns and provide a degree of customization and flexibility unavailable through a "one-size-fits-all" comprehensive PPO. Integrating several PPOs, however, results in additional complexity and administrative cost.

Q. 8:51 Who sponsors PPOs?

PPOs are sponsored by a variety of entities and organizations: hospitals, physicians, union trust funds, insurance carriers, employers, TPAs, brokers, and other entrepreneurs. In addition, joint ventures between the various entities are common, such as multi-hospital networks and hospital/physician and insurance carrier/entrepreneur joint ventures.

Provider-sponsored PPOs are typically marketed to insurance carriers, union trust funds, and self-funded plans, while insurer/TPA-sponsored PPOs are marketed exclusively to clients and policyholders.

Unless provider-based PPOs are operated by independent organizations with strong cost-management abilities, these types of PPOs can become strictly marketing ploys. It is often difficult for a hospital to screen out inefficient physicians who have privileges at the hospital, or to ignore the economic incentive to increase quantity or intensity of service. Employer- and entrepreneur-based PPOs often lack the data to identify cost-efficient providers. Insurance carrier or HMO-sponsored PPOs offer the best chance for effective provider selectivity, which is the basis for long-term savings.

Q. 8:52 How prevalent are PPOs?

By the end of 1989, there were over 800 PPOs covering an estimated 36.25 million Americans. It is, however, a highly concentrated marketplace, with the five largest PPO corporations accounting for 44% of the marketplace. [Ref.: AMCRA and Marion Managed Care Digest/PPO Edition]

PPO development is the largest growing segment of the managed care industry. Several factors are responsible for this:

- Physician surplus and low hospital occupancy rates encourage providers to develop market share through PPO participation;
- Advances in computer technology permit collection of utilization data and analysis of provider practice patterns;
- Introduction of employee cost sharing allows plan design incentives that channel patients to cost-effective providers;
- Growth of purchaser coalitions has resulted in the development of useful community average data with which to measure provider efficiency; and
- Growth in self-funding has created incentives for employers to introduce more proactive cost-management strategies, including restricting or discouraging access to inefficient providers.

Q. 8:53 Who joins PPOs?

According to the Health Insurance Association of America (HIAA), those most likely to enroll in a PPO have been employed less than one year, have no doctor or have been using their current doctor less than one year, are aged 18 through 34, are male, and are more likely to be single. Those least willing to join a PPO are those aged 55 or older and those in poor health.

Q. 8:54 What is involved in establishing a PPO?

No matter who establishes a PPO, certain steps are involved. The complexities of merging medical care with insurance make these alternative delivery systems difficult to develop successfully.

First, an adequate network of health care providers must be determined. The locations of providers selected and the various specialties required will depend on the characteristics of the group for whom PPO care is to be provided. The demographics of the group and past medical care utilization should be reviewed in order to determine the types and numbers of providers that will be needed to meet the needs of that population. For example, if the group health plan covers retirees, several geriatric specialists would be required; if the insured group includes a large percentage of dependent children, the number of pediatricians that should be available as preferred providers must be carefully determined.

Q. 8:55 How are PPO providers selected?

Selecting specific providers involves two crucial ingredients for a successful PPO: (1) selecting physicians whose practice patterns are cost-effective and whose abilities are excellent; (2) and providing the right incentives to encourage those physicians to become a part of the PPO. An intense review of practice patterns is usually performed to determine the appropriate physicians, and because of the expertise required to interpret these patterns, experienced health care consultants are normally used to perform this function.

Although the historical practice patterns of the physicians will be expected to continue if they become part of the PPO, it is still necessary to develop the utilization review (UR) controls that will help ensure cost-effective medical care from the PPO physicians and hospitals. Therefore, as the ideal list of physicians is developed, a UR plan must be developed concurrently. This plan depends on the readiness of the providers (particularly the hospital management involved) to practice by the UR standards, and must be developed jointly with the providers involved. Later, as additional providers become part of the PPO, they will be required to subscribe to the UR that is a fundamental tenet of the PPO.

In addition to the actual medical practices of physicians, the accreditation, licensure, hospital staff privileges, appropriate liability and malpractice insurance, and other administrative details must be arranged.

Q. 8:56 What else is necessary for ensuring cost-effective treatment in a PPO?

Data-processing systems that will allow the care provided to be tracked are absolutely necessary to ensure that the most cost-effective treatment is provided. Hospitals unable to collect and produce these data in a form capable of analysis would not be effective participants in a PPO.

Negotiating the price discounts that physicians and hospitals will provide to PPO participants is also paramount, and is done during the development of the provider network. The financial incentives that will encourage the providers to become involved vary, according to the medical marketplace at that time. A certain hospital may be willing to provide a discount of 10% to their per-diem rate for PPO insureds. A hospital with a large number of empty beds and a need to fill them may be willing to discount its surgical fees and its room and board fees.

Developing a mix of providers that will offer high-quality medical care at discounted fees requires a great deal of negotiation and administration. Months of negotiations are usually necessary to get the appropriate providers, a workable UR system, and discounted prices for medical services provided.

Q. 8:57 What are the incentives for doctors and hospitals to be preferred providers?

Hospitals and doctors believe that by participating in a PPO they can expect to increase their market share by increasing patient volume. Because competition for patients is fierce, providers are willing to negotiate discounts in return for the prospect of increased patient volume.

Q. 8:58 Must a PPO include UR controls?

Each PPO sponsor develops the means of monitoring and controlling participating providers' practice patterns as it sees fit. The effectiveness of the PPO in managing health care costs depends on the incentives for the PPO providers to deliver cost-effective care. Fee discounts alone will not provide this. Cost-effective PPOs, therefore, must include stringent UR controls.

Q. 8:59 Are utilization controls important when using a PPO?

Yes. Any employer contracting with a PPO should spend a considerable amount of time reviewing the utilization controls. Without effective UR, any discount is suspect, since it can be more than offset by increased utilization of services. For example, if a PPO offers a 10% discount through its participating providers, but then increases utilization by 15% over what it would have been without the PPO, the employer or union contracting for services is spending more on health care, rather than less.

UR results should be compared with community norms. It is increasingly common for employers to specify utilization targets, adjusted for their population, and to negotiate performance guarantees with the PPO.

Q. 8:60 Who does the utilization review?

Frequently, UR is done by the medical staff of the PPO. In this case, the UR function must be monitored closely in order to make sure that the review is being done effectively. Independent, external review is preferable.

Q. 8:61 Are there federally qualified PPOs?

No. The PPO concept emerged from the marketplace with no legislative impetus and, to date, there is no set of national standards for PPOs.

Q. 8:62 Do state PPO standards or laws exist?

Yes. Many states have passed or proposed laws. The laws vary from enabling legislation, which simply notes that PPOs are procompetitive and desirable, to laws that include specific discrimination tests for PPOs. Some states require that benefit payment differences between non-PPO and PPO providers fall within specified variance limits. Other laws include provisions that prohibit discrimination by classes of employees in terms of PPO versus non-PPO benefit payment percentages.

Q. 8:63 What antitrust issues affect PPO development and negotiations?

The relevant antitrust issue involved is price fixing. The fact that PPOs may eliminate competition because the same discounted fees are negotiated with many insurers (or employers or TPAs) may be construed as price fixing, which is a violation of antitrust law. However, the current stance among regulatory agencies is to enable PPO activity, mindful of, rather than confined by, the principles of antitrust law.

Q. 8:64 What incentives do employers have to include PPOs in their health plans?

PPOs allow employers to provide employees with health care benefits at lower costs than traditional plans and, also, provide some relief to employers faced with unbridled annual premium increases. The cost savings come from the price discounts and utilization review negotiated with the preferred providers. Discounts can range from 20% to 30%. Recent surveys have found that many employers believe PPOs to be more effective at controlling health care costs (or at least in moderating the rate of increase in those costs) than HMOs or conventional reimbursement plans.

Q. 8:65 What kinds of employers can expect the largest discounts from a PPO health plan?

Employers with large concentrations of workers located in areas with strong competition for patients—high physician to population ratio and excess hospital resources—have the potential to achieve large discounts. Smaller employers must identify an insurance carrier or association that is achieving large discounts due to the ability to deliver "market share."

In these instances, the smaller the PPO network, the larger the potential discount. Although large networks are an attractive selling point to employees, they are rarely as efficient in providing care, and the leverage in negotiating discounts is diluted.

Q. 8:66 Is an employer that elects a plan with a PPO sacrificing quality care for low cost?

Enough competition exists in many areas to encourage providers to lower their prices while continuing to provide high-quality care. The UR process helps ensure quality.

Since PPO providers are typically not at risk as are HMO providers, there is no incentive for skimping on care. Employers must assure, however, that there is sufficient access to employees in terms of location, a full range of medical specialties in addition to primary care, and reasonably located general and specialty hospitals.

Q. 8:67 Can any employer include a PPO in its health care plan?

No. To date, formal PPOs have been developed only in areas where there is heavy competition among providers. Many rural areas with only a few physicians and one community hospital do not justify the work involved in establishing a PPO, although providers' practice patterns and costs may be a problem.

In addition, not all insurers offer PPOs. An insurer must have a significant market share in an area in order to justify the effort required to establish a PPO. Some insurers may have other health care delivery arrangements that offer employers similar cost-management techniques.

Q. 8:68 How can an employer or union evaluate a prospective PPO?

PPO evaluation is a complex subject, and the employer or union is well-advised to seek professional help. There are a number of evaluation areas to consider, including (1) organizational considerations, (2) scope of services, (3) access, (4) utilization controls, (5) participation incentives, (6) benefits design, (7) data and performance reports, (8) financial considerations, and (9) legal issues.

The following checklist shows the steps employers or unions should take in negotiating with a PPO:

- ☐ Define scope of services.
- ☐ Develop appropriate employee participation incentives.
- ☐ Select the payment methodology.
- ☐ Include stringent utilization controls.
- ☐ Determine provider selection (and retention) criteria.
- ☐ Determine provider risk-sharing levels.
- ☐ Insist on timely, accurate, and adequate data.
- ☐ Clarify any provisions relating to workers' compensation, COB, and subrogation.
- ☐ Review any insolvency and reinsurance clauses.
- ☐ Include a hold-harmless clause to protect employees.
- ☐ Reserve the right to terminate the agreement on short notice.

Q. 8:69 How should a PPO be incorporated into an existing program?

There are two basic approaches. The simplest approach is to superimpose the PPO option on the existing plan as a voluntary option; use of preferred providers results in payment in full, while regular plan benefits continue to apply to all other providers. Unless significantly more efficient care is provided through the PPO, this approach may result in higher total plan costs if discounts are insufficient to neutralize the additional cost of in-full benefits.

The second and more successful approach involves integration or complete program redesign incorporating benefits incentives and disincentives, and utilization controls applicable to all providers.

Q. 8:70 What types of discounts are available?

The following hospital discounts are available under a PPO:

- *First dollar.* A percentage discount applies to each dollar of charge, such as a 10% discount.
- *Volume.* After a certain volume of business is directed to a provider, a discount applies.
- *Scheduled.* Fees are predetermined according to "case" or "per diem."
- *Case mix.* Similar to diagnosis-related group (DRGs)

The following physician discounts are available under a PPO:

- *Percentage of UCR.* A reimbursement is established as a percentile of "usual, reasonable, and customary" charges.
- *Relative value study (RVS).* An RVS, such as the California or New York (RVS), is used to establish the relative intensity of service. A community-sensitive conversion factor multiplied by the value determines the reimbursement amount.
- *Freeze.* Current fee levels are accepted but frozen to limit future increases.

The discounting methodology used by a PPO is an important factor in determining whether cost savings objectives can be attained. Generally, case mix and freeze approaches attract the most qualified providers.

It is critical to determine the basis of the discount as well as the method. Services should be offered at unit prices below community averages after application of the discount methodology. Independent community average information is available from local business coalitions.

Q. 8:71 When incorporating a PPO into a health plan, what employee education is necessary?

Employers should provide their employees with written material that carefully explains the reasons for the PPO plan, identifies the preferred providers, and explains the differences in reimbursement for preferred provider and nonpreferred provider care. Most employers find that continual written and visual communications are necessary. Employee meetings allow employees to ask questions and learn about the changes occurring in the health care delivery system.

Q. 8:72 What other kinds of health care delivery arrangements are available to employers?

PPOs and HMOs represent integrations of services, but there are other arrangements as well. A catchall term for these arrangements is "vertical integration." In this case, integration combines all services under one umbrella in order to meet one need—health care. Suppliers, providers, and financers of services are now joining together in various ways to deliver health care, thereby creating opportunities for increased efficiency, improved services, and lower costs for health care consumers.

For example, insurers are acquiring HMOs and integrating them into their health care plans rather than competing with them. Third-party administrators and claims payment organizations are joining forces with physicians to implement quasi-PPOs for certain large employers that need only claims administration and utilization review. Hospitals are acquiring insurance companies and equipment suppliers. Significant integration will continue.

HMOs vs. PPOs

Both HMOs and PPOs attempt to:

- Contain costs without relying heavily on participant contributions, or doing away with needed services.
- Cut back on unnecessary and overly expensive procedures by monitoring treatment, and promoting less expensive modes of treatment.

Q. 8:72   **Health Insurance Answer Book**

- Encourage more price competition among suppliers.
- Emphasize alternatives to inpatient care, such as outpatient treatment, prevention, and early detection.
- Provide incentives for providing lower-cost treatment.

HMO Advantages

- Through capitated prepayment, HMOs transfer risk from employers directly to suppliers, who are in the best position to control spending.
- Budgeting is simplified.
- HMOs offer incentives to suppliers to reduce costs.
- Through emphasis on prevention and routine care, HMOs forestall major, more costly ailments.

HMO Disadvantages

- The choice of physicians may be limited, which means that employees joining an HMO may have existing doctor/patient relationships disturbed, or may be faced with additional costs (out-of-panel charges) to keep those relationships intact.
- Centralized HMO facilities may not be as convenient as a local physician's office.
- HMO financial incentives might restrict needed care.
- Institution of an HMO can result in adverse selection.
- In the past, some HMOs have had a reputation for bad management, poor service, and financial problems.
- HMOs may not be as effective in controlling employer costs as expected.

PPO Advantages

- PPOs allow maximum flexibility in benefits program design.
- Adoption of a PPO does not necessitate a change in the mix of services, which means there is less likelihood that the issue of quality will be raised.
- PPOs have so far been judged generally more successful in braking health care cost increases than HMOs.

Managed Health Care Systems: HMOs and PPOs Q. 8:74

PPO Disadvantages

- When the PPO offers only a fee-for-service discount, there has been no shifting of risk from employer to provider.
- Without adequate controls, providers may offset discounts by revising billing schedules or prescribing increased services.

Q. 8:73 What are hybrid HMO/PPO arrangements?

Such arrangements are also called "leaky HMOs", "point-of-service-HMOs" or "open-ended HMOs". Participants in a hybrid HHO/PPO plan may use non-HMO providers at point of service and receive indemnity-type benefits, but with higher deductibles and co-insurance payments than if an HMO physician had provided services.

Q. 8:74 How prevalent are point-of service HMOs?

This is the fastest growing product in the managed care sector. According to data provided by InterStudy, the number of hybrid arrangements had increased by 14 to a total of 84 at the end of 1989 and now accounts for nearly 2 million members.

Chapter 9

Flexible Benefits

As the name denotes, flexible benefits plans come in all shapes to meet the needs of employees with diverse life styles and employers with varied objectives. This chapter covers the basic principles involved in the design and handling of flexible benefits plans, with emphasis on cafeteria plans as provided for under Section 125 of the Internal Revenue Code.

In March 1989, proposed cafeteria plan regulations were issued. The IRS has indicated that a new package of regulations for cafeteria plans can be expected in 1990, toward the end of the year.

Q. 9:1 What is a flexible benefits plan?

A flexible benefits plan is an employee benefits plan based on the concept of employee choice. Traditional benefits plans offer each employee the same benefits and the same level of coverage. Under a full flexible benefits plan, employees have the opportunity to select, individually, the type of benefits and the level of coverage desired from a menu of options offered by their employers.

Flexible benefits is a generic name given to an employee benefits plan that offers employees a choice of benefits and coverage options. If the flex plan is designed in accordance with the tax provisions of Section 125 of the Internal Revenue Code, it is legally known as a cafeteria or Section 125 plan.

Q. 9:2 How does the Internal Revenue Code define a cafeteria plan?

Under IRC Section 125, a cafeteria plan is one in which:

- All participants are employees; and
- The participants may choose (1) among two or more benefits consisting of cash and qualified benefits or (2) among two or more qualified benefits.

Q. 9:3 What are qualified benefits?

Qualified benefits include:

- Group term life insurance up to, and in excess of, the amount ($50,000) normally excludable from taxable income (IRC Section 79);
- Accident and health insurance (IRC Sections 105 and 106);
- Group legal services (IRC Section 120);
- Dependent care assistance (IRC Section 129); and
- Cash-or-deferred arrangements (CODAs) (IRC Section 401(k)).

Benefits that are not qualified include:

- Scholarships and fellowships (IRC Section 117);
- Meals and lodging (IRC Section 119);
- Van pooling (IRC Section 124);
- Educational assistance (IRC Section 127); and
- Certain other fringe benefits, such as no-additional-cost services, qualified employee discounts, working-condition fringes, and de minimis fringe benefits defined by IRC Section 132.

Q. 9:4 What are the tax advantages of a cafeteria plan?

An employer's FICA and FUTA contributions are based on its payroll, and an employee's FICA contribution and local, state, and federal tax are based on gross income. Because employee contributions to cafeteria plans are on a pretax basis, they reduce the employer's payroll and the employee's taxable income by the amount of the contribution. Consequently, the employer's FICA and FUTA contributions decrease. The employee also benefits, because he or she is able to spend these benefits dollars and not pay taxes on them.

Q. 9:5 When were flexible benefits plans first introduced?

The first flexible benefits plans were established by large companies in the early 1970s. In 1978, the first legislation that specifically allowed cafeteria plans, the Revenue Act of 1978, was enacted. The Act added Section 125 to the Internal Revenue Code, under which a plan could legally offer a choice between nontaxable benefits and taxable benefits or cash without adverse tax consequences ("constructive receipt") to employees.

Although flexible benefits have been in existence for over 10 years, only recently have they been available to small and medium-sized employers. This was due to the fact that only large companies had the resources to implement and administer flexible benefits plans. However, technological innovations have decreased the cost and have streamlined the process of administering the plans, and insurance companies have learned to adequately predict the cost and selection of the benefits offered under such plans. As a result, they are now available to companies with as few as 25 employees.

Q. 9:6 What is constructive receipt?

Taxpayers must report as taxable income any compensation or earnings realized during the year. This may include amounts not actually paid to or received by an individual if these amounts are deemed to have been "constructively received." A person is in constructive receipt of income or property if he or she has an unconditional right to take possession of it, whether he or she exercises that right or not. There is no constructive receipt, however, if possession is contingent upon surrendering some valuable right (such as the right to continue participating in the plan), or if there are other limitations on the exercise of the option.

Constructive receipt also does not apply if there is a statutory exemption. The Revenue Act of 1978 provided an exception to the doctrine of constructive receipt for cafeteria plans in IRC Section 125. Thus, an individual who could have elected cash or some other taxable benefit is not in constructive receipt when choosing a nontaxable benefit instead.

Q. 9:7 Why were flexible benefits plans developed?

Flexible benefits plans were developed as a result of two significant trends in the business world: a need to control or manage escalating employee benefits costs (see Chapter 7 on managing health insurance costs), and a changing employee population with changing needs.

Traditional benefits plans were designed in the 1950s, when 60% of the workforce consisted of men whose wives did not work. Today, this number has dropped to 34%. Only 30.5% of all wives worked in 1960; more than 60% were working by 1985. In addition, there are more women in the workforce than ever before, and there are more two-income families and single-parent families.

These demographic changes mean that a standard benefits package is inappropriate for the majority of today's workers. For example, a single person would not need or want as much life or health insurance as an older married person with children. A single parent might need day care or more life insurance. An older worker with no children might need more medical but less life insurance. Thus, different life styles give rise to different benefits needs, and workers today are asking for benefits that are more meaningful to them.

Q. 9:8 How do flexible benefits help control costs?

Flexible benefits provide a vehicle for separating the level of benefits from the cost of benefits. Employers can:

- Fix benefits costs as a percentage of payroll;
- Freeze costs at a set dollar level;
- Cover increased costs;
- Increase benefits as productivity or profits increase;
- Add new benefits without increasing the cost of the benefits program;
- Manage choices by controlling the price the employees pay for the benefits they select; or
- Control the options employees can select through plan design.

In contrast, the very structure of traditional benefits plans mandates cost increases each year, because medical care costs increase each year, and at a rate faster than the consumer price index. A plan designed to cover the reasonable and customary charge for services, as most plans are, becomes more expensive as the cost of the services increases.

An employer with a traditional plan, however, has several options for controlling costs: limiting the coverage provided, increasing the extent to which employees pay for the services provided (through increased deductible and coinsurance requirements), and increasing employees' contributions to the plan, all of which create the impression that the employee is "giving back" benefits.

Q. 9:9 How successful have flexible benefits plans been in controlling costs?

Recent surveys point to the success of flexible benefits plans in helping to control costs. A survey by A. Foster Higgins & Co. showed that in 1989 sponsors of flexible benefits plans spent 6.9% less per employee on health care than traditional plan sponsors ($2,635 versus $2,831) had, 7.9% lower indemnity medical plan costs ($2,500 versus $2,713), and had lower total health benefits costs as a percentage of payroll (8.7% vs. 9.7%).

Q. 9:10 Are there different types of flexible plans?

Yes. There are a number of different types of flexible benefits plans:

1. Salary reduction premium conversion plans;
2. Flexible spending or reimbursement accounts;
3. Modular plans;
4. Core plus plans;
5. Working spouse plans; and
6. Total flexible, or full cafeteria, plans.

Q. 9:11 What is a salary reduction premium conversion plan?

A salary reduction premium conversion plan is a very simple plan that permits employees to reduce their compensation by an amount equal to their contributions to a benefits program, such as a medical benefits plan. This has the effect of converting their contributions from after tax to pretax.

Q. 9:12 What is a flexible spending or reimbursement account?

Flexible spending or reimbursement accounts are accounts funded by employee salary reductions, employer contributions, or both. Amounts placed in these accounts are used to provide reimbursement for expenses incurred by the employee for specified benefits during the year.

Q. 9:13 What is a health care reimbursement account?

Health care reimbursement accounts, established under Section 105(h) of the Internal Revenue Code, allow participants to recover expenses on a pretax basis for those health care charges not reimbursed by any other source and not claimed on the participant's income tax return. These expenses can include, but are not limited to, medical and dental insurance deductibles and coinsurance; amounts over the reasonable and customary charges not covered by insurance; and other reimbursable expenses permitted as income tax deductions under IRC Section 213 (to the extent they exceed 7.5%), such as contact lenses, orthopedic shoes, nursing, prescription drugs, lab tests, cosmetic surgery, and hearing aids.

Q. 9:14 What is a dependent care reimbursement account?

A dependent care reimbursement account allows for the use of pretax dollars to provide benefits for the care of (1) a dependent under the age of 13 for whom a dependent deduction is allowed under the Internal Revenue Code or (2) a dependent who is physically or mentally incapable of caring for himself or herself, to enable the benefits plan participant and his or her spouse to work. This benefit works in conjunction with the dependent care deduction available on the participant's income tax return; however, expenses reimbursed through this account may not be claimed for income tax purposes.

These accounts may be used to provide up to $5,000 in dependent care assistance ($2,500 for a married individual filing separately). Amounts provided from a reimbursement account offset amounts available from the tax credit for child and dependent care expenses on a dollar-for-dollar basis. [Ref.: IRC Sections 21 and 129]

Q. 9:15 How are these reimbursement accounts structured?

Health care and dependent care reimbursement accounts can be structured through a salary reduction agreement, employer contributions to the plan, or both. The employer sets the maximum amount of contribution allowed for each account at the beginning of the plan year. Each participant may choose to contribute an amount per plan year up to that maximum. The participant submits expenses to be reimbursed periodically from funds in his or her account. Reimbursement is permitted only for services provided during the plan year. Until 1990, reimbursement was available generally only up to the amount already accumulated in the individual's account from periodic deposits. Expenses in excess of the amount accumulated were not reimbursed until funds were available. However, the cafeteria plan regulations proposed on March 7, 1989, require health care spending accounts to make the maximum reimbursement allowed available at all times. This prevents employers from limiting reimbursement to the amount of salary reduction accumulated in the individual's account and allows short-service employees to use more than they had contributed.

> **Example:** An employee elects to reduce her salary by $25 per week, effective January 1. On March 1, after depositing $200 in the spending account, the employee incurs a $1,000 qualified expense. The plan must pay the employee the full $1,000, since the maximum available benefit ($25 × 52 weeks, or $1,300) is greater, even though only $200 has been accumulated at the time of the expense. Should the employee terminate before accumulating $1,000 of salary reduction, the plan (employer) must make up the difference.

Employers cannot defer payment to the end of the plan year or until sufficient accumulation exists. In many states, the shortfall cannot be made up from other benefits distributions, such as accrued vacation, or from final pay.

Q. 9:16   What happens if the benefits paid plus administrative costs are less than the total contributions plus interest earnings?

If monies remain after all claims and expenses have been discharged, the plan is said to have an "experience gain." It can be used to reduce future contributions, in aggregate, and to improve current benefits for all participants or those allocated to participants. The return may not be based on individual claim submissions but can be either an equal amount to all employees or proportional to each participant's contribution as a percentage of total contributions.

Flexible Benefits   Q. 9:19

Q. 9:17 Are there any other special requirements for flexible spending arrangements?

Proposed cafeteria plan regulations stipulate that health care flexible spending arrangements must provide for uniform reimbursement throughout the year. This means that an employee who enters into a salary reduction agreement of $50 a month, or $600 a year, must have the full year's contributions available for reimbursement at the beginning of the year. That is, if an employee incurred $600 of reimbursable expenses in January, the full $600 would have to be made available to the employee at that time. Should this proposal become final, it presents problems for health care flexible spending accounts.

Q. 9:18 Is the uniform reimbursement approach the only one permitted under the 1989 proposed regulations?

The new uniform reimbursement approach requires that the full year's reimbursement be available on the first day of the plan year, thus placing the employer at considerable risk for insufficient contributions by short-service employees (see Question 9:17). For plan years beginning in 1990, this is the *only* approach permitted for health care spending accounts. However, dependent day care spending accounts may continue to hold claims until sufficient contributions have been collected.

Since employers are now required to assume risk as if they were providing insurance, the IRS has informally indicated that employers may charge a "risk premium." For example, an employer could charge an employee $1,500 for a $1,200 health care FSA. The additional contribution would serve to offset the losses on those who terminated after having received more in benefits than they contributed.

Q. 9:19 What new changes in family status permit participants in flexible spending arrangements to change their elections in mid-year?

The IRS has expanded the list of qualified changes in family status to include:

- An occasion where the employee's spouse commences employment, changes from part-time to full-time or from full-time to part-time, or takes an unpaid leave of absence, or
- A significant change in the coverage afforded under the spouse's employer's plan that affects the spouse and/or the employee.

In addition, the IRS has informally indicated that certain other situations would permit changes in elections because they significantly affect the need for certain benefits. For example:

- An employee changes from the day shift to the night shift and no longer needs day care for dependent children,
- An employee is transferred or moves outside an HMO service area or the HMO ceases to provide service in the employee's area,
- A dependent child ceasing to be a dependent because of age, marriage, or student status,
- A significant decrease in salary would *not* be considered a qualified basis for mid-year election change.

▶ **Planning Pointer:** Note that informal IRS indications are subject to change by the time regulations are issued and great care should be used in relying on such opinions.

Q. 9:20 Are changes in the cost of medical care options grounds for changing elections in mid—year?

The plan may permit automatic adjustment of employee premium contributions if the increase is requested by an insurance company or another third party. This adjustment feature must be properly specified in the plan document.

If such third party "significantly" increases the cost of medical coverage, the plan may allow employees to revoke their election and select another "similar" health plan. Regulations do not require the similar health plan to be of the same employer.

The IRS has informally stated that mid-year benefit election changes are not permitted when a self-insured medical plan cost is significantly increased.

Q. 9:21 What is a modular plan?

Modular flexible plans offer employees a choice of benefits packages. The employer determines combinations of coverages from which employees may choose. The employee selects the benefits package rather than choose the level of coverage within each benefit. For example, Plan A

might have life insurance equal to three times salary, a comprehensive medical plan with a $200 deductible and 80% coinsurance, and disability insurance equal to 50% of salary. Plan B might have life insurance equal to two times salary, a comprehensive medical plan with a $400 deductible and 80% coinsurance, and disability insurance equal to 60% of salary. Plan C might have life insurance equal to salary, a comprehensive medical plan with a $1,000 deductible and 80% coinsurance, and disability insurance equal to 60% of salary. Each employee could then choose Plan A, B, or C, or, if the employer allows, none of the plans. Employees could not, however, choose only part of each plan. Generally, these plans are only partially responsive to employee needs, but offer moderate control of adverse selection and price stability.

Q. 9:22 What is a core plus plan?

Core plus flexible plans require a certain level of benefits for all employees participating in the benefits plan, with employees having the option to increase one or all of the coverages. The core level is usually funded by the employer. For example, with this plan, employees would be provided with $50,000 life insurance, a comprehensive medical plan with a $500 deductible, and disability insurance equal to 50% of salary. They would then have the option to increase their life, medical, or disability insurance benefits if they so desired, or perhaps add dental, which is not included in the core. These plans are more responsive to employee needs than modular plans, but considerably less responsive than total flexible benefits plans. Adverse selection becomes more of a problem with each level of buy-up availability.

Q. 9:23 What is a working spouse plan?

Working spouse plans allow employees to drop their spousal coverage in exchange for cash or credits for other benefits. Employees would make this election when their spouses are covered by another plan, such as the spouse's employer plan.

Q. 9:24 What is a full menu or total flexible benefits plan?

Total flexible benefits plans provide employees with the greatest degree of choice and thus are most effective at meeting employee needs. Employees can select the appropriate level of coverage for each benefit offered through the plan. For example, they may be given three or four life insurance options, from which they can select one. Then they choose their medical coverage from several choices, and so on with disability, dental, and other insurance options that are provided. Only large employers should consider full menu plans, since each option offered must have sufficient participation or "spread of risk."

Q. 9:25 What types of benefits do cafeteria plans include?

Cafeteria plans include such benefits as:
- Medical benefits;
- Dental benefits;
- Health care reimbursement accounts;
- Dependent care reimbursement accounts;
- Life insurance;
- Accidental death and dismemberment (AD&D) insurance;
- Long-term disability;
- Short-term disability;

- Long-term care;
- 401(k) cash-or-deferred arrangements;
- Vision care; and
- Vacation days.

Q. 9:26 What medical insurance options are available under a cafeteria plan?

The design of medical options under a cafeteria plan is not restricted. However, offering a base plus plan as an option is not advisable if cost control is an objective. In fact, a flex plan provides an opportunity for an employer to move its plan from a base plus to a more cost-effective comprehensive plan, or to increase the deductible on a comprehensive plan, with less difficulty.

Most flexible plans offer several choices of deductibles and out-of-pocket maximums. Some include a catastrophic illness plan with a very high deductible and no coinsurance, and may allow an employee to take no medical coverage at all if he or she is covered elsewhere. The deductibles are designed with different life situations in mind and combined so that the choices among options are meaningful.

Q. 9:27 Can a flexible plan include an HMO?

Yes, an HMO can be among the medical options offered in a flexible plan. However, evidence indicates that this adversely affects the cost of the rest of the plan, whether it is insured or self-funded, since younger, healthier employees are more likely to choose the HMO. However, if a qualified HMO has taken the required steps to initiate the offer, certain employers, as described at Questions 8:33–8:34, must offer that type of HMO. To the extent that such HMOs are part of an integrated multioption plan offered by a carrier or the HMO agrees to experience rate the HMO plan, the risk of "skimming" is reduced and the impact on total employer cost is diminished.

Q. 9:28 Can a flexible plan include a PPO?

Yes, a PPO can be incorporated into one or more of the medical options offered in a flexible plan. The level of reimbursement for each person will depend on whether the insured uses a preferred provider or not, as well as on the plan option selected for the plan year. The PPO arrangement is the same as it would be for a traditional plan.

Q. 9:29 Is all the insurance provided under a flexible plan provided by one insurer, or do insurers bid for pieces?

Plans may be designed and handled either way. However, small employers often prefer to place all coverage and reimbursement accounts with one insurer, since it simplifies implementation and administration.

Q. 9:30 What are the advantages of using one carrier?

When using one carrier, integration of all parts of the plan is inherent in its design, and all procedures, including enrollment, are coordinated. This makes installation more efficient. On an ongoing basis, plan administrators deal with one set of procedures, and forms and processes can be streamlined. For example, claims submitted but not covered in full under the medical or dental insurance plan can be automatically transferred for reimbursement from the health care reimbursement account. All of this should add up to lower costs in the long run.

Q. 9:31 Does a cafeteria plan allow employees to select cash instead of benefits?

Yes, although the degree to which employees can receive cash instead of benefits varies by employer. Some employers require that employees maintain a level of insurance protection (through their spouse's plan, for example) if the employee wishes to forgo all benefits and select cash exclusively.

Q. 9:32 Can a 401(k) plan be integrated into a cafeteria plan?

Yes. The Miscellaneous Revenue Act of 1980 amended Section 125 to allow cafeteria plans to include 401(k) plans, which are "cash-or-deferred" arrangements under which employers can make nontaxable contributions to qualified defined-contribution plans. Employees can make similar contributions through salary reduction, thereby deferring taxes on a portion of their incomes. 401(k) plans are the only deferred-compensation plans allowed in cafeteria plans. Contributions to 401(k) plans are subject to FICA taxes.

Q. 9:33 What are the advantages of including a 401(k) plan in a flexible plan?

In addition to the tax advantages to both employers and employees, packaging a 401(k) plan with a flex plan makes administration of the 401(k) plan easier for the employer. The same salary reduction payroll system is used for both plans, and employees make their contributions and coverage choices at the same time. Also, employees may appreciate their benefits package more if they see the total package in an integrated manner.

Q. 9:34 Why wouldn't all employees choose the plan options that offered the best coverage?

The types of benefits provided under each option in a flexible plan are often the same or similar. What differs is the level of coverage offered and the cost of the coverage. For example, an employee can choose one of several life insurance coverage levels—the difference is in the amount of insurance protection the employee elects. With medical coverage under a flexible plan, the deductibles and the out-of-pocket maximums generally are the differentiation factors, although the coinsurance level and benefit features may also vary, especially in a catastrophic option. Athough one choice may be "richer" than another, it will cost more. Many employees prefer not to pay this extra cost.

They feel that these benefit dollars would be more wisely spent on another insurance coverage for which they have greater need, or they prefer to receive the difference in cash, as deposits to their 401(k) accounts, or as additional paid time off.

Q. 9:35 What nondiscrimination requirements must a cafeteria plan meet?

Cafeteria plans must meet nondiscrimination requirements at three levels:

1. Each of the qualified benefits must meet the specific nondiscrimination requirements for that benefit when tested singly.
2. There are rules imposed on the plan as a whole by IRC Section 125.

(See Chapter 11 for complete details on non–discrimination requirements.)

Q. 9:36 What are the requirements for qualified benefits?

No more than 25% of the total contribution under a group legal services plan, or under a dependent care reimbursement option, may be allocated to owners of more than 5% of the company, or to their dependents or spouses. In addition, the average benefit provided to nonhighly compensated individuals must be at least 55% of the average benefit provided to highly compensated individuals.

Employers have the option of testing legal services and dependent care reimbursement options as "statutory employee benefits" under the nondiscrimination rules of IRC Section 89.

Q. 9:37 What are the nondiscrimination requirements of IRC Section 125?

Cafeteria plans may not discriminate in favor of highly compensated individuals as to eligibility to participate. In addition, no more than 25% of the total nontaxable benefits may be provided to key employees. A key employee is:

- An officer earning more than 50% of the defined-benefit dollar limit (in 1990, 50% of $102,582 or $51,291);
- One of the 10 employees owning the largest interest in the employer and earning more than $30,000 annually;
- A 5% owner; or
- A 1% owner earning more than $150,000 a year.

  If the plan violates the top-heavy rule, the anti-constructive-receipt rule of Section 125 will not apply to key employees. They will be taxed as if they actually received all the taxable benefits that they could have elected to receive for the plan year.

Q. 9:38 How are plans tested to assure compliance with nondiscrimination rules?

Some nondiscrimination rules should be addressed at the plan design stage. These relate to such provisions as eligibility and equal benefits and contributions. Rules that cover participation and selection cannot be dealt with until all enrollment forms are completed. Then the insurer or administrator will test each part of the plan to be sure it is in compliance. Sometimes, changes must be made to bring the plan into compliance. For example, highly compensated employees may be required to reduce their contributions to the health care reimbursement account (alternatively, they can have the value of their benefits included in their taxable compensation).

Q. 9:39 How are flexible benefits plans funded?

Typically, flexible benefits plans are funded in three ways: employer contributions to the plan, employee contributions to the plan through a salary reduction agreement, or both. The way in which flexible benefits plans are funded does not differ from the funding of traditional employee benefits plans, with one notable exception: Employee contributions to the plan are on a pretax basis.

Q. 9:40 Must flexible benefits plans be contributory?

Any one of the options under each coverage may be fully funded by the employer either for the employee only or for family coverage, making it "noncontributory" in the traditional sense. However, other options under that coverage may require employee contributions. Thus, the plan as a whole could be looked at as "contributory." This does not preclude the possibility that given the employer's funding, an individual employee could select coverages and levels in each that would be fully noncontributory.

Q. 9:41 How does an employer determine its level of contribution to the flexible plan?

There are a number of ways for employers to determine their levels of contribution to a flexible plan, such as freezing benefits costs as a percentage of payroll, determining a set dollar amount they wish to spend on employee benefits, or contributing the same amount they did under the traditional benefits plan. All of these options, however, are based on the employer's objectives in establishing a flexible plan. Although these objectives may differ for each employer, they can generally be broken down into three categories, which are not necessarily exclusive:

1. To attract and retain the best employees;
2. To control costs; and
3. To reduce costs while maintaining an adequate benefits plan.

The contribution level will differ, just as the structure and design of the plan will vary, according to the employer's objectives. If the plan is a tool to attract and retain employees, employer contributions would probably be higher than if the objective were to reduce costs.

Q. 9:42 How are employee contribution levels determined?

Employee contributions are determined by the employer at the beginning of each plan year and vary depending on a number of factors, including the cost of the plan, the benefits each employee selects, and the level of employer contributions.

Q. 9:43 How are employer and employee contributions made in a full flexible benefits plan?

Employer contributions are commonly made by allocating credits to a "decision pool." Employee contributions consist of pretax contributions to the decision pool. A decision pool represents the combined contributions of employer and employee, and is the amount available for each employee to pay insurance premiums for chosen benefits, fund reimbursement accounts, or receive as cash instead of benefits.

Q. 9:44 Can small employers self-fund flexible benefits plans?

Small employers can self-fund their flexible benefits plans, but the adverse selection issues discussed at Question 9:46 become more acute for them. If self-funding is desired, employers need a skilled and experienced intermediary to assist with plan design, implementation, administration, and renewal. Since flex is in the early stages of development, few intermediaries have this expertise.

Q. 9:45 Is purchasing a flexible benefits plan similar to purchasing a traditional plan?

Flexible benefits plans are purchased in much the same way that traditional plans are. The employer, working with its insurance intermediary (broker, agent, or consultant), might survey employees to determine their needs, and must establish its own objectives. The intermediary then solicits quotes from insurers and selects the desired benefits provider based on those needs and objectives.

Q. 9:46 How does adverse selection affect flexible benefits plans?

With a flexible benefits plan, employees select a package of benefits that reflects their specific needs. Thus, they are most likely to select benefits they will actually use. This phenomenon is known as "adverse selection." Adverse selection does not actually cause higher utilization of benefits; employees generally use what they need, and claims remain the same. What does result is that less premium is available from those who do not use their benefits to pay for those benefits that are used.

This means, then, that pricing the benefits in a flexible benefits plan and predicting benefits utilization is a complicated process. Insurance companies and the larger cosulting firms have actuarial professionals who can estimate fairly accurately the expected cost of each flexible benefits plan component, and can make demographic predictions of who will elect certain benefits as well as who will use the benefits. In addition, the financial resources of most insurers allow them to absorb the financial consequences of some inaccurate predictions. In the future, as the accuracy of prediction of utilization increases, employers may be in a better position to consider assuming more of the risk of flexible benefits plans. Small employers will still be subject to the volatility of utilization that comes with being able to spread the risk over only a relatively few employees.

For an employer with fewer than 500 employees that is implementing a flexible benefits plan for the first time, an insurer is highly recommended, because the financial risk associated with benefits utilization in a flexible benefits plan is greater than with a traditional benefits plan.

Q. 9:47 What specific issues should an employer address in contemplating the purchase of a flexible benefits plan?

Most companies adopt flexible benefits plans to meet the needs of a diverse workforce, to attract and retain employees, to manage and control costs, and to achieve tax-effective use of their benefits dollars. However, although these are the basic reasons for purchasing a flexible plan, designing a plan to meet these objectives requires a more precise analysis.

The specific issues that employers should address before designing a plan include whether the company is interested in:

- Offering better benefits than companies competing with it for skilled labor;
- Raising employee morale by offering better benefits;
- Retaining top-level management;
- Preventing unionization;
- Improving the company's image;
- Increasing equity in benefits among employees, regardless of marital status or income;
- Increasing employees' awareness of the cost of medical care;
- Separating benefits costs from benefits levels; or
- Spending no more than a predetermined dollar amount on the benefits package for a specific period of time.

Plan features, including coverages, levels, and costs, can be designed differently to accomplish the objectives of each individual company. For example, if a company wants to offer a more attractive benefits plan than its competition, but still needs to control costs, the flexible plan can be designed so that the employer provides the same level of benefits as under its traditional plan, but gives employees the option to purchase additional benefits through pretax salary reduction. For an employer that is interested in cost control and therefore determines that it cannot spend more than a certain dollar amount on benefits, the plan can be structured so that the benefits offered remain the same, and the employer's contribution remains the same even if the cost of benefits rises. In such an example, the employee would asssume more responsibility for the purchase of the benefits if he or she wanted to maintain the previous level of benefits.

Proper design of a flexible plan requires an analysis of the company's specific situation, the employer's objectives, and the employees' benefits needs.

Q. 9:48 How can an employer determine what its employees' benefits needs are?

Employee needs can be determined by a written survey that should be administered at least six months before the proposed effective date of the flexible benefits plan. When planned and analyzed carefully by the employer, consultant, or insurer, a survey can provide valuable information for designing a flexible plan that will be well-received by employees. Just as employers must determine precisely what their needs are, it is important to determine what employees want in their benefits package.

In addition, an employee needs survey is one tool for having the employees participate in designing the plan. This involvement, in turn, will lead to greater employee acceptance of the flexible plan and the advantages it offers. However, some employers feel a survey is unnecessary. They have other reliable means of knowing their employees' needs and would prefer not to spend the time to conduct a survey.

Q. 9:49 How are flexible benefits plans implemented?

Implementation of a flexible benefits plan is generally the same as for a traditional plan: The plan is announced, employees are enrolled and receive information concerning their benefits coverages, and the plan becomes effective. However, although the basic outline for plan implementation remains the same, each of the steps involved requires different tactics. For example, the plan announcement requires more communication from the company to the employees in order to explain the new concept of flexible benefits, and the enrollment of employees is more involved.

Q. 9:50 How long does it take from the purchase of a flexible benefits plan until it can be implemented?

The preliminary analysis of employer objectives and employee needs can take somewhat longer than for a traditional benefits plan, depending on the size of the employer and the complexities involved in compensation analysis. This analysis will be done before the plan is quoted, as with traditional plans.

The time from the initial quote on the plan design to the actual effective date of the plan is usually at least four months. The first month is spent reviewing the quote for its success in meeting the employer's determined objectives. Actual implementation, once the decision to buy has been made and the final plan design settled on, requires two-and-a-half to three months.

Q. 9:51 What kinds of employee communications are advisable in advance of enrollment?

As the size of the employee group increases, so does the intensity of the communication effort involved in flexible benefits plan implementation. Regardless of size, however, careful, clear communication is essential. Employers usually use a letter from the chief executive officer or president of the company to announce the flexible benefits plan. Posters may be placed in strategic locations around the company to introduce the concept of flex. Also, in preparation for enrollment, some explanation of the concept of flexible benefits, in easily understood form, should be given to employees. A simple conceptual brochure can serve this purpose.

Q. 9:52 How do employees enroll in a plan and select their benefits?

Since understanding is so critical to making the most appropriate choices, employee meetings are usually held to explain the flexible benefits plan. They may be conducted by the employer, an intermediary, the insurer, or a combination of them. At those meetings, employees are provided with a written explanation of the process and forms on which to make their selections. The forms will typically identify the benefits options and their costs, as well as the amount of benefits dollars provided by the employer. Employees are expected to make choices and calculate their total costs, including the salary reduction that will result if selections cost more than the amount the employer provides. If an employee opts for fewer benefits than his or her benefits dollars cover, the plan might provide that he or she receive the excess as additional taxable income.

To minimize confusion to employees, particularly during the first plan year, enrollment requires a great deal of employee education, even after employee meetings have been held and the materials have been distributed. An employer representative must be knowledgeable and should be available to answer questions during the enrollment period, which is usually at least two months prior to the effective date. This educational effort takes time, but the employer's genuine concern for employee needs is communicated repeatedly, often resulting in increased employee morale.

The enrollment process can result in some dissatisfied employees, especially if previous benefits were extremely comprehensive and some new limitations are being imposed. It is advisable for management to determine what communication of compensation objectives is necessary before the flexible benefits plan is announced, to assure maximum satisfaction.

Q. 9:53 What is enrollment confirmation?

Employees are provided with a summary of their individual benefits choices and the costs associated with them. They are asked to verify the accuracy of the summary by signing and returning it to the company's personnel accounting department, which in turn directs it to the administrator of the flexible plan. Usually a short period is allowed for employees to change their choices or correct any errors or misunderstandings. Once signed, the summary serves as confirmation that the employee's choices are correct as recorded, and benefits will be paid based on the record.

Q. 9:54 What kinds of changes may an employee make during the plan year?

Tax law requires that an employee's choices in a flexible benefits plan be made in advance of the plan year. This means that after the effective date of the plan, no changes can be made (except as described below) until the next enrollment period. Changes in choices during the plan year are permitted only if a "family status" change occurs. A family status change is defined to include the following:

- Marriage;
- Divorce;
- Death of a spouse;
- Birth of a child;
- Adoption of a child; or
- Termination of employment of a spouse.

Q. 9:55 How do the cost and pricing of a flexible benefits plan compare with those of a traditional employee benefits plan?

The cost issue has two parts: (1) the cost of the benefits themselves, which incorporates the risk of adverse selection and the potential for cost management inherent in a flexible benefits plan; and (2) the cost involved in developing and implementing the program.

The cost of the benefits, if insured, will be based on the insurer's underlying price structure, which usually applies to traditional as well as flexible benefits plans. Traditional insurance allows insurers to calculate an average rate for the group to be covered and multiply it by the number of employees and dependents enrolled or, for some coverages, by the volume of insurance elected overall. Insurers' methods for flexible plan pricing vary. They must take into account selection assumptions and utilization rates that vary accordingly. The risk of adverse selection is in addition to the utilization risks in a single traditional plan. Such risk may be assumed by the employer or the insurer. An intermediary can help the employer obtain an acceptable pricing agreement with an insurer.

Cost management or cost control is most applicable to medical coverage. Decisions about features such as coinsurance variations, deductibles, and preferred provider arrangements are not inherently different for flexible benefits plan coverages, but a flexible plan, by virtue of the availability of choice, allows an employer to introduce plan features that promise long-term cost control. Furthermore, by establishing the basis for future contributions for the employee benefits plan, an employer can begin the process of long-term cost management.

Depending on who performs the services associated with design and implementation of the plan, the costs of these services may be charged separately or incorporated in the benefits cost. Excellent communication materials and enrollment assistance are available to employers of all sizes at reasonable costs. Ongoing administration costs generally depend on the frequency of the services requested, such as reimbursement account payments and reports.

Q. 9:56 How does renewal of a flexible benefits plan compare with traditional employee benefits plan renewal?

Annual reenrollment makes renewal of a flexible benefits plan somewhat more time-consuming. Renewal costs will be based on prior elections and anticipated changes, plan design adjustments, and the insurer's medical care costs in general. However, for some plans, the past experience of the total plan and its options are used separately to compute renewal costs. The process also takes more time than for traditional plans, since there are more alternatives for meeting the employer's objectives, which also may have changed.

Q. 9:57 What kinds of reports are necessary to ensure smooth implementation and administration of a flexible plan?

In addition to the standard reports associated with benefits utilization, additions and deletions of employees and dependents, and premium accounting reports, three flexible benefits plan reports are necessary. A salary impact report is usually generated after enrollment confirmation. This identifies the costs of the benefits and the salary reduction or increase associated with each employee's choices. It is the blueprint for changes to the employer's payroll system.

For plans with health care reimbursement or dependent care reimbursement accounts, periodic reports are necessary for employees and the employer to summarize available funds in each account and payments made from them. For plans with 401(k) plans, an individual periodic report showing employee contributions, employer contributions, interest, and fund balances is recommended, as well as an employer summary for the plan.

Q. 9:58 How does an employer decide who will administer the flexible benefits plan?

After understanding what is involved in administering a flexible benefits plan, an employer must evaluate the options available. Resources (both systems and people), priorities, and cost should be considered, taking into account the efficiencies of working with one source for the entire plan.

The employer may decide for simplicity's sake to select an insurer that has the ability to administer the plan as well as provide the plan design and coverage options. Insurers that do offer flexible plans to small employers will generally also offer administrative support. Some insurers also offer special software packages to small employers for plan administration.

If the employer has the systems necessary to administer the plan or is willing to invest in such areas because of anticipated cost savings, then the employer could administer the plan itself. Third-party administrators are also an option, as are brokers and consultants who have the systems available. Thus, many options are available to the employer for administering the plan.

Q. 9:59 What type of billing arrangement is used—self-accounting or home office?

Complete records of each employee's current choices must be kept, regardless of how a flexible benefits plan is billed. Generally, the first bill would identify each employee and the costs associated with his or her selections. Subsequent bills can reflect only the changes to choices as a result of the addition of new employees, termination of employees, or changes in family status. This is somewhere between what is commonly referred to as self-accounting and home-office billing by insurance companies.

Q. 9:60 What assistance is available to an employer that wants to administer its own flexible benefits plan?

There are numerous vendors that now have computerized administrative systems, as well as informational packages to assist an employer that wants to handle its own administration. Details on these packages are available from the Employers Council on Flexible Compensation.

Chapter 10

Medicare

Medicare is an important consideration for employers planning health insurance programs. This chapter explains who is covered by Medicare and what they are covered for, how that coverage affects other coverages employees may have, and how companies must coordinate these benefits.

Q. 10:1 What is Medicare?

Medicare is a system of federal reimbursement for medical care to certain eligible elderly and disabled individuals. Medicare consists of a hospital benefits plan (Part A) and supplementary medical insurance (Part B). Part A covers individuals for expenses incurred at hospitals, extended care facilities, home health care agencies, and hospices. Part A is automatic at no fee to eligible individuals. It is paid for through a hospital insurance tax that is part of the Federal Insurance Contributions Act (FICA)/ Self Employment Contribution Act (SECA) taxes.

Part B helps pay for physicians' services and other medical services not paid for under Part A. Participation in Part B is voluntary and requires premium contributions by the individual. Participation in Part A means automatic enrollment in Part B, but Part B participation is terminated if the individual files a notice that he or she no longer wishes to participate, or fails to pay a premium within the three-month grace period.

Q. 10:2 Who is eligible for Medicare coverage?

"Eligible" refers to:

- Individuals who are eligible for monthly Social Security or Railroad Retirement benefits, including retirees over the age of 65, dependents, or survivors;
- Individuals, including those who are under age 65, who have been entitled to receive Social Security disability income for two years, or receive treatment for end-stage kidney disease; and
- Persons 65 or older who are not eligible for Social Security or Railroad Retirement benefits, but who have qualified for hospital benefits by paying a monthly premium and enrolling in Part B.

The Consolidated Omnibus Budget Reconciliation Act of 1985 (COBRA) extended Medicare coverage to state and local government employees for services provided after March 31, 1986.

Q. 10:3 What services are covered under Part A?

The following services, when provided by an approved provider of services, are covered for eligible individuals:

1. Bed and board in a semiprivate room;
2. Hospital physician and nursing services;
3. Special care (e.g., intensive care);
4. Drugs in a hospital;
5. X-rays and radiation therapy;
6. Hospital laboratory tests;
7. Operating room costs (including anesthesia);
8. Recovery room costs; and
9. Inpatient rehabilitation (e.g., physical therapy or occupational therapy).

Q. 10:4 What services are covered under Part B?

Part B covers:

1. Services provided by medical doctors and osteopaths, including surgery, consultation, and visits, whether at home, in the office, or at a medical care institution;
2. Outpatient physician and hospital care, including drugs that cannot be self-administered;
3. Certain dental surgery;
4. Home health services;
5. Diagnostic x-rays and laboratory tests;
6. X-ray and radiation therapy;
7. Ambulances, if required by the patient's condition;
8. Costs of surgical devices, durable medical equipment, and prosthetic devices;
9. Colostomy supplies;
10. The first three pints of blood; and
11. Nonhospital prescription drugs (beginning in 1991).

Q. 10:5 What types of care are not covered by Medicare?

Medicare does not cover:

1. Private room in a hospital or nursing home (unless medically required);
2. Private nurse;
3. Routine physical checkups;
4. Dental services and dentures;
5. Custodial care;
6. Most services provided by optometrists, psychologists, and chiropractors;
7. Cosmetic surgery;
8. Personal comfort items, such as hospital TVs;
9. Most services provided outside the United States (except

certain emergency inpatient care), services required as a result of war, and services covered by workers' compensation;
10. Orthopedic devices; and
11. Services or devices that are not reasonable and necesary for the diagnosis or treatment of illness or injury or to improve the function of a malformed part of the body.

Medicare Order of Benefit Determination

Q. 10:6 How are Medicare benefits integrated with employer-provided benefits for older active employees?

Since 1981, several different pieces of legislation have progressively reversed the "order of benefits." Originally, Medicare eligibles received primary benefits from Medicare; any employer-provided benefits were additional. To avoid duplicating Medicare benefits, employer plan benefits were "integrated," which means that Medicare benefits were taken into account before determining supplemental benefits in one of three ways:

1. Benefits payable under the employer's plan were reduced by the benefits payable under Medicare. Generally, the employer's plan covered the same benefits as Medicare, but employer-provided benefits were reduced by the Medicare payments. This was known as "carve out."
2. Benefits payable under the employer's plan "wrapped around" Medicare, in that the employer plan was specially-designed to pay for expenses that Medicare did not cover, called "Medicare Supplement."
3. Benefits payable under the employer's plan were combined with Medicare benefits using a coordination of benefits provision, which allowed the insured to be reimbursed for up to 100% of expenses allowable under either plan.

In 1981, however, the Budget Reconciliation Act required employer plans to be primary for the first 12 months of treatment for end-stage renal disease. The Tax Equity and Fiscal Responsibility Act of 1982 (TEFRA) extended primary employer plan benefits to active employees aged 65 through 69 in addition to prohibiting benefit reductions on account of age. The Deficit Reduction Act of 1984 (DEFRA) enlarged the employer plan primary group to include any individual (employee or spouse) aged 65 through 69. This applied to a spouse even if the employee was under 65. Finally, the Consolidated Omnibus Budget Reconciliation Act of 1985 (COBRA) provided that the employer plan is primary and Medicare secondary for all active employees regardless of age, in effect eliminating the age 70 cap.

The result in almost all cases is that the employer's plan continues to be primary coverage, and older employees defer eligibility for Medicare benefits to retirement. Employees have the right, however, to reject their employer's plan and elect only Medicare coverage.

Q. 10:7   Except for treatment of end-stage renal disease, is Medicare the primary payor for disabled individuals who are less than age 65 and are not retired?

No. The Omnibus Budget Reconciliation Act of 1986 (OBRA) amended the Social Security Act to prohibit "large group health plans" (an employer that normally employs at least 100 employees on a typical business day during the prior calendar year) from taking into account any Medicare benefits received by a disabled individual who is not retired, or for which a disabled individual is eligible. This new "order of benefit determination" was effective January 1, 1987, and is scheduled to expire January 1, 1992.

OBRA '89

Q. 10:8   How did OBRA 89 change the Medicare as secondary payer rules?

OBRA 89's primary impact will be on enforcement. The law was aimed at ensuring that where an employer plan is properly the primary payor, it does not pass the obligation off on Medicare. It authorizes the Health Care Financing Administration (HCFA) to cooperate with the Social Security Administration (SSA) and the Internal Revenue Service in identifying Medicare eligibles who received wages from an employer during the preceding year. HCFA will use this information to help establish if these individuals were covered by an employer plan, as well as what benefits they were eligible for.

Q. 10:9   What information will the IRS and SSA provide?

The IRS will provide the SSA with the name, tax identification number (TIN), marital and employment status, and tax filing status of Medicare eligible employees and their spouses.

The SSA will provide information to the HCFA on the identity, TIN, and Social Security number of each Medicare beneficiary who received wages from a "qualified employer" during the preceding year, as well as the same information on the employee's spouse, if he or she received wages during the preceding year. It will also provide the name, address, and tax number of qualified employers.

Q. 10:10   Who is a "qualified employer"?

A qualified employer, subject to the Medicare-secondary rules, is one who furnishes written wage and tax statements to at least 20 persons for wages paid during a calendar year.

The the 20-employee cutoff for "qualified employers" applies even where the employer is part of a multi-employer group health plan with more than 20 member-employees overall. A "multi-employer group health plan" is a plan sponsored by more than one employer, or a union plan.

Q. 10:11   What does the HCFA do with the information it receives from the IRS and SSA?

The HCFA is empowered to contact employers, insurers, and plan administrators to determine if and when the individuals were covered under an employer plan, and what the extent of the coverage was.

Q. 10:12 What are the penalties for failure to provide information?

Employers are required to furnish information on Medicare eligible employees or spouses within 30 days of the date of the insurer's request. Failure to do so can carry penalties of up to $1000 per request.

Q. 10:13 How long are these provisions in effect?

Under the present law, the IRS and SSA disclosure requirements, as well as the penalties for employers, apply only to requests made prior to September 30, 1991.

Q. 10:14 What other changes were made to Medicare secondary rules?

The HCFA issued final regulations which clarify a number of issues regarding Medicare secondary rules:

- Employers must offer the same coverage to rehired retirees, as well as to their spouses who are over the age of 65, as they do to non-retirees. This means, however, that if the rehires are part of a class of employees where active workers do not receive health care benefits, the rehires need not receive them either. So Medicare would be the primary payor.
- The rules are intended to apply to self-insured plans as well as to insured ones.
- Self-employed persons are affected only if they had at least $400 in net earnings from self-employment in the preceding year. Self-employed clergy are included only if their churches pay FICA taxes for them.

The regulations also spell out rules for recovering payments made by Medicare which should properly have been made by the employer plan.

Q. 10:15 What are the implications of the new rules for the disabled?

This is yet another step in the process of cost shifting, that started with TEFRA in 1982. Over a period of several years, the federal government has gradually shifted payment responsibility for Medicare-eligible parties from the federal sector to the private sector. This trend has been extended to disabled employees who are under age 65.

Q. 10:16 Is this rule permanent?

This rule has a sunset provision. It is being "tested" from January 1, 1987, through December 31, 1991. During this period, the Comptroller General will conduct an impact study to determine costs, impact on business, and other factors.

Q. 10:17 Is there a penalty for failure to comply?

Yes. The penalty for noncompliance is 25% of the employer's annual contribution to noncomplying health plans. Depending on the number of persons affected, this could be a very steep price to pay for failure to comply. In addition, an individual or the government may file for damages in the case of a noncomplying employer. The claim can be for double the actual damages.

Q. 10:18 Are there any exceptions to the rule?

Yes. The end-stage renal disease program is excepted. Employers must pay for only one year.

Q. 10:19 Who is considered disabled for Social Security purposes?

Disability under Social Security means that the individual is so severely impaired, either mentally or physically, that he or she is unable to perform any substantial gainful work. This condition must be expected to last at least 12 months, or result in death. To qualify for benefits, there is a 5-month waiting period during which the individual must have been continuously disabled.

In determining whether an individual's impairment is sufficient to qualify for disability benefits, claims adjudicators at the Social Security Administration (or a state agency that performs this function for the SSA), take into account such things as:

- Current gainful employment (earning $500 per month would disqualify the person from being considered disabled); and
- The severity of the impairment or impairments. If the impairment is severe and is listed in the schedule (Appendix 1) of the regulations, then the person is deemed to be disabled. If not, additional factors are considered, such as residual functional capacity, age, education and work experience.

If the person is unable, based upon these factors, to do the type of work performed in the past 10 years, and is equally unable to perform any other types of work due to age, education and experience, then he is disabled.

Q. 10.20 What special rules apply to Medicare secondary requirements for disabled individuals?

In order for the secondary rules to apply, the individual must still be an "employee" under Health Care Financing Administration regulations.

Proposed HCFA regulations provide tests to determine if an individual who no longer comes to work (because he is disabled) is still to be considered an employee. There is an absolute test and a facts and circumstances test.

Q. 10.21 What is the absolute test?

Under this test, a disabled individual is automatically considered an employee if:

- He receives payments that are subject to Federal Insurance Contributions Act (FICA) taxation, or would be subject if the employer were not covered by a general FICA exemption, as with certain government and church employers;
- Is classified as an employee under a state or federal law, or as the result of a court decision;
- Is still characterized as an employee on the employer's records, whether or not his payroll status has been terminated.

Q. 10:22 What is the facts and circumstances test?

Where one of the three factors in the absolute test does not confer employee status automatically, a disabled individual may still be considered an employee if one or more of the following indicators applies:

- The individual receives vacation pay or accrues vacation time;
- The individual accrues sick leave;
- The individual has a contractual or legally enforceable right to return to work if the disability abates or disappears;
- The employer pays on his behalf the same taxes as are paid for active employees;
- The individual participates in an employer-sponsored benefit plan only available to employees (as opposed to one that is available to retirees as well).

Other factors not in the proposed regulations, but which have been applied before and could show up in the final regulations, are accrued years of service credits for vesting or additional pension benefits.

Q. 10:23 What other individuals are covered under the Medicare secondary rules?

The Medicare secondary rules apply to disabled dependents and self-employed individuals as well as to employees.

Q. 10:24 Which employer plans are subject to the Medicare order of benefit determination rules?

Large group health plans are those sponsored by employers who employed at least 100 employees, full-time or part-time, on at least half of their regular business days during the previous calendar year.

Plans maintained by more than one employer are affected if at least one employer meets the 100-employee test.

The rules apply to most employers, including non-profit, government, and religious organizations.

Medicare Cost Containment

Q. 10:25 What steps has Medicare taken to limit costs?

The Health Care Financing Administration began implementing a prospective payment system (PPS) for Medicare in 1983. (Some state Medicaid administrations have also implemented prospective payment systems.) Hospitals can expect a fixed reimbursement for each patient discharged, based not on the number and kinds of services delivered, but on the diagnosis of the patient. The retrospective system encourages providers to deliver more care. In contrast, PPS eliminates the incentive for hospitals to deliver unnecessary care.

Q. 10:26 How are payments determined on the basis of diagnosis?

In 1975, Yale University introduced a system of diagnosis-related groups (DRGs) for 467 diagnoses. Initially, these DRGs were meant to be used as a management and planning tool for the health care system. But because of the need for cost management, the federal government decided to apply them as a reimbursement method. Payment schedules for all DRGs were developed. Patients' conditions were translated to a DRG, and the allowable charge was determined based on the payment schedule.

Q. 10:27   Are all Medicare claims paid on a DRG basis?

Currently, only hospital care is paid on a DRG basis. There are, however, some hospitalizations that are given special consideration under the DRG system of reimbursement. These fall into two groups. First, certain kinds of hospitals are not required to subscribe to DRG rules to date. These include some teaching and psychiatric hospitals where the model for the determination of payment by diagnosis has not been developed yet, due to the different services involved and the complex issue of allowable costs of education involved at teaching hospitals. The other kinds of hospitalizations that are given special consideration are known as "outliers." Individuals whose illnesses are unique may not be classifiable under one of the DRGs. They may require care that is necessary but outside the realm of the established reimbursement norms. These cases are handled individually for Medicare reimbursement.

Q. 10:28   If the care delivered costs a hospital less than the DRG-allowed sum, does the hospital retain the difference?

Yes. It is hoped that DRGs will encourage cost-effective care. Conversely, if the care provided costs the hospital more than it is reimbursed under DRG, the hospital must make up the difference.

Q. 10:29   Are DRGs reducing the delivery of expensive, unnecessary hospital care?

There is some evidence that DRGs are having this effect. Since the institution of PPS, Medicare payments to hospitals have risen only 2% to 3% a year, compared with previous increases of up to 20% annually. There are, however, arguments by health care professionals that patients have been discharged early, and without proper care, because their DRGs would not allow the hospitals to continue care. Reconciliation of cost and quality of care under this system is still evolving.

Q. 10:30 Is Medicare the only plan that uses the DRG reimbursement system?

No. In New Jersey, New York, and Connecticut, the law requires all reimbursement by insurers to be done on a DRG basis. There may be other situations in which insurers have agreed to reimburse on a DRG basis through a private insurance arrangement at a particular hospital.

Q. 10:31 How has the DRG system affected the insurance industry?

DRGs have forced some hospitals to "cost shift" the revenue they lose from DRGs to other insurers. Many insurers—private companies as well as state Medicaid administrations—are championing the introduction of "all payor" systems, under which all insurers would pay on the same basis, although not necessarily on a DRG basis. Some states—Connecticut, Maine, Maryland, Massachusetts, New Jersey, New York, and Washington—already have such a system in effect. In other states, the federal government has granted so-called Medicare waivers, which allow providers in these states to charge Medicare on a basis other than PPS or DRG. These waivers are granted only in states where the costs to Medicare are expected to be lower than they would be otherwise. The objective is to allow experimentation with other prospective payment systems that may eventually save money for the entire health care system.

Q. 10:32 How did OBRA change the rules for Medicare physician reimbursement?

Medicare changed the rules by:
1. Placing limits on balance billing;
2. Establishing volume performance standards;
3. Establishing a resource-based relative value scale (RBRVS) system of payments; and
4. Reducing the amount Medicare will pay for certain overvalued procedures.

Q. 10:33 What is balance billing?

This is a practice whereby nonparticipating physicians charge full fees, then bill the patient for that portion of the bill not reimbursed by Medicare. Under the new rules, non-participating physician fees cannot exceed 125% of Medicare allowable costs in 1991. This ceiling drops to 120% in 1992, and 115% in 1993.

Effective April 1, 1990, balance billing will not be permitted for those whose Medicare premiums are paid by Medicaid. Beginning in 1992, this ban will be extended to Medicare beneficiaries below the federal poverty level.

Q. 10:34 What are volume performance standards?

Volume performance standards are standards intended to cut the rate of increase of Medicare Part B payments to doctors. An annual performance standard set by Congress predicts the growth rate for total Medicare physician services for the coming year. Fees for the coming year would be increased or decreased depending upon whether the prior year's actual expenditures were smaller or larger than the previous year's volume peformance standards.

Volume performance standards were set at

- 0.5% for 1990
- 1.0% for 1991
- 1.5% for 1992
- 2.0% for subsequent years.

Fees are to be updated by Congress each year based upon input from the Secretary of Health and Human Services and the Physician Payment Review Commission. Where Congress fails to act, a uniform default update will be determined based upon the Medical Economic Index.

Q. 10:35 What is the RBRVS pay system?

The Resource Based Relative Value Scale (RBRVS) system, scheduled to take effect in 1992, is a system for determining the level of Medicare payments to physicians. RBRVS will pay doctors the lesser of their actual charge, or a fee calculated using the following three factors, or relative value units:

1. A factor which takes into account the amount of work, measured by time and intensity, of the service provided;
2. A factor for practice expenses, such as office rent and employee compensation, and
3. A factor for malpractice expenses.

There will be adjustments to the practice and malpractice components, as well as to a portion of the work component, based upon geographical location. About 60% of the fee will be subject to geographical adjustments determined for urban and rural areas of each state.

Q. 10:36   When will the RBRVS system take effect?

The RBRVS system will be phased in over a 5-year period. Beginning in 1992, historical fees will be compared to the RBRVS fees. Fees that are within 15% of the RBRVS fees will be converted to RBRVS immediately. Those which vary by more than this will be adjusted by 15% the first year, with the balance of the adjustment made in equal increments over the next four years.

Q. 10:37   What effect will RBRVS have on physicians fees?

Some fees will be lowered and some will be increased. Generally, those fees charged by high cost specialists such as anesthesiologists, surgeons, radiologists and the like will come down, while those charged by internists and family practitioners will go up.

Services provided by radiologists will be reduced by 4% beginning on April 1, 1990. Anesthesiologists and registered nurse anesthetists will be paid for actual time worked, rather than time units (15-30 minute minimum increments) as is now the practice.

As Medicare procedures are often copied by commercial insurers, ultimately the RBRVS system could become the standard of payment for employer-sponsored plans as well.

Q. 10:38　What happened to the Medicare Catastrophic Coverage Act?

On November 22, 1989, The Medicare Catastrophic Coverage Act of 1988 (MCCA) was repealed entirely for the calendar year beginning in 1990 and thereafter. The pre-MCCA benefit and premium structure was reinstated with adjustments for increased medical care costs.

Q. 10:39　What is the impact of the repeal of the MCCA on Medicare benefits in 1990?

The MCCA was to phased in over a three year period. At the time of its repeal, only one year had elapsed and only Part A (hospital benefits) had been affected. Therefore, the benefit changes as a result of the repeal are relatively straightforward.

Q. 10:40　What are the resulting Part A hospital benefits?

In general, the Part A deductible, $592 in 1990, will apply "per benefit period" rather than per calendar year. The benefit period is a "spell of illness that ends when there have been 60 consecutive days without the individual being a bed patient in a hospital or an extended care facility."

The entire pre-MCCA Part A benefit structure has been reinstated. In addition to restoring the previous deductible application, the pre-MCCA hospital and skilled nursing facility coinsurance requirements and lifetime benefit limits now apply.

Q. 10:41　What are the new indexed coinsurance requirements?

The indexed coinsurance requirements for 1990 are as follows:

Inpatient Hospital	1st 60 days $592	First (per benefit period)
	61st - 90th day	$148 per day
	Lifetime reserve (up to 60 days)	$296 per day

Skilled Nursing	1st 20 days	Semi-private w/in 30 days of a hospital stay
	21st - 100th day	$74 per day

Q. 10:42 Is there a maximum dollar out-of-pocket limit on the 20% coinsurance payable for Part B (physician) expenses?

The MCCA contained a limit of $1,370 for Part B out of pocket limit that would have become effective in 1990. The repeal means that there is no limit on the out-of-pocket expense.

Q. 10:43 What are the new Medicare premiums?

The 1990 premium for Part B Medicare coverage is $28.60 per individual per month instead of $29.90, as previously announced. The $4.00 per month "catastrophic premium" will not apply in 1990, although it may have been witheld in the early months before computer reprogramming was completed. Any excess 1990 witholding will eventually be refunded.

Q. 10:44 What happens to those who reduced or eliminated Medigap insurance policies in expectation of extended Medicare benefits?

Those individuals must be given the opportunity to reinstate previous coverage levels.

Chapter 11

Nondiscrimination Rules

On November 8, 1989, President Bush signed a law that repeals IRC Section 89 which had added special non-discrimination requirements for life, accident and health, and cafeteria plans.

The repeal resurrects the previous nondiscrimination requirements that had been superseded by Section 89. Group term life, certain self-insured accident and health plans, group legal services plans, educational assistance plans, dependent day care plans, cafeteria plans and plans funded through VEBAs (Voluntary Employee Benefit Associations) are now subject to the rules that were in effect prior to the Tax Reform Act of 1986.

While not considered "health" plans, group term life plans, dependent care assistance plans, educational assistance plans and group legal service plans are often included in employee benefit plans (the first two are typically found in cafeteria plans). Therefore, information on the nondiscrimination rules applicable to such plans is included in this section

Accident and health plans

Q. 11:1 Is discrimination in health plans permitted?

With respect to *insured* accident and health plans, the only federal rules regarding benefit discrimination are those applicable to cafeteria plans. Employers must still abide by discrimination statutes that are not specifically benefit oriented and any requirements specified by a particular insurance company.

Self-insured health plans (including medical, dental and vision) must not discriminate in favor of highly compensated individuals. The plan must meet at least one of three eligibility tests and a benefits test. For the 1989 transition year, these plans have the alternative of relying on the repealed Section 89 standards.

The distinction between *insured* and *self-insured* is not as obvious as it might seem. The use of an insurance company for claim administration does not suffice to render a plan *insured*. Plans underwritten by insurance companies, such as minimum premium plans or pre-paid health care arrangements such as HMOs and PPOs may be considered partially *self-insured* unless there is a meaningful shifting of risk.

Q. 11:2 Which types of self-insured accident and health plans are not subject to discrimination testing?

The nondiscrimination rules apply only to the self-insured portion and only to the employer-provided portion of plans. Furthermore the rules do not apply to disability plans (including AD&D and travel accident plans). Plans which cover employees but *not* dependents for diagnostic procedures only, such as annual physical exams are also exempt.

Q. 11:3 What is a "highly compensated individual"?

A highly compensated individual [IRC Section 105(h)] is:

- One of the five highest paid officers,
- A shareholder who owns more than 10% of the employer's stock, or
- One of the top 25% highest paid employees.

A retiree who was highly compensated prior to retirement is considered to be a "highly compensated individual."

Q. 11:4 What are the eligibility tests applicable to self-insured accident and health plans?

A plan will be considered nondiscriminatory if it meets one of the following eligibility tests:

a. It benefits at least 70% of employees, or
b. It benefits at least 85% of those eligible, provided 70% or more are eligible, or
c. It benefits a nondiscriminatory classification of employees.

Planning Pointer: if the plan is part of a cafeteria plan it must also meet the nondiscrimination requirements of Code Section 125.

Q. 11:5 What employees are excluded in applying the eligibility tests?

In applying these tests, the following employees may be disregarded:

- Employees with less than three years of service,

- Employees under the age of 25,

- Part-time or seasonal employees (generally those working not more than 25 hours per week or 7 months per year. This group could also include those who work less than 35 hours per week or 9 months provided other employees doing essentially the same job work substantially more hours or longer periods as in the case of seasonal employees),

- Employees who are members of a collective bargaining unit which has bargained in good faith with respect to benefits provided under the plan, and

- Non-resident aliens with no income from U.S. sources.

Q. 11:6 What is the benefits test applicable to self-insured accident and health plans?

All of the benefits that are available to highly compensated employees must be made available to all other employees. The plan may not discriminate as to type or amount of benefit. Provided benefits are equally available to all participants, the fact that highly compensated individuals actually *receive* greater benefit, because they submit higher claims or have more dependents, is of no consequence. However, different waiting periods or participation costs apparently *would* result in the plan being deemed discriminatory.

Q. 11:7 What is the penalty for discrimination in a self-insured accident and health plan with respect to eligibility or benefits?

The penalty imputes additional income to the participants for tax purposes, resulting in additional income taxes. The penalty is assessed to "highly compensated" individuals to the extent of the employer-provided "excess reimbursement" benefits.

Q. 11:8 How is the penalty determined?

Determining the additional taxable income for a highly compensated individual depends on the nature of the discrimination. If the plan fails the benefits test because it provides a benefit to highly compensated employees that it does not provide to other employees, the entire amount of the reimbursement not available to all participants is includable in taxable income.

If the plan fails one of the eligibility tests, the portion of the reimbursement determined by applying the following fraction is includable in income for all highly compensated individuals:

$$\frac{\text{total reimbursements for all highly compensated individuals during the plan year}}{\text{total reimbursements during the plan year}}$$

The amount is based on reimbursement/claim payments, not the "premium" or cost.

Q. 11:9 Are all self-insured accident and health plans aggregated for the purpose of applying eligibility and benefits tests?

Employers may choose to aggregate several plans in order to apply the tests. The decision to combine or not applies to both the eligibility and benefits tests. Failure of one or the other can have significantly different penalties.

Q. 11:10 Are retiree plans subject to the same rules?

Yes, but IRS regulations are unclear on how to define a retiree, how to apply the eligibility tests, and how to treat benefits that are a function of service. However, it does appear that the benefits test applies separately to retiree plans.

Group Term Life Plans

Q. 11:11 How does the repeal of Section 89 affect group term life plans?

Group term life plans are affected in two ways. First, the $200,000 limit on income for determining the maximum nondiscriminatory benefit is eliminated. Secondly, the nondiscrimination tests and penalties for group term life insurance plans are applied with reference to "key" employees rather than "highly compensated individuals."

Q. 11:12 Who is a key employee under IRC Section 416(i)?

A *key employee* is any employee who, in the current year or any one of the four preceding plan years, was:

- A 5% owner,
- A 1% owner earning over $150,000,
- An officer earning over 50% of the IRC Section 415 defined benefit pension limit (50% of $102,582 or $51,291 in 1990), or
- One of the ten highest paid owners earning over the Section 415 defined contribution pension limit ($30,000).

Note: The number of officers who will be considered *key employees* will not exceed 50, or if less, 10% of employees (but not less than 3).

Q. 11:13 What nondiscrimination tests are applicable to group term life insurance?

Group term life insurance plans must meet one of several eligibility tests and a benefits test in order to demonstrate that the plan does not discriminate in favor of key employees.

Q. 11:14 What are the eligibility tests applicable to group term life insurance plans?

A group term life insurance plan will be considered nondiscriminatory if it meets one of the following tests:

a. It benefits at least 70% of employees, or
b. At least 85% of plan participants are not key employees, or
c. It benefits a nondiscriminatory classification of employees, or
d. The plan is part of a cafeteria plan and it meets the nondiscrimination requirements of Code Section 125.

Q. 11:15 What employees may be excluded in performing these tests?

The following employees may be excluded from testing:
- Employees with less than three years of service,

- Part-time or seasonal employees (generally those working not more than 20 hours per week or 5 months per year),
- Employees who are members of a collective bargaining unit that has bargained in good faith with respect to benefits provided under the plan, and
- Non-resident aliens.

Q. 11:16 What is the benefits test?

The benefits test requires that all of the benefits available to key employees be available to non-key employees. The plan may not discriminate as to type or amount of relative benefit. However, the IRS does permit differing benefit amounts when the benefit is based on a uniform relationship to employee compensation expressed similarly for all employees. The same definition of pay (e.g., basic, total, etc.) must be used for all employees. A plan which provides a common multiple of pay benefit (such as "2 times pay") would not be considered discriminatory.

Q. 11:17 Are all group term life insurance plans combined for testing purposes?

Yes. All plans which cover a common key employee must be tested together. This includes individual term policies which are considered group insurance for purposes of IRC Section 79.

Q. 11:18 What is the penalty for discrimination?

Normally the first $50,000 of group term life insurance benefit in a nondiscriminatory plan is exempt from taxation. Amounts in excess of $50,000 in a nondiscriminatory plan are taxed based on income imputed according to a table published by the IRS known as the Uniform Premium Table, or Table I. If the plan is discriminatory, the value of the first $50,000 of employer provided group term life insurance on key employees will be included as income for tax purposes and the total value imputed as income will be based on actual cost or the Table I rates, whichever is higher.

Recently, the IRS stated that the higher of actual cost or Table I rates would apply to amounts in excess of $50,000 for all employees even if the group term life insurance plan was nondiscriminatory, if the plan was part of a cafeteria arrangement. (Note: This contradicts current statutory language and may not be legally defensible).

Q. 11:19 Are dependent group term life benefits subject to nondiscrimination rules?

Employer-provided benefits up to $2,000 per dependent are excludable from income. Under certain conditions, dependent life benefits may be included in cafeteria plans until the end of the 1991 plan year, subject to witholding and reporting requirements. Additional IRS guidance is required to determine how to use Table I to value benefits in excess of $2,000.

Q. 11:20 Are group term life benefits for retired and former employees subject to nondiscrimination rules?

Yes. The eligibility and benefits tests are applied separately to retired and former employees. However, not all such employees need be taken into account. There are very complex "grandfathering" provisions under the Deficit Reduction Act of 1984.

Cafeteria Plans

Q. 11:21 What is the impact of the repeal of Section 89 on Cafeteria Plans?

The repeal of Section 89 reinstates the regulations proposed by the IRS in 1984. These require an eligibility test, a benefits test and a concentration test. In order to avoid constructive receipt, the plan must not discriminate in favor of highly compensated individuals, either as to eligibility or as to contributions and benefits. The definition of highly compensated individuals is different for cafeteria plans than for self-insured health plans.

Q. 11:22 Who is a highly compensated individual for the purpose of cafeteria plan nondiscrimination rules?

Highly compensated individuals [IRC Section 125(e)] are defined as either employees or participants who are:

- Officers,
- More than 5% shareholders, or
- Highly compensated based on facts and circumstances,
- Spouses or dependents of one of the above.

Q. 11:23 What is the eligibility test?

The plan may not favor highly compensated individuals as to eligibility to participate. That is, it should provide coverage to a reasonable classification of employees (see Question 11:46). The nondiscriminatory classification rules for qualified retirement plans may be considered a safe harbor in satisfying this test. If the safe harbor is used and the waiting period is less than three years, employees who have not satisfied the waiting period may be excluded for the purpose of this test.

Q. 11:24 Which employees may be excluded for purposes of the eligibility test?

Employees who have less than three years of service may be disregarded, provided:

- They are ineligible for the plan, and
- Newly eligible employees become eligible to participate not later than the beginning of the plan year following their third anniversary of employment.

This means that all eligible classes of employees must be subject to the same three year wait. That limits the utility of this rule for most plans.

Q. 11:25   What is the benefits test?

There are two parts to the benefits test. The first part is a facts and circumstances test; the plan must not favor highly compensated individuals with respect to benefits available or contributions. The second part requires that the benefits actually selected do not favor the highly compensated.

Health benefits are not discriminatory if employer contributions for each participant equal 100% of the cost of the majority of highly compensated individuals who are similarly situated (e.g., have families). Alternatively, health benefits are not discriminatory if employer contributions for each participant are at least 75% of the cost of the most expensive coverage selected by a similarly situated participant.

If employer contributions exceed the above amounts, the plan will still be nondiscriminatory provided the contributions are uniformly proportional to participant compensation.

Q. 11:26   What is the concentration test?

The concentration test states that a plan that provides key employees with more than 25% of the total nontaxable benefits will be considered discriminatory.

Q. 11:27   What is the penalty for discrimination?

The addition of Section 125 to the Internal Revenue Code protects employees who are offered the choice between taxable and nontaxable benefits from being deemed to have received the taxable benefits irrespective of their actual selection, i.e., "constructive receipt." The protection is only available in nondiscriminatory plans. If a cafeteria plan is discriminatory, the applicable favored group (highly compensated if the eligibility or benefits test is failed, key employees in the case of concentration test failure) will be taxed on the highest aggregate value of all available taxable benefits.

Q. 11:28 Does a plan that is part of a cafeteria plan have to satisfy more than one set of discrimination rules?

Yes. Plans must satisfy the rules applicable to the particular section of the Code as well as those for cafeteria plans.

Dependent Care Assistance Plans

Q. 11:29 What is the impact of the repeal of Section 89 on Dependent Care Assistance Plans?

The law that repealed Section 89 did not change the discrimination rules in effect prior to the Tax Reform Act of 1986. Those rules required an eligibility test, a benefits test and a concentration test. However it did delay until 1990 the average benefits test, added by the Tax Reform Act of 1986.

Nondiscrimination tests for dependent day care plans may be applied on a "separate line of business" basis, determined in "good faith" until regulations or additional guidance become available.

Q. 11:30 What is the eligibility test?

The plan must not discriminate in favor of highly compensated employees as defined in the Tax Reform Act of 1986 (see Question 6:169 below—this definition is different than that used for health plans or cafeteria plans). The eligibility test is satisfied if benefits are provided to a nondiscriminatory classification of employees (see Question 11:46).

The test is based on employees to whom the plan is available if the plan is part of a cafeteria arrangement. If, however, the plan is a stand-alone-plan, the test is applied to employees actually receiving benefits.

Q. 11:31 Who is a highly compensated employee with respect to dependent care assistance plans?

Any employee who, during the current year or the preceding year:

- Was a 5% owner,
- Received compensation in excess of $75,000 (adjusted for inflation),
- Received compensation in excess of $50,000 ($56,990 in 1990) and was in the top-paid 20% of the group, or
- Was an officer who received more than 50% of the [IRC Section 414 (q)] defined benefit pension limit (50% of $102,582 or $51,291 in 1990).

Q. 11:32 What employees are excluded for purposes of nondiscrimination testing?

The following nonparticipants may be excluded from testing:

- Those who are less than age 21,
- Those with less than 1 year of service,
- Members of a bargaining unit.

If the dependent care assistance plan is provided through salary reduction, for purposes of the average benefits test only, employees earning less than $25,000 may also be excluded.

Q. 11:33 What is the benefits test?

The benefits test requires that employer provided benefits or contributions must not favor highly compensated employees.

Q. 11:34 What is the concentration test?

The concentration test prohibits more-than-5%-owners from receiving more than 25% of the employer provided benefits, including salary reduction. This is in addition to the cafeteria plan concentration test applicable to key employees where the dependent day care plan is part of a cafeteria plan arrangement.

Q. 11:35 What is the average benefits test?

The average benefits test provides that non-highly compensated employees must receive an average benefit which is at least 55% of the average benefit of the highly compensated. Nonparticipants, except excludable employees, are included in this test, although employees earning less than $25,000 may be excluded in salary reduction plans.

Q. 11:36 What is the penalty for discrimination?

If any one of the tests is failed, highly compensated employees are taxed on their total dependent day care benefits.

Educational Assistance

Q. 11:37 What is an educational assistance plan?

IRC Section 127, which permits tax-free employer-provided educational assistance for employees up to $5,250 per year, expired at the end of 1988. In 1989, it was restored retroactively, but is due to expire September 30, 1990 if not extended by Congress.

Q. 11:38 What are the nondiscrimination rules that apply to educational assistance plans?

Educational assistance plans must not discriminate in favor of highly compensated employees (same definition as dependent care assistance plans) and must pass both an eligibility test and a concentration test to qualify for nontaxable status.

The eligibility test is the nondiscriminatory classification test. The concentration test prohibits more-than-5%-owners from receiving more than 5% of the employer provided benefits.

Q. 11:39 What is the penalty for failing the nondiscrimination tests?

If a plan is discriminatory, all benefits received by *all* employees are taxable.

Group Legal Services Plans

Q. 11:40 What is a qualified group legal services plan?

IRC Section 120 group legal services plans are essentially preferred provider arrangements whereby specified limited services such as will preparation, document review and representation in certain court matters are provided by a closed panel of attorneys and paralegal staff, on a prepaid basis.

Q. 11:41 What are the nondiscrimination rules that apply to group legal services plans?

Employer paid insurance premiums up to $70 per employee per year are excluded from income if the plan passes an eligibility test (the same one as for educational assistance plans), a benefits test and a concentration test.

The benefits test is a facts and circumstances test and requires that the plan not discriminate in favor of highly compensated employees (same definition as for dependent day care and educational assistance plans). Variations in contributions and benefits are not prohibited. Furthermore the IRS indicates that actual benefit utilization must be taken into account (but is not specific as to how to account for it).

The concentration test prohibits more-than-5%-owners from receiving more than 25% of the employer premium contributions.

Q. 11:42 What is the penalty for discrimination?

If a group legal services plan is discriminatory, *all* employees lose the tax exclusion.

VEBAs (Voluntary Employee Benefit Associations)

Q. 11:43 What are the nondiscrimination requirements for VEBAs?

VEBAs are subject to the nondiscrimination requirements of IRC Section 505, unless the particular benefit provided by the association has its own non-discrimination requirements under the Internal Revenue Code, such as the Section 79 requirements for group term life insurance.

The nondiscrimination rules for VEBAs do not apply to nontaxable benefits that are subject to other nondiscrimination rules. However, a benefit included in a VEBA that fails its own nondiscrimination tests would result in the loss of the VEBA's tax exempt status with the result that previously tax-free earnings would become taxable.

The VEBA nondiscrimination rules apply to all other benefits funded through the VEBA, whether taxable or nontaxable, employer paid or employee-pay-all.

IRC Section 505 requires that:

1. Each class of benefits provided by the VEBA is provided to a class of individuals set forth in the plan, and which does not discriminate in favor of highly compensated individuals (who are determined under rules "similar" to those for "highly compensated employees" as defined in IRC Section 414(q).

2. The benefits themselves do not discriminate in favor of highly compensated individuals (this does not rule out life insurance, severance pay, disability benefits, or supplemental unemployment compensation benefits that are higher for

higher paid employees, provided they bear a uniform relationship to total compensation).

For purposes of applying these tests employees with less than 3 years of service, who are less than 21 years old, who are seasonal or half time, who are covered by a collective bargaining agreement for which the benefits in question were the subject of bargaining, or who are nonresident aliens who receive no compensation from U.S. sources may be excluded.

Q. 11:44 Are there limits on compensation?

Yes, for purposes of calculating benefits, no more than $200,000 in annual compensation (adjusted for inflation) may be taken into account. Where the provided benefits are group term life insurance which must meet the IRC Section 79 nondiscrimination requirements, the $200,000 cap does not apply.

Q. 11:45 What are the penalties for discrimination?

As mentioned above, the inclusion of a discriminatory benefit in a VEBA eliminates its tax exempt status. Employees still receive nondiscriminatory nontaxable benefits tax free and are subject to the penalties described for each discriminatory benefit.

In addition, an employer who provides discriminatory postretirement medical or life insurance through a VEBA is subject to a 100% excise tax on the amount of the discriminatory benefits.

Nondiscriminatory Classification

Q. 11:46 What is a nondiscriminatory classification of employees?

There are two methods for determining what constitutes a reasonable classification of employees for nondiscrimination testing purposes:

1. *The Old Method:* The pre-Tax Reform Act of 1986 method

is somewhat subjective and based upon the procedures used in applying IRC Section 410(b) to pension plans. In addition to examining the facts and circumstances of a particular employer's plan, a quasi-mathematical test involved grouping employees by compensation brackets and determining the percentage of employees in each bracket with the percentage of participants in each bracket was employed. If the percentages were similar, bracket by bracket, or the percentage of participants was greater in the lower compensation brackets (meaning that participation was weighted in favor of lower–paid employees), the plan was deemed to cover a reasonable cross section of employees.

2. *The New Method:* With the Tax Reform Act of 1986, a new, more mathematically precise test was substituted. Proposed regulations couch the new test in terms of the relationship of two ratios:

- The percentage of non-highly compensated employees who benefit under the plan as compared to the percentage of highly compensated employees who benefit; and
- The percentage of non-highly compensated employees to total employees (less excludable employees).

After determining these ratios, they are compared to the following table of acceptable ratios:

Safe Harbor and Unsafe Harbor Percentage At Each Nonhighly Compensated Employee Concentration Percentage

Nonhighly Compensated Employee Concentration Percentage	Safe Harbor Percentage	Unsafe Harbor Percentage
0–60%	50%	40%
61%	49.25%	39.25%
62%	48.50%	38.50%
63%	47.75%	37.75%
64%	47%	37%
65%	46.25%	36.25%
66%	45.50%	35.50%
67%	44.75%	34.75%
68%	44%	34%
69%	43.25%	33.25%
70%	42.50%	32.50%
71%	41.75%	31.75%
72%	41%	31%
73%	40.25%	30.25%
74%	39.50%	29.50%

Safe Harbor and Unsafe Harbor Percentage At Each Nonhighly Compensated Employee Concentration Percentage
(Continued)

Nonhighly Compensated Employee Concentration Percentage	Safe Harbor Percentage	Unsafe Harbor Percentage
75%	38.75%	28.75%
76%	38%	28%
77%	37.25%	27.25%
78%	36.50%	26.50%
79%	35.75%	25.75%
80%	35%	25%
81%	34.25%	24.25%
82%	33.50%	23.50%
83%	32.75%	22.75%
84%	32%	22%
85%	31.25%	21.25%
86%	30.50%	20.50%
87%	29.75%	20%
88%	29%	20%
89%	28.25%	20%
90%	27.50%	20%
91%	26.75%	20%
92%	26%	20%
93%	25.25%	20%
94%	24.50%	20%
95%	23.75%	20%
96%	23%	20%
97%	22.25%	20%
98%	21.50%	20%
99%	20.75%	20%

Q. 11:47 Which method is used after the repeal of Section 89?

It is likely that the new method will be required for cafeteria plans, educational assistance plans, dependent day care plans and group legal services plans. However, Congress instructed the IRS to take the difference between welfare plans and pension plans into account when applying the reasonable calssification test. Therefore, it is possible that the old (pre-Tax Reform Act) method will be retained for certain benefits such as self-insured medical plans and group term life insurance plans.

A COMPARISON OF PRIVILEGED GROUPS
Highly Compensated Individuals (IRC Sec. 105(h)(5))

A highly compensated individual is:

a. One of the five highest paid officers;

b. A shareholder who owns more than 10 percent of the employer's stock;

c. One of the highest-paid 25% of all employees.

Highly Compensated Participants/Individuals (IRC Sec. 125 (e))

Highly compensated participants and highly compensated individuals are defined as either employees or participants, respectively, who are:

- Officers;
- More-than-5% shareholders, in terms of voting power or value of all classes of stock;
- Highly compensated employees;
- Spouses and dependents of one of the above.

Highly Compensated Employees (IRC Sec. 414(q))

This category includes any employee who during the current year or the preceding year:

- Has been a 5% owner;
- Received compensation from the employer in excess of $75,000 (adjusted for inflation to $85,485 in 1990);
- Received compensation from the employer in excess of $50,000 ($56,990 in 1990) and was in the top-paid group of employees (i.e. the highest paid 20%); or
- Has been an officer who received more than 50% of the defined benefit pension limit (that is, 50% of $102,582 or $51,291 in 1990).

Key Employees (IRC Sec. 416(i))

A key employee is:

- An officer earning more than 50% of the defined benefit pension plan limitation (that is, earning more that $51,291 in 1990, or $49,032 in 1989). The total number of officers will not exceed 50; or, if less, 10% of employees (but not less than 3);
- One of the 10 employees who own the largest interests in the company and who earn more than $30,000 a year;
- A 5% owner;
- A 1% owner earning more than $150,000.

Chapter 12

Other Benefits Issues

This chapter looks at some of the newer benefits provided to employees and the challenges they present to employers. These include substance abuse treatment, employee assistance programs, wellness and health promotion programs, retiree health care benefits, long-term care, and health care benefits for people with AIDS.

Substance Abuse Treatment

Q. 12:1 Is treatment for alcoholism and other types of substance abuse covered under typical health insurance plans?

Coverage for treatment of alcoholism and other forms of substance abuse is often limited under health plans. The limitations are similar to those for mental illnesses, and are imposed because appropriate treatment is difficult for health care professionals to define, thus making expected claims and an appropriate price for coverage difficult to establish. However, many plans extend additional coverage for treatment as a result of a referral from an employee assistance program (EAP).

Q. 12:2 How costly is substance abuse to companies and their employees?

Numerous studies reveal that somewhere between 6% and 10% of any given employee population has a problem with alco-

317

hol or another controlled substance. These data hold up whether the population is blue collar or white collar, male or female, young or old. People with substance abuse problems use health care services and other resources at much higher rates than other employees. They are also absent three times as often, are involved in more grievances, and have higher accident rates. Other costs include higher medical costs, more disability claims, more workers' compensation claims, and lost productivity.

Q. 12:3 What is the Drug-Free Workplace Act?

The Drug-Free Workplace Act of 1988 requires employers that have $25,000 or more in contracts with the federal government to certify that they are operating a drug-free workplace. Failure to comply with the law's requirements may mean termination of existing federal contracts and being barred from any such work in the future. The law requires such employers to:

- Establish an anti-drug policy;
- Educate employees on the policy and the dangers of drugs in the workplace; and
- Notify employees of the legal consequences of illegal drug involvement.

Q. 12:4 What coverage is provided for substance abuse?

Coverage for substance abuse is similar to that provided for mental health services and is often very limited, except in states such as New York, which mandate outpatient benefits. There are usually annual maximums that are separate from those for other medical services, and they are frequently low, perhaps $500 or $1,000. These constraints are a barrier to treatment, but there are nonfinancial barriers as well, such as lack of company policies and programs for identifying and referring individuals to appropriate resources. A traditional approach to treatment has been a 28-day inpatient residential program. Tracking this treatment approach, many companies (especially the larger firms) have included coverage for 28 or 30 days in their health benefits packages. However, there is a growing belief that many individuals can be treated effectively as outpatients at a much lower cost.

Q. 12:5 Why should companies consider establishing a drug testing program?

Employers should consider drug-testing programs for the following reasons:

1. To comply with legal requirements, such as the Drug-Free Workplace Act and Department of Transportation regulations.
2. To deter the use of drugs. After the U.S. Army adopted a "zero-tolerance" policy toward drug use, involving heavy command emphasis, wide publicity, and random testing, the incidence of drug use dropped from an estimated 27% of military personnel to 4.8%.
3. To promote workplace safety. According to the National Safety Council, alcohol is related to 47% of workplace accidents and 40% of workplace fatalities. A report from the Southern Pacific Transportation Co. credited post-accident testing with the sharp drop in accidents, from 22.2 per million miles in 1983, to 2.2 in 1989.
4. To avoid liability costs. Drug impaired employees are more likely to engage in acts that will injure the public, or produce products that are defective and potentially injurious to users. Reducing the use of drugs reduces the likelihood of these incidents, and the corresponding risks of liability suits.
5. Reducing employee compensation and benefits costs. Treating employee addictions cost approximately $4 billion in 1988.

Q. 12:6 Why would a company choose not to engage in substance abuse testing?

1. The evidence that testing actually accomplishes its objectives is, so far, thin. Much of it is anecdotal, and rarely is

drug testing the only factor which could have contributed to a reduction in accidents, costs, etc.

2. Cost. While simple screenings can be performed for $25 per employee or less, more accurate readings that offer conclusive evidence of drug use can more than double the cost.

3. Labor problems. There is a good chance that mandatory substance abuse testing will not be well received by employees, leading to morale problems. Where employees are members of collective bargaining units, drug testing must be negotiated, unless there is explicit, or implied permission in the agreement. (See *Consolidated Rail Corp. v. Railway Labor Executives Assn.* 109 S. Ct. 2477 (1989).)

4. Legal problems. Employees who have lost their jobs for refusing to take drug tests have filed wrongful discharge suits, and have won. While there have been a number of court cases upholding the employer's right to test, they have generally been narrow, involving matters of public safety and infractions or evidence of impairment.

5. Additional complications. Under some state laws, and at least one federal law (the Rehabilitation Act of 1973), drug abusers, drug addicts and alcoholics are considered disabled. The Americans with Disabilities Act (see the discussion above) characterizes them similarly. In these cases employer certainty about an employee's habit can lead to expensive long-term treatment and support.

Q. 12:7 What options are there for testing?

Employers have several options for testing:

1. Test job *applicants* only. This is the least likely to pose legal problems. It can also be highly effective in identifying potential drug users. Bureau of Labor Statistics figures show that drug use among job applicants can be as high as 24% in some industries.

2. Test for cause. Unusual behavior, serious accidents, would be justification for testing. There is some question, however, as to how effective after-the-fact testing is in identifying a

significant number of drug users, and preventing associated problems.
3. Test *all* employees on a regular basis. While this approach is less likely to be viewed by individuals as discriminatory, and is most likely to reach all drug users, it is also the most expensive.
4. Make unannounced random tests. A potential problem with the first three approaches is that there is some telegraphing of employer intentions to test, giving drug users the chance to practice evasion techniques, such as abstaining for sufficient periods of time or being someplace else when the test is given.

Q. 12:8 What should be included in an employer's substance abuse policies?

Employers should have a precise *written* policy that covers what is regarded as prohibited conduct, what the procedures for testing are, and what the penalties are for failing to comply. Where one or more unions are involved, the policy should receive their approval. Specifically, it should cover:

1. *Purpose of the policy:* to promote quality, safety, health, etc., and to comply with federal or state laws, in which case the standards of those laws should be included in the policy.

2. *Announcement:* what methods will be used to introduce and reinforce the policy, including employee meetings and letters.

3. *What is prohibited:* the use, possession, transportation, or sale of alcohol, narcotics, illegal drugs or drug paraphernalia by any employee while the employee is on duty, while the employee is operating a company vehicle or on the job site of a customer, or is otherwise conducting business for the company.

4. *Testing:* what it is that is being tested for.

- Who will be responsible for conducting the tests, including company personnel responsible for overseeing the program, and outside personnel (laboratories) who will actually perform the testing.

- How often the tests will be given.
- What procedures will be observed in testing, including the types of tests (e.g. urinalysis), chain-of-custody procedures for test specimens, and follow-up or secondary testing where initial tests are positive.
- What standards of confidentiality will be maintained.
- Which employees or applicants will be tested.
- When testing will be performed, and whether notice will be given.

5. *Disciplinary Penalties:* whether employees have the right to refuse to be tested, and what the consequences will be for their refusal.

- What the consequences of positive testing are (warnings, suspension, transfer, mandatory treatment, dismissal).
- What rights the employee has right to appeal or offer evidence explaining his condition.
- What records will be maintained and for how long.

Employee Assistance Programs

Q. 12:9 What is an employee assistance program?

The term "employee assistance program," or EAP, used to be a euphemism for an alcohol abuse treatment program. Today's EAP is much broader in scope. It continues to deal with alcohol and other substance abuse, but it also deals with a much wider range of employee and dependent problems. These problems can be financial, emotional, marital, or physical in nature. EAPs deal with the full range of personal problems that can and often do affect worker performance.

Q. 12:10 Is EAP coverage expensive?

An EAP can be insured or it can be a stand-alone benefit. It does not have to be expensive. Some employers pay for an initial diagnostic visit to a trained counselor. This person's role is to help the employee or family member determine a course of action. The counselor ascertains the nature of the problem and makes an appropriate referral. This referral may be to a therapist, financial counselor, community organization, or substance abuse treatment center. Some of the treatment may be covered by company insurance, such as medical care. Other treatment may be paid for by the individual. The most important aspect of the program is that it helps get people into the right system where they can obtain the help they need.

EAPs may actually save money. They can increase productivity and reduce job-related accidents, medical expenses, disabilities, absenteeism, and recruitment and training costs. They are also useful in deflecting expensive wrongful-discharge suits. Companies that have formal programs designed to help drug or alcohol addicted employees are in a much better position to show that firing the worker was a last resort after all other efforts were exhausted. Some companies report that their EAPs return several dollars for each dollar spent.

Because EAP design and services are so variable, it is difficult to generalize about cost; however, per-employee costs may be estimated to fall between $15 and $50 a year.

Q. 12:11 Do companies hire in-house counselors or use external resources?

Most companies refer individuals to an external source. This may be a community organization or one of a growing number of commercial organizations that provides EAP services on a for-profit basis. There are reputable organizations of both types. A company can justify having an in-house counselor if it has from 1,500 to 2,000 employees; this is the volume needed to warrant a full-time staff. The other reason that many companies use an outside resource is to maintain confidentiality. It is important for employees to have confidence in the discretion of the counselor, since EAPs tend to deal with the most personal of problems.

Q. 12:12 What components are needed for an effective EAP?

An effective EAP requires a solid foundation, including top management support, training for company supervisors, written company policies, adequate health care coverage, specific disciplinary actions for poor job performance (which lead to the identification of problems), understandable procedures, good counselors, and specified criteria for return to work if treatment requires hospitalization.

Q. 12:13 Other than in-house or commercially, how else may EAP services be provided?

Of growing interest to the small employer is the association or consortium EAP, in which several employers join together to sponsor an EAP. Although this can reduce costs when compared with each employer's cost of going it alone, it is important that the companies have similar needs and demographics, and/or that utilization be carefully tracked so that expenses can be fairly apportioned.

Health Promotion and Wellness

Q. 12:14 What is health promotion?

Health promotion and wellness are often used synonymously. Some specialists in the field make a distinction, with wellness being related to preventive medicine, and health promotion meaning behavioral modification programs to improve life style. These health promotion programs include nutrition, weight reduction, diet, smoking cessation, stress management, high blood pressure control, exercise, accident prevention, and employee assistance programs (EAPs).

A 1987 survey by the Health and Human Services Department (National Survey of Health Promotion Activities) found that

65.8% of worksites with more than 50 employees have at least one health promotion activity, including:

- Smoking control assistance (35.6%);
- Health risk appraisals (29.5%);
- Back care classes (28.6%);
- Stress management instruction (26.6%);
- Exercise or fitness activity (22.5%);
- On-the-job safety instruction (19.8%);
- Nutrition education (16.8%);
- High blood pressure control (16.5%); and
- Weight control programs (14.7%).

Q. 12:15 Why would an employer offer health promotion programs?

One obvious reason is the rapid escalation in health care costs. Such programs are one of many strategies that companies use to get a handle on health costs. But there are other reasons as well. Health promotion program objectives include the following:

- Improve employee morale;
- Foster better employee relations;
- Reduce absenteeism;
- Reduce benefits costs;
- Enhance recruitment efforts;
- Lower disability claims and days of disability;
- Lower workers' compensation claims;
- Reduce the number of grievances;
- Reduce turnover; and
- Promote more effective use of the health care system.

Some insurers offer discounts for healthy life styles; passing along discounts is one way of promoting wellness.

Q. 12:16 Are there advantages to offering health promotion programs at the worksite?

Yes, the worksite offers several advantages. First, the worksite is convenient, so people do not have to travel in order to benefit from the program. Second, the co-worker peer group serves as a support group, which helps the success rate of programs. This is particularly important for such programs as smoking cessation and weight reduction. Third, there is an organizational structure and a financial sponsor (the company) with a vested interest in the outcome, which also augments success rates.

Q. 12:17 How does a company select a health promotion program?

There are a few ways to choose among health promotion programs. For example, a company might conduct an employee survey to gauge interest among its employee population. A review of health and disability claims may suggest environmental problems, such as safety, that should be addressed. Another way to select a health promotion program is with the life-style cost index.

Q. 12:18 What is the life-style cost index?

The life-style cost index (LCI) is a methodology developed to pinpoint specific health problems at a given employer location. LCI was developed by the National Center for Health Promotion in cooperation with the School of Public Health at the University of Michigan. Essentially, LCI uses a combination of company-specific health claims experience and health risk factor analysis to determine which life-style-related health problems should be addressed at any given company.

Q. 12:19 Why is interest in health promotion growing?

The nature of illness has changed dramatically. Because of improvements in the detection and treatment of acute infectious disease, most of our health problems are related to life-style issues. Cardiovascular disease, cancer, and strokes account for about 70% of all deaths in the United States. These can all be affected by wellness-based interventions. Some predisposing risk factors include high cholesterol, obesity, smoking, substance abuse, lack of exercise, high blood pressure, diabetes, and exposure to toxic substances.

Q. 12:20 What is preventive care coverage?

Preventive care coverage provides for expenses incurred in the prevention, rather than the treatment, of illness or injury. It is sometimes referred to as "well care." Some preventive care expenses have traditionally been covered, such as diagnostic tests, to ascertain whether additional medication is required to control high blood pressure to prevent a stroke, and well baby care—nursery care and immunizations at birth. However, routine checkups for early detection of problems have not usually been covered.

Q. 12:21 What kinds of benefits does preventive care coverage provide when it is part of a health care plan?

Preventive care coverage can include a variety of benefits, ranging from routine checkups, immunizations, and Pap tests to health risk appraisals (HRAs) and wellness programs.

Q. 12:22 How often are routine checkups usually covered under a preventive care plan?

There is some difference of opinion in the medical profession concerning how often routine physical examinations should be conducted and how useful they are; therefore, there is a lack of uniformity regarding how often such exams are covered. Some plans cover them annually; others cover routine physicals as well as diagnostic tests and X-rays periodically, based on the insured's age.

Q. 12:23 What is the current trend with regard to routine physicals?

The trend is away from routine physicals and toward screening for particular risk factors related to age and sex, along with individual health history and status. Rather than being examined on a periodic basis (such as annually) for all health problems, each individual is profiled for particular screening. Examples would be mammograms for women based on age and history and prostate exams for men over 50.

Q. 12:24 What has caused the move away from the traditional physical?

The change has to do with both quality and cost. From a qualitative standpoint, specific screening geared toward age, sex, health history, and health status is simply more targeted and likely to produce more accurate results. Moreover, specific screening is not as expensive as a comprehensive physical.

Q. 12:25 Are there any specific guidelines available for health screening for particular risk factors?

Yes. One example is Project INSURE, developed under the sponsorship of the commercial insurance industry. This methodology uses 10 age groups and designates certain tests based on age and sex. A Canadian government task force has developed guidelines for another approach to periodic examinations.

Q. 12:26 What is a wellness program?

The most recent trend in preventive care is insurance coverage for HRAs and for exercise, nutrition, smoking cessation, and stress management programs. Because the programs encourage employees to achieve or maintain good health and well-being, they are commonly referred to as wellness programs.

Wellness programs are sometimes covered by insurance in larger companies whose claims experience significantly affects their health insurance premium rates (or when the employer is partially or fully self-funding the plan). However, some smaller employers are also being offered wellness insurance coverage as part of their plans.

Q. 12:27 In addition to behavioral modification and preventive programs, in what other ways can a company enhance health?

A company can develop specific policies on allowing employees time to participate in health programs, create optimum health benefits design, institute smoking policies, and support employee-management communication and EAPs. Companies can also provide nutritious food in their cafeterias and institute noise abatement programs and quality-of-worklife programs.

Q. 12:28 Why would an employer want to include preventive care or wellness programs in a group insurance plan?

Some state laws mandate coverage, such as well baby care. A typical benefit covers nursery care for a fixed number of days and specific tests routinely done within 48 hours of birth. Some employers include other preventive care benefits because it is often cheaper to prevent an illness or injury than it is to treat it. Thus, by investing in programs that are designed to prevent illness, employers may realize future cost savings.

Another reason for including preventive care has to do with employees' increasing concern with their health. Employers looking to provide meaningful benefits to their employees can do so by providing preventive care coverage.

Q. 12:29 Are wellness or health promotion programs usually insured?

No. Most health promotion programs are free-standing programs rather than part of the insurance package. Some preventive services are a required part of an insurance package. For example, some states mandate coverage for well baby care or alcohol and substance abuse, but most programs are optional to the employer. By offering these programs on a free-standing basis, the company has more flexibility. A company may want to offer one or two programs, but not everything; a large company may want to offer certain programs at one location and other programs at other sites.

Q. 12:30 What is a health risk appraisal?

A health risk appraisal (HRA) describes an individual's chances of death, illness, or injury in the future. A typical HRA asks the individual questions about his or her sex, age, family and individual health history, specific health practices, and life style (smoking, drinking alcohol, exercise, stress, seat-belt usage). Depending on the HRA, questions concerning the individual's reactions to everyday work and social situations may be included.

Q. 12:31 How does the HRA fit in with health promotion?

Many companies start with the HRA as another way to determine which programs to offer employees. The HRA is an inexpensive way to uncover employee needs. The typical cost is anywhere from $2.50 to $10.00 per employee. The process usually involves the HRA followed by distribution of some educational materials. At this point, a combination of HRA results, an employee interest survey, and the life-style cost index can help the company decide on a course of action. The next step often involves implementation of one or more behavioral modification programs.

Q. 12:32 Would an employer use an HRA to determine the components of its group health insurance plan?

Yes. By combining each employee's HRA scores, a total health risk profile of all employees can be produced. The employer will acquire significant information concerning the general health of the employee population in aggregate. Based on the information, the employer may decide to institute health programs or provide certain preventive care benefits. This will help employees improve their health, and may lead to cost savings to the extent medical care utilization is reduced.

Q. 12:33 Are HRA results used to set the price for health insurance coverage?

To date, this has not occurred. However, as society becomes less inclined to subsidize the health care expenses of individuals with controllable health risks, HRA-based premiums may begin to be used.

Q. 12:34 Do insurance companies provide financial incentives to companies to adopt preventive care programs?

Some insurance carriers provide financial incentives for purchasing preventive care programs. This can take the form of lower premium payments to employers that have the programs in place. Others provide deductible and coinsurance percentages related to employee health. For example, employees who control their weight and blood pressure, wear seat belts, do not smoke, and have periodic physical exams may have their annual deductible waived. Some insurance companies also provide for partial reimbursement for individuals who attend health or exercise programs.

Retiree Health Benefits

Q. 12:35 Why has health care coverage for retirees become an issue?

The population as a whole continues to age. The number of people over age 65 is expected to grow from 29 million in 1985 to 35 million in 2000—almost 13% of the population. The number of people over age 85—2.7 million in 1985—is expected to reach 5 million in the year 2000. The cost of care for people in these age groups continues to increase, and the need for coverage for the low-income elderly is also increasing.

Almost half the current health insurance plans cancel coverage for employees upon retirement. For many of these people, Medicare is their only coverage, and it pays only about 50% of an individual's health care costs (although a high percentage of acute care expenses). Medicaid varies by state, but generally requires exhaustion of almost all private resources before coverage is funded. Many employers have felt the responsibility to fund health care coverage, but some new issues have been raised recently:

- The number of individuals requiring intermediate and custodial care or skilled nursing care for longer periods has increased significantly, at a cost of $100 to $125 a day.
- Proposed accounting disclosure rules from the Financial Accounting Standards Board have made management, especially in larger companies, more aware of the cost of retiree benefits and its effect on bottom-line results.
- Court decisions have restricted the right of employers to reduce or modify postretirement benefits for already retired employees.
- Prefunding of nondiscriminatory health costs is permitted on a tax-deductible basis while employees are working, but investment income on the funds is taxable. This means that although contributions to the plan for coverage in future years are tax-deductible, the income earned on those contributions through investment is taxable. This situation makes prefunding benefits less attractive. However, if many people lose retirement benefits because of business failure, plan discontinuance, or early retirement, there may be legislation requiring prefunding.

Q. 12:36 How many employers provide health care benefits for their retirees?

Although many large companies provide health care benefits for their retirees, most companies do not. The General Accounting Office estimated that 7 million retirees were covered by such programs in 1988.

Q. 12:37 How big is the retiree health care liability for U.S. corporations?

Some accounts set the value as high as $2 trillion. The General Accounting Office, however, has estimated the value of unfunded accrued benefits at $227 billion in 1988. Annual outlays for retiree health were reckoned at $9 billion in 1988 and were expected to increase to $22 billion by the year 2008.

Q. 12:38 What are the proposed Financial Accounting Standards Board accounting rules?

The new rules were proposed in the Financial Accounting Standards Board (FASB) "Exposure Draft on Postretirement Benefits Other Than Pensions." Although the draft covers all nonpension benefits, including such things as life insurance, legal assistance, and tuition reimbursement plans, by far the most costly item is health care. The rules would require corporations to reflect the present value of future retiree health care liabilities in their financial statements, along with the value of any assets dedicated to funding those liabilities. Specifically, the draft would require:

- An actuarial estimate of the liability, to be accompanied by footnotes explaining the assumptions used in arriving at that estimate. Specifically, the footnotes must contain the health care cost trend rate assumed, as well as the effect that a 1% change in that rate would have on the estimated liability.
- The cost of the liability to be accrued over the working life of each employee.
- Any unfunded liability accrued prior to the adoption of the FASB rules to be amortized over the average remaining working life of active employees or 15 years, whichever is longer.

The rules generally would take effect in 1992; they would take effect in 1994 for nonpublic organizations with plans covering fewer than 100 participants.

> [Note: as we were going to press, the FASB announced a tentative decision to postpone the effective date one year so that calendar year taxpayers would first be affected in 1993.]

Q. 12:39   What effect would the proposed FASB rules have?

The postretirement health care obligation would prove to be some companies' single biggest liability. Because very few companies have taken steps to prefund these retiree health care obligations, there are virtually no assets available to offset the liabilities. This means that the appearance of the liability and corresponding charge against earnings would have a major impact, resulting in earnings reductions of 90% or more by some estimates. This, in turn, could seriously affect a company's creditworthiness and stock price.

Q. 12:40   How should a company respond to the new accounting rules?

Regardless of the form the FASB rules finally take, they will simply standardize accounting policy for very real liabilities that already exist. Corporations should approach the problem by:

1. Estimating the size of the liability as accurately as possible;
2. Determining whether the liability is manageable given the company's size, revenues, and overall financial situation;
3. Exploring ways of reducing or eliminating the liability if it is too large; and
4. Taking steps to set aside adequate funds to discharge the remaining liability.

Q. 12:41 How can a company limit its retiree health care benefits liability?

A company has the same types of options for limiting retiree health care costs as it does for limiting active employee costs. It may reduce the level of benefits or terminate them altogether, or increase the participants' share of overall cost by increasing contributions, deductibles, or copayments. Employers may also adopt cost-containment strategies for retiree benefits, such as:

- Mandatory second opinions;
- Preadmission review and testing (non-Medicare eligibles only);
- Utilization review;
- Preferred provider options;
- Discounted prescription drugs;
- Mandatory outpatient requirements; and
- Case management.

In a survey of employers in the Chicago area with 321,000 active and 137,000 retired employees, the General Accounting Office found that all had made one or more of these changes between 1984 and 1988. In another survey of 2,271 companies of all sizes, the Wyatt Company found that 40% were planning to change their retiree health programs by reducing coverage, increasing contributions, or both.

Some companies have applied these cost-saving features selectively to avoid legal complications, for humanitarian reasons, or to avoid political complications within the company. For example, benefits for those persons who have already retired may be left untouched; those for persons close to retirement (say within five years of retirement age) would be subject to modest adjustment; those for new hires or persons who have a specified number of years before retiring might be substantially altered or terminated altogether.

Q. 12:42 Are there limitations on a company's ability to alter retiree benefits?

Yes. Attempts to curtail retiree benefits, or to increase the cost of those benefits to retiree participants, have frequently been challenged in court. Although the results in these cases have been mixed, the right of employers to make such changes has generally been upheld by the courts (especially at the appellate level) when they had expressly reserved the right to make those changes without the consent of plan participants. This is accomplished through inclusion of clear and unambiguous language to that effect in the plan document.

Courts will look beyond the plan document itself, however, to employee communications if the plan document is ambiguous or representations to employees have been clearly misleading, fraudulent, or made in bad faith. Employee communications include the summary plan description (SPD), company newspapers, films, pamphlets, brochures, letters, and presentations. Special attention has been focused on language promising lifetime benefits at no cost.

Q. 12:43 What options are available to an employer that wants to prefund for retiree health benefits?

There is no method for advance funding retiree health plans that offers tax benefits comparable to those available for retirement income (pension) plans. Currently the best alternatives are a voluntary employees' beneficiary association (VEBA), or 501(c)(9) trust, or a separate medical benefits account under IRC Section 401(h).

Q. 12:44 What are the rules governing VEBAs?

Since 1984, the tax advantages associated with VEBAs have been limited. [Ref.: IRC Section 419A] The maximum annual deductible contribution for postretirement medical and life insurance benefits is:

- The level annual contribution spread over the working lives of covered employees necessary to fund a reserve for such benefits (determined actuarially using reasonable assumptions); or

- An annual "safe harbor" of 35% of the preceding year's medical costs, not including insurance premiums.

The projected cost of medical benefits (adjusted for health cost inflation) may not be taken into account in determining the annual deductible amount. Since health costs have been increasing at double-digit rates over much of the past decade, this is a significant restriction.

Other shortcomings of the VEBA approach include the requirement that contributions for "key employees" be paid from a separate account; such contributions offset contributions to retirement plans. In addition, earnings on assets for postretirement benefits are taxable as unrelated business income. The taxable income problem may be overcome, however, by investing in tax-deferred vehicles such as annuities.

[For more details on VEBAs, see Chapter 5.]

Q. 12:45 What is a 401(h) account?

IRC Section 401(h) permits medical benefits for retirees and their spouses and dependents to be funded through a separate account of a pension plan, provided:

- The benefits are subordinate to the retirement income (pension) benefits provided by the plan—that is, aggregate contributions for the purchase of health and life insurance benefits cannot exceed 25% of the aggregate contributions made to the plan as a whole since the medical benefits account was established. (There is an exception to the 25% rule pertaining to contributions to fund past service liabilities, but the precise meaning of this loophole is unclear.)
- Company contributions are reasonable and ascertainable.
- No part of the account is diverted for purposes other than for expenses of administering the medical benefits plan.

- Assets remaining after all liabilities are satisfied are returned to the employer.
- Benefits for key employees are separately accounted for.

Q. 12:46 Are there any other approaches to financing retiree health care?

Yes. While the foregoing methods were "benefits" approaches, there is growing interest in a "contributions" orientation to funding for postretirement health care. The difference is that under a benefits arrangement, the employer is assuming an open-ended future commitment to provide coverage for whatever medical costs might be incurred (less any costs assumed by the participant). The contributions approach, on the other hand, defines the employer's commitment in terms of a current annual contribution. Each year that contribution is invested in a fund that is available at retirement for medical insurance premium subsidy or long-term care insurance premiums, or to reimburse the retiree directly for any medical expenses incurred.

This approach has the advantage of making company outlays precisely predictable (and far more controllable). Its appeal to employers, like that of 401(k) plans as alternatives to defined-benefit plans, is understandable. It has found some adherents in Congress who favor special tax benefits for such plans. The obvious shortcoming, however, is that there is no connection between the size of the fund and the magnitude of retiree health care costs, so the accumulated assets may be inadequate to the task.

Long-Term Care

Q. 12:47 What is long-term care?

Long-term care refers to the services that would be required over an extended period of time by someone who has a chronic illness or disability. Though the types of care provided could range from home health care to hospitalization, the emphasis is on custodial and skilled nursing care, and attendant outpatient services. It can also include such things as meals-on-wheels, respite care, home health aides, and visiting nurses.

Q. 12:48 What are the special issues connected with long-term care?

It is estimated that 65% of those people over age 85 and 25% of those over age 65 will need long-term care in their lifetimes. Because of the mobility of the population and varying life styles, family support systems have been reduced, and more institutional care will therefore be necessary. Generally, neither group insurance plans that continue after retirement nor Medicare provides coverage for long-term care, except in a facility that provides skilled medical care. Even then, coverage is usually for only a limited period of time.

For most of the elderly disabled, however, the greater need is for intermediate or custodial care. Insurance companies have just begun to respond with individual policies that address the special needs of elderly former employees.

Q. 12:49 What are the different levels of long-term care?

There are three basic levels of long-term care:

1. Skilled nursing care. Care is provided by skilled medical personnel under the supervision or orders of a doctor. This includes daily nursing or rehabilitative care at a skilled nursing facility (e.g., a facility licensed by the state and approved by Medicare/Medicaid to provide skilled care).
2. Intermediate care. Nursing care on an occasional basis is provided by skilled medical personnel. Again, the care must conform to a doctor's orders.
3. Custodial care. Assistance is provided in meeting such personal needs such as bathing, dressing, and eating. It can be provided by skilled or nonskilled medical personnel. This care can be provided in skilled or intermediate nursing facilities, or, in less demanding circumstances, through a program of home health care.

Q. 12:50 How expensive is long-term care?

Nursing home costs can range from $25,000 to $50,000 or more a year, depending on geographic region and level of care provided. Minimum home health care on a five-days-a-week basis can cost $10,000 a year—more for skilled assistance.

Q. 12:51 What long-term care benefits does Medicare provide?

Medicare pays less than 2% of the nation's annual nursing home bill and provides home health or nursing home care only in limited circumstances:

- Coverage for skilled nursing care is available for up to 100 days per calendar year, and carries a copayment of $74.00 per day after the first 20 days. To be eligible, a person must be admitted within 30 days of a 3-day hospital stay.
- Part-time skilled home health care is available in limited circumstances.

Q. 12:52 What long-term care services are covered by Medicaid?

Unlike Medicare, Medicaid pays substantial benefits for nursing home care, accounting for over 40% of all nursing home payments. As a federally funded program administered by the states, Medicaid can vary in coverage. One troublesome element is the income/assets requirement (which in 1989 permitted spouses to keep $12,000 in assets and monthly income of $786). Individuals who earn or own in excess of these limits may have to "spend down" to become eligible for Medicaid.

Q. 12:53 What does a typical long-term care benefit cover?

A typical plan might provide for skilled, intermediate, and custodial care in state-licensed nursing homes, as well as home health care from Medicare-approved or state-licensed providers.

Benefits are often based on a stated dollar amount for skilled nursing care. The dollar benefit is usually an option chosen at the time the policy is written, and may range from $50 to $150 a day. Lesser types of care, such as adult day care, are usually covered at a percentage of the skilled nursing benefit (e.g., 50% of the skilled nursing benefit).

Q. 12:54 Are benefits adjusted for inflation?

Although some policies make adjustments for inflation in the level of daily benefits over time, many do not. Those that do may not fully adjust for changes in the cost of living. For example, some policies provide a flat dollar increase (e.g., $5 a day) after a specified number of years (e.g., five).

Q. 12:55 What is the tax status of custodial care?

Employer contributions to provide medical care are not taxable to employees, but contributions to provide custodial care may be. Given this, and given employer reluctance to assume significant additional employee benefits costs, long-term care is often offered as an employee-pay-all option.

Q. 12:56 Who provides long-term care insurance?

Long-term care insurance is fairly widely available from commercial insurers. In addition, HMOs, PPOs, nursing home chains, and continued care retirement communities (CCRCs) also provide long-term care plans.

Q. 12:57 How much does long-term care insurance cost?

The cost varies, depending on age at purchase, level of benefits elected, and normal variability from one insurer to another. Individual premiums may be as low as $250 annually, and can range up to $8,000 or more.

Q. 12:58 What considerations should be taken into account in evaluating long-term care insurance policies?

The following factors should be considered when evaluating long-term care policies:

1. Premium. Premiums are generally determined on an entry-age level basis, so that an older person buying long-term care insurance would pay more than a younger one, but a given individual's premium would not increase as he or she gets older. Many policies offer a "premium waiver" that continues the policy in force if the owner is unable to continue payments. Another consideration is how long the rate is guaranteed for; group policy premiums are often adjusted annually.
2. Coverage ages. Most policies have minimum and maximum coverage ages, generally ranging from 45–50 at the low end to 75–80 at the high end.
3. Duration of benefits. Policies may impose limits on the duration of care in a nursing facility (e.g., a maximum of five years of nursing home coverage). There may be a limit for each confinement, and a lifetime overall limit. Limits for custodial care and home health care may also be expressed separately. Of course, the longer the period, the higher the premium.
4. Elimination periods. Policy benefits may not cover the initial period of care, and may require a specified stay, such as 30 days, before any benefits are payable. In this example, benefits would be payable commencing with the thirty-first day.
5. Exclusions. Long-term care insurance generally does not provide coverage for preexisting conditions (from 3 to 6 months preceding, and 6 to 12 months following, the effective date of coverage), self-inflicted injuries, alcoholism, mental illness, or treatment outside the United States. One problem area is an exclusion for mental illness and nervous disorders; sometimes these disorders are further broken down into organic and nonorganic. Special care should be taken that these exclusions do not encompass Alzheimer's

disease and related impairments, since patients with these illnesses frequently require nursing home care.
6. Renewability. The policy should be guaranteed renewable and noncancelable.
7. Care levels. Some policies are specific in covering only certain types of care, such as skilled nursing care only. Since much long-term care expense is associated with custodial care, this should be avoided. Preconditions (such as prior hospitalization) for home care should be avoided as well.
8. Facilities. Some policies, while covering all levels of care, restrict coverage to certain facilities, such as skilled nursing facilities approved by Medicare. Again, since custodial care, which is often provided in an unskilled setting, is crucial, such restrictions should be avoided.
9. Benefit levels. Few policies gear benefits to actual costs incurred; instead, they pay a stated daily benefit determined by the level of care provided. Some sort of adjustment that increases the daily level over the life of the policy is necessary in order to keep the value of the policy from being overtaken by rising costs.

Impact of AIDS on Insurance

Q. 12:59 What is the impact of AIDS on health benefits and the use of medical resources?

Although the effect of acquired immune deficiency syndrome (AIDS) is only beginning to be felt, there are predictions that it will have a major impact in the future.

- The Public Health Service has estimated that the number of reported AIDS cases in the United States will reach 365,000 by 1992, with 263,000 deaths. This was based upon the assumption that somewhere between 1 million and 1.5 million Americans have been infected with the HIV virus.
- More recent estimates from the General Accounting Office suggested that these numbers were too low, and that the

number of AIDS cases would be between 300,000 and 485,000 by 1991.
- An even more recent prediction from *AIDS Insurance Reports* predicted that by 1996, 1 million people would have AIDS, and that by the year 2017, 1 million Americans would die of AIDS every year, crippling the U.S. life and health insurance industries.

Estimated costs to employers in terms of direct medical care, disability losses, and costs of premature mortality could reach .6% of payroll, or $11.8 billion in 1986 dollars. Although this is not an overwhelming number on average, the costs will not be spread evenly throughout the economy. AIDS cases are most heavily concentrated in a few major cities such as New York, San Francisco, and Los Angeles. Consequently, employers in these cities are likely to experience much higher incidences of the disease, and greater expense, than employers in other parts of the country.

How much of the cost of caring for AIDS sufferers will actually be borne by employers is difficult to estimate. The two groups most affected by the disease have been homosexuals or bisexuals, and intravenous drug users. New infections among the former group are leveling off or declining. The rate of infections among intravenous drug users may still be on the increase, but few of those at risk are covered by employer health plans.

Q. 12:60 Why will the medical costs be so high?

Early estimates of average treatment costs of AIDS patients were approximately $147,000 per patient. More recent estimates have more than halved that figure, although there is wide fluctuation from patient to patient. The reasons for the high level of expense and the variation include:
- Lengthy hospital stays. Although more and more AIDS care is being provided at home, in nursing facilities, and through volunteers—all of which serve to reduce the cost of caring for AIDS victims—there are still long periods of care in some sort of medical facility.

- Expensive drugs. Because most drugs used in the treatment of AIDS are still experimental, they are also very expensive. The cost of providing AZT to an AIDS patient may by itself add $10,000 to the annual cost of care.
- Lengthening life expectancy. The average life expectancy of a person with AIDS has been increasing. Successful treatment means longer life, which in turn means longer periods of care and more prescription drugs, all of which translates to higher costs.

Q. 12:61 What other cost increases are associated with AIDS?

Two other costs affected by AIDS are disability and insurance costs.

AIDS is generally regarded as a disability, so persons with AIDS could be entitled to benefits under a company's short- and long-term disability plans.

The high costs associated with AIDS treatment, as well as the uncertainty surrounding the future incidence of the disease, have prompted insurers to raise premiums on group life and health insurance coverage. In addition, for individual and small groups, a carrier's underwriting procedures may identify persons who have AIDS or are members of high-risk groups. Such individuals may be covered only at higher premiums (or not covered at all).

Q. 12:62 Are there restrictions on the information that may be requested to identify a person at risk for AIDS?

Yes. Although laws vary from state to state, some jurisdictions prohibit or restrict employers and/or carriers from basing coverage decisions on such things as blood/HIV antibody tests, questions about former AIDS tests, and life-style questions, particularly those surrounding sexual preference. Contractual AIDS exclusions are also prohibited.

Q. 12:63 Would all forms of care for AIDS patients be covered under an employer's health insurance program?

Not necessarily. Insurance policies tend to be quite specific about the nature of treatment covered. Because care for AIDS patients may be of an experimental nature, or may be provided through an alternative facility that is not staffed by "licensed practitioners," it may fall outside policy definitions.

Also, the plan may limit reimbursement to "actual treatment of illness or injury," which would not extend to custodial care, which is often the largest single cost item for AIDS patients. A considerable portion of such care is provided through home health care, residential facilities, or hospices. Plans that provide hospice coverage would pay for these types of expenses.

Q. 12:64 What legal protections have been extended to persons with AIDS?

AIDS as a cause for dismissal is less acceptable now for reasons beyond the humane; such an action may be considered discriminatory.

Except for certain sensitive positions, such as airline pilot, AIDS sufferers who work for the federal government or for organizations that receive federal aid are entitled to the protections of civil rights laws and the Rehabilitation Act of 1973, which protects persons with disabling physical or mental handicaps. Many states classify AIDS as a handicap under their fair employment laws.

Local agencies, such as the New York City Human Rights Commission's AIDS Discrimination Unit, also provide protection to AIDS sufferers.

Q. 12:65 Is testing for AIDS permissible?

This is an issue still being addressed by the courts, which have so far been divided. Recently:

- When the risk of disease transmission is negligible, and

such testing would have little or no effect in limiting the spread of AIDS, the employer has no justifiable interest in testing employees for the disease. [Ref.: *Glover v. Eastern Nebraska Office of Retardation*, 867 F.2d 461 (8th Cir. 1989)]
- When an employee is in an occupation covered by the Centers for Disease Control guidelines and is at medical risk for carrying AIDS, testing may be required (on pain of dismissal). [Ref.: *Leckelt v. Board of Commissioners of Hospital District No. 1*, 41 E.R. Cas. 383 (E.D. La. 1989)]

Q. 12:66 How should an employer respond to AIDS?

An employer should first establish a corporate policy on AIDS that goes beyond financial concerns to address the social environment of the workplace, and should include a program of education for other workers. Other appropriate actions include:

- Planning for the reasonable accommodation of persons with AIDS, with special attention to those working in sensitive areas such as food service, health care, laboratory, and other kinds of work that are encompassed by guidelines established by the Centers for Disease Control. Special precautions or reassignment might need to be considered.
- Making arrangements for job modifications, or alternative work assignments on a part-time or temporary basis, that would allow the individual with AIDS to continue working as long as possible.
- Contacting community agencies that will help both the employer and the person with AIDS.
- Reviewing existing insurance arrangements to see what forms of coverage are provided.
- If mandatory testing is being considered, review legal precedents to see whether it is permissible under the circumstances. Collective bargaining agreements should also be reviewed; at this writing, it is unclear whether this type of testing is subject to bargaining.

Appendix: Health Information Resources

The following is a list of resources that can provide information on various aspects of health care and insurance.

Government

Alcohol, Drug Abuse and Mental Health Administration
Parklawn Building
5600 Fishers Lane
Rockville, MD 20857
(301) 443-3783

Bureau of Labor Statistics
441 G St., NW
Washington, DC 20210
(202) 523-1222

Centers for Disease Control
1600 Clifton Road, NE
Atlanta, GA 30333
(404) 639-3311

Department of Commerce
Main Commerce Building
14th and Constitution Avenue, NW
Washington, DC 20230
(202) 377-2000

Health Insurance Answer Book

Department of Health and Human Services
200 Independence Avenue
Washington, DC 20201
(202) 619-0287

Department of Labor
200 Constitution Avenue, NW
Washington, DC 20210
(202) 523-6666

Health Care Financing Administration
6325 Security Boulevard
Baltimore, MD 21207
(301) 966-3000

Health Resources and Services Administration
Parklawn Building
5600 Fishers Lane
Rockville, MD 20857
(301) 443-5487 [6936]

Internal Revenue Service
1111 Constitution Ave, NW
Washington, D.C.
(202) 566-5000

National Center for Health Services Research and Health Care Technology Assessment
Parklawn Building
5600 Fishers Lane
Rockville, MD 20857
(301) 443-4100

National Center for Health Statistics
3700 East-West Highway
Hyattsville, MD 20782
(301) 436-8500

National Health Information Clearinghouse
PO Box 1133
Washington, DC 20013-1133
(800) 336-4797 or (301) 565-4167

National Institutes of Health
9000 Rockville Pike

Bethesda, MD 20892
(301) 496-4000

National Technical Information Service
5285 Port Royal Road
Springfield, VA 22161
(703) 487-4650

Pension and Welfare Benefits Administration
200 Constitution Avenue, NW
Washington, DC 20216
(202) 523-8921

Social Security Administration
6401 Security Boulevard
Baltimore, MD 21235
(301) 594-6660

U.S. General Accounting Office
Document Handling and Information Facility
PO Box 6015
Gaithersburg, MD 20877
(202) 275-6241

U.S. Government Printing Office
Superintendent of Documents
941 North Capital St., NE
Washington, DC 20402
(202) 783-3238

Associations/Organizations

Administrative Management Society Foundation
4622 Street Road
Trevose, PA 19047
(215) 953-1040

AFL-CIO
Occupational Safety, Health
Employee Benefits Department
815 16th Street, NW

Health Insurance Answer Book

Washington, D.C. 20006
(202) 637-5200

Alcoholics Anonymous
General Services Office
6th Floor
468 Park Avenue South
New York, NY 10016
(212) 686-1100

American Association of Health Care Consultants
11208 Waples Mill Road
Fairfax, VA 22030
(703) 691-2242

American Association of Homes for the Aging
Suite 400
1129 20th Street, NW
Washington, DC 20036-3489
(202) 296-5960

American Association of Preferred Provider Organizations
Suite 600
111 E. Wacker Dr.
Chicago, IL 60601
(312) 644-6610

American Cancer Society
1599 Clifton Road, SE
Atlanta, GA 30329
(404) 320-3333

American College of Health Care Administrators
325 S. Patrick St.
Alexandria, VA 22314
(703) 549-5822

American Health Care Association
1201 L Street, NW
Washington, DC 20005
(202) 842-4444

American Heart Association
Inquiries Section

Appendix

7320 Greenville Avenue
Dallas, TX 75231
(214) 373-6300

American Hospital Association
Office of Health Coalitions and Private Initiatives
840 North Lake Shore Drive
Chicago, IL 60611
(312) 280-6000

American Insurance Association
Suite 1000
1130 Connecticut Ave., NW
Washington, DC 20036
(202) 828-7100

American Medical Association
535 N. Dearborn St.
Chicago, IL 60610-0946
(312) 645-5000

American Medical Care and Review Association (AMCRA)
1227 25th St., NW
Suite 610
Washington, DC 20037
(202) 728-0506

Blue Cross and Blue Shield Association
676 N. St. Clair
Chicago, IL 60611
(312) 440-6000

The Center for Corporate Health Promotion
1850 Centennial Park Drive, Suite 520
Reston, VA 22091
(703) 391-1900

Employee Assistance Program Association
4601 N. Fairfax Dr. Suite 1001
Fairfax, VA 22203
(703) 522-6272

Employee Benefit Research Institute (EBRI)
Suite 600

2121 K Street, NW
Washington, DC 20037-2121
(202) 659-0670

Employers Council on Flexible Compensation (ECFC)
Suite 1000
927 15th St., NW
Washington, DC 20005
(202) 659-4300

The Financial Accounting Standards Board (FASB)
PO Box 5116
401 Merritt #7
Norwalk, CT 06856-5116
(203) 847-0700

Group Health Association of America (GHAA)
Suite 600
1129 Twentieth Street, NW
Washington, DC 20036
(202) 778-3200

Health Care Financial Management Association (HCFMA)
Suite 700
Two Westbrook Corporate Center
Westchester, IL 60153
(800) 252-4362

Health Insurance Association of America (HIAA)
1025 Connecticut Avenue, NW
Washington, DC 20004-2599
(202) 223-7780

Institute for a Drug-Free Workplace
PO Box 65708
Washington, DC 20035-5708
(202) 463-5530

Institute for Professional Health Service Administrators
1101 King St. Suite 601
Alexandria, VA 22314
(703) 684-0288

International Dental Health Foundation, Inc.
11484 Washington Place W.

Appendix

Reston, VA 22090
(703) 471-8349

International Foundation of Employee Benefit Plans (IFEBP)
18700 West Bluemound Road
PO Box 69
Brookfield, WI 53008-0069
(414) 786-6700

InterStudy
Center for Managed Care Research
5715 Christmas Lake Road
PO Box 458
Excelsior, MN 55331-0458
(612) 474-1176

Midwest Business Group on Health
8303 West Higgins Road, Suite 200
Chicago, IL 60631
(312) 380-8090

National AIDS Information Clearinghouse
PO Box 6003
Rockville, MD 20850
(800) 458-5231

National Association of Employers on Health Care Alternatives
104 Crandon Boulevard
Key Biscayne, FL 33149
(305) 361-2810

National Association of Health Data Organizations
254B N. Washington Street
Falls Church, VA 22046
(703) 532-3282

National Association of Private Psychiatric Hospitals
Suite 1000
1319 F St., NW
Washington, DC 20004
(202) 393-6700

National Association of Rehabilitation Facilities
Suite 200
1910 Association Drive

Reston, VA 22090
(703) 648-9300

The National Center for Health Promotion
3920 Varsity Drive
Ann Arbor, MI 48108
(313) 971-6077

National Coalition for Health Care Reform
555 13th St., NW
Washington, DC 20004
(202) 637-6830

National Council on Alcoholism and Drug Dependence
12 West 21st St.
New York, NY 10010
(212) 206-6770

National Employee Benefits Institute
Suite 400
2445 M Street, NW
Washington, DC 20037
(800) 558-7258

National Health Council
350 Fifth Ave.
Suite 1118
New York, NY 10118
(212) 268-8900

National Heart, Lung, and Blood Institute
Information Center
Suite 530
4733 Bethesda Ave.
Bethesda, MD 20814-4820
(301) 951-3260

National Safety Council
Box 11171
Chicago, IL 60611
(312) 527-4800

The National Wellness Institute
South Hall
1319 Fremont Street

Appendix

Stevens Point, WI 54481
(715) 346-2172

New York Business Group on Health
622 Third Avenue
New York, NY 10017
(212) 808-0550

Self Insurance Institute of America
PO Box 15466
Santa Ana, CA 92705
(714) 261-2553

Society for Human Resource Management
(formerly American Society for Personnel Administration)
606 N. Washington St.
Alexandria, VA 22314
(703) 548-3440

U.S. Chamber of Commerce
Clearinghouse on Business Coalitions for Health Action
1615 H Street, NW
Washington, DC 20062
(202) 659-6000

Washington Business Group on Health
777 N. Capitol St., NE
Suite 800
Washington, DC 20002
(202) 408-9320

HMO Quality Review Organizations

Accreditation Association for Ambulatory Health Care
9933 Lawler Avenue
Suite 512
Skokie, IL 60077-3702
(708) 676-9610

Joint Commission for Accreditation of Healthcare Organizations
1 Renaissance Blvd

Oak Brook Terr., IL 60181
(708) 916-5600

Center for Consumer Health Care Information
1821 E. Dyer Rd.
Santa Ana, CA 92075
(800) 627-2244

Glossary

The following is a list of terms, abbreviations, and acronyms (arranged in alphabetical order) intended to provide the reader with an additional guide to understanding the concepts explored in this book.

Acceptability: Consumer satisfaction with the quality and accessibility of health care services.

Accidental death and dismemberment: See AD&D.

Accreditation: Certification by a nongovernmental accrediting organization that a given health care provider meets that organization's standards.

Accumulation period: A specified period during which a covered employee must accumulate eligible medical expenses to meet the plan's deductible requirements.

Acquisition cost: The cost to an insurer of underwriting and issuing a new policy, including commissions, home-office expenses, and so forth.

Actuary: A person who mathematically analyzes and prices the risks associated with providing insurance coverage, or who calculates the costs of providing future benefits. This analysis involves the morbidity and mortality rates associated with the group, along with underlying costs, administrative expenses, and anticipated investment return.

AD&D: Accidental death and dismemberment. One of the four major components of health insurance coverage employers provide their employees. (The others are life, disability, and medical insurance.) AD&D provides coverage for death or dismemberment resulting directly from accidental causes.

ADEA: Age Discrimination in Employment Act of 1967. As amended in 1978, ADEA requires employers with 20 or more employees to offer active employees above age 40 (and their spouses) the same health insurance coverage that is provided to younger employees.

Administrative services only: See ASO.

Administrator: A person designated by an employee benefit plan sponsor to be responsible for the proper operation of the plan. When the plan sponsor makes no such designation, ERISA indicates that the plan sponsor will be considered the administrator.

Adverse selection: Also known as antiselection, this is the tendency of persons to choose health options that are financially most beneficial to them (and least beneficial to the health care program or insurer) in light of their known physical conditions. Those with known health problems elect more insurance; healthy persons elect less or none at all.

Affiliated service group: A group of related companies consisting of a service organization and other companies that have some degree of association and common ownership that is treated as a single company for nondiscrimination purposes. See also Controlled group.

Age Discrimination in Employment Act: See ADEA.

AIDS: Acquired immune deficiency syndrome.

ALOS: Average length of stay. Average number of patient days per inpatient for a given period.

ALR: Acceptable loss ratio. See TLR.

Alternative delivery system: Alternatives to traditional health care programs. See HMO; PPO.

Americans with Disabilities Act: A law enacted in 1990 which prohibits discrimination against persons with disabilities in such areas as public accommodations and terms and conditions of employment.

Annual report: Reports filed with IRS and Department of Labor on Forms 5500 and 5500-C, which summarize plan activity during a plan year.

ASO: Administrative services only. An ASO plan is a contract with an insurer to provide a fully self-insured employer with certain administrative services only; no insurance protection is provided.

Assignment of benefits: Authorization by the insured for the insurer to pay benefits directly to the medical care provider.

Glossary

Audit: A retrospective review of provider services and charges to see that all billed services were actually provided, that the charges for these services were accurate, and that the fees were reasonable.

Average length of stay: See ALOS.

Balance Billing: The practice of charging full fees in excess of Medicare reimbursable amounts, then billing the patient for that portion of the bill which Medicare does not cover.

Base plus plans: A health insurance plan that provides for basic medical coverage plus additional coverage for catastrophic health problems.

BC/BS: Blue Cross/Blue Shield. The Blues provide nonprofit health insurance to millions of Americans. Operating at the state and city levels, the Blues dominate third-party insurance reimbursement in many geographic areas because of their ability to offer reduced rates through negotiated discounts with health care providers. Blue Cross coverage was designed to provide protection against hospital costs; Blue Shield was designed to cover physician expenses and other costs.

Beneficiary: A person entitled to receive benefits under a plan, including a covered employee and his or her dependents.

Benefit period: Period over which benefits are payable under a plan or insurance contract. Alternatively, a period for satisfying a deductible requirement, usually referred to as an "accumulation period."

Bioethics: A moral and social philosophy which studies questions relating to when life begins and ends, and how choices regarding the allocation of medical and health care resources would be made.

Blanket medical expense: A provision in loss-of-income (e.g., disability) policies that provides a specific maximum reimbursement for all types of care, with no individual limits.

Blue Cross/Blue Shield: See BC/BS.

Broker: A licensed insurance professional who represents the insurance purchaser (e.g., plan sponsors) in the acquisition of insurance coverage. This contrasts with an agent, who represents the insurer.

Cafeteria plan: A flexible benefits plan, generally one that complies with the requirements of IRC Section 125 and offers a choice of two or more "qualified benefits," or a choice between cash and one or more qualified benefits.

Capitation: A form of payment used by HMOs. Members pay a preset fixed fee for which they receive as much health care service as needed. This is an alternative to a fee-for-service arrangement.

Carryover deductible: An arrangement that allows expenses incurred in the last three months of the plan year, which were applied to that year's deductible, to be carried over to the following year and counted toward satisfying the new year's deductible.

Case management: A form of utilization review used with high-cost cases that monitors and manages treatment and suggests alternatives to lengthy hospital stays.

Cash-or-deferred arrangement: See CODA.

CCRC: Continuing care retirement community. A community which, in exchange for an entrance fee and a monthly charge, guarantees lifetime housing and nursing care as required.

Certificate of insurance: A booklet or statement from an insurer that provides a covered employee with a summary of coverage.

Churning: A form of code gaming where the same procedure is billed for more than once.

Claim: The request for reimbursement from an insurer or plan for a covered expense.

Claims services only: See CSO.

Closed panel: A health care program that requires participants to use providers or pharmacies from a list of such providers provided by the plan, with whom the plan has established a contractual relationship. The alternative is an open panel.

Coalitions: An employer health care coalition is an association of health care sponsors that pool resources to gather information on and negotiate with insurers and other health care providers.

COB: Coordination of benefits. COB is a cost-control mechanism to prevent an employee from receiving duplicate benefits from two or more group insurance or health plans.

COBRA: Consolidated Omnibus Budget Reconciliation Act of 1985. COBRA permits covered employees and beneficiaries to continue their health care coverage for a period of up to 36 months after it would normally terminate. The continuation of coverage requires the individual to pay a premium.

CODA: Cash-or-deferred arrangement. A provision that permits employees to elect to take cash compensation, or to defer the receipt of the income (and the taxes on it) by directing it to a tax-exempt trust. These arrangements, also known as 401(k) plans, can be made available through cafeteria plans.

Glossary

Code Gaming: The use of incorrect billing codes to increase provider income, or to enable a patient to receive reimbursement for a treatment which would otherwise be nonreimbursable.

Coinsurance: An arrangement that apportions expenses between the covered individual and an insurer; for example, 80% to be paid by the health insurer and 20% by the employee.

COLAs: Cost-of-living adjustments. Changes (increases) in the level of benefits provided under an income replacement or reimbursement program which are proportional to changes in a price index, such as the consumer price index (CPI).

Community rating: The determination of a single average premium rate based on the characteristics and claims experience of the entire membership (in an HMO or insurance pool), rather than separate premiums for individual member groups. See also Experience rating.

Comprehensive medical plan: A plan that provides medical coverage under a single reimbursement formula rather than two, as with a base plus plan.

Concurrent review: A form of utilization review in which hospital admissions are reviewed and certified within 24 hours following admission, and are monitored for appropriateness thereafter.

Consolidated Omnibus Budget Reconciliation Act: See COBRA.

Constructive receipt: The tax principle that compensation is taxable when made available, even if not actually received, such as when an individual is offered taxable income but elects nontaxable benefits instead. The doctrine does not apply to cafeteria plans because of the exception granted in IRC Section 125.

Continued stay review: A form of utilization review that monitors the continued appropriateness of hospital stays. See Discharge planning.

Controlled group: Two or more companies with a defined level of common ownership that are treated as a single company for coverage and nondiscrimination purposes. See also Affiliated service group.

Conversion privilege: The right of a terminating employee to convert from group coverage to an individual policy without providing evidence of insurability.

Coordination of benefits: See COB.

Core benefits: The central components of a health care plan, generally comprehensive major medical and hospitalization benefits. These may be supplemented by additional "noncore" benefits. Dental and vision benefits are examples of noncore benefits.

Core plus plan: A type of flexible benefits plan that provides a minimum level of benefits to all employees. Individuals then have the option of increasing the levels of some or all of these benefits above the minimums.

Cost containment: Any activity or practice aimed at holding down health care costs or reducing their rate of increase.

Cost sharing: The apportioning of health care costs between a health care plan and individual participants through employee contributions, deductibles, and coinsurance.

Cost shifting: The increase of charges to a patient or group of patients to make up for losses incurred in providing care to other patients.

Cost-of-Living Adjustments: See COLAs

Coverage: The types and amounts of benefits provided under a plan, or an insurance contract.

Covered expenses: An expense for which a health care plan will provide reimbursement.

CPT: Current Procedural Technology. A coding system developed by the American Medical Association to categorize medical procedures for billing purposes.

Credibility: The confidence in a given set of prior claims experience data as an indicator of future claims experience.

CSO: Claims services only. A CSO plan is a contract designed for fully self-insured employers that need very little administrative assistance. Under a CSO arrangement, the insurer administers only the claims portion of the plan.

Current Procedural Technology: See CPT.

DCAP: Dependent care assistance plan. A program governed by IRC Section 129 which provides for tax-free child care assistance either from an employer or a reimbursement account.

Deductible: An amount that a covered individual must pay before an insurance program begins reimbursing for expenses.

Deferred premium plan: A funding arrangement that extends the grace period beyond the normal 31 days, usually to 60 or 90 days.

DEFRA: Deficit Reduction Act of 1984.

Glossary

Dental services corporation: A nonprofit corporation that provides or contracts to provide dental care.

Dependent Care Assistance Plan: See DCAP.

Diagnosis-related groups: See DRGs.

Direct reimbursement: A noninsured dental program in which an employer agrees to pay for a specified percentage or amount of dental expenses.

Disability: The inability to perform all or some portion of the duties of one's occupation or, alternatively, any occupation as a result of a physical or mental impairment. See also Short-term disability and Long-term disability.

Discharge planning: A form of utilization review that is intended to ensure that a patient stays in a hospital only as long as medically necessary.

DRGs: Diagnosis-related groups. A system of classifying patients according to categories of diagnosis which should require very similar programs of treatment and lengths of hospital stays. DRGs are used to determine the amount Medicare reimburses for hospital stays. DRGs were developed at Yale University in 1975 and have been adopted by several states.

Drug-Free Workplace Act: A federal law which requires employers with $25,000 or more in government contracts to certify that they are running a drug-free workplace.

Dual choice: The requirement that, upon request, certain employers must offer a federally qualified HMO as an alternative to its conventional health plan.

Duplication of benefits: Similar or identical coverages provided to the same insured by two or more plans.

EAP: Employee assistance program. A program of counseling and other forms of assistance to employees suffering from alcoholism, substance abuse, or emotional and family problems.

Eligibility: The conditions imposed for coverage under a plan, such as full-time status and length of service.

Elimination period: A period that must elapse before benefits become payable under a disability or health plan for the onset of a covered illness.

Employee assistance programs: See EAP.

Employee Retirement Income Security Act: See ERISA.

Employee welfare benefit plan: A plan that provides benefits other than pension benefits, such as death, disability, and medical benefits. Defined in ERISA Section 3(1).

End-stage renal disease: A terminal kidney disease whose sufferers are eligible for Medicare benefits.

Enrolled group: Individuals who have signed up and are therefore eligible for benefits under a plan.

EOB: Explanation of benefits. A document that accompanies a claims check and summarizes how reimbursement was determined and, among other things, explains the claims appeal process.

EPO: Exclusive provider organization. A more rigid type of PPO, closely related to an HMO, that requires the employee to use only designated providers or sacrifice reimbursement altogether. (PPOs generally encourage employees to use preferred providers through more generous reimbursement, but will still reimburse for nonpreferred providers.)

ERISA: Employee Retirement Income Security Act of 1974. Primarily enacted to effect pension equality, ERISA also contains provisions to protect the interests of group insurance plan participants and beneficiaries. It requires, among other things, that insurance plans be established pursuant to a written instrument that describes the benefits provided under the plan, names the persons responsible for the operation of the plan, and spells out the arrangements for funding and amending the plan.

Evidence of insurability: A personal description that lists factors regarding a person's physical condition, medical history, and other information on which an insurer could base an underwriting decision. Although evidence of insurability is required for individual insurance coverage, it is seldom required for group policies other than very small ones.

Excess benefits: Benefits exceeding the maximum permitted under nondiscrimination requirements; they must be included in the taxable incomes of highly compensated employees.

Exclusions: Specific illnesses or treatments that are expressly not covered by a plan or insurance contract.

Exclusive provider organization: See EPO.

Executive Medical Plans: See medical reimbursement plans.

Glossary

Experience rating: A method of determining premiums that adjusts a group's rate based on the demographic characteristics and utilization experience of that particular group, as opposed to using averaged data for multiple groups.

Explanation of benefits: See EOB.

Exploding: A form of code gaming. A billing practice which bills separately for each test performed on a given laboratory specimen.

Extended benefits: Benefits that continue, or become payable, after an insurance contract terminates, such as for an injury that occurred prior to the termination.

Extended care facility: An institution that provides skilled nursing, intermediate, or custodial care.

FASB: Financial Accounting Standards Board. An organization that establishes standards for accounting statements. Recently its attention has been focused on accounting for retiree health care liabilities.

Fiduciary: Under ERISA, any person who exercises discretionary authority or control over a plan or plan assets.

Financial Accounting Standards Board: See FASB.

First dollar coverage: A plan that covers health care expenses with no deductible.

501(c)(9) trust: See VEBA.

Flexible benefits plan: A plan that offers employees a choice among a number of alternative benefits. Also called a flex plan. See also Cafeteria plan.

Flexible spending (or reimbursement) account: An account funded by an employee salary reduction, employer contribution, or both, used to pay the employee's share of the cost of certain benefits, or to reimburse him or her for expenses. It is a device for converting after-tax expenses to pretax ones.

FMCs: Foundations for medical care. A forerunner program to utilization review, these watchdog organizations were established in the early 1960s for Medicare recipients.

Foundations for medical care: See FMCs.

401(h) account: A separate account of a pension plan that, under provisions of IRC Section 401(h), may be used to fund medical benefits for retirees and dependents.

Fully insured plan: A plan in which a policyholder tranfers risk and responsibility for all claims to an insurer in exchange for payment of a regular premium.

GHAA: Group Health Association of America.

Grace period: A period that follows the due date of the premium after which the policy continues in force.

Group insurance: A single program insuring a group of associated individuals against financial loss resulting from illness, injury, or death.

Guaranteed issue underwriting: The provision of insurance up to stated amounts of coverage without evidence of insurability, common with group policies.

Guaranteed renewable: The right to continue a policy in force up to a stated age simply by making timely premium payments. During that time, the insurer may not change the policy, except to change policies for a class of policyholders.

HCEs: Highly compensated employees. One of several definitions of employees who are not permitted to receive benefits disproportionately larger than other employees under the nondiscrimination rules applicable to employee benefit plans. As defined by IRC Section 414(q) HCEs include 5% owners, employees who earned more than $85,485 (in 1990), the top paid 20% of employees who earn more than $56,990 (in 1990), and officers earning more than $51,291 (in 1990). [See also Highly compensated individual, Highly compensated participant, and Key employee.]

HCFA: Health Care Financing Administration.

Health maintenance organization: See HMO.

Health promotion: Behavioral modification programs intended to modify life styles and habits to promote better health. See also Wellness.

Health risk appraisal: See HRA.

High self-insured deductible: See HSID.

Highly compensated employees: See HCEs.

Highly compensated individuals: As defined by IRC Section 105(h)(5), one of the 5 highest paid officers, a shareholder who owns more than 10% of employer stock, or one of the 25 highest paid employees. [See also HCE, Highly compensated participant, and Key employee.]

Glossary

Highly compensated participant: As defined by IRC Section 125(e), an officer, a more-than-5% shareholder, a highly compensated employee, or spouses or dependents of one of the former.

HMO: Health maintenance organization. An HMO is an organization that, for a prepaid fee, provides comprehensive health care services to a voluntarily enrolled membership. HMOs are sponsored by large employers, labor unions, medical schools, hospitals, medical clinics, and even insurance companies. Development of HMOs was spurred by the federal government in the 1970s as a means to correct the structural, inflationary problems with conventional health care payment.

Home health care: A program that provides skilled nursing care to patients in their homes.

Hospice: A facility that provides care for the terminally ill in the form of relieving pain, providing counseling, and custodial care.

Hospital indemnity: A program that pays fixed benefits for hospital stays on a daily, weekly, or monthly basis. The payment is in no way related to actual expenses incurred.

HRA: Health risk appraisal. A survey used by employers to determine the likelihood of an insured experiencing death, illness, or injury in the future. It helps employers decide whether wellness and other preventive care programs are necessary.

HSID: High self-insured deductible. Also known as shared funding, HSID is a way for employers to improve cash flow by self-funding the first tier of any employee's health care expenses. Employers can thus retain funds that would normally be paid to the insurance company to cover current and future claims.

IBNR: Incurred but not reported. Claims that have been incurred but have not been reported to the insurer as of some specific date.

ICM: Individual case management. See Case management.

ILP: Independent living program. A program of housing assistance, job retraining, and other types of assistance to help disabled individuals live as independently as possible.

Incurred but not reported: See IBNR.

Indemnity: Any benefits paid to cover a loss insured against by a policy.

Independent living program: See ILP.

Individual insurance: As opposed to group insurance, coverage provided under a contract issued to one individual at a time, usually requiring evidence of insurability.

Individual practice association model: See IPA model.

Intermediary: A knowledgeable benefits professional, such as a benefits consultant, who assists plan sponsors in designing, purchasing, and administering health insurance programs.

Intermediate care facility: A facility that provides health care or nursing services to patients who do not require the level of care offered by hospitals or skilled nursing facilities.

IPA model: Individual practice association model. One of the four different models by which HMOs are organized. The others are the group model, the network model, and the staff model. The IPA model is a mixture of physicians from solo and group practices.

IRC: Internal Revenue Code.

IRS: Internal Revenue Service.

Key employees: Individuals who may not receive benefits disproportional to those of other employees under a cafeteria plan. As defined by IRC Section 416(i), a key employee is a 5% owner, a 1% owner earning more than $150,000, an officer earning more than $51,291 (in 1990) or one of the 10 largest owners earning over $30,000. [See also HCE, Highly compensated individual, and Highly compensated participant.]

Lag: The period of time between the incurring of a claim and the payment of that claim.

Lapse: The termination of insurance coverage for failure to pay premiums.

LCI: Life-style cost index. A methodology that uses a combination of company-specific health claims experience and health risk factor analysis to pinpoint specific health problems at any given company.

Life-style cost index: See LCI.

Lifetime aggregate: The maximum benefit provided under a major medical plan.

Lifetime benefit: A benefit provided for an indefinite period, up to the lifetime of the individual, such as a lifetime disability benefit.

Load: The amount added to an insurance premium to cover administrative expenses, acquisition costs, taxes, contingency reserves, and profits.

Glossary

Long-term care: The services that would be required over an extended period of time by someone with a chronic illness or disability, such as skilled nursing care, intermediate care, or custodial care.

Long-term disability: See LTD.

Loss ratio: The ratio of claims to premium.

LTD: Long-term disability. A significant period of disability generally ranging from six months to life.

Maintenance of benefits: See MOB.

Maintenance of effort: See MOE.

Major medical insurance: Coverage characterized by larger maximum limits, which is intended to cover the costs associated with a major illness or injury.

Managed care: A health care program which imposes some controls on the utilization of health care services, the providers who offer such care, and/or the fees charged for such services. Managed care is provided through HMOs, PPOs, managed indemnity plans, etc.

Mandated benefit: A specific coverage that an insurer or plan sponsor is required to offer by law. Mandated benefits in insurance contracts vary from state to state according to each state's insurance laws.

Mandated offering: Similar to a mandated benefit, except that instead of being a requirement in each policy, the coverage need only be offered to a policyholder, who is not required to purchase it.

MCCA: Medicare Catastrophic Coverage Act of 1988, which added significant coverage and substantially increased the cost of Medicare. The MCCA was repealed in 1989.

Medicaid: A medical benefits program paid for by the federal government but administered by the states. Medicaid provides medical benefits to persons who meet certain criteria and whose incomes fall below specified maximums.

Medical reimbursement plan: A employer plan which reimburses employees for medical expenses directly from employer funds, and not through a policy of health or accident insurance. These programs were usually extended to executives and other key employees.

Medicare: A federal program of medical care benefits, generally for those over age 65. See also Part A and Part B.

Medicare Catastrophic Coverage Act: See MCCA.

Medicare supplement (Medigap): An insurance program that is specifically to cover those costs not covered by Medicare.

Medigap: See Medicare supplement.

MET: Multiple employer trust. A mechanism that allows small employers in the same or a related industry to provide group insurance to their employees under a trust arrangement.

Minimum premium plan: See MPP.

MOB: Maintenance of benefits. A type of coordination of benefits that limits the total reimbursement from all health plans to a given individual for a program of treatment.

Modular plan: A type of flexible benefits plan that offers a choice of benefits packages rather than a selection of individual levels of coverage.

MOE: Maintenance of effort. A requirement that employers increase benefits or provide refunds to Medicare primary employees to compensate for the reduced wraparound plan costs that resulted from the increased Medicare coverages of the MCCA.

Morbidity: An actuarial concept applied to setting health and disability insurance rates that shows the average incidence of illness occurring in a large group of people.

Mortality: An actuarial concept applied to setting life and disability insurance rates that shows the average death rates for a large group of people.

MPP: Minimum Premium Plan. A way of self-funding to improve cash flow, whereby the employer assumes responsibility for funding most benefits and the insurer assumes liability for benefits above a predetermined level.

Multiemployer plan: An employee benefits plan established or maintained for employees of two or more employers pursuant to terms of a collective bargaining agreement.

Multiple employer trust: See MET.

NAIC: National Association of Insurance Commissioners. An organization that assists state insurance departments. A major function is the drafting of model laws.

Nondiscrimination: The general requirement that employee benefits plans not provide significantly greater benefits to higher paid employees and owners than to lower paid employees. Although some disparity is permitted, there are limits.

Glossary

OASDI: Old Age, Survivors' and Disability Insurance Act. The 1965 amendment to OASDI established Medicare, effective July 1966.

OBRA: Omnibus Budget Reconciliation Act of 1986 or 1989. OBRA 86 made employer plans primary for Medicare eligible participants. OBRA 89 clarified COBRA rules.

OOP maximum: Out-of-pocket maximum. The maximum amount that an insured employee will have to pay for covered expenses under the plan. It is usually $500, $1,000, or $2,000.

Open panel: A health care program that permits participants to purchase services or drugs from a provider of his or her choice. See closed panel.

OSHA: Occupational Safety and Health Act. OSHA provides national standards for health and safety in a workplace.

Out-of-pocket maximum: See OOP maximum.

Part A: The portion of Medicare that covers expenses incurred in hospitals, extended care facilities, hospices, etc.

Part B: The portion of Medicare that covers physicians' services and other types of care not covered under Part A.

Partial disability: A disability that prevents an employee from performing one or more, but not necessarily all, material duties of his or her job.

PAT: Preadmission testing. A cost-control mechanism intended to reduce hospital stays by encouraging employees to have routine hospital testing done on an outpatient basis before being admitted to the hospital. Reimbursement is sometimes made on a more generous basis for PAT.

Pool: A large number of small groups that are analyzed and rated as a single large group.

PPA: Preferred provider arrangement. A PPA differs from a PPO in that it is an agreement between providers and another entity, whereas a PPO is an organization of providers.

PPO: Preferred provider organization. A health care provider arrangement whereby a third-party payor contracts with a group of medical care providers that agrees to furnish services at negotiated fees in return for prompt payment and a guaranteed patient volume. PPOs control costs by keeping fees down and curbing excessive service through stringent utilization control.

PPS: Prospective payment system. A standardized payment system implemented in 1983 by Medicare to help manage health care reimbursement whereby the incentive for hospitals to deliver unnecessary care is eliminated. Hospitals can expect a fixed reimbursement based not on the number and kinds of services delivered but on the diagnosis of the patient.

Preadmission certification: A form of utilization review that requires a patient to receive authorization from a medical review agent prior to being admitted to a hospital.

Preadmission testing: See PAT.

Preemption: The application of ERISA to state regulation of employee benefits plans. Generally, ERISA provides that federal law shall govern such plans, which means that state laws regarding such plans are of no effect (there are exceptions).

Preexisting condition: A condition that existed, or for which a participant was being treated, before coverage under a current health or disability plan commenced, and for which benefits under the plan are not available or are limited.

Preferred provider arrangement: See PPA.

Preferred provider organization: See PPO.

Pregnancy Discrimination Act: The PDA is an amendment to Title VII of the Civil Rights Act of 1964 which requires employers to treat pregnancy-related disability like any other form of disability.

Premium tax: A state tax on insurance premiums, including group insurance premiums.

Prepaid group practice plan: A plan wherein participating physicians provide specified services to plan members in exchange for a fixed payment in advance. This is one form of HMO.

Primary care: Routine medical care provided by a family physician, normally in the doctor's office. Referral to specialized secondary care may be made as necessary.

Professional standards review organization: See PSRO.

Prospective payment system: See PPS.

Prospective rating: The setting of rates for a future period, prior to the incurring of claims, based upon experience in a prior period. See also Retrospective rating.

PSRO: Professional standards review organization. The successors of FMCs; 200 of these watchdog organizations were created to provide for review of all federally financed patient care in acute care hospitals.

Glossary

Qualified beneficiary: An individual covered by a group health plan, or a dependent of such an individual, as of the day before a COBRA qualifying event takes place.

Qualified benefits: Nontaxable benefits that are includible in a cafeteria plan—group term life insurance, accident and health insurance, dependent care assistance, and cash-or-deferred arrangements.

Qualifying event: An event that terminates an individual's normal coverage under a health care plan, but that qualifies the employee or beneficiary to continued coverage under COBRA. Examples include death, termination of employment, and divorce.

RBRVS: Resource Based Relative Value Scale. A system for determining the level of Medicare payments to physicians based upon the amount of work involved in the treatment, the skill level of the physician, and the medical malpractice risk.

R&C: Reasonable and customary charge; also known as usual, customary, and reasonable (UCR) charge. The maximum amount an insurer will consider eligible for reimbursement under group health insurance plans. Insurers use R&C charges to control claims costs.

Reasonable and customary charge: See R&C.

Recurring clause: An contract provision that treats a relapse or recurrence of a condition occuring within a specified period of time as a continuation of the prior period of confinement or disability.

Reinstatement provision: An insurance contract provision that provides for resumption of coverage within a stated period after a policy has lapsed. Also, a contract provision that adjusts aggregate lifetime expenses, in effect reinstating some portion of the maximum lifetime limit that had previously been used up.

Reserve reduction agreement: An agreement between an insurer and a policyholder that modifies or eliminates the insurer's liability for claims after contract termination in exchange for reduced premiums.

Reserves: Amounts set aside by insurers to assure adequate funds to meet incurred but not reported future claims, extension of benefit claims, and expenses. Residential care facility: A facility that provides adults with food and shelter and some additional services.

Respite care: Temporary care provided in a patient's home to provide the primary caregiver with time off from the demands of taking care of a family member.

Retention: The portion of an insurance premium allocated to expenses and profit.

Retrospective rating: The determination of insurance rates at the end of the coverage period, based on actual plan experience for that period. Retrospective rates are usually subject to a preset minimum and maximum.

Return-to-work program: A program of rehabilitation, job modification, and monitoring to get disabled employees back to work as soon as possible.

Right of direct payment: A type of mandated benefit that requires a plan to pay for services not prescribed by a licensed physician (such as the services of a midwife).

Risk: The possibility that costs associated with insuring a particular group will exceed expected levels, thereby resulting in losses for an insurance carrier or self-insurer.

Salary reduction agreement: An agreement between an employee and employer to reduce the employee's taxable income. The amount of the reduction is generally applied to the employee's share of the cost of providing nontaxable benefits.

SAR: Summary annual report. A summary of key information included in the Form 5500 Annual Report, which must be distributed to plan participants.

Schedule of insurance: A listing of the maximum amounts insurer will pay for specified medical procedures.

Second surgical opinion: See SSO.

Section 89: A section of the Internal Revenue Code that set out certain written minimum requirements for welfare benefit plans to meet, as well as establishing highly specific nondiscrimination requirements. Section 89 was repealed in 1989.

Self-funding: An arrangement under which some or all of the risk associated with providing of benefits is not covered by an insurance contract. The plan sponsor establishes the necessary reserves, often through a VEBA, to assure payment of claims.

Shared funding: See HSID.

Short-term disability: See STD.

Skilled nursing facility: See SNF.

Glossary

SNF: Skilled nursing facility. A facility that provides inpatient care for persons requiring skilled nursing care, either as part of a hospital or as a separate nursing home.

SPD: Summary plan description. A document containing specific information about the health plan. Each plan participant and the Department of Labor must be provided with an SPD.

SSO: Second surgical opinion. A cost-control mechanism to reduce unnecessary surgery by encouraging individuals to seek a second opinion for elective surgery.

STD: Short-Term disability. A temporary period of disability usually not exceeding six months.

Stop-loss insurance: Insurance that reimburses a plan or plan sponsor for losses in excess of certain limits, usually expressed as a percentage of expected claims, or a specified dollar amount.

Substandard or special class: Individual health or life insurance coverage provided to an individual who does not meet the physical or other criteria for a standard rating. The policy provides less coverage, higher premiums, or both.

Summary annual report: See SAR.

Summary plan description: See SPD.

Surgical schedule: A list of amounts payable by a health insurance program for different types of surgery.

TAMRA: Technical and Miscellaneous Revenue Act of 1988, which revised the Section 89 nondiscrimination rules and amended the penalties for noncompliance with COBRA.

Tax Equity and Fiscal Responsibility Act: See TEFRA.

Tax Reform Act of 1986: See TRA '86.

Technical and Miscellaneous Revenue Act of 1988: See TAMRA.

TEFRA: Tax Equity and Fiscal Responsibility Act of 1982. TEFRA was enacted to prevent discrimination against elderly employees with regard to health insurance. It amended the Social Security Act to make Medicare secondary to employer group health plans for active employees and spouses aged 65 through 69. TEFRA also amended ADEA to require employers to offer older employees and dependents the same coverage available to younger employees.

Third-party administrator: See TPA.

TLR: Tolerable loss ratio. The loss ratio the insurer can fund without losing money on the group. See also Loss ratio.

Tolerable loss ratio: See TLR.

TPA: Third-party administrator. A person or organization that provides certain administrative services to group benefits plans, including premium accounting, claims review and payment, claims utilization review, maintenance of employee eligibility records, and negotiations with insurers that provide stop-loss protection for large claims.

TRA '86: Tax Reform Act of 1986, which imposed the comprehensive nondiscrimination rules of IRC Section 89.

UCR: Usual, customary, and reasonable charges. See R&C.

Unbundling: A form of code gaming where each step of a medical procedure is billed as a separate item.

Unrelated Business Income: Earnings from activities which do not relate to a fund's tax-exempt purpose. Such earnings are taxable.

Upcoding: A form of code gaming also known as code creep where a medical procedure is redefined so that it falls into a billing category which qualifies for a higher reimbursement.

UR: Utilization review. A cost-control mechanism used by some insurers and employers in recent years that evaluates health care on the basis of appropriateness, necessity, and quality. For hospital review, it can include preadmission certification, concurrent review with discharge planning, and retrospective review.

Utilization review: See UR.

VEBA: Voluntary employees' beneficiary association. Also known as a 501(c)(9) trust, a VEBA is a tax-efficient means of funding an employee benefits plan. It is used almost exclusively by large employers.

Volume Performance Standards: Estimates of the annual rate of growth for Medicare physician services. The relationship of these estimates to actual experience will be used in adjusting Medicare physician fees.

Voluntary employees' beneficiary association: See VEBA.

Waiting period: The period of time between an employee's hire and his or her enrollment in a program (eligibility to receive benefits).

Waiver of premium: A contract provision that exempts an individual from the requirement to pay premiums while he or she is disabled.

Wellness: Programs that reduce health care costs by encouraging fitness, preventive care, and early detection of illness.

Workers' compensation: State programs that require employers to carry insurance to compensate employees for work-related injuries or disabilities.

Wraparound: A supplementary plan designed to pay for benefits not provided under a basic plan, such as Blue Cross or Medicare.

Index

(References in the index are to Question numbers.)

- A -

Accidental death and dismemberment, 1:8
Actuary, 5:6–5:7
ADEA, 3:16
Administration of plan
  annual reports, 6:12
  appeal of claims determination, 6:38
  application for coverage, 6:1
  assignment of benefits to provider, 6:30–6:31
  audit by insurer, 6:27
  benefit check receipt, 6:36
  billing, 6:24–6:27
  certificate of insurance claims submitted prior to, 6:29
  defined, 6:8
  change of coverage, 6:41–6:42, 6:45, 6:48
  claims submission procedure, 6:28
  COBRA. See COBRA
  computers for, 6:133, 6:135
  detailed coverage information required, 6:5
  effective date of coverage, 6:2
  enrollment. See Enrollment
  explanation of benefits, 6:14, 6:37
  flexible benefits plans, 9:54–9:57
  information for employee about plan, 6:7
  material provided by insurer, 6:15
  materials issued to employees, 6:9
  OBRA. See OBRA
  pre-claim determination of coverage, 6:33
  rejection of an application, 6:3–6:4
  renewal of coverage, 6:40, 6:42–6:44
  setup, 6:1–6:15
  summary plan description, 6:12–6:14
  terminated employee, coverage, 6:49
  termination of coverage by employer, 6:46–6:47
  third-party administrator. See Third-party administrator
Adverse selection, 2:4, 8:24–8:28, 9:43
Agent, 2:11
AIDS
  care covered, 12:63
  costs associated with, 12:60–12:61
  employers' recommended response, 12:65

Health Insurance Answer Book

(References in the index are to Question numbers.)

AIDS *(cont.)*
  identification of at-risk people, 12:62
  impact on health benefits, 12:59
  legal protections for sufferers, 12:64
  testing for, 12:65

Americans with Disabilities Act
  adverse effect on businesses, 3:53
  business size, 3:50
  employers and employees, generally, 3:49
  purpose of Act, 3:48
  qualifications, 3:52
  reasonable accommodation requirement, 3:52

Association plan, 1:18

- B -

Base plus plan
  advantages, 4:4
  availability, 4:6
  defined, 4:2

Benefits. *See also* particular types, e.g., Medicare
  AIDS. *See* AIDS
  assignment to provider, 6:30–6:31
  coordination of, 7:27–7:32
  death, 4:79–4:81
  deductible. *See* Deductible
  dental. *See* Dental plans
  disability. *See* Disability insurance, group
  diverse needs, 3:60
  duplication, 3:63
  employee assistance programs. *See* Employee assistance programs
  explanation of, 6:14, 6:37
  flexible. *See* Cafeteria plan; Flexible benefits plan
  health promotion. *See* Health promotion programs
  hearing evaluation and aids, 4:50
  hospital. *See* Hospital benefits
  key employees, enhanced coverage, 3:65
  life insurance, 4:79–4:81
  long-term care. *See* Long-term care
  mandated, 3:8–3:9
  medical. *See* Medical benefits
  mental health. *See* Mental health
  pregnancy. *See* Pregnancy Discrimination Act
  prescriptions. *See* Prescription drug plans
  preventive care coverage. *See* Preventive care coverage
  qualified, defined, 9:3
  reasonable and customary (R&C) charges, 4:16
  reimbursement. *See* Reimbursement
  retirement. *See* Retirement
  scheduling. *See* Schedule of insurance
  substance abuse treatment, 12:1–12:4
  taxation of, 3:57
  vision care, 4:49
  wellness programs. *See* Wellness programs

Birthday rule, 7:30–7:31

Blue Cross/Blue Shield plans
  comparison with private insurers, 4:8–4:11
  major medical supplements to, 4:9
  PPO compared, 8:47
  premium rates, 4:10
  reimbursement level, 4:11

Broker, 2:10

- C -

Cafeteria plan
  benefits included, 9:25
  cash option, 9:31

Index

(References in the index are to Question numbers.)

defined, 9:2
401(k) plan, integration of, 9:32
medical insurance options, 9:26
nondiscrimination requirements, 9:35, 9:37–9:38
  benefits test, 11:25
  concentration test, 11:26
  eligibility test, 11:23–11:24
  highly compensated employee, 11:22
  penalties, 11:27
  repeal of section 89, 11:21
  safeharbor/unsafe harbor, 11:47
qualified benefits, 9:3, 9:36
tax advantages, 9:4
Carryover deductible, 4:25
Case management
  individual, 7:43–7:45
  mental health services, 4:77
Certificate of insurance, 6:8, 6:29
Claims
  actuarial estimate of, 5:7
  appeal, 6:38
  benefit check receipt, 6:36
  counted toward experience, 5:25
  credibility, 5:20
  expected, 5:3–5:5
    affected by plan design, 5:8
    employer with several locations, 5:11
    margin for higher, 5:12
    medical services cost protection, 5:10
  form, assistance in completing, 6:32
  lag, 5:34–5:35
  loss ratio, 5:30–5:32
  paid after contract termination, 5:4
  paid/incurred distinction, 5:33
  payment by employer under minimum premium plan, 5:65
  pool, 5:26, 5:44
  prior determination of coverage, 6:33
  prior to receiving certificate of insurance, 6:29
  processing time, 6:35
  reimbursement turnaround time, 6:34
  shock, 5:64
  submission procedure, 6:28
Client service representative, 2:6
Closed-panel drug plan, 4:59
COBRA. *See also* OBRA
  collectively bargained plan, 6:91
  computers for administration, 6:135
  continuation coverage
    deductibles, 6:76
    defined, 6:56
    duration of availability, 6:77–6:84
    election period, 6:69
    options, 6:66–6:67, 6:71
    premium payment, 6:72–6:75
  conversion privilege, 6:85
  core coverage, 6:64
  covered employee defined, 6:62
  deferral of coverage, 6:86
  defined, 6:53
  effective date, 6:90
  employer defined, 6:57
  excluded group health plans, 6:60
  federal law applicable, 6:54
  flexible benefits plan, impact on, 6:87
  group conversion privilege, effect on, 6:51
  group health plan defined, 6:59
  new family members, coverage of, 6:68
  noncompliance, 6:92
  noncore coverage, 6:65
  qualified beneficiary, 6:63
  qualifying events, 6:61, 6:70
  small employer plan, 6:58
  state continuation requirements, effect on, 6:88–6:89
  terminology of, 6:55

Health Insurance Answer Book

(References in the index are to Question numbers.)

COBRA *(cont.)*
  unresolved issues, 6:93
Coinsurance
  defined, 4:27
  maximum out-of-pocket limit, 4:28–4:30
  typical percentages, 7:20
Commissions
  schedules, 2:18
  vesting of, 2:19
Community rating system, 8:32
Comparable plans defined, 6:104
Comprehensive plan
  advantages, 4:5
  availability, 4:6
  defined, 4:3
Computers
  for COBRA administration, 6:135
  communications programs, 6:137
  features to look for, 6:138
  flexible benefits plan administration, 6:136
  to manage health plans, 6:133
  for nondiscrimination testing, 6:134
Constructive receipt, 9:6
Contraceptives, 4:54
Contributory plans, 3:69–3:70
Controlled group defined, 6:104
Core benefits defined, 6:104
Core plus plan, 9:19
Cost management. *See also* Health maintenance organization; Preferred provider organization
  capitative payment structure. *See* Health maintenance organization
  coinsurance percentages, 7:20
  coordination of benefits
    birthday rule, 7:30–7:31
    claim cost management, 7:28
    defined, 7:27
    innovations, 7:32
    maintenance of benefits, 7:29
  cost-effective designs, 7:26

  cost-sharing strategies, 7:18–7:26
  dental plans, 4:43, 4:45
  determination of need, 7:19, 7:53
  education of employees, 7:54
  employee contributions, 7:24–7:25
  extended care facilities, 7:51
  health care data, 7:11–7:17
  home health care, 7:51
  hospice care, 7:52
  hospital bill audit, 7:55
  mental health care, 4:72
  merger of services, 8:2
  negotiations with providers, 7:56
  outpatient surgery, 7:33
  preadmission testing, 7:34
  preventive programs, 7:10
  reduction in care purchased, 7:7
  second surgical opinions, 7:35–7:38
  small employer, 7:8
  utilization review. *See* Utilization review
  workers' compensation, 3:20, 3:21, 3:22
Cost shifting, 7:4
Costs. *See also* Cost management; Funding of plan; Premiums
  AIDS associated, 12:60–12:61
  Catastrophic Coverage Act, 10:19, 10:24
  comparison of plans, 8:38
  contribution of traditional reimbursement system, 8:1
  contributory plans, 3:69–3:70
  disability benefits, 4:82, 4:91
  employer's, with third-party administrator, 2:24
  health insurance, 3:68–3:69
  increased, factors for, 7:1, 7:5
  legal constraints on cost sharing, 3:71
  limiting reimbursements, 7:2–7:3
  Medicare, 10:25
  prescription drug plans, 4:52
  self-funded plans, 3:72

Index

(References in the index are to Question numbers.)

shifting, 7:4
substance abuse, 11:2
unnecessary care, 7:6
Covered expense, 4:31–4:33
Credibility, 5:20
Custodial care. *See* Long-term care

- D -

Death benefits, 4:76–4:78
Deductible
  carryover, 4:25
  COBRA continuation coverage, 6:76
  defined, 4:24
  expenses applied toward, 4:30
  front-end, 7:22–7:23
  HMOs, 8:14
  maximum out-of-pocket expenses, 4:29
  Medicare, 10:25, 10:39
  satisfaction of dependents', 4:26
  typical, 7:19
"Deep cut" retro, 5:54
Deferred premium arrangements, 5:45–5:47
Dental plans
  cost-management features, 4:43, 4:45
  direct reimbursement, 4:40
  incentives, 4:46
  inclusion with health insurance, 4:37–4:39
  orthodontics, 4:44
  precertification, 4:47
  services covered, 4:42
  services excluded, 4:48
  services provided, 4:41
Dependent care assistance plans
  average benefit test, 11:35
  benefits test, 11:33
  concentration test, 11:34
  eligibility test, 11:30
  employees excluded for purposes of nondiscriminatory testing, 11:32
  highly compensated employee, 11:31
  penalty for discrimination, 11:36
  repeal of Section 89, 11:29
  Americans with Disabilities Act. *See* Americans with Disabilities Act
  disabled beneficiaries, 6:79–6:80
  medicare secondary rules, 10:15–10:24
Dependent care reimbursement account, 9:14
Dependents
  deductible satisfaction, 4:26
  premium determination, 5:29
  reimbursement account, 9:14
Diagnosis-related groups (DRGs)
  excess reimbursement, 10:12
  hospital care reduction resulting from, 10:14
  insurance industry, effect on, 10:16
  Medicare claims paid on basis of, 10:11
  payment determination, 10:10
  physician reimbursement, 10:13
  plans using, 10:15
Direct payment, right of, 3:11
Disability insurance, group
  benefit amounts, 4:90
  cost, 4:82, 4:91
  disability defined, 4:88
  long-term plan, 4:87, 4:89, 4:91
  loss of income protection, 1:9
  need for coverage, 4:83–4:84
  programs available, 4:85
  short-term plan, 4:86
  taxation of benefits, 4:92
Disability management
  causes of disabilities, 4:84
  effective, 4:87
  independent living program, 4:101
  prevention program, 4:94
  rehabilitation, 4:95–4:100
  return-to-work program, 4:100

(References in the index are to Question numbers.)

DRGs. *See* Diagnosis-related groups
Drug card plan, 4:61–4:64
Drug-Free Workplace Act, 11:3
Drugs. *See* Prescription drug plans
Drug testing, 12:5–12:8
Dual choice mandate, 8:33–8:34

- E -

Eligibility. *See* Participation
Eligible employee, 3:26
Employee
  assistance. *See* Employee assistance programs
  covered, COBRA definition, 6:62
  dependents. *See* Dependents
  disabilities, 4:83–4:84
  eligible, defined, 3:59
  enrollment. *See* Enrollment
  inactive, at time of change in coverage, 6:48
  key, 3:65
  nondiscriminatory classification, 11:46
  participation. *See* Participation
  part-time and temporary, 3:64
  pregnancy. *See* Pregnancy Discrimination Act
  responsibility for excess of R&C charges, 4:17
  retired. *See* Retirement
  taxation of benefits, 3:56–3:57, 4:92
  terminated, 6:49–6:52
Employee assistance programs
  components needed, 12:12
  cost of coverage, 12:10
  defined, 12:9
  provision of services, 12:11, 12:13
Employee benefits consultant, 2:12
Employer. *See also* Administration of plan; Cost management; Costs
  COBRA definition, 6:57
  disability management, 4:93–4:101
  small
    COBRA plan, defined, 6:58
    cost management, 7:8
    reserve reduction agreements, 5:61
    self-funded plans, 3:74, 9:44
Employer health care coalition, 2:28
Employer-provided benefit defined, 6:104, 6:125
Enrollment. *See also* Participation
  administrator, 6:19
  encouragement of, 6:16
  flexible benefits plan, 9:51–9:53
  forms, completion of, 6:20–6:21
  information required, 6:17
  late, 6:21–6:22
  obligatory, 6:18
  reenrollment, 6:23
  state or federal government, filing requirements, 6:10
ERISA, 3:18
  pre-emption, 8:38, 8:39
Exclusive provider organization, 8:49
Experience rate, 5:23–5:25
Extended care facilities. *See* Long-term care

- F -

Federal regulations
  ADEA, 3:24
  changes in, 3:5
  COBRA. *See* COBRA
  employer reports, 6:12–6:14
  ERISA, 3:26
  general, 3:3, 3:23
  HMO Act, 3:42, 8:29
  legally required insurance, 3:1
  maternal benefits, 3:19
  PPOs, 8:61
  retired employees, 3:25
  self-funded plans, 3:4

Index

(References in the index are to Question numbers.)

taxation of employees, 3:55–3:57
taxation of employers, 3:55
Financial Accounting Standards Board, 11:34–11:36
administration
  assistance available, 9:60
  billing arrangements, 9:59
  reports necessary, 9:57
  selection of administrator, 9:58
adverse selection, 9:46
cafeteria plan. *See* Cafeteria plan
changes by employee during plan year, 9:54
COBRA's impact on, 6:87
computers for administration, 6:136
constructive receipt, 9:6
contributions
  employee's, 9:42–9:43
  employer's, 9:41, 9:43
  optional, 9:40
core plus plan, 9:19
cost comparison with traditional plans, 9:55
cost control, 9:8–9:9
coverage options, 9:34
defined, 9:1
development, 9:5, 9:7
employees' benefit needs, determination of, 9:48
enrollment
  communication with employees prior to, 9:51
  confirmation, 9:53
  selection of benefits, 9:52
flexible spending accounts, 9:12–9:17
401(k) plan, inclusion of, 9:33
full menu, 9:24
funding, 9:39
HMOs, 9:27
implementation, 9:49–9:50
insurance provider, 9:29
issues to consider, 9:47
modular plan, 9:18
PPOs, 9:28
purchasing procedure, 9:45
reimbursement accounts, 9:12–9:17
renewal, 9:56
salary reduction premium conversion plan, 9:11
self-funding, 9:44
single insurer, 9:30
total, 9:24
types, 9:10
working spouse plan, 9:23
Flexible spending account, 9:12–9:17
401(h) account, 11:41
401(k) plans
  cafeteria plan, integration into, 9:32
  flexible plan, inclusion in, 9:33
Fully insured plan
  funding, 5:2–5:35
  third-party administrator with, 2:23
Funding of plan
  actuaries, 5:6–5:7
  alternative vehicles
    deferred premium arrangements, 5:45–5:47
    difference from fully funded, 5:37
    general, 5:36–5:40
    minimum premium plans (MPPs), 5:62–5:69
    reserve reduction agreements, 5:57–5:61
    retrospective premium arrangements, 5:52–5:56
    shared funding arrangements, 5:48–5:51
    stop-loss insurance, 5:41–5:44
  cost components, 5:2
  credibility, 5:20
  deficit reimbursement, 5:15
  defined, 5:1
  expected claims, 5:3–5:5
    affected by plan design, 5:8
    employer with several

(References in the index are to Question numbers.)

Funding of plan
  expected claims (cont.)
    locations, 5:11
    margin for higher, 5:12
    medical services cost
      projection, 5:10
  expense projection, 5:18
  experience rate, 5:23–5:25
  flexible benefits plans, 9:36
  fully insured, 5:2–5:35
  lag study, 5:35
  loss ratio, 5:30–5:32
  manual rate, 5:21, 5:25
  pool, 5:22, 5:26
  profit for insurer, 5:19
  prospective rating, 5:13
  rate guarantee period's effect, 5:9
  reserves, 5:15–5:17
  retention, 5:27
  retrospective rating, 5:14

- G -

Group insurance
  accidental death and
    dismemberment, 1:8
  association plan, 1:18
  availability, 1:15
  base plus plan. *See* Base plus
    plan
  benefits. *See* Benefits
  Blue Cross/Blue Shield plans.
    See Blue Cross/Blue Shield
    plans
  characteristics, 1:7–1:8, 1:11
  comprehensive plan. *See*
    Comprehensive plan
  disability, 1:9
  federal regulations, 3:23–3:42
  health, general, 1:10–1:14,
    4:12–4:19, 4:23, 8:72
  individual insurance compared
    with, 1:2–1:3
  intermediaries. *See*
    Intermediaries

  life insurance, 1:7
  multiple employer trust, 1:16
  nonlegal factors, general, 3:58
  overview, 1:1–1:18
  participation. *See* Participation
  plan design, factors affecting,
    3:1–3:74
  prevalence of, 1:4, 1:12
  rationale for, 1:5
  restrictions on coverage,
    3:61–3:67
  sales, 2:5
  state regulations, 3:6–3:14
  taxation, 3:54–3:57
  types of protection, 1:1, 1:6,
    1:10, 4:1–4:11
  union plan, 1:17
Group sales representative, 2:5,
  2:8
Group term life insurance
  benefits test, 11:16–11:17
  dependent group term life
    benefits, 11:19
  eligibility test, 11:14–11:15
  key employee, 11:12, 11:16
  nondiscrimination tests, 11:13
  penalty for discrimination, 11:18
  repeal of Section 89, 11:11

- H -

Health care coalition, employer,
  2:29, 7:15–7:16
**Health care reimbursement
  account**, 9:13
**Health maintenance organization
  (HMO)**
  adverse selection, 8:24–8:28
  capitative payment structure,
    8:10
  community rating system, 8:32
  conventional plan, effect on cost
    of, 8:25
  cost-effectiveness, 8:20
  coverage, 8:13

Index

(References in the index are to Question numbers.)

deductible, 8:14
defined, 2:26, 8:3
development of, 8:4–8:5
dual choice mandate, 8:33–8:34
employer contribution required, 8:35
employer costs, 8:23
ERISA pre-emption, 8:39
evaluation of, 8:40–8:43
federal funding, role in development, 8:36
federal standards, 8:30
federally qualified, prevalence of, 8:31
financial difficulties, 8:42
flexible benefits plan, inclusion in, 9:24
Health Maintenance Act, 8:29
hospitalization, 8:15
hybrid HMO/PPO arrangements, 8:73
information sources, 8:41
legal standards, 8:29–8:37
models defined, 8:9
organization, 8:8
outside care, 8:16
participation
  age and health factors, 8:26
  deciding upon, 8:18
  duplicate, 8:19
  increase in, 8:22
  physicians', 8:7
  75% requirement, effect of, 8:21
  timing of, 8:17
plan option, 4:23
point-of-service, 8:74
PPO compared, 8:42, 8:72
prevalence, 8:6
provisions of act affecting plans, 3:20
quality of care, 8:41
sponsors, 8:5
state regulations, 8:37
Health promotion programs
advantages of worksite program, 12:16
defined, 12:14
health risk appraisal, 12:31
insurance for, 12:29
interest in, 12:19
life-style cost index, 12:18
objectives, 12:15
selection criteria, 12:17
Health risk appraisal (HRA)
components of group health plan determined by, 12:32
coverage price, effect upon, 12:33
defined, 12:30
health promotion's relation to, 12:31
Hearing evaluation and aids, 4:50
HMO. See Health maintenance organization
Home health care, 7:51
Hospice care, 7:52
Hospital benefits
alternatives to, 4:20
general plan coverage, 4:14
HMOs, 8:15
nonsurgical physicians' services, 4:19
outpatient, 4:21
recent changes in care, 4:18
surgery, 4:14
Hospital discharge planning, 7:45
HRA. See Health risk appraisal

- I -

Implementation. See Administration of plan
Incentives, dental plan, 4:46
Income, loss of, 1:9
Independent living program, 4:101
Individual case management, 7:43–7:45
Individual insurance, 1:2–1:3
Intermediaries
agent, 2:11
broker, 2:10

Health Insurance Answer Book

(References in the index are to Question numbers.)

Intermediaries *(cont.)*
  commissions. *See* Commissions
  compensation of, 2:17
  defined, 2:7
  employee benefits consultant, 2:12
  group sales representatives' interaction with, 2:8
  personal or business advisor serving as, 2:16
  regulation of, 2:20
  role of, 2:1
  selection, 2:13, 2:15, 2:23
  self-funding plan, 2:21
  services provided, 2:9
  third-party administrator (TPA). *See* Third-party administrator

- K -

Key employees
  enhanced coverage, 3:32

- L -

Lag, 5:34–5:35
Life insurance, group
  characteristics, 1:7
  survivor benefits, 4:79–4:81
Life-style cost index, 12:18
Long-term care
  benefit coverage, 4:22, 8:51
  cost, 11:46
  cost-management factors, 7:51
  custodial care, 12:55
  defined, 12:47
  evaluation of insurance policies, 12:58
  inflation-adjusted benefits, 12:54
  insurance cost, 12:57
  issues involved, 12:48
  levels of, 4:20, 12:49
  Medicaid provisions, 12:52
  Medicare provisions, 12:51
  providers of insurance, 12:56
Long-term disability (LTD) plan, 4:88, 4:89, 4:91
Loss of income, protection against, 1:9
Loss ratio, 5:30–5:32

- M -

Mail-order drug plan, 4:60
Major medical plans
  Blue Cross/Blue Shield supplements, 4:8
  prescription medications, 4:65
Mandated benefits, 3:8–3:9
Mandated offerings, 3:10
Manual rate, 5:21, 5:25
Medicaid
  cost control, 7:3
  long-term care, 12:52
Medical benefits
  Blue Cross/Blue Shield plans, 4:7–4:11
  coverage, 4:12–4:19
  long-term care. *See* Long-term care
  outpatient care, 4:20–4:21
  types of plans available, 4:1–4:6, 4:23
Medical billing codes
  code gaming, 7:59
  defined, 7:57
Medicare
  balance billing, 10:33
  Catastrophic Coverage Act. *See* Catastrophic Coverage Act
  cost control, 7:3, 10:25
  defined, 10:1
  diagnosis-related groups. *See* Diagnosis-related groups
  disabled nonretired individuals, 10:7
  election of over employer plan, 10:8
  eligibility, 10:2
  excluded services, 10:5

Index

(References in the index are to Question numbers.)

indexed coinsurance requirements for 1990, 10:41
integration with employer-provided benefits, 10:6
IRS and SSA, information provided by, 10:9, 10:11, 10:13
Medicare Catastrophic Coverage Act, 10:39
medigap insurance policies, 10:44–10:45
Part A services, 10:3
Part B services, 10:4
penalties for failure to provide information, 10:12
physician reimbursement under OBRA, 10:32
PPO compared, 8:47
premiums for 1990, 10:43
qualified employer, 10:11
secondary payer rules, 10:8–10:14
  disabled persons, 10:15–10:24
volume performance standards, 10:34
Medical review organizations
charges for services, 7:63
defined, 7:60
hiring of, 7:61
services provided by, 7:62
Mental health
cost management, 4:72, 4:74–4:76
coverage by health plans, 4:67–4:68
management of services, 4:73–4:77
need for care, 4:70–4:71
overutilization of inpatient care, 4:69
prepaid plan, 4:78
Minimum premium plans (MPPs)
benefits to employer, 5:66
claims payment by employer, 5:65
defined, 5:62
disadvantages to employer, 5:67
employers electing, 5:68
insurer's liability level, 5:63
shock claim under, 5:64
third-party administrators in, 5:69
Modular plan, 9:18
Multiple employer trust, 1:16

- N -

Nondiscrimination testing.
aggregation, 6:11
cafeteria plans. See Cafeteria plans
computers' role, 6:134
dependent care assistance plans. See Dependent care assistance plans
educational assistance plans, 11:37–11:39
group legal services plans, 11:40–11:42
group term life insurance. See Group term life insurance
health plans, benefit discrimination, 11:1
highly-compensated individual, defined, 11:3
nondiscriminatory classification of employees, 11:46
penalties, 11:7–11:8
self-funded plans. See Self-funded plans
self-insured accident plans, 11:2
VEBAs, 11:43–11:45
Nonsurgical physicians' services, 4:19

- O -

OBRA
continuation coverage, 6:82–6:83
disabled beneficiaries,

391

Health Insurance Answer Book

(References in the index are to Question numbers.)

OBRA
  disabled beneficiaries *(cont.)*
    continuation coverage, 6:79–6:80
    Medicare physician reimbursement, 10:32
  secondary payer rules, 10:8
Occupational Safety and Health Act (OSHA)
  booklets explaining provisions of Act, 3:47
  business requirements, 3:44
  inspections, 3:46
  notification and recordkeeping, 3:45
  purpose of Act, 3:43
Offerings, mandated, 3:10
Open-panel drug plan, 4:58
Orthodontics, 4:44
Out-of-pocket (OOP) expenses, maximum
  covered expenses, 4:30
  deductible in determination, 4:29
  defined, 4:28
Outpatient care, 4:20–4:21, 7:33

- P -

Participation
  eligible employee, 3:59
  exclusions, 3:61–3:62, 3:66
  HMOs. *See* Health maintenance organization
  maximum, 3:14
  minimum, 3:13
  part-time and temporary employees, 3:64
  reporting requirements, 6:12
  state regulation, 3:12–3:14
  welfare plan reporting, 6:11
Part-time employees, 3:64
Pool, 5:22, 5:26, 5:44
PPA. *See* Preferred provider arrangement
PPO. *See* Preferred provider organization

Preadmission testing, 7:34
Precertification, 4:47, 7:46–7:47
Preferred provider arrangement (PPA), 8:48
Preferred provider organization (PPO)
  antitrust issues, 8:63
  availability, 8:67
  Blue Cross/Blue Shield, Medicare compared, 8:47
  cost-effective treatment in, 8:56
  defined, 2:27, 8:44
  discounts available, 8:70
  discounts, employers receiving largest, 8:65
  employee education, 8:71
  employee incentives, 8:64
  enrollment, 8:53
  establishment, 4:23, 8:45
  establishment procedures, 8:54
  evaluation, 8:68
  exclusive provider organization, 8:49
  federal standards, 8:61
  flexible benefits plan, inclusion in, 9:25
  HMO compared, 8:46, 8:72
  hybrid HMO/PPO arrangements, 8:73
  incorporation into existing program, 8:69
  PPA distinguished, 8:48
  prevalence, 8:52
  provider incentives, 8:57
  quality of care, 8:66
  selection of providers, 8:55
  services provided, 8:50
  sponsors, 8:51
  state standards, 8:62
  utilization review, 8:58–8:60
Pregnancy Discrimination Act (PDA)
  abortions, 3:34
  dependents, 3:33
  employers subject to, 3:30
  family leave policies, 3:41

Index

(References in the index are to Question numbers.)

HMO Act of 1973 as affecting, 3:42
married employees, 3:31
maternity leave, 3:35–3:36
parental or family leave, 3:38–3:39
purpose of act, 3:28
spouses of employees, 3:32
state law as pre-empting, 3:37
"The same" treatment for pregnancy-related condition, 3:29
Premiums
 billing of employers, 6:24
 Blue Cross/Blue Shield rates, 4:10
 calculation, 6:25
 COBRA continuation coverage, 6:72–6:75
 contributory plans, 3:69–3:70
 cost estimate, 3:68
 deferred, 5:45–5:47
 dependent rate, 5:29
 experience rate, 5:23–5:25
 late payment, 6:26
 loss ratio, 5:30–5:32
 manual rate, 5:21, 5:25
 minimum premium plans (MPPs). *See* Minimum premium plans
 pool, 5:22
 prepayment of services through, 8:11–8:12
 profit for insurer, 5:19
 rate-guarantee period, 5:9
 reasonableness, determination of, 5:28
 renewal rate, 6:44
 reserves, 5:16–5:17
 retention, 5:27
 retrospective, 5:52–5:56
 timely payment, 6:79
Prepaid mental health plan, 4:75
Prescription drug plans
 closed-panel, 4:59
 concern for insurance planners, 4:51
 cost, 4:52
 drug card, 4:61–4:64
 drugs covered, 4:53–4:54
 mail-order, 4:60
 major medical coverage, 4:65
 open-panel, 4:58
 separate from medical plan, 4:55–4:56
 sources, 4:66
 types, 4:57–4:61
Preventive care coverage
 benefits provided, 12:21
 defined, 12:20
 financial incentives for, 12:34
 rationale for, 12:28
 risk factor screening, 12:25
 routine checkups, 12:22–12:24
Professionals, insurance
 client service representative, 2:6
 employer health care coalition, 2:29
 group sales representative, 2:5
 HMOs, 2:27
 intermediaries. *See* Intermediaries; Third-party administrator (TPA)
 PPOs, 2:28
 underwriter, 2:2
Prospective rating, 5:13

- R -

RBRVS pay system, 10:35–10:38
Reasonable and customary (R&C) charges
 defined, 4:34
 excess paid by employee, 4:17
 scheduling of benefits compared, 4:16
Regulation. *See* Federal regulations; State regulations; specific subject headings
Rehabilitation programs, 3:16, 4:92–4:97

Health Insurance Answer Book

(References in the index are to Question numbers.)

Reimbursement
  accounts, defined, 9:12–9:17
  covered expenses, 4:32
  dependents' deductible satisfaction, 4:26
  diagnosis-related groups as basis, 10:12, 10:30
  direct, for dental care, 4:40
  drug card plan compared, 4:63
  excess with diagnosis-related groups, 10:12
  level, Blue Cross/Blue Shield compared with private insurers, 4:11
  limit to individual, 4:36
  limiting to control costs, 7:2–7:3
  policyholder funding deficit, 5:15
  traditional system, contribution to rising costs, 8:1
  turnaround time, 6:34
Reserves
  defined, 5:16
  determination of, 5:16
  reduction agreements as alternative funding, 5:57–5:61
Retention, 5:27
Retirement
  alternative health care financing methods, 12:46
  change in benefits, 12:42
  COBRA. *See* COBRA
  corporate health care liability, 12:37, 12:41
  coverage provided, 12:36
  federal regulation of coverage, 3:25
  Financial Accounting Standards Board proposed rules, 12:38–12:40
  401(h) account, 12:45
  Medicare. *See* Medicare
  need for benefits, 12:35
  OBRA. *See* OBRA
  prefunding of benefits, 12:43
  VEBAs, 12:44
Retrospective premium arrangements, 5:52–5:56
Retrospective rating, 5:14
Return-to-work program, 4:100
Risk, 2:3

- S -

Salary reduction premium conversion plan, 9:11
Schedule of insurance
  defined, 4:35
  reasonable and customary charges compared, 4:16
Second surgical opinion programs, 7:35–7:38
Self-funded plans
  benefits test, 11:6, 11:9
  costs, 3:39
  discrimination testing, 11:2
  dual choice mandate, 8:34
  eligibility tests, 11:4–11:5, 11:9
  federal regulation, 3:4
  insurance professional needed, 2:21
  prevalence, 3:73
  retiree plans, 11:10
  small employer, 3:74, 9:41
  state regulation, 3:4
Self-insured plans. *See* Self-funded plans
Shared funding arrangements, 5:48–5:51
Short-term disability (STD) plan, 4:83
Skilled nursing facilities. *See* Long-term care
Small employer plan, 6:58
State regulations
  administrative agency, responsibilities, 3:6
  changes in, 3:5
  COBRA's effect on continuation requirements, 6:88–6:89
  employer reports, 6:12

394

Index

(References in the index are to Question numbers.)

general, 3:3
HMOs, 8:37
legally required insurance, 3:2
mandated benefits, 3:8–3:9
mandated offerings, 3:10
participation. *See* Participation
PPOs, 8:62
right of direct payment, 3:11
self-funded plans, 3:4
similarities among states, 3:7
taxation, 3:54
Stop-loss insurance
aggregate/specific distinction, 5:42
defined, 5:41
pooling compared, 5:44
source, 5:43
Substance abuse treatment, 11:1–11:4
Summary plan description, 6:12–6:14
Surgery
inpatient. *See* Hospital benefits
outpatient, 7:33
second opinion programs, 7:35–7:38
Survivor benefits, 3:16, 4:76–4:78
bankruptcy proceedings affecting, 6:78

- T -

Taxation
death benefits, 4:78
disability benefits, 4:89
employer contribution as taxable income to employee, 3:56
federal, 3:55
health benefits, 3:57
state, 3:54
Temporary employees, 3:64
Third-party administrator (TPA)
compensation of, 2:25
defined, 2:14
employer's cost when using, 2:24

fully insured plan, need for, 2:22
minimum premium plans, 5:69
selection of over insurance company, 2:23
services provided, 6:6
Tolerable loss ratio, 5:31–5:32

- U -

Underwriter, 2:2
Uniform reimbursement, 9:18–9:20
Union plan, 1:17
Utilization review
concurrent review, 7:48
cost savings, 7:50
defined, 7:39
individual case management
  defined, 7:43
  hospital discharge planning differentiated, 7:45
  procedure, 7:44
PPOs, 8:56–8:58
preadmission certification, 7:46–7:47
prevalence of process, 7:41
procedure, 7:40
retrospective review, 7:49
types, 7:42

- V -

VEBAs
nondiscrimination requirements, 11:43–11:45
rules governing, 12:44
Vesting of commissions, 2:19
Vision care, 4:49

- W -

Waiting periods, 3:67
Wellness programs
defined, 12:26
insurance for, 12:29

Health Insurance Answer Book

(References in the index are to Question numbers.)

Wellness programs *(cont.)*
  options, 12:27
  rationale for, 12:28
Workers' compensation
  defined, 3:15
  employer, costs to, 3:20, 3:21, 3:22
  integration with employer benefits, 3:18
  state law governing availability, 3:17
  taxation under section 104, 3:19
Working spouse plan, 9:23